# CRIMINAL PROCEDURE: ADJUDICATION

## CASES AND MATERIALS

### Second Edition

■　■　■

**Cynthia Lee**

*Charles Kennedy Poe Research Professor of Law*
*The George Washington University Law School*

**L. Song Richardson**

*Dean and Professor of Law*
*UC Irvine School of Law*

**Tamara Lawson**

*Associate Dean of Academic Affairs and Professor of Law*
*St. Thomas University School of Law*

**AMERICAN CASEBOOK SERIES®**

*American Casebook Series* is a trademark registered in the U.S. Patent and Trademark Office.

© 2018 LEG, Inc. d/b/a West Academic
    444 Cedar Street, Suite 700
    St. Paul, MN 55101
    1-877-888-1330

West, West Academic Publishing, and West Academic are trademarks of West Publishing Corporation, used under license.

Printed in the United States of America

**ISBN:** 978-1-64020-857-5

*This book is dedicated to*

*Kenichi Haramoto*

*Tuck and Dorothea Lee*

*Barbara A. Lawson*

*Kurt Kieffer*

*Song Yim and Nehemiah Richardson*

# ACKNOWLEDGMENTS

Cynthia Lee would like to thank several people for their help in making this casebook possible. First and foremost, she thanks Matt Halldorson, who served as her Research Assistant from the summer of his first year in law school at The George Washington University Law School until he graduated in May 2016. Matt helped gather excerpts for possible inclusion in the casebook. He put cases into casebook format, made sure the formatting was consistent throughout, edited cases, drafted the Index, and proofread numerous drafts. This casebook could not have been produced without Matt's help. Additionally, Professor Lee thanks Masako Yoshioka, Carrie James, and Mario Kolev, students at The George Washington University Law School who served as Professor Lee's Research Assistants and assisted with the production of the first edition of this casebook. She also thanks Stephanie Hansen, Leanza Bethel, and Payal Patel who helped proofread the page proofs for the second edition of this casebook and Stephanie Hansen and Payal Patel for proofreading the final page proofs in October. Finally, she thanks administrative assistants Katey Mason from the University of California at Hastings and Elizabeth Moulton from The George Washington University Law School, who provided tireless administrative support to Professor Lee in the production of the first edition of this casebook and Prerna Balasundarum from The George Washington University Law School who provided administrative support in the production of the second edition of this casebook.

L. Song Richardson extends her deepest gratitude to her Research Assistants Sean Corpstein, Elizabeth Etchells, and Grant Lientz from the University of Iowa College of Law and Ariela-Rutkin Becker and Sierra Nelson from the University of California, Irvine School of Law who worked tirelessly to help bring this casebook to completion.

Tamara F. Lawson sincerely thanks her Research Assistants Kathryn Lecusay, Gamila Elmaadawy, Matthew Carcano, Oscar Quintero, and Alexa Bontkowski from St. Thomas University School of Law in Miami, Florida. She is grateful for their diligent commitment to the casebook project and their conscientious assistance as a team. She also thanks her family and friends for their continued support.

# SUMMARY OF CONTENTS

# TABLE OF CONTENTS

# TABLE OF CASES

The principal cases are in bold type.

---

# CRIMINAL PROCEDURE: ADJUDICATION

## CASES AND MATERIALS

### Second Edition

# CHAPTER 1

# INTRODUCTION TO THE CRIMINAL JUSTICE PROCESS

■ ■ ■

## A. SOURCES OF CRIMINAL PROCEDURE LAW

This casebook presents the leading Supreme Court cases on the criminal justice process. In each distinct phase of this process, procedures exist to achieve fair adjudication of criminal allegations and to prevent government oppression of liberty and privacy interests. Many of these procedures can be found in state criminal codes and the Federal Rules of Criminal Procedure. The most important criminal procedure protections, however, are found in the Bill of Rights or the first ten amendments to the United State Constitution. In interpreting these provisions, the Supreme Court sets a constitutional floor for government behavior. States are free to provide more protection to their citizens, but cannot provide less than the constitutional minimum. Because so much of criminal procedure derives from the U.S. Constitution, the basic criminal procedure class is often referred to as constitutional criminal procedure.

This chapter provides an overview of the criminal justice process. It is important to keep in mind that every state has its own specific procedures for the processing of a criminal defendant, so the steps outlined in this chapter may not reflect what takes place in every state. Moreover, procedures often differ depending on the seriousness of the crime. The procedures outlined in this chapter are the most common procedures in place for the processing of a person charged with a felony offense.

## B. THE INVESTIGATION OF THE CRIME

It is typical for the police to conduct an investigation once a crime occurs. The police may question witnesses to the crime, take photos of the crime scene, and gather forensic evidence in the hopes of determining who committed the crime. At some point during the investigation of the crime, the police will begin to focus their attention on a suspect or several suspects.

As part of the investigation process, the police may wish to search a suspect's home, car, and other belongings. Whether such a search can take place without a warrant turns on U.S. Supreme Court case law interpreting the Fourth Amendment. These cases tell us what kind of government action constitutes a "search" within the meaning of the Fourth Amendment, the requirements for a valid search warrant, and when police can conduct a search without obtaining a search warrant in advance. When evidence is obtained in violation of the Fourth Amendment, it can be excluded at trial.

Another investigative technique is the interrogation of a suspect. Police officers will often question an individual suspected of having committed a crime in an effort to get the suspect to confess or make incriminating statements. Police who question suspects must abide by certain rules. For instance, the Supreme Court has held that it violates due process if the police beat a suspect in order to obtain a confession. The Supreme Court has also held that under certain circumstances, police may not question a suspect without the suspect's attorney being present. These and other "rules" of interrogation are examined in the cases that follow.

Police may also place a suspect in a lineup. The purpose of a lineup is to see if an eyewitness to the crime can identify the person who committed the crime. To conduct a lineup, police will usually put the suspect and other individuals who are physically similar to the suspect in a line with their backs against a wall so they are all facing towards a one-way mirror behind which is the eyewitness. Each person in the lineup is asked to step forward, and the eyewitness is asked whether the person who has stepped forward is the person who committed the crime. Sometimes, the police will show an eyewitness a photographic array—a photo of the suspect's face along with photos of the faces of other individuals with similar features—instead of conducting a live physical lineup. A positive witness identification can provide both probable cause to support an arrest and evidence at trial to support a conviction. The "rules" governing lineups are also examined within this casebook.

## C.  THE ARREST

An arrest is a seizure of a person who is suspected of having broken the law. If the offense in question is a minor offense, the arrestee may be released with an order to appear in court at some later date. For more serious offenses, the arrestee will remain in custody, at least temporarily.

An arrest must be based on probable cause to believe that a crime has been committed and the person being arrested committed that crime. An arrest can either be warrantless, in which case it will be based upon the police officer's determination of probable cause, or pursuant to an arrest warrant issued by a judicial magistrate. If an arrest warrant is needed, a police officer must supply a magistrate with an affidavit articulating specific facts to support a finding of probable cause prior to making the arrest. If the magistrate finds probable cause to arrest, the magistrate will issue a warrant for the suspect's arrest. You will learn about the "rules" governing arrests within.

## D.   JUDICIAL DETERMINATION OF PROBABLE CAUSE

If an individual is arrested and taken into custody without an arrest warrant, a prompt judicial determination of probable cause must be made after the arrest. A magistrate judge will review the facts and circumstances underlying the arrest to ensure that the officer had probable cause to support the arrest. The judicial determination of probable cause is presumed to be sufficiently prompt if it occurs within 48 hours of the arrest. If the magistrate judge finds that the arrest is not supported by probable cause, the arrestee will be released from custody.

## E.  THE PROSECUTOR'S DECISION TO CHARGE

Once an individual has been arrested, the prosecutor must decide whether to formally charge the arrestee. The prosecutor's charge might be the same or different from the original charge for which the individual was arrested. In some cases, the prosecutor may send the case back to the police for further investigation. In other cases, the prosecutor may simply decline to file any charges at all. If the prosecutor decides to go forward with prosecution, the prosecutor will file a criminal complaint with the court. The complaint serves as the initial charging document.

In exercising its charging discretion, the prosecutor should follow ethical obligations articulated in the Model Rules of Professional Conduct (or her state's ethics code). Section 3–1.2(b) of the ABA Criminal Justice System: Standards for the Prosecution Function reminds prosecutors of these ethical obligations:

> The primary duty of the prosecutor is to seek justice within the bounds of the law, not merely to convict. The prosecutor serves the public interest and should act with integrity and balanced judgment to increase public safety both by pursuing appropriate criminal charges of appropriate severity, and by exercising discretion to not pursue criminal charges in appropriate circumstances. The prosecutor should seek to protect the innocent and convict the guilty, consider the interests of victims and witnesses, and respect the constitutional and legal rights of all persons, including suspects and defendants.

The prosecutor's decision to charge is completely discretionary. Before the case can go to trial, however, either a magistrate judge through a preliminary hearing or a grand jury will assess the case for probable cause. The preliminary hearing and the grand jury proceeding act as checks on the prosecutor's charging discretion. Additionally, most prosecutors serve as elected officials. As such, they are subject to voter referendum for their charging decisions.

## F.   INITIAL APPEARANCE OR ARRAIGNMENT ON THE COMPLAINT

An arrestee who is taken into custody and charged must be brought before a magistrate judge within a short time after the arrest. At this initial appearance, sometimes called the arraignment on the complaint, the magistrate judge will inform the defendant of the charge or charges against him and of various constitutional rights, such as the right to remain silent. In many jurisdictions, the magistrate judge will also decide at this initial appearance whether to release the defendant on bail or continue to keep the defendant in custody pending trial. If the defendant is indigent and the government is seeking jail time, the magistrate judge will assign a court appointed attorney. The magistrate will also set a date for the preliminary hearing at this time.

## G.  THE PRELIMINARY HEARING

The preliminary hearing is an adversarial proceeding conducted by a magistrate judge who is charged with evaluating the case to determine whether there is probable cause to support the charges contained in the complaint. The defendant has a right to be present at the preliminary hearing, a right to counsel, and a right to cross-examine the prosecution's witnesses. The defendant may also testify at the preliminary hearing and present evidence. It is not common for a defendant to present a full blown case at the preliminary hearing because the government's burden of proof is so low. The government just needs to convince the magistrate judge that there is probable cause to believe a crime has been committed and that the defendant committed it. It does not need to establish every element of the charged offense or offenses beyond a reasonable doubt as it would at trial. In most cases, the magistrate judge will find probable cause and bind the defendant over for trial.

Rather than reveal too much of its defense strategy, the defense will usually use the preliminary hearing to obtain a preview of the prosecution's case and lock in the testimony of the prosecution's witnesses. If the magistrate judge finds that the case lacks probable cause, she will dismiss the case. If the magistrate judge finds probable cause, the defendant will be bound over for trial. If grand jury review is not required, a document drafted by the prosecutor, called an information, will replace the complaint as the formal charging document in the case.

## H.  THE GRAND JURY

The Fifth Amendment to the U.S. Constitution gives felony defendants the right to an indictment by a grand jury. The Supreme Court has declined to apply this right to the states through the Due Process Clause of the Fourteenth Amendment. This means that in most states, it is up to the prosecutor whether to proceed by way of preliminary hearing or grand jury proceeding.

A grand jury proceeding is a one-sided proceeding at which the prosecutor presents evidence to the grand jurors without participation by defense counsel. The grand jury is tasked with deciding whether there is probable cause to support the indictment, which the prosecutor has drafted. If the grand jury does not find probable cause to support the charges, it will issue a no bill, and the charges will be dropped. If the grand jury finds probable cause, it may return the indictment, which will replace the complaint as the formal charging document in the case once it is filed with the court.

## I.    ARRAIGNMENT ON THE INFORMATION OR INDICTMENT

After an information or indictment has been filed, the defendant will be arraigned before the trial court. At this proceeding, the defendant will be informed of the charges against him and asked to enter a plea. The defendant may plead guilty, not guilty, or nolo contendere (no contest). If the defendant pleads guilty or nolo contendere, the judge must assure that the plea is voluntary and that the defendant understands the charges, the constitutional rights that the defendant is waiving by entering a plea, and the consequences of the plea, before accepting the plea. If the defendant pleads not guilty, the judge will set a date for trial.

## J.  PRETRIAL MOTIONS

In preparation for trial, both the defense and prosecution may file pretrial motions. For example, a defendant may file a motion to suppress physical evidence obtained in a police search, arguing that the government violated his Fourth Amendment rights in obtaining the evidence. The defendant may move to exclude incriminating statements he made to the police from being admitted at trial, arguing that they were obtained in violation of due process or his Fifth Amendment privilege against self-incrimination. Either side may file a motion to exclude evidence that the other side plans to present on the ground that it is not relevant or reliable.

# K.  DISCOVERY

Discovery is the name for the process through which prosecutors and defense attorneys share information about the case. The discovery process is predominantly governed by rules and statutes. In federal court, for instance, Rule 16 of the Federal Rules of Criminal Procedure explains the obligations of both the prosecution and the defense to disclose information. Sometimes, discovery is governed by the U.S. Constitution. For example, under what is known as the *Brady* rule, the prosecutor has a constitutional duty to disclose evidence that is both favorable to the accused and material to guilt or punishment.

Discovery in criminal cases is much more limited than discovery in civil cases, even though a defendant's liberty is often at stake in a criminal case. Regardless of the limitations set forth in the discovery rules, some prosecutor's offices engage in open file discovery, which means the office will allow the defendant access to all of the information in its files, aside from attorney work-product. Other offices will only disclose the bare minimum required by the rules and statutes governing discovery.

# L.  PLEA NEGOTIATIONS

Most criminal cases are resolved by a guilty plea instead of a trial. The process of negotiating a plea, wherein the defendant usually agrees to plead guilty to a lesser offense in exchange for some concession from the prosecution, is commonly known as plea bargaining. The benefit of plea bargaining from the prosecution's standpoint is a guaranteed conviction. The benefit to the defendant is a reduction in criminal liability or jail time.

A plea bargain can be reached at any stage of the process, even as late as during jury deliberations. Most plea agreements, however, are reached prior to trial. Before a judge will accept a defendant's guilty plea, the judge will have a conversation with the defendant on the record, known as the plea colloquy, in order to make sure the defendant understands his constitutional rights and is knowingly and voluntarily waiving those rights. Additionally, the court[a] must be assured that the plea bargain is voluntary and that the defendant has been advised by competent legal counsel.

# M.  TRIAL, SENTENCING, AND APPEAL

At trial, the government carries the burden of proving every element of the charged offense beyond a reasonable doubt. Although the Sixth Amendment to the U.S. Constitution guarantees a right to a trial by an

---

[a]   When you see a reference to "the court," this sometimes means the institution of the court in which the defendant is being prosecuted. At other times, "the court" is just another way of referring to the judge.

impartial jury in all criminal prosecutions, the Supreme Court has held that the jury trial right applies only to defendants charged with a non-petty offense.[b]

At the beginning of the trial, both sides will make an opening statement. The opening statement serves as a summary of what each side believes the evidence will show. The prosecutor goes first because it bears the ultimate burden of proof. After both sides have made their opening statements, the prosecution will present its case.

At the close of the prosecution's case, the defense may make a motion to dismiss the case, also known as a motion for a judgment of acquittal, arguing that no reasonable jury could find the defendant guilty beyond a reasonable doubt based on the evidence presented. In considering the motion, the court must review the evidence in the light most favorable to the prosecution. If the court grants this motion, the charges against the defendant will be dismissed, and the court will enter a judgment of acquittal. If the court denies the motion, the trial will continue and the defense will be given an opportunity to present its case. The defense is not required to present any witnesses, nor is the defendant required to testify. If the defendant elects not to testify, the court will usually instruct the jurors not to make any negative inferences from the defendant's decision not to testify. At the close of the defendant's case-in-chief, the prosecution may present rebuttal witnesses.

After both sides rest, the parties will give their closing arguments. The prosecution will present its closing argument first. The defense will follow with its closing argument. The prosecution will be allowed to have the final word.

After closing arguments, the defense can renew or make a motion for a judgment of acquittal for the first time. Importantly, the failure to make such a motion can foreclose the defendant's ability to appeal a guilty verdict based on a claim that the evidence was insufficient to convict. If the motion is granted, the court will enter a judgment of acquittal. If the motion is denied, the court will proceed to instruct the jury on the law applicable to the case. The exact language of the instructions given to the jury is a matter that is litigated outside the presence of the jury. Both sides can propose jury instructions, but the judge will make the final decision as to the wording of the jury instructions. Any objections to the instructions will be preserved on the record in case of error and appeal.

After the judge instructs the jury, the jury will retire to deliberate on its verdict. The jury will typically enter either a verdict of guilty or not guilty. The jury is not required to give an explanation for its verdict. If the

---

[b]   Blanton v. City of North Las Vegas, 489 U.S. 538 (1989). With the consent of the prosecutor, the defendant can waive his right to a trial by jury and elect to be tried by a judge. Singer v. United States, 380 U.S. 24 (1965). A trial before a judge is called a bench trial.

verdict is not guilty, the charges will be dismissed, and the defendant will be released. As a general matter, the Double Jeopardy Clause will protect the defendant who has been acquitted from being retried for the same offense. If the verdict is guilty, the court will enter a judgment of conviction and set a date for sentencing.

In preparation for sentencing, often a probation officer will prepare a presentence report for the court. The report will provide a summary of the case, information about the defendant's criminal history, and a recommendation as to sentence. The court has broad discretion to choose whatever it feels is the appropriate sentence, as long as it complies with any applicable statutory minimums or maximums set by the legislature. The court may sentence the defendant to a term of imprisonment and/or order the defendant to pay a fine. If the court feels a term of incarceration is unnecessary, the court may sentence the defendant to probation or order the defendant to perform community service. The court can also order the defendant to pay restitution to the victim. In federal court, the sentencing judge will usually consult the federal sentencing guidelines and sentence the defendant within the applicable guideline range.

Following sentencing, the defendant may file an appeal to the intermediate court of appeals to try to overturn his conviction. The appellate court can either affirm the conviction or reverse it. If the appellate court reverses the conviction, it will usually order a new trial. Sometimes, however, the appellate court will reverse the conviction and order the charges dismissed. If the intermediate court of appeals affirms the conviction, the defendant can try to appeal to the supreme court of the state in which he was convicted. Review by the state supreme court is completely discretionary, which means the state supreme court can choose not to hear the case without providing any reason for its action. A judgment of conviction becomes final after the highest court of the state affirms the conviction or declines to hear the case.[c]

---

[c] If the case involves an issue of broad significance, the defendant may try to appeal to the U.S. Supreme Court. Review by the U.S. Supreme Court is also completely discretionary. After exhausting the appeal process, the defendant may try to get released from custody by filing a petition for habeas corpus. A petition for habeas corpus in federal court must be based upon an alleged violation of the U.S. Constitution other than the Fourth Amendment. Stone v. Powell, 428 U.S. 465 (1976). Proceeding by way of habeas corpus is often called collateral review because it is done outside the appeal process.

# CHAPTER 21

## LINEUPS AND OTHER PRETRIAL IDENTIFICATION PROCEDURES

■ ■ ■

Both the Sixth Amendment and the Due Process Clause of the Fourteenth Amendment place limits on the state's use of pretrial identification procedures. The first two cases in this chapter address the protections afforded to the accused by the Sixth Amendment. The last two cases address the protections afforded by the Due Process Clause.

In *United States v. Wade*, the Court considers whether to recognize a right to counsel at a pretrial lineup that occurs after the filing of the indictment. In order to answer this question, the Court examines whether a post-indictment lineup is a "critical stage" of the proceeding. In *Kirby v. Illinois*, the Court has to decide whether to extend its holding in *Wade* to an identification procedure that also takes place pretrial, but before the defendant has been formally charged with a criminal offense.

The remaining materials in this chapter involve the protections of the Due Process Clause. In *Manson v. Brathwaite*, the Court considers which of two tests should be used to admit or exclude evidence obtained by an unnecessarily suggestive pretrial identification procedure. Sandra Guerra Thompson explains and critiques the *Manson v. Brathwaite* decision in *Eyewitness Identifications and State Courts as Guardians against Wrongful Convictions*. Next is an article from Forbes Magazine on cross-racial identification, discussing the increased likelihood of misidentification when a witness of one race tries to identify a suspect of another race. In *Using an Expert to Evaluate Eyewitness Identification Evidence*, Shirley K. Duffy also examines problems posed by cross-racial identifications. Finally, in *Perry v. New Hampshire*, the Court considers whether the Due Process Clause is violated when a suggestive pretrial identification procedure is involved, but the police were not responsible for arranging the suggestive procedure.

## UNITED STATES v. WADE

Supreme Court of the United States
388 U.S. 218, 87 S.Ct 1926, 18 L.Ed.2d 1149 (1967)

JUSTICE BRENNAN delivered the opinion of the Court.

The question here is whether courtroom identifications of an accused at trial are to be excluded from evidence because the accused was exhibited to the witnesses before trial at a post-indictment lineup conducted for identification purposes without notice to and in the absence of the accused's appointed counsel.

The federally insured bank in Eustace, Texas, was robbed on September 21, 1964. A man with a small strip of tape on each side of his face entered the bank, pointed a pistol at the female cashier and the vice president, the only persons in the bank at the time, and forced them to fill a pillowcase with the bank's money. The man then drove away with an accomplice who had been waiting in a stolen car outside the bank. On March 23, 1965, an indictment was returned against respondent, Wade, and two others for conspiring to rob the bank, and against Wade and the accomplice for the robbery itself. Wade was arrested on April 2, and counsel was appointed to represent him on April 26. Fifteen days later an FBI agent, without notice to Wade's lawyer, arranged to have the two bank employees observe a lineup made up of Wade and five or six other prisoners and conducted in a courtroom of the local county courthouse. Each person in the line wore strips of tape such as allegedly worn by the robber and upon direction each said something like "put the money in the bag," the words allegedly uttered by the robber. Both bank employees identified Wade in the lineup as the bank robber.

At trial the two employees, when asked on direct examination if the robber was in the courtroom, pointed to Wade. The prior lineup identification was then elicited from both employees on cross-examination. At the close of testimony, Wade's counsel moved for a judgment of acquittal or, alternatively, to strike the bank officials' courtroom identifications on the ground that conduct of the lineup, without notice to and in the absence of his appointed counsel, violated * * * his Sixth Amendment right to the assistance of counsel. The motion was denied, and Wade was convicted. The Court of Appeals for the Fifth Circuit reversed the conviction and ordered a new trial * * *. We granted certiorari, and set the case for oral argument with *Gilbert v. State of California*, and *Stovall v. Denno*, which present similar questions.

* * * [I]n this case it is urged that the assistance of counsel at the lineup was indispensable to protect Wade's most basic right as a criminal defendant—his right to a fair trial at which the witnesses against him might be meaningfully cross-examined.

\* \* \* [O]ur cases have construed the Sixth Amendment guarantee to apply to "critical" stages of the proceedings. The guarantee reads: "In all criminal prosecutions, the accused shall enjoy the right \* \* \* to have the Assistance of Counsel for his defence." \* \* \* The plain wording of this guarantee thus encompasses counsel's assistance whenever necessary to assure a meaningful "defence."

\* \* \* [To determine whether a pretrial stage of the proceeding is critical], we scrutinize [that] pretrial confrontation of the accused to determine whether the presence of his counsel is necessary to preserve the defendant's basic right to a fair trial as affected by his right meaningfully to cross-examine the witnesses against him and to have effective assistance of counsel at the trial itself. It calls upon us to analyze whether potential substantial prejudice to defendant's rights inheres in the particular confrontation and the ability of counsel to help avoid that prejudice.

The Government characterizes the lineup as a mere preparatory step in the gathering of the prosecution's evidence, not different—for Sixth Amendment purposes—from various other preparatory steps, such as systematized or scientific analyzing of the accused's fingerprints, blood sample, clothing, hair, and the like. We think there are differences which preclude such stages being characterized as critical stages at which the accused has the right to the presence of his counsel. Knowledge of the techniques of science and technology is sufficiently available, and the variables in techniques few enough, that the accused has the opportunity for a meaningful confrontation of the Government's case at trial through the ordinary processes of cross-examination of the Government's expert witnesses and the presentation of the evidence of his own experts. \* \* \*

But the confrontation compelled by the State between the accused and the victim or witnesses to a crime to elicit identification evidence is peculiarly riddled with innumerable dangers and variable factors which might seriously, even crucially, derogate from a fair trial. The vagaries of eyewitness identification are well-known; the annals of criminal law are rife with instances of mistaken identification. \* \* \* A major factor contributing to the high incidence of miscarriage of justice from mistaken identification has been the degree of suggestion inherent in the manner in which the prosecution presents the suspect to witnesses for pretrial identification. \* \* \* Moreover, "[i]t is a matter of common experience that, once a witness has picked out the accused at the line-up, he is not likely to go back on his word later on, so that in practice the issue of identity may (in the absence of other relevant evidence) for all practical purposes be determined there and then, before the trial."

The pretrial confrontation for purpose of identification may take the form of a lineup, also known as an "identification parade" or "showup," as in the present case, or presentation of the suspect alone to the witness. \* \* \*

It is obvious that risks of suggestion attend either form of confrontation and increase the dangers inhering in eyewitness identification. But as is the case with secret interrogations, there is serious difficulty in depicting what transpires at lineups and other forms of identification confrontations. * * * [T]he defense can seldom reconstruct the manner and mode of lineup identification for judge or jury at trial. * * * [N]either witnesses nor lineup participants are apt to be alert for conditions prejudicial to the suspect. And if they were, it would likely be of scant benefit to the suspect since neither witnesses nor lineup participants are likely to be schooled in the detection of suggestive influences. Improper influences may go undetected by a suspect, guilty or not, who experiences the emotional tension which we might expect in one being confronted with potential accusers. Even when he does observe abuse, if he has a criminal record he may be reluctant to take the stand and open up the admission of prior convictions. Moreover, any protestations by the suspect of the fairness of the lineup made at trial are likely to be in vain; the jury's choice is between the accused's unsupported version and that of the police officers present. In short, the accused's inability effectively to reconstruct at trial any unfairness that occurred at the lineup may deprive him of his only opportunity meaningfully to attack the credibility of the witness' courtroom identification.

What facts have been disclosed in specific cases about the conduct of pretrial confrontations for identification illustrate both the potential for substantial prejudice to the accused at that stage and the need for its revelation at trial. A commentator provides some striking examples:

> In a Canadian case * * * the defendant had been picked out of a lineup of six men, of which he was the only Oriental. On other cases, a black-haired suspect was placed among a group of light-haired persons, tall suspects have been made to stand with short nonsuspects, and, in a case where the perpetrator of the crime was known to be a youth, a suspect under twenty was placed in a lineup with five other persons, all of whom were forty or over.

Similarly state reports, in the course of describing prior identifications admitted as evidence of guilt, reveal numerous instances of suggestive procedures, for example, that all in the lineup but the suspect were known to the identifying witness, that the other participants in a lineup were grossly dissimilar in appearance to the suspect, that only the suspect was required to wear distinctive clothing which the culprit allegedly wore, that the witness is told by the police that they have caught the culprit after which the defendant is brought before the witness alone or is viewed in jail, that the suspect is pointed out before or during a lineup, and that the participants in the lineup are asked to try on an article of clothing which fits only the suspect.

The potential for improper influence is illustrated by the circumstances, insofar as they appear, surrounding the prior identifications in the three cases we decide today. In the present case, the testimony of the identifying witnesses elicited on cross-examination revealed that those witnesses were taken to the courthouse and seated in the courtroom to await assembly of the lineup. The courtroom faced on a hallway observable to the witnesses through an open door. The cashier testified that she saw Wade "standing in the hall" within sight of an FBI agent. Five or six other prisoners later appeared in the hall. The vice president testified that he saw a person in the hall in the custody of the agent who "resembled the person that we identified as the one that had entered the bank."

The lineup in *Gilbert* was conducted in an auditorium in which some 100 witnesses to several alleged state and federal robberies charged to Gilbert made wholesale identifications of Gilbert as the robber in each other's presence, a procedure said to be fraught with dangers of suggestion. And the vice of suggestion created by the identification in *Stovall*, was the presentation to the witness of the suspect alone handcuffed to police officers. It is hard to imagine a situation more clearly conveying the suggestion to the witness that the one presented is believed guilty by the police.

The few cases that have surfaced therefore reveal the existence of a process attended with hazards of serious unfairness to the criminal accused and strongly suggest the plight of the more numerous defendants who are unable to ferret out suggestive influences in the secrecy of the confrontation. We do not assume that these risks are the result of police procedures intentionally designed to prejudice an accused. Rather we assume they derive from the dangers inherent in eyewitness identification and the suggestibility inherent in the context of the pretrial identification. * * *

Insofar as the accused's conviction may rest on a courtroom identification in fact the fruit of a suspect pretrial identification which the accused is helpless to subject to effective scrutiny at trial, the accused is deprived of that right of cross-examination which is an essential safeguard to his right to confront the witnesses against him. And even though cross-examination is a precious safeguard to a fair trial, it cannot be viewed as an absolute assurance of accuracy and reliability. Thus in the present context, where so many variables and pitfalls exist, the first line of defense must be the prevention of unfairness and the lessening of the hazards of eyewitness identification at the lineup itself. The trial which might determine the accused's fate may well not be that in the courtroom but that at the pretrial confrontation, with the State aligned against the accused, the witness the sole jury, and the accused unprotected against the overreaching, intentional or unintentional, and with little or no effective appeal from the judgment there rendered by the witness—"that's the man."

Since it appears that there is grave potential for prejudice, intentional or not, in the pretrial lineup, which may not be capable of reconstruction at trial, and since presence of counsel itself can often avert prejudice and assure a meaningful confrontation at trial, there can be little doubt that for Wade the postindictment lineup was a critical stage of the prosecution at which he was "as much entitled to such aid [of counsel] . . . as at the trial itself." Thus both Wade and his counsel should have been notified of the impending lineup, and counsel's presence should have been a requisite to conduct of the lineup, absent an "intelligent waiver." * * *

We come now to the question whether the denial of Wade's motion to strike the courtroom identification by the bank witnesses at trial because of the absence of his counsel at the lineup required, as the Court of Appeals held, the grant of a new trial at which such evidence is to be excluded. We do not think this disposition can be justified without first giving the Government the opportunity to establish by clear and convincing evidence that the in-court identifications were based upon observations of the suspect other than the lineup identification. Where, as here, the admissibility of evidence of the lineup identification itself is not involved, a per se rule of exclusion of courtroom identification would be unjustified. A rule limited solely to the exclusion of testimony concerning identification at the lineup itself, without regard to admissibility of the courtroom identification, would render the right to counsel an empty one. The lineup is most often used, as in the present case, to crystallize the witnesses' identification of the defendant for future reference. We have already noted that the lineup identification will have that effect. The State may then rest upon the witnesses' unequivocal courtroom identifications, and not mention the pretrial identification as part of the State's case at trial. Counsel is then in the predicament in which Wade's counsel found himself—realizing that possible unfairness at the lineup may be the sole means of attack upon the unequivocal courtroom identification, and having to probe in the dark in an attempt to discover and reveal unfairness, while bolstering the government witness' courtroom identification by bringing out and dwelling upon his prior identification. Since counsel's presence at the lineup would equip him to attack not only the lineup identification but the courtroom identification as well, limiting the impact of violation of the right to counsel to exclusion of evidence only of identification at the lineup itself disregards a critical element of that right.

* * * [T]he proper test to be applied in these situations is * * * "[W]hether, granting establishment of the primary illegality, the evidence to which instant objection is made has been come at by exploitation of that illegality or instead by means sufficiently distinguishable to be purged of the primary taint." * * * Application of this test in the present context

requires consideration of various factors; for example, the prior opportunity to observe the alleged criminal act, the existence of any discrepancy between any pre-lineup description and the defendant's actual description, any identification prior to lineup of another person, the identification by picture of the defendant prior to the lineup, failure to identify the defendant on a prior occasion, and the lapse of time between the alleged act and the lineup identification. It is also relevant to consider those facts which, despite the absence of counsel, are disclosed concerning the conduct of the lineup. * * *

On the record now before us we cannot make the determination whether the in-court identifications had an independent origin. This was not an issue at trial, although there is some evidence relevant to a determination. That inquiry is most properly made in the District Court. We therefore think the appropriate procedure to be followed is to vacate the conviction pending a hearing to determine whether the in-court identifications had an independent source, or whether, in any event, the introduction of the evidence was harmless error, and for the District Court to reinstate the conviction or order a new trial, as may be proper. * * *

[CHIEF JUSTICE WARREN's opinion, concurring in part and dissenting in part, JUSTICE DOUGLAS' opinion, concurring in part and dissenting in part, JUSTICE FORTAS' opinion, concurring in part and dissenting in part, JUSTICE CLARK's concurring opinion, JUSTICE BLACK's opinion, dissenting in part and concurring in part, and JUSTICE WHITE's opinion, concurring in part and dissenting in part, have been omitted.]

## KIRBY v. ILLINOIS

Supreme Court of the United States
406 U.S. 682, 92 S.Ct. 1877, 32 L.Ed.2d 411 (1972)

JUSTICE STEWART announced the judgment of the Court and an opinion in which the CHIEF JUSTICE, JUSTICE BLACKMUN, and JUSTICE REHNQUIST join.

* * * In the present case we are asked to extend the *Wade-Gilbert per se* exclusionary rule to identification testimony based upon a police station showup that took place *before* the defendant had been indicted or otherwise formally charged with any criminal offense.

On February 21, 1968, a man named Willie Shard reported to the Chicago police that the previous day two men had robbed him on a Chicago street of a wallet containing, among other things, traveler's checks and a Social Security card. On February 22, two police officers stopped the petitioner and a companion, Ralph Bean, on West Madison Street in Chicago. When asked for identification, the petitioner produced a wallet that contained three traveler's checks and a Social Security card, all bearing the name of Willie Shard. Papers with Shard's name on them were also found in Bean's possession. When asked to explain his possession of Shard's property, the petitioner first said that the traveler's checks were "play money," and then told the officers that he had won them in a crap game. The officers then arrested the petitioner and Bean and took them to a police station.

Only after arriving at the police station, and checking the records there, did the arresting officers learn of the Shard robbery. A police car was then dispatched to Shard's place of employment, where it picked up Shard and brought him to the police station. Immediately upon entering the room in the police station where the petitioner and Bean were seated at a table, Shard positively identified them as the men who had robbed him two days earlier. No lawyer was present in the room, and neither the petitioner nor Bean had asked for legal assistance, or been advised of any right to the presence of counsel.

More than six weeks later, the petitioner and Bean were indicted for the robbery of Willie Shard. Upon arraignment, counsel was appointed to represent them, and they pleaded not guilty. A pretrial motion to suppress Shard's identification testimony was denied, and at the trial Shard testified as a witness for the prosecution. In his testimony he described his identification of the two men at the police station on February 22, and identified them again in the courtroom as the men who had robbed him on February 20. He was cross-examined at length regarding the circumstances of his identification of the two defendants. The jury found both defendants guilty, and the petitioner's conviction was affirmed on appeal. The Illinois appellate court held that the admission of Shard's testimony was not error, relying upon an earlier decision of the Illinois Supreme Court, holding that the *Wade-Gilbert per se* exclusionary rule is not applicable to preindictment confrontations. We granted certiorari, limited to this question. * * *

The *Wade-Gilbert* exclusionary rule * * * stems from * * * the guarantee of the right to counsel contained in the Sixth and Fourteenth Amendments. Unless all semblance of principled constitutional adjudication is to be abandoned, therefore, it is to the decisions construing that guarantee that we must look in determining the present controversy.

In a line of constitutional cases in this Court stemming back to the Court's landmark opinion in *Powell v. Alabama*, it has been firmly established that a person's Sixth and Fourteenth Amendment right to counsel attaches only at or after the time that adversary judicial proceedings have been initiated against him.

This is not to say that a defendant in a criminal case has a constitutional right to counsel only at the trial itself. The *Powell* case makes clear that the right attaches at the time of arraignment, and the Court has recently held that it exists also at the time of a preliminary hearing. But the point is that, while members of the Court have differed as to existence of the right to counsel in the contexts of some of the above cases, all of those cases have involved points of time at or after the initiation of adversary judicial criminal proceedings—whether by way of formal charge, preliminary hearing, indictment, information, or arraignment. * * *

The initiation of judicial criminal proceedings is far from a mere formalism. It is the starting point of our whole system of adversary criminal justice. For it is only then that the government has committed itself to prosecute, and only then that the adverse positions of government and defendant have solidified. It is then that a defendant finds himself faced with the prosecutorial forces of organized society, and immersed in the intricacies of substantive and procedural criminal law. It is this point, therefore, that marks the commencement of the "criminal prosecutions" to which alone the explicit guarantees of the Sixth Amendment are applicable.

In this case we are asked to import into a routine police investigation an absolute constitutional guarantee historically and rationally applicable only after the onset of formal prosecutorial proceedings. We decline to * * * impos[e] a *per se* exclusionary rule upon testimony concerning an identification that took place long before the commencement of any prosecution whatever.

What has been said is not to suggest that there may not be occasions during the course of a criminal investigation when the police do abuse identification procedures. Such abuses are not beyond the reach of the Constitution [since the] Due Process Clause of the Fifth and Fourteenth Amendments forbids a lineup that is unnecessarily suggestive and conducive to irreparable mistaken identification. * * *

The judgment is affirmed.

JUSTICE BRENNAN, with whom JUSTICE DOUGLAS and JUSTICE MARSHALL join, dissenting. * * *

While it should go without saying, it appears necessary, in view of the plurality opinion today, to re-emphasize that *Wade* did not require the presence of counsel at pretrial confrontations for identification purposes simply on the basis of an abstract consideration of the words "criminal prosecutions" in the Sixth Amendment. Counsel is required at those confrontations because "the dangers inherent in eyewitness identification and the suggestibility inherent in the context of the pretrial identification" mean that protection must be afforded to the "most basic right (of) a criminal defendant—his right to a fair trial at which the witnesses against him might be meaningfully cross-examined." * * * Hence, "the initiation of adversary judicial criminal proceedings," is completely irrelevant to whether counsel is necessary at a pretrial confrontation for identification in order to safeguard the accused's constitutional rights to confrontation and the effective assistance of counsel at his trial.

In view of *Wade*, it is plain, and the plurality today does not attempt to dispute it, that there inhere[s] in a confrontation for identification conducted after arrest the identical hazards to a fair trial that inhere in such a confrontation conducted "after the onset of formal prosecutorial proceedings." The plurality apparently considers an arrest, which for present purposes we must assume to be based upon probable cause, to be nothing more than part of "a routine police investigation," and thus not "the starting point of our whole system of adversary criminal justice." * * * If these propositions do not amount to "mere formalism," it is difficult to know how to characterize them. An arrest evidences the belief of the police that the perpetrator of a crime has been caught. A post-arrest confrontation for identification is not "a mere preparatory step in the gathering of the prosecution's evidence." A primary, and frequently sole, purpose of the confrontation for identification at that stage is to accumulate proof to buttress the conclusion of the police that they have the offender in hand. The plurality offers no reason, and I can think of none, for concluding that a post-arrest confrontation for identification, unlike a post-charge confrontation, is not among those "critical confrontations of the accused by the prosecution at pretrial proceedings where the results might well settle the accused's fate and reduce the trial itself to a mere formality."

The highly suggestive form of confrontation employed in this case underscores the point. This showup was particularly fraught with the peril of mistaken identification. In the setting of a police station squad room where all present except petitioner and Bean were police officers, the danger was quite real that Shard's understandable resentment might lead him too readily to agree with the police that the pair under arrest, and the only persons exhibited to him, were indeed the robbers. "It is hard to imagine a situation more clearly conveying the suggestion to the witness that the one presented is believed guilty by the police." The State had no case without Shard's identification testimony, and safeguards against [the risk of mistaken identification] were therefore of critical importance. Shard's testimony itself demonstrates the necessity for such safeguards. On direct examination, Shard identified petitioner and Bean not as the alleged robbers on trial in the courtroom, but as the pair he saw at the police station. * * *

[CHIEF JUSTICE BURGER's concurring opinion, JUSTICE POWELL's opinion concurring in the result, and JUSTICE WHITE's dissenting opinion have been omitted.]

# MANSON V. BRATHWAITE

Supreme Court of the United States
432 U.S. 98, 97 S.Ct. 2243, 53 L.Ed.2d 140 (1977)

JUSTICE BLACKMUN delivered the opinion of the Court.

This case presents the issue as to whether the Due Process Clause of the Fourteenth Amendment compels the exclusion * * * of pretrial identification evidence obtained by a police procedure that was both suggestive and unnecessary. * * *

Jimmy D. Glover, a full-time trooper of the Connecticut State Police, in 1970 was assigned to the Narcotics Division in an undercover capacity. On May 5 of that year, about 7:45 p.m., * * * and while there was still daylight, Glover and Henry Alton Brown, an informant, went to an apartment building at 201 Westland, in Hartford, for the purpose of purchasing narcotics from "Dickie Boy" Cicero, a known narcotics dealer. * * * Glover and Brown entered the building, observed by back-up Officers D'Onofrio and Gaffey, and proceeded by stairs to the third floor. Glover knocked at the door. * * * The area was illuminated by natural light from a window in the third floor hallway. The door was opened 12 to 18 inches in response to the knock. Glover observed a man standing at the door and, behind him, a woman. Brown identified himself. Glover then asked for "two things" of narcotics. The man at the door held out his hand, and Glover gave him two $10 bills. The door closed. Soon the man returned and handed Glover two glassine bags. While the door was open, Glover stood within two feet of the person from whom he made the purchase and observed his face. Five to seven minutes elapsed from the time the door first opened until it closed the second time.

Glover and Brown then left the building. This was about eight minutes after their arrival. Glover drove to headquarters where he described the seller to D'Onofrio and Gaffey. Glover at that time did not know the identity of the seller. He described him as being "a colored man, approximately five feet eleven inches tall, dark complexion, black hair, short Afro style, and having high cheekbones, and of heavy build. He was wearing at the time blue pants and a plaid shirt." D'Onofrio, suspecting from this description that respondent might be the seller, obtained a photograph of respondent from the Records Division of the Hartford Police Department. He left it at Glover's office. D'Onofrio was not acquainted with respondent personally, but did know him by sight and had seen him "[s]everal times" prior to May 5. Glover, when alone, viewed the photograph for the first time upon his return to headquarters on May 7; he identified the person shown as the one from whom he had purchased the narcotics. * * *

Respondent was charged, in a two-count information, with possession and sale of heroin. * * * At his trial in January 1971, the photograph from which Glover had identified respondent was received in evidence without objection on the part of the defense. Glover also testified that, although he had not seen respondent in the eight months that had elapsed since the sale, "there (was) no doubt whatsoever" in his mind that the person shown on the photograph was respondent. Glover also made a positive in-court identification without objection. * * *

Respondent * * * testified that on May 5, the day in question, he had been ill at his Albany Avenue apartment * * * and that at no time on that particular day had he been at 201 Westland. His wife testified that she recalled, after her husband had refreshed her memory, that he was home all day on May 5. * * *

The jury found respondent guilty on both counts of the information. He received a sentence of not less than six nor more than nine years. * * * [After his conviction was affirmed on appeal,] respondent filed a petition for habeas corpus in the United States District Court for the District of Connecticut. He alleged that the admission of the identification testimony at his state trial deprived him of due process of law to which he was entitled under the Fourteenth Amendment. The District Court * * * dismissed respondent's petition. On appeal, the United States Court of Appeals for the Second Circuit reversed. * * * We granted certiorari.

*Stovall v. Denno*, decided in 1967, concerned a petitioner who had been convicted in a New York court of murder. He was arrested the day following the crime and was taken by the police to a hospital where the victim's wife, also wounded in the assault, was a patient. After observing Stovall and hearing him speak, she identified him as the murderer. She later made an in-court identification. * * * On the identification issue, the Court reviewed the practice of showing a suspect singly for purposes of identification, and the claim that this was so unnecessarily suggestive and conducive to irreparable mistaken identification that it constituted a denial of due process of law. The Court noted that the practice "has been widely condemned," but it concluded that "a claimed violation of due process of law in the conduct of a confrontation depends on the totality of the circumstances surrounding it." In that case, showing Stovall to the victim's spouse "was imperative." The Court then quoted the observations of the Court of Appeals, to the effect that the spouse was the only person who could possibly exonerate the accused; that the hospital was not far from the courthouse and jail; that no one knew how long she might live; that she was not able to visit the jail; and that taking Stovall to the hospital room was the only feasible procedure, and, under the circumstances, "the usual police station line-up . . . was out of the question."

*Neil v. Biggers*, decided in 1972, concerned a respondent who had been convicted in a Tennessee court of rape, on evidence consisting in part of the victim's visual and voice identification of Biggers at a station-house showup seven months after the crime. The victim had been in her assailant's presence for some time and had directly observed him indoors and under a full moon outdoors. She testified that she had "no doubt" that Biggers was her assailant. She previously had given the police a description of the assailant. She had made no identification of others presented at previous showups, lineups, or through photographs. * * * [This] Court concluded that * * * "admission of evidence of a showup without more does not violate due process." * * * The "central question," * * * [is] "whether under the totality of the circumstances the identification was reliable even though the confrontation procedure was suggestive." * * *

*Biggers* well might be seen to provide an unambiguous answer to the question before us * * *. In one passage, however, the Court observed that the challenged procedure occurred pre-*Stovall* * * *. The question before us, then, is simply whether the *Biggers* analysis applies to post-*Stovall* confrontations as well to those pre-*Stovall*. * * *

Petitioner at the outset acknowledges that "the procedure in the instant case was suggestive (because only one photograph was used) and unnecessary" (because there was no emergency or exigent circumstance). The respondent * * * proposes a per se rule of exclusion that he claims is dictated by the demands of the Fourteenth Amendment's guarantee of due process. * * *

Since the decision in *Biggers*, the Courts of Appeals appear to have developed at least two approaches to such evidence. The first, or per se approach, employed by the Second Circuit in the present case, focuses on the procedures employed and requires exclusion of the out-of-court identification evidence, without regard to reliability, whenever it has been obtained through unnecessarily suggestive confrontation procedures. The justifications advanced are the elimination of evidence of uncertain reliability, deterrence of the police and prosecutors, and the stated "fair assurance against the awful risks of misidentification."

The second, or more lenient, approach is one that continues to rely on the totality of the circumstances. It permits the admission of the confrontation evidence if, despite the suggestive aspect, the out-of-court identification possesses certain features of reliability. * * * This second approach, in contrast to the other, is ad hoc and serves to limit the societal costs imposed by a sanction that excludes relevant evidence from consideration and evaluation by the trier of fact. * * *

There are, of course, several interests to be considered and taken into account. * * * [First is] the concern that the jury not hear eyewitness testimony unless that evidence has aspects of reliability. It must be observed that both approaches before us are responsive to this concern. The per se rule, however, goes too far since its application automatically and peremptorily, and without consideration of alleviating factors, keeps evidence from the jury that is reliable and relevant.

The second factor is deterrence. Although the per se approach has the more significant deterrent effect, the totality approach also has an influence on police behavior. * * *

The third factor is the effect on the administration of justice. Here the per se approach suffers serious drawbacks. Since it denies the trier reliable evidence, it may result, on occasion, in the guilty going free. Also, because of its rigidity, the per se approach may make error by the trial judge more likely than the totality approach. * * * Certainly, inflexible rules of exclusion that may frustrate rather than promote justice have not been viewed recently by this Court with unlimited enthusiasm. * * *

The standard * * * is that of fairness as required by the Due Process Clause of the Fourteenth Amendment. * * * We therefore conclude that reliability is the linchpin in determining the admissibility of identification testimony for both pre-and post-*Stovall* confrontations. The factors to be considered are set out in *Biggers*. These include the opportunity of the witness to view the criminal at the time of the crime, the witness' degree of attention, the accuracy of his prior description of the criminal, the level of certainty demonstrated at the confrontation, and the time between the crime and the confrontation. Against these factors is to be weighed the corrupting effect of the suggestive identification itself.

We turn, then, to the facts of this case and apply the analysis:

1.   The opportunity to view. Glover testified that for two to three minutes he stood at the apartment door, within two feet of the respondent. The door opened twice, and each time the man stood at the door. The moments passed, the conversation took place, and payment was made. Glover looked directly at his vendor. It was near sunset, to be sure, but the sun had not yet set, so it was not dark or even dusk or twilight. * * * There was natural light. * * *

2.   The degree of attention. Glover was not a casual or passing observer. * * * Trooper Glover was a trained police officer. * * * Glover himself was a Negro. * * * [A]s a specially trained, assigned, and experienced officer, he could be expected to pay scrupulous attention to detail, for he knew that subsequently he would have to find and arrest his vendor. In addition, he knew that his claimed observations would be subject later to close scrutiny and examination at any trial.

3.   The accuracy of the description. Glover's description was given to D'Onofrio within minutes after the transaction. It included the vendor's race, his height, his build, the color and style of his hair, and the high cheekbone facial feature. It also included

clothing the vendor wore. No claim has been made that respondent did not possess the physical characteristics so described. * * *

4.   The witness' level of certainty. * * * Glover, in response to a question whether the photograph was that of the person from whom he made the purchase, testified: "There is no question whatsoever." This positive assurance was repeated.

5.   The time between the crime and the confrontation. Glover's description of his vendor was given to D'Onofrio within minutes of the crime. The photographic identification took place only two days later. * * *

These indicators of Glover's ability to make an accurate identification are hardly outweighed by the corrupting effect of the challenged identification itself. * * * Although it plays no part in our analysis, all this assurance as to the reliability of the identification is hardly undermined by the facts that respondent was arrested in the very apartment where the sale had taken place * * *. Surely, we cannot say that under all the circumstances of this case there is "a very substantial likelihood of irreparable misidentification." Short of that point, such evidence is for the jury to weigh. * * *

We conclude that the criteria laid down in *Biggers* are to be applied in determining the admissibility of evidence offered by the prosecution concerning a post-*Stovall* identification, and that those criteria are satisfactorily met and complied with here.

The judgment of the Court of Appeals is reversed.

*It is so ordered.*

JUSTICE MARSHALL, with whom JUSTICE BRENNAN joins, dissenting.

* * * Relying on little more than a strong distaste for "inflexible rules of exclusion," the Court rejects the per se test. In so doing, the Court disregards two significant distinctions between the per se rule advocated in this case and the exclusionary remedies for certain other constitutional violations.

First, the per se rule here is not "inflexible." Where evidence is suppressed, for example, as the fruit of an unlawful search, it may well be forever lost to the prosecution. Identification evidence, however, can by its very nature be readily and effectively reproduced. * * * [W]hen a prosecuting attorney learns that there has been a suggestive confrontation, he can easily arrange another lineup conducted under scrupulously fair conditions. * * *

Second, other exclusionary rules have been criticized for preventing jury consideration of relevant and usually reliable evidence in order to serve interests unrelated to guilt or innocence, such as discouraging illegal searches or denial of counsel. Suggestively obtained eyewitness testimony is excluded, in contrast, precisely because of its unreliability and concomitant irrelevance. Its exclusion both protects the integrity of the truth-seeking function of the trial and discourages police use of needlessly inaccurate and ineffective investigatory methods.

Indeed, impermissibly suggestive identifications are not merely worthless law enforcement tools. They pose a grave threat to society at large in a more direct way than most governmental disobedience of the law. For if the police and the public erroneously conclude, on the basis of an unnecessarily suggestive confrontation, that the right man has been caught and convicted, the real outlaw must still remain at large. Law enforcement has failed in its primary function and has left society unprotected from the depredations of an active criminal.

For these reasons, I conclude that adoption of the per se rule would enhance, rather than detract from, the effective administration of justice. In my view, the Court's totality test will allow seriously unreliable and misleading evidence to be put before juries. * * * [Nonetheless,] assuming applicability of the totality test enunciated by the Court, the facts of the present case require [exclusion of Officer Glover's identification testimony.]

I consider first the opportunity that Officer Glover had to view the suspect. Careful review of the record shows that he could see the heroin seller only for the time it took to speak three sentences of four or five short words, to hand over some money, and later after the door reopened, to receive the drugs in return. The entire face-to-face transaction could have taken as little as 15 or 20 seconds. But during this time, Glover's attention was not focused exclusively on the seller's face. He observed that the door was opened 12 to 18 inches, that there was a window in the room behind the door, and, most importantly, that there was a woman standing behind the man. Glover was, of course, also concentrating on the details of the transaction—he must have looked away from the seller's face to hand him the money and receive the drugs. The observation during the conversation thus may have been as brief as 5 or 10 seconds.

As the Court notes, Glover was a police officer trained in and attentive to the need for making accurate identifications. Nevertheless, both common sense and scholarly study indicate that while a trained observer such as a police officer "is somewhat less likely to make an erroneous identification than the average untrained observer, the mere fact that he has been so trained is no guarantee that he is correct in a specific case. Police identification testimony should be scrutinized just as carefully as that of the normal witness." Moreover, "identifications made by policemen in highly competitive activities, such as undercover narcotic agents . . . , should be scrutinized with special care." Yet it is just such a searching inquiry that the Court fails to make here.

Another factor on which the Court relies, the witness' degree of certainty in making the identification, is worthless as an indicator that he is correct. Even if Glover had been unsure initially about his identification of respondent's picture, by the time he was called at trial to present a key piece of evidence for the State that paid his salary, it is impossible to imagine his responding negatively to such questions as "is there any doubt in your mind whatsoever" that the identification was correct. As the Court noted in *Wade*: "It is a matter of common experience that, once a witness has picked out the accused at the (pretrial confrontation), he is not likely to go back on his word later on."

Next, the Court finds that because the identification procedure took place two days after the crime, its reliability is enhanced. While such temporal proximity makes the identification more reliable than one occurring months later, the fact is that the greatest memory loss occurs within hours after an event. After that, the dropoff continues much more slowly. Thus, the reliability of an identification is increased only if it was made within several hours of the crime. If the time gap is any greater, reliability necessarily decreases.

Finally, the Court makes much of the fact that Glover gave a description of the seller to D'Onofrio shortly after the incident. Despite the Court's assertion that because "Glover himself was a Negro and unlikely to perceive only general features of 'hundreds of Hartford black males,' as the Court of Appeals stated," the description given by Glover was actually no more than a general summary of the seller's appearance. [Aside from describing the seller's clothing,] Glover merely described vaguely the seller's height, skin color, hairstyle, and build. He did say that the seller had "high cheekbones," but there is no other mention of facial features, nor even an estimate of age. Conspicuously absent is any indication that the seller was a native of the West Indies, certainly something which a member of the black community could immediately recognize from both appearance and accent.

From all of this, I must conclude that the evidence of Glover's ability to make an accurate identification is far weaker than the Court finds it. In contrast, the procedure used to identify respondent was both extraordinarily suggestive and strongly conducive to error. * * * By displaying a single photograph of respondent to the witness Glover under the circumstances in this record almost everything that could have been done wrong was done wrong.

In the first place, there was no need to use a photograph at all. Because photos are static, two-dimensional, and often outdated, they are "clearly inferior in reliability" to corporeal procedures. * * * [T]he poor reliability of photos makes their use inexcusable where any other means of identification is available. Here, since Detective D'Onofrio believed that he knew the seller's identity, further investigation without resort to a photographic showup was easily possible. With little inconvenience, a corporeal lineup including Brathwaite might have been arranged. * * *

Worse still than the failure to use an easily available corporeal identification was the display to Glover of only a single picture, rather than a photo array. With good reason, such single-suspect procedures have "been widely condemned." They give no assurance that the witness can identify the criminal from among a number of persons of similar appearance, surely the strongest evidence that there was no misidentification. * * *

The use of a single picture (or the display of a single live suspect, for that matter) is a grave error, of course, because it dramatically suggests to the witness that the person shown must be the culprit. Why else would the police choose the person? And it is deeply ingrained in human nature to agree with the expressed opinions of others particularly others who should be more knowledgeable when making a difficult decision. In this case, moreover, the pressure was not limited to that inherent in the display of a single photograph. Glover, the identifying witness, was a state police officer on special assignment. He knew that D'Onofrio, an experienced Hartford narcotics detective, presumably familiar with local drug operations, believed respondent to be the seller. There was at work, then, both loyalty to another police officer and deference to a better-informed colleague. * * *

The Court discounts this overwhelming evidence of suggestiveness, however. It reasons that because D'Onofrio was not present when Glover viewed the photograph, there was "little pressure on the witness to acquiesce in the suggestion." That conclusion blinks psychological reality. There is no doubt in my mind that even in D'Onofrio's absence, a clear and powerful message was telegraphed to Glover as he looked at respondent's photograph. He was emphatically told that "this is the man," and he responded by identifying respondent then and at trial "whether or not he was in fact 'the man.'"

I must conclude that this record presents compelling evidence that there was "a very substantial likelihood of misidentification" of respondent Brathwaite. The suggestive display of respondent's photograph to the witness Glover likely erased any independent memory that Glover had retained of the seller from his barely adequate opportunity to observe the criminal. * * *

[JUSTICE STEVENS' concurring opinion has been omitted.]

### NOTE

The photographic identification procedure in *Manson v. Brathwaite* took place before Brathwaite was indicted. If the photographic identification had taken place after Brathwaite was indicted, would Brathwaite have been able to challenge the identification as violating his Sixth Amendment right to counsel?

In *United States v. Ash*, 413 U.S. 300 (1973), the Court answered this question in the negative, holding that a defendant has no right to have counsel present at a post-indictment photographic identification procedure in which his picture is presented to a witness. The Court explained that a photo identification is not a critical stage of the proceeding because it is not a trial-like confrontation where the guiding hand of counsel is needed. Because the defendant is not present at a photo identification procedure, "no possibility arises that the accused might be misled by his lack of familiarity with the law or overpowered by his professional adversary." *Id.* at 317. The Court further noted that equality of access to photographs "remove[s] any inequality in the adversary process." *Id.* at 319. Defense counsel can seek its own witnesses and conduct its own photographic displays. Justice Stewart, concurring, added that "there are substantially fewer possibilities of impermissible suggestion when photographs are used, and those unfair influences can be readily reconstructed at trial." *Id.* at 324. If a defendant's photograph is substantially different from the others displayed, "this unfairness can be demonstrated at trial from an actual comparison of the photographs used or from the witness's description of the display." *Id.*

In his dissent, Justice Brennan noted various ways impermissible suggestion might occur in the context of a photographic display. For example, the police officer or the prosecutor's "inflection, facial expressions, physical motions, and myriad other almost imperceptible means of communication might tend, intentionally or unintentionally, to compromise the witness's objectivity" and lead to an erroneous identification. *Id.* at 333–34. The defense, however, would not be able to reconstruct at trial the exact mode and manner of the photographic identification. *Id.* at 335. Justice Brennan also pointed out that precisely because the accused is not present at a photographic identification, this reduces "the likelihood that it regularities in the procedure will ever come to light." *Id.* at 336.

*Ash* is significant in light of the fact that police "have mostly stopped using live lineups because it is so difficult and time-consuming to find people who look similar to a suspect." Brandon L. Garrett, *Eyewitnesses and Exclusion*, 65 VAND. L. REV. 451, 459 (2012). Police today tend to use photo arrays rather than live lineups.

## EYEWITNESS IDENTIFICATIONS AND STATE COURTS AS GUARDIANS AGAINST WRONGFUL CONVICTION

Sandra Guerra Thompson
7 Ohio St. J. Crim. L. 603 (2010)

It is fascinating to read the Supreme Court's Due Process jurisprudence on eyewitness identifications—now well over thirty years old—from a perspective which is informed by the lessons of hundreds of wrongful convictions and by the massive body of social science literature that has since developed. Long before the advent of DNA evidence and the release of so many wrongly convicted people, a rich dialogue had existed in the jurisprudence of eyewitness identifications about the risks of misidentification and the role the courts should play in protecting the innocent. In the early 1970's, federal district and circuit courts were apparently more inclined than now to exclude identification testimony on Due Process grounds. In *Manson v. Brathwaite*, the Supreme Court, clearly signaling its intent to take a hands-off approach, reversed several such decisions and, in the process, set in place a "more lenient" Due Process standard that has failed to provide any meaningful protection against wrongful convictions, despite the fact that the Court declared reliability to be the "linchpin" of its approach.

Upon a showing that the identification procedure is impermissibly suggestive, the Court then considers the "totality of the circumstances" to determine whether the identification is nonetheless reliable. To assess the totality of the circumstances, the Court instructs lower courts to consider five factors (taken from its earlier decision in *Neil v. Biggers*): "the opportunity of the witness to view the criminal at the time of the crime, the witness' degree of attention, the accuracy of his prior description of the criminal, the level of certainty demonstrated at the confrontation, and the time between the crime and the confrontation." The Court also called for the weighing of these factors against "the corrupting effect of the suggestive identification itself." However, courts have generally not undertaken to measure the extent to which suggestive practices might have undermined reliability. The Supreme Court has not revisited this jurisprudence in the three decades since it was established, so it continues to govern in federal courts and is followed in most state courts as well. * * *

The Supreme Court's Due Process test focuses first on the question of police suggestiveness before turning to the question of reliability. If there is no suggestion introduced by the police procedures, then there is no Due Process claim. The test, thus, completely ignores unreliability if there is no evidence of police suggestion. This is a gaping hole in the protection against mistaken identification and erroneous conviction. If the Due Process clause serves to protect against unfair trials due to unreliable evidence, then the *Brathwaite* test applies too narrowly. A great deal of unreliability is caused by factors inherent to the eyewitnesses (age, lighting, weapon-focus, cross-race bias, etc.). * * * However, the Supreme Court's Due Process protection only applies if the defense first crosses the threshold of suggestive police practices. * * *

The Supreme Court instructs courts to consider the "totality of the circumstances" in determining reliability, but this "totality" turns out to be restricted to a checklist of five factors (which, again, do not include suggestiveness). * * * [T]he list of factors is problematic. First, it includes the consideration of the witness's level of certainty as an indication of reliability, when scientific studies show witness certainty does not correlate with reliability. Second, it fails to include many other important * * * variables such as cross-race identification and weapon-focus, which have a strong impact on reliability. By limiting the courts to a restrictive list of factors, the Supreme Court's test has actually hamstrung the lower courts in their ability to evaluate the true "totality" of the circumstances. * * *

## 'THEY ALL LOOK ALIKE': THE OTHER-RACE EFFECT

Steven Ross Pomeroy
Forbes Magazine (January 28, 2014)

If somebody says, "Well, they all look alike," one might assume that person to be a closet bigot. But in all likelihood, he's simply being honest about a well-known limitation that plagues people of all colors: we humans are notoriously poor at distinguishing between the members of races different from our own.

The Other-Race Effect, as this psychological shortcoming is called, has been studied for decades. Originally realized during times of mass immigration, it was first recognized by science a century ago. Theories to explain it abound, but two clearly have an edge. The first hypothesis goes something like this: we generally spend more time with people of our own race and thus gain "perceptual expertise" for the characteristics of people who look like us. For example, since Caucasians sport wide variability in hair color, they may grow accustomed to differentiating strangers by looking at their hair. On the other hand, black people show more variability in skin tone, so they might instinctively use skin tone to tell others apart.

The second hypothesis states that people think more categorically about members of other races. Basically, we take notice that they're different from us, but tune out less noticeable characteristics. "The problem is not that we can't code the details of cross-race faces—it's that we don't," Daniel Levin, a cognitive psychologist at Kent State University explained to the American Psychological Association.

Concrete evidence is often hard to come by in psychology, so it's unlikely that either theory will ever be "proven" conclusively. We can, however, switch gears and examine a couple of things that don't factor in to the Other-Race Effect.

First, it's not simply because some races are more homogenous. Available evidence suggests that humans belonging to all ethnicities differ in a multitude of ways. "Cognitive psychologists have pointed to the fact that faces are not all alike; they differ from each other in terms of specific features like width, length, size of nose, and color of eyes," Professor Lawrence White of Beloit College says.

Second, the Other Race effect is not necessarily fueled by racist thinking. "Studies have found that racial attitudes don't predict performance in cross-race identification tasks; prejudiced and non-prejudiced people are equally likely to fall victim to the other-race effect," White says.

Many might scoff at the idea of studying the Other-Race Effect, but it certainly merits examination. The effect is ubiquitous, and has real-world, life and death implications. Take eyewitness testimony, for example. The Other-Race effect suggests that witnesses of one race would not be very skilled at identifying suspects of another. Published research bears this out. In one study, investigators examined 40 participants in a racially diverse area of the United States. Participants watched a video of a crime being committed, then, over the following 24 hours, were asked to pick a suspect out of a photo line-up. The majority of participants either misidentified the suspect or stated the suspect was not in the line-up at all. However, correct identification of the suspect occurred more often when the eyewitness and the suspect were of the same race.

Is there any way to prevent or minimize the Other-Race Effect? Absolutely. Recent research points to a sensitive period in which the effect develops. If infants regularly see and interact with people of other races before nine months of age, the Other-Race Effect may never emerge. But for those who are already inept at distinguishing between people of other ethnicities, don't fret, there's still hope. According to University of London psychologist Gizelle Anzures, "The Other-Race Effect can be prevented, attenuated, and even reversed given experience with a novel race class." So broaden your horizons! Get out there any meet some new people!

*This article originally appeared on RealClearScience.*

## USING AN EXPERT TO EVALUATE EYEWITNESS IDENTIFICATION EVIDENCE

Shirley K. Duffy
83–JUN N.Y. St. B.J. 41 (2011)

A cross-racial identification occurs where a victim/witness of one race identifies a suspect of another race as a perpetrator. A problem exists because cross-racial identifications by witnesses are more likely to result in wrongful convictions. This greater tendency to misidentify suspects of another race has been dubbed the "other-race effect" or "own-race bias." There is some support that the own-race effect is strongest when a white witness must identify a black face. While the majority of research has been conducted using white and black subjects, a recent study has noted the other-race effect between black and Hispanic subjects. * * *

In the last 20 years, research has been conducted in an attempt to discern whether the effect has a social or cognitive explanation. Some researchers have suggested that the inability to accurately encode and recognize other-race faces stems from a simple lack of contact with persons of other races. This theory has not been heavily supported, however, and many studies have argued that it is the quality—not the quantity—of the contact that results in increased ability to recognize other-race faces. Originally, prejudice and racism were thought to be an explanation for lower recognition rates; however, recent studies have found no correlation.

A cognitive interpretation for the "other-race effect" focuses on the physiognomic variability of faces. Specifically, the type of variability in faces, and not the amount of variability, is what accounts for differences in recognition accuracy. Because different races can differ in the type of variability among their faces (e.g., hair color in whites, skin tone in blacks, etc.), relying on the facial cues that lead to variability in one's own race will be ineffective for encoding and recognition of an other-race face.

Whatever the reason for the other-race effect, it has been extensively documented in laboratory research and has been shown to exist outside the lab as well. If cross-racial identification errors cannot be precluded at the source, then they need to be identified and remedied in the courtroom. * * *

Cross-racial-identification error poses unique problems in the realm of eyewitness testimony, primarily because most witnesses either do not know it exists or do not know that they suffer from it. The problem is magnified by the fact that the potential problems with recognition and identification are lost on most jurors. Further, because traditional safeguards against the admission of inaccurate eyewitness testimony (suppression hearings, cross-examination and closing arguments) fail to bring out the existence of any bias, attorneys who are aware of the other-race effect cannot educate the jurors properly. The use of expert testimony and special jury instructions has shown some promise; however, they carry an inherent ineffectiveness because they attempt to make jurors aware of the problem after the fact, with only mixed results.

### PERRY V. NEW HAMPSHIRE

Supreme Court of the United States

565 U.S. 228, 132 S.Ct. 716, 181 L.Ed.2d 691 (2012)

JUSTICE GINSBURG delivered the opinion of the Court.

\* \* \*

Around 3 a.m. on August 15, 2008, Joffre Ullon called the Nashua, New Hampshire, Police Department and reported that an African-American male was trying to break into cars parked in the lot of Ullon's apartment building. Officer Nicole Clay responded to the call. Upon arriving at the parking lot, Clay heard what "sounded like a metal bat hitting the ground." She then saw petitioner Barion Perry standing between two cars. Perry walked toward Clay, holding two car-stereo amplifiers in his hands. A metal bat lay on the ground behind him. Clay asked Perry where the amplifiers came from. "[I] found them on the ground," Perry responded.

Meanwhile, Ullon's wife, Nubia Blandon, woke her neighbor, Alex Clavijo, and told him she had just seen someone break into his car. Clavijo immediately went downstairs to the parking lot to inspect the car. * * * [H]e discovered that the speakers and amplifiers from his car stereo were missing, as were his bat and wrench. * * *

By this time, another officer had arrived at the scene. Clay asked Perry to stay in the parking lot with that officer, while she and Clavijo went to talk to Blandon. * * * They met Blandon in the hallway just outside the open door to her apartment.

Asked to describe what she had seen, Blandon stated that, around 2:30 a.m., she saw from her kitchen window a tall, African-American man roaming the parking lot and looking into cars. Eventually, the man circled Clavijo's car, opened the trunk, and removed a large box.

Clay asked Blandon for a more specific description of the man. Blandon pointed to her kitchen window and said the person she saw breaking into Clavijo's car was standing in the parking lot, next to the police officer. Perry's arrest followed this identification.

About a month later, the police showed Blandon a photographic array that included a picture of Perry and asked her to point out the man who had broken into Clavijo's car. Blandon was unable to identify Perry.

Perry was charged in New Hampshire state court with one count of theft by unauthorized taking and one count of criminal mischief.[a] Before trial, he moved to suppress Blandon's identification on the ground that admitting it at trial would violate due process. Blandon witnessed what amounted to a one-person showup in the parking lot, Perry asserted, which all but guaranteed that she would identify him as the culprit.

The New Hampshire Superior Court denied the motion. * * * [T]he Superior Court concluded [that] Blandon's identification of Perry on the night of the crime did not result from an unnecessarily suggestive procedure "manufacture[d] . . . by the police." Blandon pointed to Perry "spontaneously," the court noted, "without any inducement from the police." * * *

The Superior Court recognized that there were reasons to question the accuracy of Blandon's identification: the parking lot was dark in some locations; Perry was standing next to a police officer; Perry was the only

---

[a]   In order to be found guilty of criminal mischief in the state of New Hampshire, one must, when "having no right to do so nor any reasonable basis for belief of having such a right, purposely or recklessly damage property of another." N.H. REV. STAT. ANN. § 634:2 (2008).

African-American man in the vicinity; and Blandon was unable, later, to pick Perry out of a photographic array. But "[b]ecause the police procedures were not unnecessarily suggestive," the court ruled that the reliability of Blandon's testimony was for the jury to consider. At the ensuing trial, Blandon and Clay testified to Blandon's out-of-court identification. The jury found Perry guilty of theft and not guilty of criminal mischief. On appeal, * * * [t]he New Hampshire Supreme Court rejected Perry's argument and affirmed his conviction.

We granted certiorari to resolve a division of opinion on the question whether the Due Process Clause requires a trial judge to conduct a preliminary assessment of the reliability of an eyewitness identification made under suggestive circumstances not arranged by the police. * * *

[W]e set forth in *Neil v. Biggers*, and reiterated in *Manson v. Brathwaite*, the approach appropriately used to determine whether the Due Process Clause requires suppression of an eyewitness identification tainted by police arrangement. The Court emphasized, first, that due process concerns arise only when law enforcement officers use an identification procedure that is both suggestive and unnecessary. Even when the police use such a procedure, the Court next said, suppression of the resulting identification is not the inevitable consequence.

A rule requiring automatic exclusion, the Court reasoned, would "g[o] too far," for it would "kee[p] evidence from the jury that is reliable and relevant," and "may result, on occasion, in the guilty going free."

Instead of mandating a *per se* exclusionary rule, the Court held that the Due Process Clause requires courts to assess, on a case-by-case basis, whether improper police conduct created a "substantial likelihood of misidentification." "[R]eliability [of the eyewitness identification] is the linchpin" of that evaluation, the Court stated in *Brathwaite*. Where the "indicators of [a witness'] ability to make an accurate identification" are "outweighed by the corrupting effect" of law enforcement suggestion, the identification should be suppressed. Otherwise, the evidence (if admissible in all other respects) should be submitted to the jury.

Applying this "totality of the circumstances" approach, the Court held in *Biggers* that law enforcement's use of an unnecessarily suggestive showup did not require suppression of the victim's identification of her assailant. Notwithstanding the improper procedure, the victim's identification was reliable: She saw her assailant for a considerable period of time under adequate light, provided police with a detailed description of her attacker long before the showup, and had "no doubt" that the defendant was the person she had seen. Similarly, the Court concluded in *Brathwaite* that police use of an unnecessarily suggestive photo array did not require exclusion of the resulting identification. The witness, an undercover police officer, viewed the defendant in good light for several minutes, provided a thorough description of the suspect, and was certain of his identification. Hence, the "indicators of [the witness'] ability to make an accurate identification [were] hardly outweighed by the corrupting effect of the challenged identification."

Perry concedes that * * * law enforcement officials did not arrange the suggestive circumstances surrounding Blandon's identification. He contends, however, that it was mere happenstance that each of the [previously discussed] cases involved improper police action. The rationale underlying our decisions, Perry asserts, supports a rule requiring trial judges to prescreen eyewitness evidence for reliability any time an identification is made under suggestive circumstances. We disagree.

Perry's argument depends, in large part, on the Court's statement in *Brathwaite* that "reliability is the linchpin in determining the admissibility of identification testimony." If reliability is the linchpin of admissibility under the Due Process Clause, Perry maintains, it should make no difference whether law enforcement was responsible for creating the suggestive circumstances that marred the identification.

Perry has removed our statement in *Brathwaite* from its mooring, and thereby attributes to the statement a meaning a fair reading of our opinion does not bear. * * * The due process check for reliability, *Brathwaite* made plain, comes into play only after the defendant establishes improper police conduct. The very purpose of the check, the Court noted, was to avoid depriving the jury of identification evidence that is reliable, notwithstanding improper police conduct. * * * A primary aim of excluding identification evidence obtained under unnecessarily suggestive circumstances, the Court said, is to deter law enforcement use of improper lineups, showups, and photo arrays in the first place. * * *

Perry's argument, reiterated by the dissent, thus lacks support in the case law he cites. Moreover, his position would open the door to judicial preview, under the banner of due process, of most, if not all, eyewitness identifications. External suggestion is hardly the only factor that casts doubt on the trustworthiness of an eyewitness' testimony. As one of Perry's amici points out, many other factors bear on "the likelihood of misidentification,"—for example, the passage of time between exposure to and identification of the defendant, whether the witness was under stress when he first encountered the suspect, how much time the witness had to observe the suspect, how far the witness was from the suspect, whether the suspect carried a weapon, and the race of the suspect and the witness. There is no reason why an identification made by an eyewitness with poor vision, for example, or one who harbors a grudge against the defendant, should be regarded as inherently more reliable, less of a "threat to the fairness of trial," than the identification Blandon made in this case. To embrace Perry's view would thus entail a vast enlargement of the reach of due process as a constraint on the admission of evidence. * * *

In urging a broadly applicable due process check on eyewitness identifications, Perry maintains that eyewitness identifications are a uniquely unreliable form of evidence. We do not doubt * * * the fallibility of eyewitness identifications. * * * The fallibility of eyewitness evidence does not, without the taint of improper state conduct, warrant a due process rule requiring a trial court to screen such evidence for reliability before allowing the jury to assess its creditworthiness.

Our unwillingness to enlarge the domain of due process as Perry and the dissent urge rests, in large part, on our recognition that the jury, not the judge, traditionally determines the reliability of evidence. We also take account of other safeguards built into our adversary system that caution juries against placing undue weight on eyewitness testimony of questionable reliability. * * *

Many of the safeguards * * * were at work at Perry's trial. During her opening statement, Perry's court-appointed attorney cautioned the jury about the vulnerability of Blandon's identification. While cross-examining Blandon and Officer Clay, Perry's attorney constantly brought up the weaknesses of Blandon's identification. She highlighted: (1) the significant distance between Blandon's window and the parking lot, (2) the lateness of the hour, (3) the van that partly obstructed Blandon's view, (4) Blandon's concession that she was "so scared [she] really didn't pay attention" to what Perry was wearing, (5) Blandon's inability to describe Perry's facial features or other identifying marks, (6) Blandon's failure to pick Perry out of a photo array, and (7) Perry's position next to a uniformed, gun-bearing police officer at the moment Blandon made her identification Perry's counsel reminded the jury of these frailties during her summation.

After closing arguments, the trial court read the jury a lengthy instruction on identification testimony and the factors the jury should consider when evaluating it. The court also instructed the jury that the defendant's guilt must be proved beyond a reasonable doubt, and specifically cautioned that "one of the things the State must prove [beyond a reasonable doubt] is the identification of the defendant as the person who committed the offense."

Given the safeguards generally applicable in criminal trials, protections availed of by the defense in Perry's case, we hold that the Due Process Clause does not require a preliminary judicial inquiry into the reliability of an eyewitness identification when the identification was not procured under unnecessarily suggestive circumstances arranged by law enforcement. Accordingly, the judgment of the New Hampshire Supreme Court is

*Affirmed.*

JUSTICE SOTOMAYOR, dissenting. * * *

The majority today creates a novel and significant limitation on our longstanding rule: Eyewitness identifications so impermissibly suggestive that they pose a very substantial likelihood of an unreliable identification will be deemed inadmissible at trial only if the suggestive circumstances were "police-arranged." Absent "improper police arrangement," "improper police conduct," or "rigging," the majority holds, our two-step inquiry does not even "com[e] into play." I cannot agree.

The majority does not simply hold that an eyewitness identification must be the product of police action to trigger our ordinary two-step inquiry. Rather, the majority maintains that the suggestive circumstances giving rise to the identification must be "police-arranged," "police rigg[ed]," "police-designed," or "police-organized." Those terms connote a degree of intentional orchestration or manipulation. The majority categorically exempts all eyewitness identifications derived from suggestive circumstances that were not police-manipulated—however suggestive, and however unreliable—from our due process check. The majority thus appears to graft a *mens rea* requirement onto our existing rule.

As this case illustrates, police intent is now paramount. As the Court acknowledges, Perry alleges an "accidental showup." He was the only African-American at the scene of the crime standing next to a police officer. For the majority, the fact that the police did not intend that showup, even if they inadvertently caused it in the course of a police procedure, ends the inquiry. The police were questioning the eyewitness, Blandon, about the perpetrator's identity, and were intentionally detaining Perry in the parking lot—but had not intended for Blandon to identify the perpetrator from her window. Presumably, in the majority's view, had the police asked Blandon to move to the window to identify the perpetrator, that could have made all the difference.

I note, however, that the majority leaves what is required by its arrangement-focused inquiry less than clear. In parts, the opinion suggests that the police must arrange an identification "procedure," regardless of whether they "inten[d] the arranged procedure to be suggestive." Elsewhere, it indicates that the police must arrange the "suggestive circumstances" that lead the witness to identify the accused. Still elsewhere it refers to "improper" police conduct, connoting bad faith. * * *

The arrangement-focused inquiry will sow needless confusion. If the police had called Perry and Blandon to the police station for interviews, and Blandon saw Perry being questioned, would that be sufficiently "improper police arrangement"? If Perry had voluntarily come to the police station, would that change the result? Today's opinion renders the applicability of our ordinary inquiry contingent on a murky line-drawing exercise. Whereas our two-step inquiry focuses on overall reliability—and could account for the spontaneity of the witness' identification and degree of police manipulation under the totality of the circumstances—today's opinion forecloses that assessment by establishing a new and inflexible step zero.

* * * [T]he majority emphasizes that we should rely on the jury to determine the reliability of evidence. But our cases are rooted in the assumption that eyewitness identifications upend the ordinary expectation that it is "the province of the jury to weigh the credibility of competing witnesses." As noted, jurors find eyewitness evidence unusually powerful and their ability to assess credibility is hindered by a witness' false confidence in the accuracy of his or her identification. That disability in no way depends on the intent behind the suggestive circumstances. * * *

The empirical evidence demonstrates that eyewitness misidentification is "the single greatest cause of wrongful convictions in this country." Researchers have found that a staggering 76% of the first 250 convictions overturned due to DNA evidence since 1989 involved eyewitness misidentification. Study after study demonstrates that eyewitness recollections are highly susceptible to distortion by postevent information or social cues; that jurors routinely overestimate the accuracy of eyewitness identifications; that jurors place the greatest weight on eyewitness confidence in assessing identifications even though confidence is a poor gauge of accuracy; and that suggestiveness can stem from sources beyond police-orchestrated procedures. The majority today nevertheless adopts an artificially narrow conception of the dangers of suggestive identifications at a time when our concerns should have deepened. * * *

[JUSTICE THOMAS' concurring opinion has been omitted.]

# CHAPTER 22

# THE PROSECUTOR'S CHARGING DISCRETION

■ ■ ■

As the Supreme Court has often said, the decision whether to prosecute and what charge or charges to file rests entirely within the prosecutor's discretion. The prosecutor's charging discretion, however, is not unfettered. It is subject to constitutional constraints. *United States v. Armstrong* examines one of these constitutional constraints: the Equal Protection Clause. A defendant who believes she has been unfairly charged because of her race, gender, national origin, or other protected class status can assert a selective prosecution claim. A selective prosecution claim is an affirmative defense that can lead to a dismissal of the indictment or a reversal of a conviction. The *Armstrong* Court explains the requirements for a selective prosecution claim and decides what showing is necessary for a defendant to obtain discovery in support of a selective prosecution claim.[a]

In *United States v. Batchelder*, the Court examines a case involving overlapping statutes, i.e., two statutes that are identical except for the penalty that is authorized by each statute. The *Batchelder* Court considers whether it violates the Constitution for the prosecutor to charge a defendant with violating the statute with the greater penalty. As part of this inquiry, the Court considers whether the rule of lenity and/or the void for vagueness doctrine require the prosecutor to charge the defendant with violating the offense with the lesser sentence.

In *United States v. Goodwin*, we learn about another constitutional constraint on the prosecutor's charging discretion: the Due Process Clause. The Due Process Clause prohibits the prosecution from using its charging discretion to retaliate against a defendant for exercising a constitutional or statutory right. A defendant who believes he is being retaliated against or punished for exercising a constitutional or statutory right may assert a claim of vindictive prosecution. Because it is almost always impossible to prove a retaliatory motive, courts may apply a presumption of vindictiveness in cases involving a realistic likelihood of vindictiveness. In

---

[a] Discovery is the process in which the parties obtain information about the witnesses and evidence that the other side has, usually before trial. *See* American Bar Association, Division for Public Education, How Courts Work, *available at* http://www.americanbar.org/groups/public_education/resources/law_related_education_network/how_courts_work/discovery.html. We will study the rules governing discovery in criminal cases in a later chapter.

these cases, the defendant need only show that he exercised a constitutional or statutory right, and that this was followed by additional or more serious charges. The prosecutor can overcome a presumption of vindictiveness by presenting objective information supporting the additional or more serious charges. If a presumption of vindictiveness does not apply, the defendant must show actual vindictiveness, i.e., that the prosecutor filed the additional or more serious charges to punish him for doing something that the law allowed him to do.

The prosecutor is also subject to ethical constraints. As noted in the American Bar Association's Criminal Justice Standards for the Prosecution Function, "The primary duty of the prosecutor is to seek justice within the bounds of the law, not merely to convict." *See* Standard 3–1.2 (a) in Appendix. Under these standards, "A prosecutor should . . . file criminal charges only if the prosecutor reasonably believes that the charges are supported by probable cause, that admissible evidence will be sufficient to support a conviction beyond a reasonable doubt, and that the decision to charge is in the interests of justice." *See* Standard 3–4.3 (a) in Appendix.

In *Racial Fairness in the Criminal Justice System: The Role of the Prosecutor*, Angela Davis explains how racial considerations can affect prosecutorial charging decisions, even when the prosecutor is not consciously intending to discriminate based on race. Davis's article examines the traditional factors that inform the prosecutor's charging decision, and shows how race and class can have an impact on these seemingly race-neutral factors. A note on the prosecutor's charging discretion in relation to the 2012 shooting death of Trayvon Martin, an unarmed Black male teenager, by George Zimmerman, a Neighborhood Watch volunteer, follows this excerpt.

## UNITED STATES V. ARMSTRONG

Supreme Court of the United States
517 U.S. 456, 116 S.Ct. 1480, 134 L.Ed.2d 687 (1996)

CHIEF JUSTICE REHNQUIST delivered the opinion of the Court. * * *

In April 1992, respondents were indicted in the United States District Court for the Central District of California on charges of conspiring to possess with intent to distribute more than 50 grams of cocaine base (crack) and conspiring to distribute the same, in violation of 21 U.S.C. §§ 841 and 846, and federal firearms offenses. For three months prior to the indictment, agents of the Federal Bureau of Alcohol, Tobacco, and Firearms and the Narcotics Division of the Inglewood, California, Police Department had infiltrated a suspected crack distribution ring by using three confidential informants. On seven separate occasions during this period, the informants had bought a total of 124.3 grams of crack from respondents and witnessed respondents carrying firearms during the sales. The agents searched the hotel room in which the sales were transacted, arrested respondents Armstrong and Hampton in the room, and found more crack and a loaded gun. The agents later arrested the other respondents as part of the ring.

In response to the indictment, respondents filed a motion for discovery or for dismissal of the indictment, alleging that they were selected for federal prosecution because they are black. In support of their motion, they offered only an affidavit by a "Paralegal Specialist," employed by the Office of the Federal Public Defender representing one of the respondents. The only allegation in the affidavit was that, in every one of the 24 § 841 or § 846 cases closed by the office during 1991, the defendant was black. Accompanying the affidavit was a "study" listing the 24 defendants, their race, whether they were prosecuted for dealing cocaine as well as crack, and the status of each case.

The Government opposed the discovery motion, arguing, among other things, that there was no evidence or allegation "that the Government has acted unfairly or has prosecuted non-black defendants or failed to prosecute them." The District Court granted the motion. It ordered the Government (1) to provide a list of all cases from the last three years in which the Government charged both cocaine and firearms offenses, (2) to identify the race of the defendants in those cases, (3) to identify what levels of law enforcement were involved in the investigations of those cases, and (4) to explain its criteria for deciding to prosecute those defendants for federal cocaine offenses.

The Government moved for reconsideration of the District Court's discovery order. With this motion it submitted affidavits and other evidence to explain why it had chosen to prosecute respondents and why respondents' study did not support the inference that the Government was singling out blacks for cocaine prosecution. The federal and local agents participating in the case alleged in affidavits that race played no role in their investigation. An Assistant United States Attorney explained in an affidavit that the decision to prosecute met the general criteria for prosecution, because

> there was over 100 grams of cocaine base involved, over twice the threshold necessary for a ten year mandatory minimum sentence; there were multiple sales involving multiple defendants, thereby indicating a fairly substantial crack cocaine ring; . . . there were multiple federal firearms violations intertwined with the narcotics trafficking; the overall evidence in the case was extremely strong, including audio and videotapes of defendants; . . . and several of the defendants had criminal histories including narcotics and firearms violations.

The Government also submitted sections of a published 1989 Drug Enforcement Administration report which concluded that "[l]arge-scale, interstate trafficking networks controlled by Jamaicans, Haitians and Black street gangs dominate the manufacture and distribution of crack."

In response, one of respondents' attorneys submitted an affidavit alleging that an intake coordinator at a drug treatment center had told her that there are "an equal number of caucasian users and dealers to minority users and dealers." Respondents also submitted an affidavit from a criminal defense attorney alleging that in his experience many nonblacks are prosecuted in state court for crack offenses, and a newspaper article reporting that federal "crack criminals . . . are being punished far more severely than if they had been caught with powder cocaine, and almost every single one of them is black."

The District Court denied the motion for reconsideration. When the Government indicated it would not comply with the court's discovery order, the court dismissed the case. * * * [An] en banc panel [of the Court of Appeals] affirmed the District Court's order of dismissal, holding that "a defendant is not required to demonstrate that the government has failed to prosecute others who are similarly situated." We granted certiorari to determine the appropriate standard for discovery for a selective-prosecution claim. * * *

A selective-prosecution claim is not a defense on the merits to the criminal charge itself, but an independent assertion that the prosecutor has brought the charge for reasons forbidden by the Constitution. Our cases delineating the necessary elements to prove a claim of selective prosecution have taken great pains to explain that the standard is a demanding one. * * *

A selective-prosecution claim asks a court to exercise judicial power over a "special province" of the Executive. The Attorney General and United States Attorneys retain "broad discretion" to enforce the Nation's criminal laws. They have this latitude because they are designated by statute as the President's delegates to help him discharge his constitutional responsibility to "take Care that the Laws be faithfully executed." As a result, "[t]he presumption of regularity supports" their prosecutorial decisions and, "in the absence of clear evidence to the contrary, courts presume that they have properly discharged their official duties." In the ordinary case, "so long as the prosecutor has probable cause to believe that the accused committed an offense defined by statute, the decision whether or not to prosecute, and what charge to file or bring before a grand jury, generally rests entirely in his discretion."

Of course, a prosecutor's discretion is "subject to constitutional constraints." One of these constraints, imposed by the equal protection component of the Due Process Clause of the Fifth Amendment, is that the decision whether to prosecute may not be based on "an unjustifiable standard such as race, religion, or other arbitrary classification." A defendant may demonstrate that the administration of a criminal law is "directed so exclusively against a particular class of persons . . . with a mind so unequal and oppressive" that the system of prosecution amounts to "a practical denial" of equal protection of the law.

In order to dispel the presumption that a prosecutor has not violated equal protection, a criminal defendant must present "clear evidence to the contrary." We explained in *Wayte* why courts are "properly hesitant to examine the decision whether to prosecute." Judicial deference to the decisions of these executive officers rests in part on an assessment of the relative competence of prosecutors and courts. "Such factors as the strength of the case, the prosecution's general deterrence value, the Government's enforcement priorities, and the case's relationship to the Government's overall enforcement plan are not readily susceptible to the kind of analysis the courts are competent to undertake." It also stems from a concern not to unnecessarily impair the performance of a core executive constitutional function. "Examining the basis of a prosecution delays the criminal proceeding, threatens to chill law enforcement by subjecting the prosecutor's motives and decisionmaking to outside inquiry, and may undermine prosecutorial effectiveness by revealing the Government's enforcement policy."

The requirements for a selective-prosecution claim draw on "ordinary equal protection standards." The claimant must demonstrate that the federal prosecutorial policy "had a discriminatory effect and that it was motivated by a discriminatory purpose." To establish a discriminatory effect in a race case, the claimant must show that similarly situated individuals of a different race were not prosecuted. This requirement has been established in our case law since *Ah Sin v. Wittman*. Ah Sin, a subject of China, petitioned a California state court for a writ of habeas corpus, seeking discharge from imprisonment under a San Francisco County ordinance prohibiting persons from setting up gambling tables in rooms barricaded to stop police from entering. He alleged in his habeas petition "that the ordinance is enforced 'solely and exclusively against persons of the Chinese race and not otherwise.' " We rejected his contention that this averment made out a claim under the Equal Protection Clause, because it did not allege "that * * * there were other offenders against the ordinance than the Chinese as to whom it was not enforced."

The similarly situated requirement does not make a selective-prosecution claim impossible to prove. Twenty years before *Ah Sin,* we invalidated an ordinance, also adopted by San Francisco, that prohibited the operation of laundries in wooden buildings. The plaintiff in error [in *Yick Wo*] successfully demonstrated that the ordinance was applied against Chinese nationals but not against other laundry-shop operators. The authorities had denied the applications of 200 Chinese subjects for permits to operate shops in wooden buildings, but granted the applications of 80 individuals who were not Chinese subjects to operate laundries in wooden buildings "under similar conditions." * * *

Having reviewed the requirements to prove a selective-prosecution claim, we turn to the showing necessary to obtain discovery in support of such a claim. If discovery is ordered, the Government must assemble from its own files documents which might corroborate or refute the defendant's claim. Discovery thus imposes many of the costs present when the Government must respond to a prima facie case of selective prosecution. It will divert prosecutors' resources and may disclose the Government's prosecutorial strategy. The justifications for a rigorous standard for the elements of a selective-prosecution claim thus require a correspondingly rigorous standard for discovery in aid of such a claim.

The parties, and the Courts of Appeals which have considered the requisite showing to establish entitlement to discovery, describe this showing with a variety of phrases, like "colorable basis," "substantial threshold showing," "substantial and concrete basis," or "reasonable likelihood." However, the many labels for this showing conceal the degree of consensus about the evidence necessary to meet it. The Courts of Appeals "require some evidence tending to show the existence of the essential elements of the defense," discriminatory effect and discriminatory intent.

In this case we consider what evidence constitutes "some evidence tending to show the existence" of the discriminatory effect element. The Court of Appeals held that a defendant may establish a colorable basis for discriminatory effect without evidence that the Government has failed to prosecute others who are similarly situated to the defendant. We think it was mistaken in this view. The vast majority of the Courts of Appeals require the defendant to produce some evidence that similarly situated defendants of other races could have been prosecuted, but were not, and this requirement is consistent with our equal protection case law. As the three-judge panel explained, " '[s]elective prosecution' implies that a selection has taken place." * * *

In the case before us, respondents' "study" did not constitute "some evidence tending to show the existence of the essential elements of" a selective-prosecution claim. The study failed to identify individuals who were not black and could have been prosecuted for the offenses for which respondents were charged, but were not so prosecuted. This omission was not remedied by respondents' evidence in opposition to the Government's motion for reconsideration. The newspaper article, which discussed the discriminatory effect of federal drug sentencing laws, was not relevant to an allegation of discrimination in decisions to prosecute. Respondents' affidavits, which recounted one attorney's conversation with a drug treatment center employee and the experience of another attorney defending drug prosecutions in state court, recounted hearsay and reported personal conclusions based on anecdotal evidence. The judgment of the Court of Appeals is therefore reversed, and the case is remanded for proceedings consistent with this opinion.

*It is so ordered.*

JUSTICE STEVENS, dissenting.

Federal prosecutors are respected members of a respected profession. Despite an occasional misstep, the excellence of their work abundantly justifies the presumption that "they have properly discharged their official duties." Nevertheless, the possibility that political or racial animosity may infect a decision to institute criminal proceedings cannot be ignored. For that reason, it has long been settled that the prosecutor's broad discretion to determine when criminal charges should be filed is not completely unbridled. As the Court notes, however, the scope of judicial review of particular exercises of that discretion is not fully defined. * * *

The District Judge's order should be evaluated in light of three circumstances that underscore the need for judicial vigilance over certain types of drug prosecutions. First, the Anti-Drug Abuse Act of 1986 and subsequent legislation established a regime of extremely high penalties for the possession and distribution of so-called "crack" cocaine. Those provisions treat one gram of crack as the equivalent of 100 grams of powder cocaine. The distribution of 50 grams of crack is thus punishable by the same mandatory minimum sentence of 10 years in prison that applies to the distribution of 5,000 grams of powder cocaine. The Sentencing Guidelines extend this ratio to penalty levels above the mandatory minimums: For any given quantity of crack, the guideline range is the same as if the offense had involved 100 times that amount in powder cocaine. These penalties result in sentences for crack offenders that average three to eight times longer than sentences for comparable powder offenders.[a]

Second, the disparity between the treatment of crack cocaine and powder cocaine is matched by the disparity between the severity of the punishment imposed by federal law and that imposed by state law for the same conduct. For a variety of reasons, often including the absence of mandatory minimums, the existence of parole, and lower baseline penalties, terms of imprisonment for drug offenses tend to be substantially

---

[a] For years, the U.S. Sentencing Commission tried without success to get Congress to eliminate the 100 to 1 ratio between sentences for crack cocaine and sentences for powder cocaine because of the disproportionate impact this was having on Blacks. Ellis Cose, *Closing the Gap: Obama Could Fix Cocaine Sentencing*, NEWSWEEK, July 20, 2009, at 25. Finally, more than two decades after passage of the Anti-Drug Abuse Act of 1986, Congress passed the Fair Sentencing Act in July of 2010, reducing the 100 to 1 disparity between crack and powder cocaine to approximately 18 to 1. Fair Sentencing Act of 2010, 21 U.S.C. §§ 841, 960 (2012). *See also* Jim Abrams, *Congress Passes Bill to Reduce Disparity in Crack, Powder Cocaine Sentencing*, WASH. POST, July 29, 2010, at A9.

lower in state systems than in the federal system. The difference is especially marked in the case of crack offenses. The majority of States draw no distinction between types of cocaine in their penalty schemes; of those that do, none has established as stark a differential as the Federal Government. For example, if respondent Hampton is found guilty, his federal sentence might be as long as a mandatory life term. Had he been tried in state court, his sentence could have been as short as 12 years, less worktime credits of half that amount.

Finally, it is undisputed that the brunt of the elevated federal penalties falls heavily on blacks. While 65% of the persons who have used crack are white, in 1993 they represented only 4% of the federal offenders convicted of trafficking in crack. Eighty-eight percent of such defendants were black. During the first 18 months of full guideline implementation, the sentencing disparity between black and white defendants grew from preguideline levels: Blacks on average received sentences over 40% longer than whites. Those figures represent a major threat to the integrity of federal sentencing reform, whose main purpose was the elimination of disparity (especially racial) in sentencing. The Sentencing Commission acknowledges that the heightened crack penalties are a "primary cause of the growing disparity between sentences for Black and White federal defendants."

The extraordinary severity of the imposed penalties and the troubling racial patterns of enforcement give rise to a special concern about the fairness of charging practices for crack offenses. Evidence tending to prove that black defendants charged with distribution of crack in the Central District of California are prosecuted in federal court, whereas members of other races charged with similar offenses are prosecuted in state court, warrants close scrutiny by the federal judges in that district. In my view, the District Judge, who has sat on both the federal and the state benches in Los Angeles, acted well within her discretion to call for the development of facts that would demonstrate what standards, if any, governed the choice of forum where similarly situated offenders are prosecuted.

Respondents submitted a study showing that of all cases involving crack offenses that were closed by the Federal Public Defender's Office in 1991, 24 out of 24 involved black defendants. To supplement this evidence, they submitted affidavits from two of the attorneys in the defense team. The first reported a statement from an intake coordinator at a local drug treatment center that, in his experience, an equal number of crack users and dealers were caucasian as belonged to minorities. The second was from David R. Reed, counsel for respondent Armstrong. Reed was both an active court-appointed attorney in the Central District of California and one of the directors of the leading association of criminal defense lawyers who practice before the Los Angeles County courts. Reed stated that he did not recall "ever handling a [crack] cocaine case involving non-black defendants" in federal court, nor had he even heard of one. He further stated that "[t]here are many crack cocaine sales cases prosecuted in state court that *do* involve racial groups other than blacks." (emphasis in original).

The majority discounts the probative value of the affidavits, claiming that they recounted "hearsay"[b] and reported "personal conclusions based on anecdotal evidence." But the Reed affidavit plainly contained more than mere hearsay; Reed offered information based on his own extensive experience in both federal and state courts. Given the breadth of his background, he was well qualified to compare the practices of federal and state prosecutors. In any event, the Government never objected to the admission of either affidavit on hearsay or any other grounds. It was certainly within the District Court's discretion to credit the affidavits of two members of the bar of that Court, at least one of whom had presumably acquired a reputation by his frequent appearances there, and both of whose statements were made on pains of perjury.

The criticism that the affidavits were based on "anecdotal evidence" is also unpersuasive. I thought it was agreed that defendants do not need to prepare sophisticated statistical studies in order to receive mere discovery in cases like this one. Certainly evidence based on a drug counselor's personal observations or on an attorney's practice in two sets of courts, state and federal, can "ten[d] to show the existence" of a selective prosecution.

Even if respondents failed to carry their burden of showing that there were individuals who were not black but who could have been prosecuted in federal court for the same offenses, it does not follow that the District Court abused its discretion in ordering discovery. There can be no doubt that such individuals exist, and indeed the Government has never denied the same. In those circumstances, I fail to see why the District Court was unable to take judicial notice of this obvious fact and demand information from the Government's files to support or refute respondents' evidence.

* * * In this case, the evidence was sufficiently disturbing to persuade the District Judge to order discovery that might help explain the conspicuous racial pattern of cases before her court. I cannot accept the majority's conclusion that the District Judge either exceeded her power or abused her discretion when she did so. I therefore respectfully dissent.

---

[b]    Black's Law Dictionary defines hearsay as "1. Traditionally, testimony that is given by a witness who relates not what he or she knows personally, but what others have said, and that is therefore dependent on the credibility of someone other than the witness. Such testimony is generally inadmissible under the rules of evidence. 2. In federal law, a statement . . . other than one made by the declarant while testifying at the trial or hearing, offered in evidence to prove the truth of the matter asserted." BLACK'S LAW DICTIONARY 838 (10th ed. 2014).

[JUSTICE SOUTER's concurring opinion, JUSTICE GINSBURG's concurring opinion, and JUSTICE BREYER's concurring opinion have been omitted.]

## NOTE

Does *Armstrong* make it impossible for defendants to get discovery to support a selective prosecution claim? Richard McAdams points out that the *Armstrong* Court provides only one case, *Yick Wo v. Hopkins*, as support for its claim that it is not impossible to satisfy the requirement that the defendant show that similarly situated individuals could have been, but were not prosecuted. Richard H. McAdams, *Race and Selective Prosecution: Discovering the Pitfalls of* Armstrong, 73 CHI.-KENT L. REV. 605, 615 (1998). *Yick Wo*, however, was decided in 1886, more than 100 years before *Armstrong*, and the Court was unable to find any other case in which the defendant succeeded in meeting this standard.

## UNITED STATES V. BATCHELDER

Supreme Court of the United States
442 U.S. 114, 99 S.Ct. 2198, 60 L.Ed.2d 755 (1979)

JUSTICE MARSHALL delivered the opinion of the Court.

At issue in this case are two overlapping provisions of the Omnibus Crime Control and Safe Streets Act of 1968 (Omnibus Act). Both prohibit convicted felons from receiving firearms, but each authorizes different maximum penalties. We must determine whether a defendant convicted of the offense carrying the greater penalty may be sentenced only under the more lenient provision when his conduct violates both statutes.

Respondent, a previously convicted felon, was found guilty of receiving a firearm that had traveled in interstate commerce, in violation of 18 U.S.C. § 922(h).[7] The District Court sentenced him under 18 U.S.C. § 924(a) to five years' imprisonment, the maximum term authorized for violation of § 922(h).[8]

---

[7]   In pertinent part, 18 U.S.C. § 922(h) provides:
"It shall be unlawful for any person—
    (1) who is under indictment for, or who has been convicted in any court of, a crime punishable by imprisonment for a term exceeding one year;
    (2) who is a fugitive from justice;
    (3) who is an unlawful user of or addicted to marihuana or any depressant or stimulant drug . . . or narcotic drug . . . ; or
    (4) who has been adjudicated as a mental defective or who has been committed to any mental institution; to receive any firearm or ammunition which has been shipped or transported in interstate or foreign commerce."

[8]   Title 18 U.S.C. § 924(a) provides in relevant part:
    "Whoever violates any provision of this chapter . . . shall be fined not more than $5,000, or imprisoned not more than five years, or both, and shall become eligible for parole as the Board of Parole shall determine."

The Court of Appeals affirmed the conviction but, by a divided vote, remanded for resentencing. The majority recognized that respondent had been indicted and convicted under § 922(h) and that § 924(a) permits five years' imprisonment for such violations. However, noting that the substantive elements of § 922(h) and 18 U.S.C.App. § 1202(a) are identical as applied to a convicted felon who unlawfully receives a firearm, the court interpreted the Omnibus Act to allow no more than the 2-year maximum sentence provided by § 1202(a).[4] In so holding, the Court of Appeals relied on [several] principles of statutory construction. Because, in its view, the "arguably contradict[ory]" penalty provisions for similar conduct and the "inconclusive" legislative history raised doubt whether Congress had intended the two penalty provisions to coexist, the court first applied the doctrine that ambiguities in criminal legislation are to be resolved in favor of the defendant. Second, the court determined that since § 1202(a) was "Congress' last word on the issue of penalty," it may have implicitly repealed the punishment provisions of § 924(a). * * *

We granted certiorari, and now reverse the judgment vacating respondent's 5-year prison sentence.

This Court has previously noted the partial redundancy of §§ 922(h) and 1202(a), both as to the conduct they proscribe and the individuals they reach. However, we find nothing in the language, structure, or legislative history of the Omnibus Act to suggest that because of this overlap, a defendant convicted under § 922(h) may be imprisoned for no more than the maximum term specified in § 1202(a). As we read the Act, each substantive statute, in conjunction with its own sentencing provision, operates independently of the other.

Section 922(h), contained in Title IV of the Omnibus Act, prohibits four categories of individuals from receiving "any firearm or ammunition which has been shipped or transported in interstate or foreign commerce." Persons who violate Title IV are subject to the penalties provided by § 924(a), which authorizes a maximum fine of $5,000 and imprisonment for up to five years. Section 1202(a), located in Title VII of the Omnibus Act, forbids five categories of individuals from "receiv[ing], possess[ing], or

---

[4]    Section 1202(a) states:

"Any person who—

(1) has been convicted by a court of the United States or of a State or any political subdivision thereof of a felony, or

(2) has been discharged from the Armed Forces under dishonorable conditions, or

(3) has been adjudged by a court of the United States or of a State or any political subdivision thereof of being mentally incompetent, or

(4) having been a citizen of the United States has renounced his citizenship, or

(5) being an alien is illegally or unlawfully in the United States,

and who receives, possesses, or transports in commerce or affecting commerce, after the date of enactment of this Act, any firearm shall be fined not more than $10,000 or imprisoned for not more than two years, or both." 18 U.S.C.App. § 1202(a).

transport[ing] in commerce or affecting commerce . . . any firearm." This same section authorizes a maximum fine of $10,000 and imprisonment for not more than two years. * * *

In construing § 1202(a) to override the penalties authorized by § 924(a), the Court of Appeals relied, we believe erroneously, on [several] principles of statutory interpretation. First, the court invoked the well-established doctrine that ambiguities in criminal statutes must be resolved in favor of lenity. Although this principle of construction applies to sentencing as well as substantive provisions, in the instant case there is no ambiguity to resolve. Respondent unquestionably violated § 922(h), and § 924(a) unquestionably permits five years' imprisonment for such a violation. That § 1202(a) provides different penalties for essentially the same conduct is no justification for taking liberties with unequivocal statutory language. By its express terms, § 1202(a) limits its penalty scheme exclusively to convictions obtained under that provision. Where as here, "Congress has conveyed its purpose clearly, . . . we decline to manufacture ambiguity where none exists."

Nor can § 1202(a) be interpreted as implicitly repealing § 924(a) whenever a defendant's conduct might violate both Titles. For it is "not enough to show that the two statutes produce differing results when applied to the same factual situation." Rather, the legislative intent to repeal must be manifest in the "positive repugnancy between the provisions." In this case, however, the penalty provisions are fully capable of coexisting because they apply to convictions under different statutes. * * *

In resolving the statutory question, the majority below expressed "serious doubts about the constitutionality of two statutes that provide different penalties for identical conduct." Specifically, the court suggested that the statutes might (1) be void for vagueness, (2) implicate "due process and equal protection interest[s] in avoiding excessive prosecutorial discretion and in obtaining equal justice," and (3) constitute an impermissible delegation of congressional authority. We find no constitutional infirmities.

It is a fundamental tenet of due process that "[n]o one may be required at peril of life, liberty or property to speculate as to the meaning of penal statutes." A criminal statute is therefore invalid if it "fails to give a person of ordinary intelligence fair notice that his contemplated conduct is forbidden." So too, vague sentencing provisions may post constitutional questions if they do not state with sufficient clarity the consequences of violating a given criminal statute.

The provisions in issue here, however, unambiguously specify the activity proscribed and the penalties available upon conviction. That this particular conduct may violate both Titles does not detract from the notice afforded by each. Although the statutes create uncertainty as to which crime may be charged and therefore what penalties may be imposed, they do so to no greater extent than would a single statute authorizing various alternative punishments. So long as overlapping criminal provisions clearly define the conduct prohibited and the punishment authorized, the notice requirements of the Due Process Clause are satisfied.

This Court has long recognized that when an act violates more than one criminal statute, the Government may prosecute under either so long as it does not discriminate against any class of defendants. Whether to prosecute and what charge to file or bring before a grand jury are decisions that generally rest in the prosecutor's discretion.

The Court of Appeals acknowledged this "settled rule" allowing prosecutorial choice. Nevertheless, relying on the dissenting opinion in *Berra v. United States*, the court distinguished overlapping statutes with identical standards of proof from provisions that vary in some particular. In the court's view, when two statutes prohibit "exactly the same conduct," the prosecutor's "selection of which of two penalties to apply" would be "unfettered." Because such prosecutorial discretion could produce "unequal justice," the court expressed doubt that this form of legislative redundancy was constitutional. We find this analysis factually and legally unsound.

Contrary to the Court of Appeals' assertions, a prosecutor's discretion to choose between §§ 922(h) and 1202(a) is not "unfettered." Selectivity in the enforcement of criminal laws is, of course, subject to constitutional constraints. And a decision to proceed under § 922(h) does not empower the Government to predetermine ultimate criminal sanctions. Rather, it merely enables the sentencing judge to impose a longer prison sentence than § 1202(a) would permit and precludes him from imposing the greater fine authorized by § 1202(a). More importantly, there is no appreciable difference between the discretion a prosecutor exercises when deciding whether to charge under one of two statutes with different elements and the discretion he exercises when choosing one of two statutes with identical elements. In the former situation, once he determines that the proof will support conviction under either statute, his decision is indistinguishable from the one he faces in the latter context. The prosecutor may be influenced by the penalties available upon conviction, but this fact, standing alone, does not give rise to a violation of the Equal Protection or Due Process Clause. Just as a defendant has no constitutional right to elect which of two applicable federal statutes shall be the basis of his indictment and prosecution, neither is he entitled to choose the penalty scheme under which he will be sentenced.

Approaching the problem of prosecutorial discretion from a slightly different perspective, the Court of Appeals postulated that the statutes might impermissibly delegate to the Executive Branch the Legislature's responsibility to fix criminal penalties. We do not agree. The provisions at issue plainly demarcate the range of penalties that prosecutors and judges may seek and impose. In light of that specificity, the power that Congress has delegated to those officials is no broader than the authority they routinely exercise in enforcing the criminal laws. * * *

Accordingly, the judgment of the Court of Appeals is

*Reversed.*

## UNITED STATES v. GOODWIN
Supreme Court of the United States
457 U.S. 368, 102 S.Ct. 2485, 73 L.Ed.2d 74 (1982)

JUSTICE STEVENS delivered the opinion of the Court. * * *

Respondent Goodwin was stopped for speeding by a United States Park Policeman on the Baltimore-Washington Parkway. Goodwin emerged from his car to talk to the policeman. After a brief discussion, the officer noticed a clear plastic bag underneath the armrest next to the driver's seat of Goodwin's car. The officer asked Goodwin to return to his car and to raise the armrest. Respondent did so, but as he raised the armrest he placed the car into gear and accelerated rapidly. The car struck the officer, knocking him first onto the back of the car and then onto the highway. The policeman returned to his car, but Goodwin eluded him in a high-speed chase.

The following day, the officer filed a complaint in the District Court charging respondent with several misdemeanor and petty offenses, including assault. Goodwin was arrested and arraigned before a United States Magistrate. The Magistrate set a date for trial, but respondent fled the jurisdiction. Three years later Goodwin was found in custody in Virginia and was returned to Maryland.

Upon his return, respondent's case was assigned to an attorney from the Department of Justice, who was detailed temporarily to try petty crime and misdemeanor cases before the Magistrate. The attorney did not have authority to try felony cases or to seek indictments from the grand jury. Respondent initiated plea negotiations with the prosecutor, but later advised the Government that he did not wish to plead guilty and desired a trial by jury in the District Court.

The case was transferred to the District Court and responsibility for the prosecution was assumed by an Assistant United States Attorney. Approximately six weeks later, after reviewing the case and discussing it with several parties, the prosecutor obtained a four-count indictment charging respondent with one felony count of forcibly assaulting a federal officer and three related counts arising from the same incident.[2] A jury convicted respondent on the felony count and on one misdemeanor count.

Respondent moved to set aside the verdict on the ground of prosecutorial vindictiveness, contending that the indictment on the felony charge gave rise to an impermissible appearance of retaliation. The District Court denied the motion, finding that "the prosecutor in this case has adequately dispelled any appearance of retaliatory intent."

Although the Court of Appeals readily concluded that "the prosecutor did not act with actual vindictiveness in seeking a felony indictment," it nevertheless reversed. Relying on our decisions in *North Carolina v. Pearce* and *Blackledge v. Perry*, the court held that the Due Process Clause of the Fifth Amendment prohibits the Government from bringing more serious charges against a defendant after he has invoked his right to a jury trial, unless the prosecutor comes forward with objective evidence to show that the increased charges could not have been brought before the defendant exercised his rights. Because the court believed that the circumstances surrounding the felony indictment gave rise to a genuine risk of retaliation, it adopted a legal presumption designed to spare courts the "unseemly task" of probing the actual motives of the prosecutor.

To punish a person because he has done what the law plainly allows him to do is a due process violation "of the most basic sort." In a series of cases beginning with *North Carolina v. Pearce* and culminating in *Bordenkircher v. Hayes*, the Court has recognized this basic—and itself uncontroversial—principle. For while an individual certainly may be penalized for violating the law, he just as certainly may not be punished for exercising a protected statutory or constitutional right.

* * * Motives are complex and difficult to prove. As a result, in certain cases in which action detrimental to the defendant has been taken after the exercise of a legal right, the Court has found it necessary to "presume" an improper vindictive motive. Given the severity of such a presumption, however—which may operate in the absence of any proof of an improper motive and thus may block a legitimate response to criminal conduct—the Court has done so only in cases in which a reasonable likelihood of vindictiveness exists.

In *North Carolina v. Pearce*, the Court held that neither the Double Jeopardy Clause nor the Equal Protection Clause prohibits a trial judge from imposing a harsher sentence on retrial after a criminal defendant

---

[2] By affidavit, the Assistant United States Attorney later set forth his reasons for this action: (1) he considered respondent's conduct on the date in question to be a serious violation of law, (2) respondent had a lengthy history of violent crime, (3) the prosecutor considered respondent's conduct to be related to major narcotics transactions, (4) the prosecutor believed that respondent had committed perjury at his preliminary hearing, and (5) respondent had failed to appear for trial as originally scheduled. The Government attorney stated that his decision to seek a felony indictment was not motivated in any way by Goodwin's request for a jury trial in District Court.

successfully attacks an initial conviction on appeal. The Court stated, however, that "[i]t can hardly be doubted that it would be a flagrant violation [of the Due Process Clause] of the Fourteenth Amendment for a state trial court to follow an announced practice of imposing a heavier sentence upon every reconvicted defendant for the explicit purpose of punishing the defendant for his having succeeded in getting his original conviction set aside." The Court continued:

> Due process of law, then, requires that vindictiveness against a defendant for having successfully attacked his first conviction must play no part in the sentence he receives after a new trial. And since the fear of such vindictiveness may unconstitutionally deter a defendant's exercise of the right to appeal or collaterally attack his first conviction, due process also requires that a defendant be freed of apprehension of such a retaliatory motivation on the part of the sentencing judge.

In order to assure the absence of such a motivation, the Court concluded:

> [W]henever a judge imposes a more severe sentence upon a defendant after a new trial, the reasons for his doing so must affirmatively appear. Those reasons must be based upon objective information concerning identifiable conduct on the part of the defendant occurring after the time of the original sentencing proceeding.[a] And the factual data upon which the increased sentence is based must be made part of the record, so that the constitutional legitimacy of the increased sentence may be fully reviewed on appeal.

In sum, the Court applied a presumption of vindictiveness, which may be overcome only by objective information in the record justifying the increased sentence.

In *Blackledge v. Perry*, the Court confronted the problem of increased punishment upon retrial after appeal in a setting different from that considered in *Pearce*. Perry was convicted of assault in an inferior court having exclusive jurisdiction for the trial of misdemeanors. The court imposed a 6-month sentence. Under North Carolina law, Perry had an absolute right to a trial *de novo* in the Superior Court, which possessed felony jurisdiction. After Perry filed his notice of appeal, the prosecutor obtained a felony indictment charging him with assault with a deadly weapon. Perry pleaded guilty to the felony and was sentenced to a term of five to seven years in prison.

---

[a] In a later case, the Court retreated from this statement, noting that "[r]estricting justifications for a sentence increase to *only* 'events that occurred subsequent to the original sentencing proceedings' could in some circumstances lead to absurd results." *Texas v. McCullough*, 475 U.S. 134, 141 (1986).

In reviewing Perry's felony conviction and increased sentence this Court first stated the essence of the holdings in *Pearce* and the cases that had followed it:

> The lesson that emerges from *Pearce* [and other cases] is that the Due Process Clause is not offended by all possibilities of increased punishment upon retrial after appeal, but only by those that pose a realistic likelihood of "vindictiveness."

The Court held that the opportunities for vindictiveness in the situation before it were such "as to impel the conclusion that due process of law requires a rule analogous to that of the *Pearce* case." * * *

The Court emphasized in *Blackledge* that it did not matter that no evidence was present that the prosecutor had acted in bad faith or with malice in seeking the felony indictment. As in *Pearce*, the Court held that the likelihood of vindictiveness justified a presumption that would free defendants of apprehension of such a retaliatory motivation on the part of the prosecutor.[8] * * *

In *Bordenkircher v. Hayes*, the Court for the first time considered an allegation of vindictiveness that arose in a pretrial setting. In that case the Court held that the Due Process Clause of the Fourteenth Amendment did not prohibit a prosecutor from carrying out a threat, made during plea negotiations, to bring additional charges against an accused who refused to plead guilty to the offense with which he was originally charged. The prosecutor in that case had explicitly told the defendant that if he did not plead guilty and "save the court the inconvenience and necessity of a trial" he would return to the grand jury to obtain an additional charge that would significantly increase the defendant's potential punishment.[9] The defendant refused to plead guilty and the prosecutor obtained the indictment. It was not disputed that the additional charge was justified by the evidence, that the prosecutor was in possession of this evidence at the time the original indictment was obtained, and that the prosecutor sought the additional charge because of the accused's refusal to plead guilty to the original charge.

In finding no due process violation, the Court in *Bordenkircher* considered the decisions in *Pearce* and *Blackledge*, and stated:

> In those cases the Court was dealing with the State's unilateral imposition of a penalty upon a defendant who had chosen to exercise a legal right to attack his original conviction—a situation

---

[8]    The presumption again could be overcome by objective evidence justifying the prosecutor's action. The Court noted: "This would clearly be a different case if the State had shown that it was impossible to proceed on the more serious charge at the outset * * *."

[9]    The prosecutor advised the defendant that he would obtain an indictment under the Kentucky Habitual Criminal Act, which would subject the accused to a mandatory sentence of life imprisonment by reason of his two prior felony convictions. Absent the additional indictment, the defendant was subject to a punishment of 2 to 10 years in prison.

"very different from the give-and-take negotiation common in plea bargaining between the prosecution and defense, which arguably possess relatively equal bargaining power."

The Court stated that the due process violation in *Pearce* and *Blackledge* "lay not in the possibility that a defendant might be deterred from the exercise of a legal right . . . but rather in the danger that the State might be retaliating against the accused for lawfully attacking his conviction."

The Court held, however, that there was no such element of punishment in the "give-and-take" of plea negotiation, so long as the accused "is free to accept or reject the prosecution's offer." The Court noted that, by tolerating and encouraging the negotiation of pleas, this Court had accepted as constitutionally legitimate the simple reality that the prosecutor's interest at the bargaining table is to persuade the defendant to forgo his constitutional right to stand trial. The Court concluded:

> We hold only that the course of conduct engaged in by the prosecutor in this case, which no more than openly presented the defendant with the unpleasant alternatives of forgoing trial or facing charges on which he was plainly subject to prosecution, did not violate the Due Process Clause of the Fourteenth Amendment.
> * * *

This case, like *Bordenkircher*, arises from a pretrial decision to modify the charges against the defendant. Unlike *Bordenkircher*, however, there is no evidence in this case that could give rise to a claim of *actual* vindictiveness; the prosecutor never suggested that the charge was brought to influence the respondent's conduct. The conviction in this case may be reversed only if a *presumption* of vindictiveness—applicable in all cases—is warranted.

There is good reason to be cautious before adopting an inflexible presumption of prosecutorial vindictiveness in a pretrial setting. In the course of preparing a case for trial, the prosecutor may uncover additional information that suggests a basis for further prosecution or he simply may come to realize that information possessed by the State has a broader significance. At this stage of the proceedings, the prosecutor's assessment of the proper extent of prosecution may not have crystallized. In contrast, once a trial begins—and certainly by the time a conviction has been obtained—it is much more likely that the State has discovered and assessed all of the information against an accused and has made a determination, on the basis of that information, of the extent to which he should be prosecuted. Thus, a change in the charging decision made after an initial trial is completed is much more likely to be improperly motivated than is a pretrial decision.

In addition, a defendant before trial is expected to invoke procedural rights that inevitably impose some "burden" on the prosecutor. Defense counsel routinely file pretrial motions to suppress evidence; to challenge the sufficiency and form of an indictment; to plead an affirmative defense; to request psychiatric services; to obtain access to government files; to be tried by jury. It is unrealistic to assume that a prosecutor's probable response to such motions is to seek to penalize and to deter. The invocation of procedural rights is an integral part of the adversary process in which our criminal justice system operates.

Thus, the timing of the prosecutor's action in this case suggests that a presumption of vindictiveness is not warranted. A prosecutor should remain free before trial to exercise the broad discretion entrusted to him to determine the extent of the societal interest in prosecution. * * *

In declining to apply a presumption of vindictiveness, we of course do not foreclose the possibility that a defendant in an appropriate case might prove objectively that the prosecutor's charging decision was motivated by a desire to punish him for doing something that the law plainly allowed him to do. In this case, however, the Court of Appeals stated: "On this record we readily conclude that the prosecutor did not act with actual vindictiveness in seeking a felony indictment." Respondent does not challenge that finding. Absent a presumption of vindictiveness, no due process violation has been established. * * *

JUSTICE BLACKMUN, concurring in the judgment.

Like Justice Brennan, I believe that our precedents mandate the conclusion that "a realistic likelihood of 'vindictiveness'" arises in this context. The Assistant United States Attorney responsible for increasing the charges against respondent was aware of the initial charging decision; he had the means available to discourage respondent from electing a jury trial in District Court; he had a substantial stake in dissuading respondent from exercising that option; and he was familiar with, and sensitive to, the institutional interests that favored a trial before the Magistrate.

Moreover, I find no support in our prior cases for any distinction between pretrial and post-trial vindictiveness. As I have said before: "Prosecutorial vindictiveness in any context is still prosecutorial vindictiveness. The Due Process Clause should protect an accused against it, however it asserts itself." And, as Justice Brennan points out, *Bordenkircher* does not dictate the result here. In fact, in *Bordenkircher* the Court expressly distinguished and left *unresolved* cases such as this one, "where the prosecutor without notice brought an additional and more serious charge after plea negotiations relating only to the original [charges] had ended with the defendant's insistence on pleading not guilty."

The Court's ruling in *Bordenkircher* did not depend on a distinction between the pretrial and post-trial settings: rather, the Court declined to apply its prior opinions in *Blackledge* and *North Carolina v. Pearce* because those cases involved "the State's unilateral imposition of a penalty," rather than "the give-and-take negotiation common in plea bargaining." Here, as in *Pearce* and *Blackledge*, the prosecutor unilaterally imposed a penalty in response to respondent's exercise of a legal right.

* * * [T]he Due Process Clause does not deprive a prosecutor of the flexibility to add charges after a defendant has decided not to plead guilty and has elected a jury trial in District Court—so long as the adjustment is based on "objective information concerning identifiable conduct on the part of the defendant occurring after the time of the original" charging decision. In addition, I believe that the prosecutor adequately explains an increased charge by pointing to objective information that he could not reasonably have been aware of at the time charges were initially filed.

Because I find that the Assistant United States Attorney's explanation for seeking a felony indictment satisfies these standards, I conclude that the Government has dispelled the appearance of vindictiveness and, therefore, that the imposition of additional charges did not violate respondent's due process rights. Accordingly, I concur in the judgment.

JUSTICE BRENNAN, with whom JUSTICE MARSHALL joins, dissenting. * * *

The salient facts of this case are quite simple. Respondent was originally charged with several petty offenses and misdemeanors—speeding, reckless driving, failing to give aid at the scene of an accident, fleeing from a police officer, and assault by striking a police officer—arising from his conduct on the Baltimore-Washington Parkway. Assuming that respondent had been convicted on every count charged in this original complaint, the maximum punishment to which he conceivably could have been exposed was fines of $3,500 and 28 months in prison. Because all of the charges against respondent were petty offenses or misdemeanors, they were scheduled for trial before a magistrate, who was not authorized to conduct jury trials. In addition, the case was assigned to a prosecutor who, owing to inexperience, was not even authorized to try felony cases. Thus the Government recognized that respondent's alleged crimes were relatively minor, and attempted to dispose of them in an expedited manner. But respondent frustrated this attempt at summary justice by demanding a jury trial in Federal District Court. This was his right, of course, not only under the applicable statute, but also under the Constitution.

Respondent's demand required that the case be transferred from the Magistrate's Court in Hyattsville to the District Court in Baltimore, and that the prosecution be reassigned to an Assistant United States Attorney, who was authorized to prosecute cases in the District Court. The new prosecutor sought and obtained a second, four-count indictment, in which the same conduct originally charged as petty-offense and misdemeanor counts was now charged as a misdemeanor and two felonies: assaulting, resisting, or impeding a federal officer with a deadly weapon, and assault with a dangerous weapon. If we assume (as before) that respondent was convicted on all of these charges, his maximum exposure to punishment had now become fines of $11,500 and 15 years in prison. Respondent's claim below was that such an elevation of the charges against him from petty offenses to felonies, following his exercise of his statutory and constitutional right to a jury trial, reflected prosecutorial vindictiveness that denied him due process of law. * * *

I would analyze respondent's claim in the terms employed by our precedents. Did the elevation of the charges against respondent "pose a realistic likelihood of 'vindictiveness?'" Is it possible that "the fear of such vindictiveness may unconstitutionally deter" a person in respondent's position from exercising his statutory and constitutional right to a jury trial? The answer to these questions is plainly "Yes." * * *

The truth of my conclusion, and the patent fallacy of the Court's, is particularly evident on the record before us. The practical effect of respondent's demand for a jury trial was that the Government had to transfer the case from a trial before a Magistrate in Hyattsville to a trial before a District Judge and jury in Baltimore, and had to substitute one prosecutor for another. The Government thus suffered not only administrative inconvenience: It also lost the value of the preparation and services of the first prosecutor, and was forced to commit a second prosecutor to prepare the case from scratch. Thus, just as in *Blackledge*, respondent's election had the effect of "clearly requir[ing] increased expenditures of prosecutorial resources before the defendant's conviction" could finally be achieved. And, to paraphrase *Blackledge*,

> if the prosecutor has the means readily at hand to discourage such [elections]—by "upping the ante" through a felony indictment . . .
> —the State can insure that only the most hardy defendants will brave the hazards of a [jury] trial.

I conclude that the facts of this case easily support the inference of "a realistic likelihood of vindictiveness." * * *

### NOTE

Although *United States v. Goodwin* might be interpreted as holding that a presumption of vindictiveness can never be applied in the pretrial setting, it does not lay down such a rigid rule. Lower courts can decide that the circumstances in an individual case merit finding a realistic likelihood of vindictiveness, and then apply a presumption of vindictiveness. *See United States v. LaDeau*, 734 F.3d 561 (6th Cir. 2013) (finding that a presumption of vindictiveness was appropriately applied in the pretrial context).

## RACIAL FAIRNESS IN THE CRIMINAL JUSTICE SYSTEM: THE ROLE OF THE PROSECUTOR

Angela J. Davis
39 Colum. Hum. Rts. L. Rev. 202 (2007)

Prosecutors exercise a tremendous amount of discretion in charging and plea bargaining processes with no external oversight and very little accountability to the constituents they serve. Charging and plea bargaining decisions frequently predetermine the outcome of criminal cases, especially in cases involving mandatory minimum sentences. Since over ninety-five percent of criminal cases are resolved with guilty pleas, the impact of prosecutorial discretion cannot be understated. * * *

Prosecutors can, and frequently do, decide not to charge individuals who have been arrested, even if there is probable cause to believe they have committed a crime. This decision is completely within their discretion. If they do decide to charge, prosecutors have complete discretion in deciding what crime or crimes to charge and are restrained only by the criminal codes of their jurisdictions. * * *

Most prosecutors would vehemently deny that they take race into account in any way in the exercise of their prosecutorial duties, and most probably do not consciously consider race. Nonetheless, prosecutors rely on legitimate, race-neutral factors that sometimes have racial effects. The American Bar Association (ABA) Standards for the Prosecution Function have endorsed several such factors. A report to the ABA noted that legitimate factors include: the seriousness of the offense, the defendant's prior criminal record, the victim's interest in prosecution, the strength of the evidence, the likelihood of conviction, and the availability of alternative dispositions.

The factor that many prosecutors consider most important is the seriousness of the offense: the more serious the offense, the more likely the prosecutor will charge the accused. For example, a prosecutor may decide to dismiss a simple assault while zealously pursuing the prosecution of an aggravated assault involving serious injury. Few would question this decision, regardless of the race of the defendant or victim. The more difficult issue arises when two defendants are charged differently in cases involving similar facts, except with defendants or victims of different races. At this point, the issue of unconscious racism becomes relevant. If, for example, a defendant in a case involving a white victim is charged with capital murder while a similarly situated defendant in a case involving a black victim is charged with second-degree murder, questions arise about the value the prosecutors placed on the lives of the respective victims.[a] A

---

[a]  Empirical research suggests that Black defendants charged with killing White victims are far more likely to receive the death penalty than defendants charged with killing Black victims. For example, the well-known Baldus study, discussed in *McCleskey v. Kemp, infra*, found that defendants charged with killing White victims received the death penalty in 11 percent of the

prosecutor may unconsciously consider a case involving a white victim as more serious than a case involving a black victim, and this may influence the charging, plea bargaining, and other related decisions.[b]

If a prosecutor initially deems a particular case to be more serious than others, she will invest more time and resources investigating the case and preparing for trial. This will yield more evidence, making it less likely that the prosecutor will offer a plea bargain and more likely that she will succeed in obtaining a conviction at trial. The likelihood of conviction is another consideration endorsed by the ABA. Thus, although the strength of the evidence and the likelihood of conviction are facially race-neutral factors, they may be influenced by initial, unconscious racial valuations.

The victim's interest in prosecution is another factor that prosecutors legitimately consider in making charging and plea bargaining decisions. If the victim of a crime has no interest in the prosecution of his case and no desire to see the defendant punished, the prosecutor may dismiss the case based on these views, especially if the prosecutor believes that the defendant does not pose a danger to society and that there are no other legitimate reasons for pursuing the prosecution. Few would question this decision, especially if the victim of the crime considered the prosecution process too onerous and difficult.

On the other hand, should a prosecutor pursue a prosecution in a case that she would otherwise dismiss for legitimate reasons simply because the victim demonstrates an interest in prosecution? Or should a prosecutor assume that a victim is not interested in prosecution when the victim does not appear for witness conferences or respond to a subpoena? Prosecutors are more likely to pursue prosecutions in cases involving crime victims who are comfortable navigating the criminal process and who have time to attend grand jury hearings, witness conferences, and status hearings. The poor, who are disproportionately people of color, are less able to take time off from work to attend these hearings. They may also feel less comfortable participating in the process, especially since they are more likely to have family or friends involved in the system as criminal defendants. Thus, race and class may have an unintended effect on this factor as well.

The prior record of the defendant is another seemingly race-neutral factor considered by prosecutors in the charging and plea bargaining process. Prosecutors understandably are more likely to charge and less likely to offer a favorable plea bargain to defendants with prior arrest and conviction records; defendants who are recidivists are arguably more deserving of prosecution. Race, however, may affect the existence of a prior

---

cases, whereas defendants charged with killing Black victims received the death penalty in only 1 percent of the cases.

[b]   *See* Robert J. Smith, et al., *Implicit White Favoritism in the Criminal Justice System*, 66 ALA. L. REV. 871 (2015) (arguing that even if we eliminated negative stereotyping of Blacks, automatic associations of positive stereotypes with White Americans would still exist).

criminal record even in the absence of recidivist tendencies on the part of the suspect because of racial profiling at the arrest stage of the process.

Race often plays a role in the decision to detain and/or arrest a suspect. In addition, policy decisions about where police officers should be deployed and what offenses they should investigate have racial ramifications. A white defendant with no criminal arrest or conviction record may have engaged in criminal behavior. If he lives in a community that resolves certain criminal offenses (drug use, assault, etc.) without police intervention, he may be a recidivist without a record. Likewise, a black defendant who lives in a designated "high crime" area may have been detained and arrested on numerous occasions even if he has not engaged in criminal behavior. Thus, the existence or nonexistence of an arrest or conviction record may not reflect criminality. A prosecutor without knowledge of or sensitivity to this issue may give prior arrests undue consideration in making charging and plea bargaining decisions.

The ABA standards also suggest that prosecutors consider the availability of alternative dispositions before bringing criminal charges. Many prosecutors' offices have diversion programs or other alternatives that allow for the dismissal of a case combined with alternative resolutions such as restitution, rehabilitative treatment or community service. Most of these alternatives are available for first offenders only and benefit not only the defendant but all parties. The victim may be compensated if restitution is involved, and the alternatives have the added benefit of eliminating the time and expense of trying another case for the prosecutor, the defense attorney, and the court. As with other seemingly legitimate considerations, however, this factor may have class and race ramifications. Wealthier defendants have a greater ability to make restitution or pay for drug, alcohol, or psychiatric treatment. Since people of color are disproportionately poor, this seemingly race neutral factor can have racial effects.

Arbitrary, unsystematic decision-making, exacerbated by unconscious race and class predilections, sometimes results in disparate treatment of similarly situated victims and defendants. That prosecutors do not intend to cause racial disparities does not excuse them from responsibility for the harmful effects of their decisions. The U.S. Supreme Court, however, has repeatedly blocked efforts to hold prosecutors accountable for unintentional discrimination. * * *

### *NOTE*

"While the decision to arrest is often the responsibility of law enforcement personnel, the decision to institute formal criminal proceedings is the responsibility of the prosecutor."[a] The question whether to charge George Zimmerman, a white Hispanic male, with criminal homicide in the shooting death of Trayvon Martin, an unarmed Black male teenager, was wrought with much controversy, including allegations of racial bias.

The shooting took place on February 26, 2012, in Sanford, Florida. Martin had been walking back to the apartment where he was staying while visiting his father and was talking on his cell phone with a friend when Zimmerman first began following him in his car. Zimmerman called 911 and told the dispatcher that he thought Martin "looked suspicious" and was "up to no good." When Martin started running away, Zimmerman got out of his car and followed Martin on foot. A physical altercation ensued and Zimmerman found himself on the ground on his back with Martin on top. Zimmerman claimed he shot Martin in self-defense because he thought Martin was going to kill him. A haunting 911 call from a neighbor concerned about the altercation, which captured a desperate scream for help immediately before the fatal shot, initially put Zimmerman's self-defense claim into question. Zimmerman, however, claimed he was the one screaming for help because he feared for his life. Martin's parents asserted the screams were from their son.[b]

Once the case caught the attention of the press, it was widely covered both domestically and internationally. President Barack Obama weighed in on the shooting, saying: "I can only imagine what these parents are going through. . . . If I had a son, he'd look like Trayvon."[c] The case triggered criminal investigations by both federal and state officials. The federal investigation of the case was focused on whether to charge the case as a hate crime or a violation of Martin's civil rights. The U.S. Department of Justice ultimately concluded there was insufficient evidence to file federal charges.

The response at the state level was mixed on whether to charge Zimmerman with criminal homicide. Although the lead detective on the case recommended that Zimmerman be arrested on charges of manslaughter, Norm Wolfinger, the State Attorney, instructed the police not to arrest Zimmerman because he had concerns about the strength of the evidence. Both the Sanford

---

[a] ABA STANDARDS FOR CRIMINAL JUSTICE: PROSECUTION AND DEF. FUNCTION § 3–4.2(a) (AM. BAR ASS'N 2015).

[b] For additional commentary on the shooting of Trayvon Martin, see Darren Lenard Hutchinson, "Continually Reminded of their Inferior Position": Social Dominance, Implicit Bias, Criminality, and Race, 46 WASH. U. J.L. & POL'Y 23 (2014); Cynthia Lee, Making Race Salient: Trayvon Martin and Implicit Bias in a Not Yet Post-Racial Society, 91 N.C. L. REV. 1555 (2013); L. Song Richardson & Phillip Atiba Goff, Self-Defense and the Suspicion Heuristic, 98 IOWA L. REV. 293 (2012); Tamara F. Lawson, A Fresh Cut in an Old Would—A Critical Analysis of the Trayvon Martin Killing: The Public Outcry, the Prosecutors' Discretion, and the Stand Your Ground Law, 23 U. FLA. J.L. & PUB. POL'Y 271 (2012); Valena Elizabeth Beety, What the Brain Saw: The Case of Trayvon Martin and the Need for Eyewitness Identification Reform, 90 DENV. U. L. REV. 331 (2012). See also Josephine Ross, Cops on Trial: Did Fourth Amendment Case Law Help George Zimmerman's Claim of Self-Defense?, 40 SEATTLE UNIV. L. REV. 1 (2016).

[c] Sam Stein, Obama on Trayvon Martin Case: "If I Had a Son, He'd Look Like Trayvon," HUFFINGTON POST, March 23, 2012, http://www.huffingtonpost.com/2012/03/23/obama-trayvon-martin_n_1375083.html.

Police Department and Wolfinger were harshly criticized for the initial decision not to arrest or charge Zimmerman with any crime.

The case split the public along racial lines, at least initially. One study conducted by USA Today reported that 73% of Blacks believed that George Zimmerman should have been arrested, while only 33% of Whites felt the same way.[d] As the case attracted national attention, however, individuals of all races came together to demand Zimmerman's arrest. Scores of people held vigils in honor of Trayvon Martin. Many wore T-shirts emblazoned with a photo of Martin and the words, "I am Trayvon." The case sparked a national dialogue regarding the exercise of prosecutorial discretion and race.

Professor Tamara Lawson describes the impact of the initial charging decision on Black Americans as a reinjuring of an "old wound" reminiscent of a historic era in which impunity was common for the killing of Black men and boys in America.

> [The response to] Trayvon Martin's killing [and the lack of criminal charges] was becoming a national movement * * *. Communities [across the country] were chanting the slogan: "I am Trayvon." Students of Trayvon's age group and younger were walking out of school in symbolic rage regarding the fact that nothing was being done to vindicate his killing. People from all walks of life were wearing hoodies in solidarity with the perceived injustice of the treatment of the case. Although the initial outcry was primarily led by the Black community, the expression of outrage was not limited to Black people. Joe Scarborough, a well-known white conservative [R]epublican [television] commentator * * * also called for charges to be filed. Scarborough * * * felt [Florida officials] should intervene to correct this injustice. Scarborough, along with * * * others * * * implored the government to do something. At that point, it was still uncertain whether or not the something would be to charge Trayvon's killer with murder.[e]

After numerous public protests, then Florida Governor Rick Scott appointed Special Prosecutor Angela Corey to take over the case and re-evaluate the charging decision. Within twenty days of being appointed as Special Prosecutor, Corey decided to charge George Zimmerman with second degree murder. Corey insisted that her charging decision was not influenced by public opinion, but was governed solely by the facts of the case and the laws of the state of Florida.

After a three-week trial, a jury acquitted Zimmerman of all charges. Does the acquittal suggest that Corey made the wrong charging decision?

---

[d]   Yamiche Alcindor, *Poll Shows Racial Divide on Views of Trayvon Martin Case*, USA TODAY, April 6, 2012, http://usatoday30.usatoday.com/news/nation/story/2012-04-05/trayvon-martin-poll/54047512/1.

[e]   Tamara F. Lawson, *A Fresh Cut in an Old Wound—A Critical Analysis of the Trayvon Martin Killing: The Public Outcry, the Prosecutors' Discretion, and the Stand Your Ground Law*, 23 U. FLA. J. L. & PUB. POL'Y 271, 274, 283–84 (2012).

Why was Corey's charging decision so different from Wolfinger's when both reviewed the same facts and same laws? According to the American Bar Association, the minimum requirements for filing and maintaining criminal charges are as follows: "A prosecutor should seek or file criminal charges only if the prosecutor reasonably believes that the charges are supported by probable cause, that admissible evidence will be sufficient to support conviction beyond a reasonable doubt, and that the decision to charge is in the interests of justice." ABA STANDARDS FOR CRIMINAL JUSTICE: PROSECUTION AND DEFENSE FUNCTION, STANDARD § 3–4.3(a) (4th ed. 2015). Standard 3–1.2(c) states: "[T]he primary duty of the prosecutor is to seek justice within the bounds of the law, not merely to convict." Did Corey appropriately exercise the prosecutorial obligation to "seek justice" in the Zimmerman case? Did Wolfinger? Is it possible that both Wolfinger and Corey correctly exercised their duties even though their charging decisions were different? The Zimmerman case illustrates the breadth of prosecutorial discretion as well as the political, social, and cultural dynamics that may impact it.

# Chapter 23

# Grand Jury

■ ■ ■

The Fifth Amendment to the U.S. Constitution provides:

No person shall be held to answer for a capital, or otherwise infamous crime, unless on a presentment or indictment of a Grand Jury . . . .

The Fifth Amendment right to an indictment[a] by a grand jury applies only to defendants in federal court. A defendant in state court does not have a right under the U.S. Constitution to an indictment by a grand jury.[b]

It is often said that the grand jury operates as both a sword and a shield. The grand jury acts as a sword when it helps the government investigate and bring charges against individuals. The grand jury acts as a shield when it declines to return an indictment, even in cases where there is probable cause to support an indictment. In this way, the grand jury can protect individuals from unjust prosecutions.

In contrast to the trial and the preliminary hearing, which are adversarial proceedings at which both the government and the defense have the right to present evidence, the grand jury proceeding is a one-sided proceeding at which the government alone presents evidence. Generally speaking, the target of the investigation (the defendant-to-be) has no right to present evidence to the grand jury, including his own testimony, unless he is called by the government to testify.[c] Unlike most criminal trials,

---

[a] An indictment is a charging document drawn up by the prosecutor. If a majority of the grand jury finds probable cause to believe the defendant committed the crimes in the indictment, it will return the indictment to the prosecutor. When the grand jury returns an indictment, this action is called returning a true bill. If a majority of the grand jury does not think the evidence presented supports a finding of probable cause, they will return a no bill. In cases involving a no bill, the indictment drawn up by the prosecutor will be considered invalid and cannot be used to commence a prosecution.

[b] *Hurtado v. California*, 110 U.S. 516 (1884) (declining to apply the Fifth Amendment right to indictment by a grand jury to the states through the Due Process Clause). In a majority of the states, the prosecutor can choose to proceed either by grand jury indictment or by preliminary hearing. A minority of states require a grand jury indictment in felony cases as a matter of state law. YALE KAMISAR ET AL., MODERN CRIMINAL PROCEDURE (13th ed. West).

[c] Some states permit the target of the investigation to testify before the grand jury as a matter of state law. *See* IND. CODE. ANN. § 35–34–2–9(b) (West 1999) ("A target of a grand jury investigation shall be given the right to testify before the grand jury, provided he signs a waiver of immunity"); NEV. REV. STAT. § 172.241(1) (1999) ("a person whose indictment the district attorney intends to seek . . . may testify before the grand jury if the person requests to do so . . ."); N.M. STAT. ANN. § 31–6–11(B) (Michie 2000) ("the target of a grand jury investigation shall be notified in writing of . . . the target's right to testify . . ."); N.Y. CRIM. PROC. LAW § 190.50(5)(a)

which are open to the public, grand jury proceedings are closed to the public. Indeed, under Rule 6 of the Federal Rules of Criminal Procedure, grand jurors are required to keep secret anything that is said during the grand jury proceeding.

The grand jury differs in many other respects from the trial jury, also known as the petit jury. In the federal system, the grand jury consists of 16 to 23 persons whereas the petit jury usually consists of 12 persons.[d] The grand jury may sit for up to 18 months. In contrast, a petit jury will only sit for the duration of the trial. Even though the grand jury may sit for a longer period of time than a petit jury, grand jurors are not called into session every day. Some grand juries meet just once a month. Others meet once a week. A petit jury usually meets every day until the trial is concluded.[e]

The first case in this chapter, *Vasquez v. Hillery*, considers whether automatic reversal of a conviction is appropriate when racial discrimination occurs in the selection of the grand jury. The next few cases deal with questions concerning what evidence the grand jury can and should consider. *Costello v. United States* addresses whether the grand jury should be allowed to consider hearsay evidence. *United States v. Williams* discusses whether the prosecutor must advise the grand jury of any exculpatory evidence in its possession.

## VASQUEZ V. HILLERY
Supreme Court of the United States
474 U.S. 254, 106 S.Ct. 617, 88 L.Ed.2d 598 (1986)

JUSTICE MARSHALL delivered the opinion of the Court.

The Warden of San Quentin State Prison asks this Court to retire a doctrine of equal protection jurisprudence first announced in 1880. The time has come, he urges, for us to abandon the rule requiring reversal of the conviction of any defendant indicted by a grand jury from which members of his own race were systematically excluded.

In 1962, the grand jury of Kings County, California, indicted respondent, Booker T. Hillery, for a brutal murder. Before trial in Superior Court, respondent moved to quash the indictment on the ground that it had been issued by a grand jury from which blacks had been systematically

---

(Consol. 1996) ("When a criminal charge against a person is being or is about to be or has been submitted to a grand jury, such person has a right to appear before such grand jury as a witness in his own behalf").

   [d] As you will learn in the chapter on the right to a trial by jury, the states are free to have as few as 6 persons on a jury. Williams v. Florida, 399 U.S. 78 (1970).

   [e] For helpful information about the grand jury, *see* Jeffrey Fagan & Bernard E. Harcourt, *Professors Fagan and Harcourt Provide Facts on Grand Jury Practice in Light of Ferguson Decision*, COLUMBIA LAW SCHOOL, http://www.law.columbia.edu/media_inquiries/news_events/2014/november2014/Facts-on-Ferguson-Grand-Jury or https://perma.cc/DP94-77F2.

excluded.[a] A hearing on respondent's motion was held by Judge Meredith Wingrove, who was the sole Superior Court Judge in the county and had personally selected all grand juries, including the one that indicted respondent, for the previous seven years. Absolving himself of any discriminatory intent, Judge Wingrove refused to quash the indictment. Respondent was subsequently convicted of first-degree murder.

For the next 16 years, respondent pursued appeals and collateral relief in the state courts, raising at every opportunity his equal protection challenge to the grand jury that indicted him. Less than one month after the California Supreme Court foreclosed his final avenue of state relief in 1978, respondent filed a petition for a writ of habeas corpus in federal court, raising that same challenge. The District Court concluded that respondent had established discrimination in the grand jury, and granted the writ. The Court of Appeals affirmed, and we granted certiorari. * * *

On the merits, petitioner urges this Court to find that discrimination in the grand jury amounted to harmless error in this case,[b] claiming that the evidence against respondent was overwhelming and that discrimination no longer infects the selection of grand juries in Kings County. Respondent's conviction after a fair trial, we are told, purged any taint attributable to the indictment process. Our acceptance of this theory would require abandonment of more than a century of consistent precedent.

In 1880, this Court reversed a state conviction on the ground that the indictment charging the offense had been issued by a grand jury from which blacks had been excluded. We reasoned that deliberate exclusion of blacks "is practically a brand upon them, affixed by the law, an assertion of their inferiority, and a stimulant to that race prejudice which is an impediment to securing to individuals of the race that equal justice which the law aims to secure to all others."

Thereafter, the Court has repeatedly rejected all arguments that a conviction may stand despite racial discrimination in the selection of the grand jury. Only six years ago, the Court explicitly addressed the question whether this unbroken line of case law should be reconsidered in favor of a

---

[a]   Hillery was a Black farmhand. Miles Corwin, *Man Guilty of Slaying—24 Years After Crime*, L.A. TIMES, Dec. 19, 1986, http://articles.latimes.com/1986-12-19/news/mn-3565_1_kings-county.

[b]   Under the doctrine of harmless error, a conviction may stand "where the reviewing court believes the defect in the proceeding was harmless beyond a reasonable doubt." Roger A. Fairfax, Jr., *Harmless Constitutional Error and the Institutional Significance of the Jury*, 76 FORDHAM L. REV. 2027, 2029 (2008). If, however, the reviewing court finds that the conviction was infected by structural error, the conviction is subject to automatic reversal rather than harmless error review. *Id.* The Supreme Court has recognized only a few errors as structural errors subject to automatic reversal, including *inter alia* bias of the trial judge, denial of the right to counsel, racial discrimination in the selection of the grand jury, and denial of the right to a public trial. *Id.* at 2029 n.3. All other errors—those that are not structural errors—are considered trial errors, which are subject to harmless error review. *Arizona v. Fulminante*, 499 U.S. 279, 306–08 (1991).

harmless-error standard, and determined that it should not. We reaffirmed our conviction that discrimination on the basis of race in the selection of grand jurors "strikes at the fundamental values of our judicial system and our society as a whole," and that the criminal defendant's right to equal protection of the laws has been denied when he is indicted by a grand jury from which members of a racial group purposefully have been excluded.

Petitioner argues here that requiring a State to retry a defendant, sometimes years later, imposes on it an unduly harsh penalty for a constitutional defect bearing no relation to the fundamental fairness of the trial. Yet intentional discrimination in the selection of grand jurors is a grave constitutional trespass, possible only under color of state authority, and wholly within the power of the State to prevent. Thus, the remedy we have embraced for over a century—the only effective remedy for this violation—is not disproportionate to the evil that it seeks to deter. If grand jury discrimination becomes a thing of the past, no conviction will ever again be lost on account of it.

Nor are we persuaded that discrimination in the grand jury has no effect on the fairness of the criminal trials that result from that grand jury's actions. The grand jury does not determine only that probable cause exists to believe that a defendant committed a crime, or that it does not. In the hands of the grand jury lies the power to charge a greater offense or a lesser offense; numerous counts or a single count; and perhaps most significant of all, a capital offense or a noncapital offense—all on the basis of the same facts. Moreover, "[t]he grand jury is not bound to indict in every case where a conviction can be obtained."[c] Thus, even if a grand jury's determination of probable cause is confirmed in hindsight by a conviction on the indicted offense, that confirmation in no way suggests that the discrimination did not impermissibly infect the framing of the indictment and, consequently, the nature or very existence of the proceedings to come.

When constitutional error calls into question the objectivity of those charged with bringing a defendant to judgment, a reviewing court can neither indulge a presumption of regularity nor evaluate the resulting harm. * * * [W]hen a petit jury has been selected upon improper criteria or has been exposed to prejudicial publicity, we have required reversal of the conviction because the effect of the violation cannot be ascertained. Like these fundamental flaws, which never have been thought harmless, discrimination in the grand jury undermines the structural integrity of the criminal tribunal itself, and is not amenable to harmless-error review.

Just as a conviction is void under the Equal Protection Clause if the prosecutor deliberately charged the defendant on account of his race, a

---

[c] When a grand jury declines to indict when there is probable cause to indict, it may be engaging in "grand jury nullification," which is within its authority and power. Roger A. Fairfax, Jr. *Grand Jury Discretion and Constitutional Design*, 93 CORNELL L. REV. 703 (2008).

conviction cannot be understood to cure the taint attributable to a charging body selected on the basis of race. Once having found discrimination in the selection of a grand jury, we simply cannot know that the need to indict would have been assessed in the same way by a grand jury properly constituted. The overriding imperative to eliminate this systemic flaw in the charging process, as well as the difficulty of assessing its effect on any given defendant, requires our continued adherence to a rule of mandatory reversal. * * *

The judgment of the Court of Appeals, accordingly, is affirmed. * * *

JUSTICE POWELL, with whom The Chief Justice and JUSTICE REHNQUIST join, dissenting.

Respondent, a black man, was indicted by a grand jury having no black members for the stabbing murder of a 15-year-old girl. A petit jury found respondent guilty of that charge beyond a reasonable doubt, in a trial the fairness of which is unchallenged here. Twenty-three years later, we are asked to grant respondent's petition for a writ of habeas corpus—and thereby require a new trial if that is still feasible—on the ground that blacks were purposefully excluded from the grand jury that indicted him. It is undisputed that race discrimination has long since disappeared from the grand jury selection process in Kings County, California. It is undisputed that a grand jury that perfectly represented Kings County's population at the time of respondent's indictment would have contained only one black member. Yet the Court holds that respondent's petition must be granted, and that respondent must be freed unless the State is able to reconvict, more than two decades after the murder that led to his incarceration.

It is difficult to reconcile this result with a rational system of justice. The Court nevertheless finds its decision compelled by a century of precedent and by the interests of respondent and of society in ending race discrimination in the selection of grand juries. I dissent for two reasons. First, in my view, any error in the selection of the grand jury that indicted respondent is constitutionally harmless. Second, even assuming that the harmless-error rule does not apply, reversal of respondent's conviction is an inappropriate remedy for the wrong that prompts this case.

* * * In this case, the Court misapplies *stare decisis* because it relies only on decisions concerning grand jury discrimination. There is other precedent, including important cases of more recent vintage than those cited by the Court, that should control this case. Those cases hold, or clearly imply, that a conviction should not be reversed for constitutional error where the error did not affect the outcome of the prosecution. * * *

In *Chapman v. California*, the Court held that a trial judge's improper comment on the defendant's failure to testify—a clear violation of the Fifth and Fourteenth Amendments—was not a proper basis for reversal if harmless. Since *Chapman*, "the Court has consistently made clear that it is the duty of a reviewing court to consider the trial record as a whole and to ignore errors that are harmless, including most constitutional violations." This rule has been applied to a variety of constitutional violations. * * *

In *Rose v. Mitchell*, the Court contended that the principle of these cases is inapplicable to grand jury discrimination claims, because grand jury discrimination "destroys the appearance of justice and thereby casts doubt on the integrity of the judicial process." But *every* constitutional error may be said to raise questions as to the "appearance of justice" and the "integrity of the judicial process." * * * Grand jury discrimination is a serious violation of our constitutional order, but so also are the deprivations of rights guaranteed by the Fourth, Fifth, Sixth, and Fourteenth Amendments to which we have applied harmless-error analysis or an analogous prejudice requirement. * * * The Court does not adequately explain why grand jury discrimination affects the "integrity of the judicial process" to a greater extent than the deprivation of equally vital constitutional rights, nor why it is exempt from a prejudice requirement while other constitutional errors are not. * * *

No one questions that race discrimination in grand jury selection violates the Equal Protection Clause of the Fourteenth Amendment. The issue in this case is not whether the State erred, but what should be done about it. The question is whether reversal of respondent's conviction either is compelled by the Constitution or is an appropriate, but not constitutionally required, remedy for racial discrimination in the selection of grand jurors. * * *

The Court * * * decides that discrimination in the selection of the grand jury potentially harmed respondent, because the grand jury is vested with broad discretion in deciding whether to indict and in framing the charges, and because it is impossible to know whether this discretion would have been exercised differently by a properly selected grand jury. The point appears to be that an all-white grand jury from which blacks are systematically excluded might be influenced by race in determining whether to indict and for what charge. Since the State may not imprison respondent for a crime if one of its elements is his race, the argument goes, his conviction must be set aside.

This reasoning ignores established principles of equal protection jurisprudence. We have consistently declined to find a violation of the Equal Protection Clause absent a finding of intentional discrimination. There has been no showing in this case—indeed, respondent does not even allege—that the Kings County grand jury indicted respondent because of his race, or that the grand jury declined to indict white suspects in the face of similarly strong evidence. Nor is it sensible to assume that impermissible discrimination might have occurred simply because the grand jury had no black members. This Court has never suggested that the racial composition of a grand jury gives rise to the inference that indictments are racially motivated, any more than it has suggested that a suspect arrested by a policeman of a different race may challenge his subsequent conviction on that basis. But the Court now holds that relief is justified in part because of the bare potential, unsupported by any evidence, that an all-white grand jury charged respondent because of his race.

Twenty-three years ago, respondent was fairly convicted of the most serious of crimes. * * * For that reason alone, the Court should reverse the Court of Appeals' decision. * * *

[JUSTICE O'CONNOR's concurring opinion has been omitted.]

## NOTE

In a part of his dissent not included in the excerpt of *Vasquez v. Hillery* above, Justice Powell argued that, "when relief is granted many years after the original conviction . . . the State may find itself severely handicapped in its ability to carry its heavy burden of proving guilt beyond a reasonable doubt." Notwithstanding the risk that Hillery might have escaped conviction if reprosecuted so many years after the first trial, a majority of the Supreme Court affirmed the reversal of Hillery's conviction. Justice Marshall responded to Justice Powell's criticism of the majority's application of the automatic reversal rule and the risk that the Court would be letting a guilty man go free by noting, "If grand jury discrimination becomes a thing of the past, no conviction will ever again be lost on account of it."

In the end, Hillery did not go free. Despite the handicap to the State that Justice Powell feared given the more than 20 year time span between Hillery's conviction in the 1960s and the reversal of that conviction in 1986, the State secured another conviction when they reprosecuted Hillery. Miles Corwin, *Man Guilty of Slaying—24 Years After Crime*, L.A. TIMES, Dec. 19, 1986, http:// articles.latimes.com/1986-12-19/news/mn-3565_1_kings-county (noting that "[o]ne remarkable aspect of the case [was] that the Kings County Sheriff's Department held onto more than one hundred pieces of evidence from the Hillery case, including photographs of the crime scene, fiber and paint samples and Hillery's car."); *Killer, Twice Convicted, Due Parole Hearing*, L.A. TIMES, Feb. 28, 1987, http://articles.latimes.com/1987-02-28/news/mn-6520_1_parole-hearing. An all-white jury found Hillery guilty on December 18, 1986, and he was sentenced to life in prison. *Id.* Public outrage against Hillery for the murder of Marlene Miller, a white fifteen-year-old girl who was at home alone making a dress to wear to a party when she was stabbed to death with her own sewing scissors, remained high for many years. Miles Corwin, *Man Guilty of Slaying—24 Years After Crime*, L.A. TIMES, Dec. 19, 1986, http:// articles.latimes.com/1986-12-19/news/mn-3565_1_kings-county. As of 1993, Hillery continued to be denied parole. *Man Who Killed Girl, 15, in 1962 is*

*Denied Parole*, L.A. TIMES, July 30, 1993, http://articles.latimes.com/1993-07-30/news/mn-18501_1_parole-hearing.

## COSTELLO V. UNITED STATES
Supreme Court of the United States
350 U.S. 359, 76 S.Ct. 406, 100 L.Ed. 397 (1956)

JUSTICE BLACK delivered the opinion of the Court.

We granted certiorari in this case to consider a single question: "May a defendant be required to stand trial and a conviction be sustained where only hearsay evidence was presented to the grand jury which indicted him?"

Petitioner, Frank Costello, was indicted for wilfully attempting to evade payment of income taxes due the United States for the years 1947, 1948 and 1949. The charge was that petitioner falsely and fraudulently reported less income than he and his wife actually received during the taxable years in question. Petitioner promptly filed a motion for inspection of the minutes of the grand jury and for a dismissal of the indictment. His motion was based on an affidavit stating that he was firmly convinced there could have been no legal or competent evidence before the grand jury which indicted him since he had reported all his income and paid all taxes due. The motion was denied. At the trial which followed the Government offered evidence designed to show increases in Costello's net worth in an attempt to prove that he had received more income during the years in question than he had reported. To establish its case the Government called and examined 144 witnesses and introduced 368 exhibits. All of the testimony and documents related to business transactions and expenditures by petitioner and his wife. The prosecution concluded its case by calling three government agents. Their investigations had produced the evidence used against petitioner at the trial. They were allowed to summarize the vast amount of evidence already heard and to introduce computations showing, if correct, that petitioner and his wife had received far greater income than they had reported. * * *

Counsel for petitioner asked each government witness at the trial whether he had appeared before the grand jury which returned the indictment. This cross-examination developed the fact that the three investigating officers had been the only witnesses before the grand jury. After the Government concluded its case, petitioner again moved to dismiss the indictment on the ground that the only evidence before the grand jury was "hearsay," since the three officers had no firsthand knowledge of the transactions upon which their computations were based. Nevertheless the trial court again refused to dismiss the indictment, and petitioner was convicted. The Court of Appeals affirmed. * * * Petitioner here urges: (1) that an indictment based solely on hearsay evidence violates that part of the Fifth Amendment providing that "No person shall be held to answer for a capital, or otherwise infamous crime, unless on a presentment or indictment of a Grand Jury . . . ," and (2) that if the Fifth Amendment does not invalidate an indictment based solely on hearsay we should now lay down such a rule for the guidance of federal courts.

\* \* \* [N]either the Fifth Amendment nor any other constitutional provision prescribes the kind of evidence upon which grand juries must act. \* \* \* The basic purpose of the English grand jury was to provide a fair method for instituting criminal proceedings against persons believed to have committed crimes. Grand jurors were selected from the body of the people and their work was not hampered by rigid procedural or evidential rules. In fact, grand jurors could act on their own knowledge and were free to make their presentments or indictments on such information as they deemed satisfactory. \* \* \* And in this country as in England of old the grand jury has convened as a body of laymen, free from technical rules, acting in secret, pledged to indict no one because of prejudice and to free no one because of special favor. \* \* \*

In *Holt v. United States*, this Court had to decide whether an indictment should be quashed because supported in part by incompetent evidence. Aside from the incompetent evidence "there was very little evidence against the accused." The Court refused to hold that such an indictment should be quashed, pointing out that "The abuses of criminal practice would be enhanced if indictments could be upset on such a ground." The same thing is true where as here all the evidence before the grand jury was in the nature of "hearsay." If indictments were to be held open to challenge on the ground that there was inadequate or incompetent evidence before the grand jury, the resulting delay would be great indeed. The result of such a rule would be that before trial on the merits a defendant could always insist on a kind of preliminary trial to determine the competency and adequacy of the evidence before the grand jury. This is not required by the Fifth Amendment. An indictment returned by a legally constituted and unbiased grand jury, \* \* \* is enough to call for trial of the charge on the merits. The Fifth Amendment requires nothing more.

Petitioner urges that this Court should exercise its power to supervise the administration of justice in federal courts and establish a rule permitting defendants to challenge indictments on the ground that they are not supported by adequate or competent evidence. No persuasive reasons are advanced for establishing such a rule. It would run counter to the whole history of the grand jury institution, in which laymen conduct their inquiries unfettered by technical rules. Neither justice nor the concept of a fair trial requires such a change. In a trial on the merits, defendants are entitled to a strict observance of all the rules designed to bring about a fair verdict. Defendants are not entitled, however, to a rule which would result in interminable delay but add nothing to the assurance of a fair trial.

Affirmed.

JUSTICE CLARK and JUSTICE HARLAN took no part in the consideration or decision of this case.

[JUSTICE BURTON's concurring opinion has been omitted.]

## UNITED STATES V. WILLIAMS

Supreme Court of the United States
504 U.S. 36, 112 S.Ct. 1735, 118 L.Ed.2d 352 (1992)

JUSTICE SCALIA delivered the opinion of the Court.

The question presented in this case is whether a district court may dismiss an otherwise valid indictment because the Government failed to disclose to the grand jury "substantial exculpatory evidence" in its possession.

* * * [R]espondent John H. Williams, Jr., * * * was indicted * * * [for] "knowingly mak[ing] [a] false statement or report . . . for the purpose of influencing . . . the action [of a federally insured financial institution]," * * *. According to the indictment, * * * Williams supplied four Oklahoma banks with "materially false" statements that variously overstated the value of his current assets and interest income in order to influence the banks' actions on his loan requests.

* * * [T]he District Court granted Williams' motion for disclosure of all exculpatory portions of the grand jury transcripts. Upon reviewing this material, Williams demanded that the District Court dismiss the indictment, alleging that the Government had failed to fulfill its obligation under the Tenth Circuit's prior decision in *United States v. Page* to present "substantial exculpatory evidence" to the grand jury. His contention was that evidence which the Government had chosen not to present to the grand jury * * * belied an intent to mislead the banks, and thus directly negated an essential element of the charged offense.

The District Court * * * ordered the indictment dismissed without prejudice. It found * * * that the withheld evidence was "relevant to an essential element of the crime charged," created "a reasonable doubt about [respondent's] guilt," and thus "render[ed] the grand jury's decision to indict gravely suspect." Upon the Government's appeal, the Court of Appeals affirmed the District Court's order * * *. It first sustained * * * the District Court's determination that the Government had withheld "substantial exculpatory evidence" from the grand jury. It then found that the Government's behavior "substantially influence[d]" the grand jury's decision to indict, or at the very least raised a "grave doubt that the decision to indict was free from such substantial influence." [The Court of Appeals also found that] * * * it was not an abuse of discretion for the District Court to require the Government to begin anew before the grand jury. We granted certiorari. * * *

Respondent does not contend that the Fifth Amendment itself obliges the prosecutor to disclose substantial exculpatory evidence in his possession to the grand jury. Instead, building on our statement that the federal courts "may, within limits, formulate procedural rules not specifically required by the Constitution or the Congress," he argues that imposition of the Tenth Circuit's disclosure rule is supported by the courts' "supervisory power." We think not.

* * * Because the grand jury is an institution separate from the courts, over whose functioning the courts do not preside, we think it clear that, as a general matter at least, no such "supervisory" judicial authority exists, and that the disclosure rule applied here exceeded the Tenth Circuit's authority.

"[R]ooted in long centuries of Anglo-American history," the grand jury is mentioned in the Bill of Rights, but not in the body of the Constitution. It has not been textually assigned, therefore, to any of the branches described in the first three Articles. It "is a constitutional fixture in its own right." In fact the whole theory of its function is that it belongs to no branch of the institutional Government, serving as a kind of buffer or referee between the Government and the people. Although the grand jury normally operates, of course, in the courthouse and under judicial auspices, its institutional relationship with the Judicial Branch has traditionally been, so to speak, at arm's length. Judges' direct involvement in the functioning of the grand jury has generally been confined to the constitutive one of calling the grand jurors together and administering their oaths of office.

The grand jury's functional independence from the Judicial Branch is evident both in the scope of its power to investigate criminal wrongdoing and in the manner in which that power is exercised. "Unlike [a] [c]ourt, whose jurisdiction is predicated upon a specific case or controversy, the grand jury 'can investigate merely on suspicion that the law is being violated, or even because it wants assurance that it is not.'" It need not identify the offender it suspects, or even "the precise nature of the offense" it is investigating. The grand jury requires no authorization from its constituting court to initiate an investigation, nor does the prosecutor require leave of court to seek a grand jury indictment. And in its day-to-day functioning, the grand jury generally operates without the interference of a presiding judge. It swears in its own witnesses, and deliberates in total secrecy. * * *

No doubt in view of the grand jury proceeding's status as other than a constituent element of a "criminal prosecutio[n]," we have said that certain constitutional protections afforded defendants in criminal proceedings have no application before that body. The Double Jeopardy Clause of the Fifth Amendment does not bar a grand jury from returning an indictment when a prior grand jury has refused to do so. We have twice suggested, though not held, that the Sixth Amendment right to counsel does not attach when an individual is summoned to appear before a grand jury, even if he is the subject of the investigation. And although "the grand jury may not force a witness to answer questions in violation of [the Fifth Amendment's] constitutional guarantee" against self-incrimination, our cases suggest that an indictment obtained through the use of evidence previously obtained in violation of the privilege against self-incrimination "is nevertheless valid." * * *

Respondent argues that the Court of Appeals' rule can be justified as a sort of Fifth Amendment "common law," a necessary means of assuring the constitutional right to the judgment "of an independent and informed grand jury." Respondent makes a generalized appeal to functional notions: Judicial supervision of the quantity and quality of the evidence relied upon by the grand jury plainly facilitates, he says, the grand jury's performance of its twin historical responsibilities, *i.e.,* bringing to trial those who may be justly accused and shielding the innocent from unfounded accusation and prosecution. We do not agree. The rule would neither preserve nor enhance the traditional functioning of the institution that the Fifth Amendment demands. To the contrary, requiring the prosecutor to present exculpatory as well as inculpatory evidence would alter the grand jury's historical role, transforming it from an accusatory to an adjudicatory body.

It is axiomatic that the grand jury sits not to determine guilt or innocence, but to assess whether there is adequate basis for bringing a criminal charge. That has always been so; and to make the assessment it has always been thought sufficient to hear only the prosecutor's side. As Blackstone described the prevailing practice in 18th-century England, the grand jury was "only to hear evidence on behalf of the prosecution[,] for the finding of an indictment is only in the nature of an enquiry or accusation, which is afterwards to be tried and determined." So also in the United States. According to the description of an early American court, three years before the Fifth Amendment was ratified, it is the grand jury's function not "to enquire . . . upon what foundation [the charge may be] denied," or otherwise to try the suspect's defenses, but only to examine "upon what foundation [the charge] is made" by the prosecutor. As a consequence, neither in this country nor in England has the suspect under investigation by the grand jury ever been thought to have a right to testify or to have exculpatory evidence presented. * * *

We accepted Justice Nelson's description in *Costello v. United States,* where we held that "[i]t would run counter to the whole history of the grand jury institution" to permit an indictment to be challenged "on the ground that there was inadequate or incompetent evidence before the grand jury."

And we reaffirmed this principle recently in *Bank of Nova Scotia,* where we held that "the mere fact that evidence itself is unreliable is not sufficient to require a dismissal of the indictment," and that "a challenge to the reliability or competence of the evidence presented to the grand jury" will not be heard. It would make little sense, we think, to abstain from reviewing the evidentiary support for the grand jury's judgment while scrutinizing the sufficiency of the prosecutor's presentation. A complaint about the quality or adequacy of the evidence can always be recast as a complaint that the prosecutor's presentation was "incomplete" or "misleading." Our words in *Costello* bear repeating: Review of facially valid indictments on such grounds "would run counter to the whole history of the grand jury institution[,] [and] [n]either justice nor the concept of a fair trial requires [it]."

* * * For the reasons set forth above, however, we conclude that courts have no authority to prescribe such a duty pursuant to their inherent supervisory authority over their own proceedings. The judgment of the Court of Appeals is accordingly reversed, and the cause is remanded for further proceedings consistent with this opinion. * * *

JUSTICE STEVENS, with whom JUSTICE BLACKMUN and JUSTICE O'CONNOR join, and with whom JUSTICE THOMAS joins as to Parts II and III, dissenting. * * *

## II

We do not protect the integrity and independence of the grand jury by closing our eyes to the countless forms of prosecutorial misconduct that may occur inside the secrecy of the grand jury room. After all, the grand jury is not merely an investigatory body; it also serves as a "protector of citizens against arbitrary and oppressive governmental action." * * * It blinks reality to say that the grand jury can adequately perform this important historic role if it is intentionally misled by the prosecutor—on whose knowledge of the law and facts of the underlying criminal investigation the jurors will, of necessity, rely.

Unlike the Court, I am unwilling to hold that countless forms of prosecutorial misconduct must be tolerated—no matter how prejudicial they may be, or how seriously they may distort the legitimate function of the grand jury—simply because they are not proscribed by Rule 6 of the Federal Rules of Criminal Procedure or a statute that is applicable in grand jury proceedings. Such a sharp break with the traditional role of the federal judiciary is unprecedented, unwarranted, and unwise. Unrestrained prosecutorial misconduct in grand jury proceedings is inconsistent with the administration of justice in the federal courts and should be redressed in appropriate cases by the dismissal of indictments obtained by improper methods.

## III

What, then, is the proper disposition of this case? I agree with the Government that the prosecutor is not required to place all exculpatory evidence before the grand jury. A grand jury proceeding is an *ex parte* investigatory proceeding to determine whether there is probable cause to believe a violation of the criminal laws has occurred, not a trial. Requiring the prosecutor to ferret out and present all evidence that could be used at trial to create a reasonable doubt as to the defendant's guilt would be inconsistent with the purpose of the grand jury proceeding and would place significant burdens on the investigation. But that does not mean that the prosecutor may mislead the grand jury into believing that there is probable cause to indict by withholding clear evidence to the contrary. * * *

Although I question whether the evidence withheld in this case directly negates respondent's guilt, I need not resolve my doubts because the Solicitor General did not ask the Court to review the nature of the evidence withheld. Instead, he asked us to decide the legal question whether an indictment may be dismissed because the prosecutor failed to present exculpatory evidence. Unlike the Court and the Solicitor General, I believe the answer to that question is yes, if the withheld evidence would plainly preclude a finding of probable cause. I therefore cannot endorse the Court's opinion. * * *

### NOTE

Despite the holding in *United States v. Williams*, some states require their prosecutors to present exculpatory evidence to the grand jury as a matter of state law. *See, e.g. State v. Herrera*, 601 P.2d 75, 77 (N.M. Ct. App. 1979) (holding that "due process requires the presentation of evidence to the grand jury which tends to negate guilt" because the basic duty of the prosecutor is to seek a just result).

The 2014 deaths of Michael Brown in Ferguson, Missouri, and Eric Garner in New York City, New York, drew public attention to the use of the grand jury in charging decisions involving police officers. In each of these high profile cases, the grand jury failed to indict the officers involved. The "no bill" for Michael Brown's death in Missouri was returned first, followed a few days later by the "no bill" in New York for Eric Garner's death.

Notably, the events leading up to Garner's death—the officer putting Garner into a chokehold and Garner, who suffered from asthma, crying out, "I can't breathe; I can't breathe"—were captured on video. Thus, many were surprised when no indictment was returned by the grand jury. The no bill was particularly surprising given that the New York City Police Department prohibits its officers from using chokeholds.[a] In the Ferguson case, there were

---

[a]    Alissa Scheller, *The Chokehold is Banned by NYPD, but Complaints about its Use Persist*, HUFFINGTON POST, Dec. 5, 2014 (4:14 PM ET), http://www.huffingtonpost.com/2014/12/05/nyc-police-chokeholds_n_6272000.html or https://perma.cc/999L-SBLB; Ian Fisher, *Kelley Bans*

allegations of prosecutorial error, such as instructing the grand jurors on an outdated version of the use-of-force law.[b] Moreover, the prosecutor admitted he presented the grand jury with evidence he knew was false.[c]

In both cases, the decisions by each of the grand juries resulted in strong public reaction. The Pew Research Center conducted public opinions polls that gauged the public's reaction to the decisions and found that a majority of Whites (64%) felt the grand jury's decision not to indict Officer Darren Wilson in the death of Michael Brown was the right decision, while an overwhelming majority of Blacks (80%) felt the grand jury's decision in the Ferguson case was the wrong decision.[d] In the New York case, Whites and Blacks were more aligned in feeling that the grand jury's decision not to indict the officer involved in Eric Garner's death was the wrong decision. Nonetheless, only 47% of Whites polled felt the no bill in Garner's case was the wrong decision compared to an overwhelming majority of Blacks (90%) who felt the no bill was the wrong decision.

*Chokeholds by Officers*, N.Y. TIMES, Nov. 24, 1993, http://www.nytimes.com/1993/11/24/nyregion/kelly-bans-choke-holds-by-officers.html or https://perma.cc/EJ6A-6ADC.

[b] Jeffrey Fagan & Bernard E. Harcourt, *Professors Fagan and Harcourt Provide Facts on Grand Jury Practice in Light of Ferguson Decision*, Columbia Law School, http://www.law.columbia.edu/media_inquiries/news_events/2014/november2014/Facts-on-Ferguson-Grand-Jury or https://perma.cc/DP94-77F2. It appears this criticism may have been misplaced since the initial instruction instructed grand jurors on the use of force law in effect in Missouri at the time. In 2014, Missouri was still operating under the old common law rule, which permitted police officers to use deadly force to prevent the escape of a fleeing felon even if the individual was not posing an imminent threat of death or serious bodily injury to anyone. *See* Chad Flanders and Joseph Welling, *Police Use Of Deadly Force: State Statutes 30 Years After Garner*, 35 ST. LOUIS U. PUB. L. Rev. 109, 124–26 (2015) (explaining that the ruling in *Tennessee v. Garner* controls in Section 1983 civil rights actions, but a state's use of force law controls in its criminal prosecutions). In 2016, Missouri finally abandoned the common law rule and changed its use of force statute to comport with *Tennessee v. Garner*. H.B. 2332, 98th Gen, Assemb. Reg. Sess. (Mo. 2016).

[c] Judd Legum, *A Startling Admission By the Ferguson Prosecutor Could Restart The Case Against Darren Wilson*, ThinkProgress (Dec. 21, 2014, 2:32 PM), http://thinkprogress.org/justice/2014/12/21/3606084/how-a-startling-admission-from-the-ferguson-prosecutor-could-restart-the-case-against-darren-wilson/ (noting that prosecutor Bob McCulloch admitted in a radio interview that he presented witnesses to the grand jury who clearly were not telling the truth); Josh Levs, *One challenge for Ferguson grand jury: Some witnesses' credibility*, CNN (Dec. 14, 2014, 3:53 PM), http://www.cnn.com/2014/12/14/justice/ferguson-witnesses-credibility/ or https://perma.cc/FY7D-AJFE.

[d] *Sharp Racial Divisions in Reactions to Brown, Garner Decisions*, Pew Research Ctr. (Dec. 8, 2014), http://www.people-press.org/2014/12/08/sharp-racial-divisions-in-reactions-to-brown-garner-decisions or https://perma.cc/GE8Z-CZ82.

# CHAPTER 24

# BAIL

▪ ▪ ▪

"Bail"[a] is the process for releasing a defendant from jail with conditions to ensure that the defendant will make future court appearances and not endanger the community. NATIONAL INSTITUTE OF CORRECTIONS, FUNDAMENTALS OF BAIL: A RESOURCE GUIDE FOR PRETRIAL PRACTITIONERS AND A FRAMEWORK FOR AMERICAN PRETRIAL REFORM 2 (August 2014). Since 1900, the bail system in the United States has primarily relied upon financial conditions as the means for ensuring court appearances and safety of the community. While the court can release the defendant on the defendant's own recognizance or personal promise to appear, also known as OR (own recognizance) release, in most cases, the court will set financial conditions for release and require the defendant to post bond before the defendant is released pending trial.

There is no express right to bail in the U.S. Constitution. The Eighth Amendment to the U.S. Constitution, however, provides that "[e]xcessive bail shall not be required." In the first case in this chapter, *Stack v. Boyle*, the Court explains when bail is excessive in violation of the Eighth Amendment.

Prior to 1984, it was understood that the purpose of setting financial conditions upon release was to secure the defendant's appearance at trial. In 1984, Congress passed the Federal Bail Reform Act of 1984, *see* Appendix, which authorizes the pretrial detention of a defendant to ensure either the appearance of the defendant or the safety of any other person or the community. When a defendant is incarcerated prior to or pending trial to assure the safety of the community, this type of detention is known as "preventive detention." In *United States v. Salerno*, the Court considers whether preventive detention violates either the Due Process Clause or the Eighth Amendment's proscription against excessive bail.

The chapter ends with two articles. In the first article, Chris Ingraham points out how wealth, or lack thereof, has a huge impact on who ends up

---

[a]  The term "bail" is often used as shorthand for "bail bond," which is an agreement between the defendant and the court (or a private bail bondsman) in which the defendant promises to appear in court as required. The defendant agrees to forfeit a certain amount of money to the court (or to a bail bondsman) if he does not fulfill his promise to appear. In exchange, the court (or the bail bondsman who charges the defendant a percentage of the full amount and agrees to pay the full amount owed if the defendant does not appear) allows the defendant to be released pending trial.

being detained pending trial. In the second article, Cynthia Jones summarizes the results of research studies from 1970 to the present, all showing that Black defendants are subjected to pretrial detention at higher rates and are subjected to higher bail amounts than White defendants with similar charges and similar criminal histories.

## STACK V. BOYLE

Supreme Court of the United States
342 U.S. 1, 72 S.Ct. 1, 96 L.Ed. 3 (1951)

CHIEF JUSTICE VINSON delivered the opinion of the Court.

Indictments have been returned in the Southern District of California charging the twelve petitioners with conspiring to violate the Smith Act. Upon their arrest, bail was fixed for each petitioner in the widely varying amounts of $2,500, $7,500, $75,000 and $100,000. On motion of petitioner Schneiderman following arrest in the Southern District of New York, his bail was reduced to $50,000 before his removal to California. On motion of the Government to increase bail in the case of other petitioners, and after several intermediate procedural steps not material to the issues presented here, bail was fixed in the District Court for the Southern District of California in the uniform amount of $50,000 for each petitioner.

Petitioners moved to reduce bail on the ground that bail as fixed was excessive under the Eighth Amendment.[8] In support of their motion, petitioners submitted statements as to their financial resources, family relationships, health, prior criminal records, and other information. The only evidence offered by the Government was a certified record showing that four persons previously convicted under the Smith Act in the Southern District of New York had forfeited bail. No evidence was produced relating those four persons to the petitioners in this case. At a hearing on the motion, petitioners were examined by the District Judge and cross-examined by an attorney for the Government. Petitioners' factual statements stand uncontroverted.

After their motion to reduce bail was denied, petitioners filed applications for habeas corpus in the same District Court. Upon consideration of the record on the motion to reduce bail, the writs were denied. The Court of Appeals for the Ninth Circuit affirmed.

* * * [F]rom the passage of the Judiciary Act of 1789 to the present Federal Rules of Criminal Procedure, Rule 46(a)(1), federal law has unequivocally provided that a person arrested for a non-capital offense shall be admitted to bail. This traditional right to freedom before conviction permits the unhampered preparation of a defense, and serves to prevent

---

[8] "Excessive bail shall not be required, nor excessive fines imposed, nor cruel and unusual punishments inflicted." U.S. Const. Amend. VIII.

the infliction of punishment prior to conviction. Unless this right to bail before trial is preserved, the presumption of innocence, secured only after centuries of struggle, would lose its meaning.

The right to release before trial is conditioned upon the accused's giving adequate assurance that he will stand trial and submit to sentence if found guilty. Like the ancient practice of securing the oaths of responsible persons to stand as sureties for the accused, the modern practice of requiring a bail bond or the deposit of a sum of money subject to forfeiture serves as additional assurance of the presence of an accused. Bail set at a figure higher than an amount reasonably calculated to fulfill this purpose is "excessive" under the Eighth Amendment.

Since the function of bail is limited, the fixing of bail for any individual defendant must be based upon standards relevant to the purpose of assuring the presence of that defendant. The traditional standards as expressed in the Federal Rules of Criminal Procedure[3] are to be applied in each case to each defendant. * * * Upon final judgment of conviction, petitioners face imprisonment of not more than five years and a fine of not more than $10,000. It is not denied that bail for each petitioner has been fixed in a sum much higher than that usually imposed for offenses with like penalties and yet there has been no factual showing to justify such action in this case. The Government asks the courts to depart from the norm by assuming, without the introduction of evidence, that each petitioner is a pawn in a conspiracy and will, in obedience to a superior, flee the jurisdiction. To infer from the fact of indictment alone a need for bail in an unusually high amount is an arbitrary act. Such conduct would inject into our own system of government the very principles of totalitarianism which Congress was seeking to guard against in passing the statute under which petitioners have been indicted.

If bail in an amount greater than that usually fixed for serious charges of crimes is required in the case of any of the petitioners, that is a matter to which evidence should be directed in a hearing so that the constitutional rights of each petitioner may be preserved. In the absence of such a showing, we are of the opinion that the fixing of bail before trial in these cases cannot be squared with the statutory and constitutional standards for admission to bail. * * *

The Court concludes that bail has not been fixed by proper methods in this case and that petitioners' remedy is by motion to reduce bail, with right of appeal to the Court of Appeals. Accordingly, the judgment of the Court of Appeals is vacated and the case is remanded to the District Court with

---

[3] Rule 46(c). "AMOUNT. If the defendant is admitted to bail, the amount thereof shall be such as in the judgment of the commissioner or court or judge or justice will insure the presence of the defendant, having regard to the nature and circumstances of the offense charged, the weight of the evidence against him, the financial ability of the defendant to give bail and the character of the defendant."

directions to vacate its order. * * * Petitioners may move for reduction of bail in the criminal proceeding so that a hearing may be held for the purpose of fixing reasonable bail for each petitioner.

It is so ordered.

By JUSTICE JACKSON, whom JUSTICE FRANKFURTER joins. * * *

The practice of admission to bail, as it has evolved in Anglo-American law, is not a device for keeping persons in jail upon mere accusation until it is found convenient to give them a trial. On the contrary, the spirit of the procedure is to enable them to stay out of jail until a trial has found them guilty. Without this conditional privilege, even those wrongly accused are punished by a period of imprisonment while awaiting trial and are handicapped in consulting counsel, searching for evidence and witnesses, and preparing a defense. To open a way of escape from this handicap and possible injustice, Congress commands allowance of bail for one under charge of any offense not punishable by death, Fed.Rules Crim.Proc. 46(a)(1) providing: "A person arrested for an offense not punishable by death shall be admitted to bail . . ." before conviction. * * *

It is complained that the District Court fixed a uniform blanket bail chiefly by consideration of the nature of the accusation and did not take into account the difference in circumstances between different defendants. If this occurred, it is a clear violation of Rule 46(c). Each defendant stands before the bar of justice as an individual. Even on a conspiracy charge defendants do not lose their separateness or identity. While it might be possible that these defendants are identical in financial ability, character and relation to the charge—elements Congress has directed to be regarded in fixing bail—I think it violates the law of probabilities. Each accused is entitled to any benefits due to his good record, and misdeeds or a bad record should prejudice only those who are guilty of them. The question when application for bail is made relates to each one's trustworthiness to appear for trial and what security will supply reasonable assurance of his appearance.

* * * [T]he defect in the proceedings below appears to be, that, provoked by the flight of certain Communists after conviction, the Government demands and public opinion supports a use of the bail power to keep Communist defendants in jail before conviction. Thus, the amount is said to have been fixed not as a reasonable assurance of their presence at the trial, but also as an assurance they would remain in jail. There seems reason to believe that this may have been the spirit to which the courts below have yielded, and it is contrary to the whole policy and philosophy of bail. This is not to say that every defendant is entitled to such bail as he can provide, but he is entitled to an opportunity to make it in a reasonable amount. I think the whole matter should be reconsidered by the appropriate judges in the traditional spirit of bail procedure. * * *

## United States v. Salerno

Supreme Court of the United States
481 U.S. 739, 107 S.Ct. 2095, 95 L.Ed.2d 697 (1987)

Chief Justice Rehnquist delivered the opinion of the Court.

The Bail Reform Act of 1984 (Act) allows a federal court to detain an arrestee pending trial if the Government demonstrates by clear and convincing evidence after an adversary hearing that no release conditions "will reasonably assure ... the safety of any other person and the community." The United States Court of Appeals for the Second Circuit struck down this provision of the Act as facially unconstitutional, because, in that court's words, this type of pretrial detention violates "substantive due process." We granted certiorari because of a conflict among the Courts of Appeals regarding the validity of the Act. We hold that, as against the facial attack mounted by these respondents, the Act fully comports with constitutional requirements. We therefore reverse.

Responding to "the alarming problem of crimes committed by persons on release," Congress formulated the Bail Reform Act of 1984, as the solution to a bail crisis in the federal courts. The Act represents the National Legislature's considered response to numerous perceived deficiencies in the federal bail process. By providing for sweeping changes in both the way federal courts consider bail applications and the circumstances under which bail is granted, Congress hoped to "give the courts adequate authority to make release decisions that give appropriate recognition to the danger a person may pose to others if released."

To this end, § 3141(a) of the Act requires a judicial officer to determine whether an arrestee shall be detained. Section 3142(e) provides that "[i]f, after a hearing pursuant to the provisions of subsection (f), the judicial officer finds that no condition or combination of conditions will reasonably assure the appearance of the person as required and the safety of any other person and the community, he shall order the detention of the person prior to trial." Section 3142(f) provides the arrestee with a number of procedural safeguards. He may request the presence of counsel at the detention hearing, he may testify and present witnesses in his behalf, as well as proffer evidence, and he may cross-examine other witnesses appearing at the hearing. If the judicial officer finds that no conditions of pretrial release can reasonably assure the safety of other persons and the community, he must state his findings of fact in writing, and support his conclusion with "clear and convincing evidence."

The judicial officer is not given unbridled discretion in making the detention determination. Congress has specified the considerations relevant to that decision. These factors include the nature and seriousness of the charges, the substantiality of the Government's evidence against the arrestee, the arrestee's background and characteristics, and the nature and seriousness of the danger posed by the suspect's release. Should a judicial officer order detention, the detainee is entitled to expedited appellate review of the detention order.

Respondents Anthony Salerno and Vincent Cafaro were arrested on March 21, 1986, after being charged in a 29-count indictment alleging various Racketeer Influenced and Corrupt Organizations Act (RICO) violations, mail and wire fraud offenses, extortion, and various criminal gambling violations. The RICO counts alleged 35 acts of racketeering activity, including fraud, extortion, gambling, and conspiracy to commit murder. At respondents' arraignment, the Government moved to have Salerno and Cafaro detained pursuant to § 3142(e), on the ground that no condition of release would assure the safety of the community or any person. The District Court held a hearing at which the Government made a detailed proffer of evidence. The Government's case showed that Salerno was the "boss" of the Genovese crime family of La Cosa Nostra and that Cafaro was a "captain" in the Genovese family. According to the Government's proffer, based in large part on conversations intercepted by a court-ordered wiretap, the two respondents had participated in wide-ranging conspiracies to aid their illegitimate enterprises through violent means. The Government also offered the testimony of two of its trial witnesses, who would assert that Salerno personally participated in two murder conspiracies. Salerno opposed the motion for detention, challenging the credibility of the Government's witnesses. He offered the testimony of several character witnesses as well as a letter from his doctor stating that he was suffering from a serious medical condition. Cafaro presented no evidence at the hearing, but instead characterized the wiretap conversations as merely "tough talk."

The District Court granted the Government's detention motion, concluding that the Government had established by clear and convincing evidence that no condition or combination of conditions of release would ensure the safety of the community or any person:

> The activities of a criminal organization such as the Genovese Family do not cease with the arrest of its principals and their release on even the most stringent of bail conditions. The illegal businesses, in place for many years, require constant attention and protection, or they will fail. Under these circumstances, this court recognizes a strong incentive on the part of its leadership to continue business as usual. When business as usual involves threats, beatings, and murder, the present danger such people pose in the community is self-evident.

Respondents appealed, contending that to the extent that the Bail Reform Act permits pretrial detention on the ground that the arrestee is likely to commit future crimes, it is unconstitutional on its face. Over a dissent, the United States Court of Appeals for the Second Circuit agreed. Although the court agreed that pretrial detention could be imposed if the defendants were likely to intimidate witnesses or otherwise jeopardize the trial process, it found "§ 3142(e)'s authorization of pretrial detention [on the ground of future dangerousness] repugnant to the concept of substantive due process, which we believe prohibits the total deprivation of liberty simply as a means of preventing future crimes." The court concluded that the Government could not, consistent with due process, detain persons who had not been accused of any crime merely because they were thought to present a danger to the community. It reasoned that our criminal law system holds persons accountable for past actions, not anticipated future actions. * * *

Respondents present two grounds for invalidating the Bail Reform Act's provisions permitting pretrial detention on the basis of future dangerousness. First, they rely upon the Court of Appeals' conclusion that the Act exceeds the limitations placed upon the Federal Government by the Due Process Clause of the Fifth Amendment. Second, they contend that the Act contravenes the Eighth Amendment's proscription against excessive bail. We treat these contentions in turn.

The Due Process Clause of the Fifth Amendment provides that "No person shall . . . be deprived of life, liberty, or property, without due process of law. . . ." This Court has held that the Due Process Clause protects individuals against two types of government action. So-called "substantive due process" prevents the government from engaging in conduct that "shocks the conscience," or interferes with rights "implicit in the concept of ordered liberty." When government action depriving a person of life, liberty, or property survives substantive due process scrutiny, it must still be implemented in a fair manner. This requirement has traditionally been referred to as "procedural" due process.

Respondents first argue that the Act violates substantive due process because the pretrial detention it authorizes constitutes impermissible punishment before trial. The Government, however, has never argued that pretrial detention could be upheld if it were "punishment." The Court of Appeals assumed that pretrial detention under the Bail Reform Act is regulatory, not penal, and we agree that it is.

As an initial matter, the mere fact that a person is detained does not inexorably lead to the conclusion that the government has imposed punishment. To determine whether a restriction on liberty constitutes impermissible punishment or permissible regulation, we first look to legislative intent. Unless Congress expressly intended to impose punitive restrictions, the punitive/regulatory distinction turns on "whether an alternative purpose to which [the restriction] may rationally be connected is assignable for it, and whether it appears excessive in relation to the alternative purpose assigned [to it]."

We conclude that the detention imposed by the Act falls on the regulatory side of the dichotomy. The legislative history of the Bail Reform Act clearly indicates that Congress did not formulate the pretrial detention provisions as punishment for dangerous individuals. Congress instead perceived pretrial detention as a potential solution to a pressing societal problem. There is no doubt that preventing danger to the community is a legitimate regulatory goal.

Nor are the incidents of pretrial detention excessive in relation to the regulatory goal Congress sought to achieve. The Bail Reform Act carefully limits the circumstances under which detention may be sought to the most serious of crimes. See 18 U.S.C. § 3142(f) (detention hearings available if case involves crimes of violence, offenses for which the sentence is life imprisonment or death, serious drug offenses, or certain repeat offenders). The arrestee is entitled to a prompt detention hearing, and the maximum length of pretrial detention is limited by the stringent time limitations of the Speedy Trial Act. Moreover, * * * the conditions of confinement envisioned by the Act "appear to reflect the regulatory purposes relied upon by the" Government. * * * [T]he statute at issue here requires that detainees be housed in a "facility separate, to the extent practicable, from persons awaiting or serving sentences or being held in custody pending appeal." We conclude, therefore, that the pretrial detention contemplated by the Bail Reform Act is regulatory in nature, and does not constitute punishment before trial in violation of the Due Process Clause. * * *

Respondents also contend that the Bail Reform Act violates the Excessive Bail Clause of the Eighth Amendment. The Court of Appeals did not address this issue because it found that the Act violates the Due Process Clause. We think that the Act survives a challenge founded upon the Eighth Amendment.

The Eighth Amendment addresses pretrial release by providing merely that "[e]xcessive bail shall not be required." This Clause, of course, says nothing about whether bail shall be available at all. Respondents nevertheless contend that this Clause grants them a right to bail calculated solely upon considerations of flight. They rely on *Stack v. Boyle*, in which the Court stated that "[b]ail set at a figure higher than an amount reasonably calculated [to ensure the defendant's presence at trial] is 'excessive' under the Eighth Amendment." In respondents' view, since the Bail Reform Act allows a court essentially to set bail at an infinite amount for reasons not related to the risk of flight, it violates the Excessive Bail Clause. Respondents concede that the right to bail they have discovered in the Eighth Amendment is not absolute. A court may, for example, refuse bail in capital cases. And, as the Court of Appeals noted and respondents admit, a court may refuse bail when the defendant presents a threat to the judicial process by intimidating witnesses. Respondents characterize these exceptions as consistent with what they claim to be the sole purpose of bail—to ensure the integrity of the judicial process.

While we agree that a primary function of bail is to safeguard the courts' role in adjudicating the guilt or innocence of defendants, we reject the proposition that the Eighth Amendment categorically prohibits the government from pursuing other admittedly compelling interests through regulation of pretrial release. The above-quoted *dictum* in *Stack v. Boyle* is far too slender a reed on which to rest this argument.

* * * Nothing in the text of the Bail Clause limits permissible Government considerations solely to questions of flight. The only arguable substantive limitation of the Bail Clause is that the Government's proposed conditions of release or detention not be "excessive" in light of the perceived evil. Of course, to determine whether the Government's response is excessive, we must compare that response against the interest the Government seeks to protect by means of that response. Thus, when the Government has admitted that its only interest is in preventing flight, bail must be set by a court at a sum designed to ensure that goal, and no more. We believe that when Congress has mandated detention on the basis of a compelling interest other than prevention of flight, as it has here, the Eighth Amendment does not require release on bail.

In our society liberty is the norm, and detention prior to trial or without trial is the carefully limited exception. We hold that the provisions for pretrial detention in the Bail Reform Act of 1984 fall within that carefully limited exception. The Act authorizes the detention prior to trial of arrestees charged with serious felonies who are found after an adversary hearing to pose a threat to the safety of individuals or to the community which no condition of release can dispel. The numerous procedural safeguards detailed above must attend this adversary hearing. We are unwilling to say that this congressional determination, based as it is upon that primary concern of every government—a concern for the safety and indeed the lives of its citizens—on its face violates either the Due Process Clause of the Fifth Amendment or the Excessive Bail Clause of the Eighth Amendment.

The judgment of the Court of Appeals is therefore

*Reversed.*

JUSTICE MARSHALL, with whom JUSTICE BRENNAN joins, dissenting.

This case brings before the Court for the first time a statute in which Congress declares that a person innocent of any crime may be jailed indefinitely, pending the trial of allegations which are legally presumed to be untrue, if the Government shows to the satisfaction of a judge that the accused is likely to commit crimes, unrelated to the pending charges, at any time in the future. Such statutes, consistent with the usages of tyranny and the excesses of what bitter experience teaches us to call the police state, have long been thought incompatible with the fundamental human rights protected by our Constitution. Today a majority of this Court holds otherwise. Its decision disregards basic principles of justice established centuries ago and enshrined beyond the reach of governmental interference in the Bill of Rights.

* * * The Eighth Amendment, as the majority notes, states that "[e]xcessive bail shall not be required." The majority then declares, as if it were undeniable, that: "[t]his Clause, of course, says nothing about whether bail shall be available at all." If excessive bail is imposed the defendant stays in jail. The same result is achieved if bail is denied altogether. Whether the magistrate sets bail at $1 million or refuses to set bail at all, the consequences are indistinguishable. It would be mere sophistry to suggest that the Eighth Amendment protects against the former decision, and not the latter. * * *

The essence of this case may be found, ironically enough, in a provision of the Act to which the majority does not refer. Title 18 U.S.C. § 3142(j) (1982 ed., Supp. III) provides that "[n]othing in this section shall be construed as modifying or limiting the presumption of innocence." But the very pith and purpose of this statute is an abhorrent limitation of the presumption of innocence. The majority's untenable conclusion that the present Act is constitutional arises from a specious denial of the role of the Bail Clause and the Due Process Clause in protecting the invaluable guarantee afforded by the presumption of innocence.

"The principle that there is a presumption of innocence in favor of the accused is the undoubted law, axiomatic and elementary, and its enforcement lies at the foundation of the administration of our criminal law." Our society's belief, reinforced over the centuries, that all are innocent until the state has proved them to be guilty, like the companion principle that guilt must be proved beyond a reasonable doubt, is "implicit in the concept of ordered liberty," and is established beyond legislative contravention in the Due Process Clause.

The statute now before us declares that persons who have been indicted may be detained if a judicial officer finds clear and convincing evidence that they pose a danger to individuals or to the community. The statute does not authorize the Government to imprison anyone it has evidence is dangerous; indictment is necessary. But let us suppose that a defendant is indicted and the Government shows by clear and convincing evidence that he is dangerous and should be detained pending a trial, at which trial the defendant is acquitted. May the Government continue to hold the defendant in detention based upon its showing that he is dangerous? The answer cannot be yes, for that would allow the Government to imprison someone for uncommitted crimes based upon "proof" not beyond a reasonable doubt. The result must therefore be that once the indictment has failed, detention cannot continue. But our fundamental principles of justice declare that the defendant is as innocent on the day before his trial as he is on the morning after his acquittal. Under this statute an untried indictment somehow acts to permit a detention, based on other charges, which after an acquittal would be unconstitutional. * * *

It is not a novel proposition that the Bail Clause plays a vital role in protecting the presumption of innocence. Reviewing the application for bail pending appeal by members of the American Communist Party convicted under the Smith Act, Justice Jackson wrote:

> Grave public danger is said to result from what [the defendants] may be expected to do, in addition to what they have done since their conviction. If I assume that defendants are disposed to commit every opportune disloyal act helpful to Communist countries, it is still difficult to reconcile with traditional American law the jailing of persons by the courts because of anticipated but as yet uncommitted crimes. Imprisonment to protect society from predicted but unconsummated offenses is . . . unprecedented in this country and . . . fraught with danger of excesses and injustice. . . .

As Chief Justice Vinson wrote for the Court in *Stack v. Boyle:* "Unless th[e] right to bail before trial is preserved, the presumption of innocence, secured only after centuries of struggle, would lose its meaning." * * *

"It is a fair summary of history to say that the safeguards of liberty have frequently been forged in controversies involving not very nice people." Honoring the presumption of innocence is often difficult; sometimes we must pay substantial social costs as a result of our commitment to the values we espouse. But at the end of the day the presumption of innocence protects the innocent; the shortcuts we take with those whom we believe to be guilty injure only those wrongfully accused and, ultimately, ourselves. * * *

I dissent.

[JUSTICE STEVENS' dissenting opinion has been omitted.]

## SHOULD MORE DEFENDANTS GET OUT OF JAIL FREE?

Chris Ingraham
Washington Post, June 14, 2015, at F2

At any given time, roughly 480,000 people sit in America's local jails awaiting their day in court, according an estimate by the London-based

International Centre for Prison Studies. These are people who have been charged with a crime but not convicted. They remain innocent in the eyes of the law.

Some are violent criminals who need to await their trials behind bars in the interest of public safety—murderers, rapists and the like. But most (three quarters of them, according to the National Conference of State Legislatures) are nonviolent offenders, arrested for traffic violations or property crimes or simple drug possession. And many of them will be found not guilty. A 2013 Bureau of Justice Statistics report found that one-third of felony defendants in the nation's largest counties were not ultimately convicted of any crime.

That same report found that defendants who were detained before trial waited a median of 68 days in jail. Often, that is simply because they can't afford to post bail. A 2013 analysis by the Drug Policy Alliance found that was the case for nearly 40 percent of New Jersey's jail population.

The idea of bail makes a lot of intuitive sense: When someone is charged with a crime, you make them put down a deposit to ensure they show up in court for trial. If they don't put the money down, they have to wait in jail. But in practice this means that plenty of people sit behind bars not because they are dangerous or because they're a flight risk, but simply because they can't come up with the cash.

For low-income people, the consequences of a pre-trial detention, even a brief one, can be disastrous. Miss too much work and you're out of a job. Fall behind on your rent and you're out of a home, too. Plus, in many cases, these people will eventually be found not guilty.

For reasons like this, some civil rights reformers advocate abolishing bail. Maya Schenwar, editor in chief of independent news site Truthout, says bail policies are tantamount to "locking people up for being poor." HBO's John Oliver recently noted that while a poor person might not be able to post a $1,000 dollar bail for a minor infraction, a wealthy murder suspect like Robert Durst can post a $250,000 bail and walk free.

Eliminating bail is not as radical as it sounds. The District [of Columbia] effectively stopped using bail in the late 1960s. Instead, the city's Pretrial Services Agency determines the best option for dealing with defendants before they go to court. According to the agency, 12 to 15 percent of defendants are held before trial for various reasons, including flight risk or danger to others. Others are released. The overwhelming majority of released defendants, 88 percent of them, make all scheduled court appearances and remain arrest-free while awaiting trial.[a]

---

[a]   The District of Columbia permits preventive detention (pretrial detention on the basis of danger to the community), but prohibits detention based upon inability to pay. KiDeuk Kim & Megan Denver, *A Case Study on the Practice of Pretrial Services and Risk Assessment in Three Cities* 3 (December 2011). If financial conditions are imposed, defendants are entitled to a bail bond

If you're not convinced by the civil rights argument, consider the economic one: We spend about $17 billion dollars annually to keep innocent people locked up as they await trial. Here's how I arrived at that number: U.S. taxpayers spent $26 billion on county and municipal jails in 2012, the most recent year for which the Bureau of Justice Statistics has data. And 64 percent of those in jail are awaiting trial, thus the estimate that we're spending about $17 billion each year on pre-trial detentions. That's just a back-of-the-envelope estimate, but it gives us a sense. For comparison, that amount is a little less than NASA's annual budget.

## "GIVE US FREE": ADDRESSING RACIAL DISPARITIES IN BAIL DETERMINATIONS

Cynthia E. Jones
16 N.Y.U. J. Legis. & Pub. Pol'y 919 (2013)

Over the last fifty years, research studies have consistently found that African American defendants receive significantly harsher bail outcomes than those imposed on white defendants. * * * [N]early every study on the impact of race in bail determinations has concluded that African Americans are subjected to pretrial detention at a higher rate and are subjected to higher bail amounts than are white arrestees with similar charges and similar criminal histories. The adverse impact of the defendant's race on the outcome of the bail determination is not a new or recent problem, nor is it confined to specific types of cases. Criminologists and researchers have published over twenty five studies documenting racial disparities in bail determinations in state cases, federal cases, and juvenile delinquency proceedings. The adverse impact of race in bail determinations also is not isolated to particular regions of the country. The problem is pervasive. Researchers documented racial disparities in bail determinations in studies of northeast urban areas, mid-western urban areas, southern counties, mid-western counties, and northern counties. Researchers also documented similar patterns of ethnic disparities in bail determinations for Latino defendants.

### A. The First Generation Studies of Race and Bail: 1970–2000

In 2003, Professor Marvin D. Free, Jr. completed a meta-analysis of twenty-five different studies on the impact of race in bail determinations published between 1970 and 2000. In each study, researchers identified representative samples of criminal cases, isolated particular legal and extra-legal factors, and employed various metrics and statistical analyses

---

they can meet, and money is not supposed to be used to ensure community safety. *Id.* As a result, the District of Columbia releases about 85 percent of all arrestees. Clifford T. Keenan, *We Need More Bail Reform* (Pretrial Services Agency for the District of Columbia Sept. 2013). About 88 percent of arrestees are not arrested again prior to trial and appear for trial. *Id.* Of those who are re-arrested, less than 1 percent are alleged to have committed a violent crime. *Id.* The use of preventive detention is limited to approximately 15 percent of all accused persons in the District of Columbia. *Id.*

to determine whether race played a role in bail determinations. In eighteen studies, researchers concluded that African American defendants were subjected to more severe treatment than white defendants. * * * For example, one major national study examined bail determinations in over 5000 felony cases adjudicated in the federal district courts in Brooklyn, Manhattan, Chicago, Philadelphia, Baltimore, Dallas, Kansas City, Atlanta, Los Angeles and Detroit. Researchers compared the bail outcomes for African American and white defendants, all of whom had prior felony convictions. * * * The researchers found that white defendants with a prior felony conviction received more favorable bail outcomes than similarly-situated African American defendants. * * *

Other first generation studies found that African Americans were charged a higher money bond to secure their pretrial release than were white defendants. * * * Also, local community ties, generally viewed as a positive factor in determining risk of flight, were found to decrease the bond amount for white residents, but not African American defendants. More recent studies have likewise found that bail officials generally tend to impose higher bail amounts on African American defendants.

## B. The Second Generation Studies of Race and Bail: 2001–2012

The second generation of research studies on the role of race in bail determinations relies primarily on the volume of national criminal justice data compiled by the Department of Justice as part of the State Court Processing Statistics Project (SCPS). One study examined bail determinations in over 30,000 property, drug, and violent criminal cases filed in over forty-five counties across the country. Controlling for important legal and extralegal factors relevant to bail determinations, the study found that African Americans were sixty-six percent more likely to be in jail pretrial than were white defendants, and that Latino defendants were ninety-one percent more likely to be detained pretrial. Overall, the odds of similarly-situated African American and Latino defendants being held on bail because they were unable to pay the bond amounts imposed were twice that of white defendants.

Another 2005 study examined bail determinations in over 36,000 felony state court cases across the country. The study found that "being Black increases a defendant's odds of being held in jail pretrial by 25%." Similar to earlier studies, this study also concluded that poverty plays a role in pretrial outcomes.

* * * The two most recent studies—both published since 2010—found that African American defendants face higher bail amounts than white arrestees with similar criminal charges and criminal histories and, when race is combined with other legally relevant factors, African Americans

have lower odds of non-financial release and greater odds of pretrial detention.

## C. The Cause of Racial Disparities in Bail Determinations

There is relative agreement among criminologists regarding the reasons for the persistent pattern of racial disparities in bail determinations. * * * [B]ail officials are vested with tremendous discretionary authority, have very few legal constraints, and possess scant relevant background information on the defendant when making bail determinations. Criminologists believe this combination of factors forces bail officials to create their own internal guidelines, relying on racial stereotypes and biases to assist them in deciding whether a defendant is dangerous or a flight risk, and what amount of bond should be imposed. Criminologist Stephen DeMuth explains:

> Legal decision making is complex, repetitive, and often constrained by information, time and resources in ways that produce considerable ambiguity or uncertainty for arriving at a "satisfactory" decision. As an adaptation to these constraints, a "perceptual shorthand" for decision making emerges that allows for more simple and efficient processing of cases by court actors. . . . [L]egal agents may rely on the defendant's current offense and criminal history, but also on stereotypes linked to the defendant's race. . . . On the basis of these stereotypes, judges may project behavioral expectations about such things as the offender's risk of recidivism or danger to the community. Once in place and continuously reinforced, such patterned thinking and acting are resistant to change and may result in the inclusion of racial and ethnic biases in criminal case processing.

## *NOTE*

In *Race, Prediction, and Pretrial Detention*, Frank McIntyre and Shima Baradaran use empirical methods to suggest that the large racial gap in pretrial detention outcomes is not due to racial bias against Black defendants, but is the result of differing probabilities of rearrest for violent crime. *See* Frank McIntyre & Shima Baradaran, *Race, Prediction, and Pretrial Detention*, 10 J. EMPIRICAL LEGAL STUD. 741 (2013). Does the McIntyre and Baradaran study undermine the concerns raised in the Cynthia Jones article?

# CHAPTER 25

# THE RIGHT TO A SPEEDY TRIAL

■ ■ ■

The defendant's right to a speedy trial is usually covered by statute or court rule. In addition to a statutory right to a speedy trial, however, a defendant has a constitutional right to a speedy trial. The Sixth Amendment to the U.S. Constitution provides, "In all criminal prosecutions, the accused shall enjoy the right to a speedy . . . trial. . . ."

In *Barker v. Wingo*, the first case in this chapter, the Supreme Court outlines the factors that a court should consider in deciding whether a defendant's Sixth Amendment right to a speedy trial has been violated. In *Betterman v. Montana*, the Court decides whether the Sixth Amendment's speedy trial right applies to a delay between conviction and sentencing.

The Sixth Amendment right to a speedy trial typically covers delays between accusation and trial. If the defendant has been subjected to a lengthy preindictment delay, the defendant cannot allege a violation of the Sixth Amendment right to a speedy trial. Instead, the defendant can allege a violation of the Due Process Clause. The last case in this chapter, *United States v. Lovasco*, examines a defendant's claim that his due process rights were violated by an 18-month delay in the Government's filing of an indictment against him and sheds light on what a defendant needs to do in order to prevail when asserting a due process violation due to preindictment delay.

## BARKER V. WINGO
Supreme Court of the United States
407 U.S. 514, 92 S.Ct. 2182, 33 L.Ed.2d 101 (1972)

JUSTICE POWELL delivered the opinion of the Court.

Although a speedy trial is guaranteed the accused by the Sixth Amendment to the Constitution,[9] this Court has dealt with that right on infrequent occasions. The Court's opinion in *Kloper v. North Carolina*, established that the right to a speedy trial is "fundamental" and is imposed

---

[9]   The Sixth Amendment provides: "In all criminal prosecutions, the accused shall enjoy the right to a speedy and public trial, by an impartial jury of the State and district wherein the crime shall have been committed, which district shall have been previously ascertained by law, and to be informed of the nature and cause of the accusation; to be confronted with the witnesses against him; to have compulsory process for obtaining Witnesses in his favor, and to have the Assistance of Counsel for his defense."

by the Due Process Clause of the Fourteenth Amendment on the States. As Mr. Justice Brennan pointed out in his concurring opinion in *Dickey*, in none of these cases have we attempted to set out the criteria by which the speedy trial right is to be judged. This case compels us to make such an attempt.

On July 20, 1958, in Christian County, Kentucky, an elderly couple was beaten to death by intruders wielding an iron tire tool. Two suspects, Silas Manning and Willie Barker, the petitioner, were arrested shortly thereafter. The grand jury indicted them on September 15. Counsel was appointed on September 17, and Barker's trial was set for October 21. The Commonwealth had a stronger case against Manning, and it believed that Barker could not be convicted unless Manning testified against him. Manning was naturally unwilling to incriminate himself. Accordingly, on October 23, the day Silas Manning was brought to trial, the Commonwealth sought and obtained the first of what was to be a series of 16 continuances of Barker's trial. Barker made no objection. By first convicting Manning, the Commonwealth would remove possible problems of self-incrimination and would be able to assure his testimony against Barker.

The Commonwealth encountered more than a few difficulties in its prosecution of Manning. The first trial ended in a hung jury. A second trial resulted in a conviction, but the Kentucky Court of Appeals reversed because of the admission of evidence obtained by an illegal search. At his third trial, Manning was again convicted, and the Court of Appeals again reversed because the trial court had not granted a change of venue. A fourth trial resulted in a hung jury. Finally, after five trials, Manning was convicted, in March 1962, of murdering one victim, and after a sixth trial, in December 1962, he was convicted of murdering the other.

The Christian County Circuit Court holds three terms each year—in February, June, and September. Barker's initial trial was to take place in the September term of 1958. The first continuance postponed it until the February 1959 term. The second continuance was granted for one month only. Every term thereafter for as long as the Manning prosecutions were in process, the Commonwealth routinely moved to continue Barker's case to the next term. When the case was continued from the June 1959 term until the following September, Barker, having spent 10 months in jail, obtained his release by posting a $5,000 bond. He thereafter remained free in the community until his trial. Barker made no objection, through his counsel, to the first 11 continuances.

When on February 12, 1962, the Commonwealth moved for the twelfth time to continue the case until the following term, Barker's counsel filed a motion to dismiss the indictment. The motion to dismiss was denied two weeks later, and the Commonwealth's motion for a continuance was granted. The Commonwealth was granted further continuances in June 1962 and September 1962, to which Barker did not object.

In February 1963, the first term of court following Manning's final conviction, the Commonwealth moved to set Barker's trial for March 19. But on the day scheduled for trial, it again moved for a continuance until the June term. It gave as its reason the illness of the ex-sheriff who was the chief investigating officer in the case. To this continuance, Barker objected unsuccessfully.

The witness was still unable to testify in June, and the trial, which had been set for June 19, was continued again until the September term over Barker's objection. This time the court announced that the case would be dismissed for lack of prosecution if it were not tried during the next term. The final trial date was set for October 9, 1963. On that date, Barker again moved to dismiss the indictment, and this time specified that his right to a speedy trial had been violated. The motion was denied; the trial commenced with Manning as the chief prosecution witness; Barker was convicted and given a life sentence.

Barker appealed his conviction to the Kentucky Court of Appeals, relying in part on his speedy trial claim. The court affirmed. * * * We granted Barker's petition for certiorari.

The right to a speedy trial is generically different from any of the other rights enshrined in the Constitution for the protection of the accused. In addition to the general concern that all accused persons be treated according to decent and fair procedures, there is a societal interest in providing a speedy trial which exists separate from, and at times in opposition to, the interests of the accused. The inability of courts to provide a prompt trial has contributed to a large backlog of cases in urban courts which, among other things, enables defendants to negotiate more effectively for pleas of guilty to lesser offenses and otherwise manipulate the system. In addition, persons released on bond for lengthy periods awaiting trial have an opportunity to commit other crimes. It must be of little comfort to the residents of Christian County, Kentucky, to know that Barker was at large on bail for over four years while accused of a vicious and brutal murder of which he was ultimately convicted. Moreover, the longer an accused is free awaiting trial, the more tempting becomes his opportunity to jump bail and escape. Finally, delay between arrest and punishment may have a detrimental effect on rehabilitation.

If an accused cannot make bail, he is generally confined, as was Barker for 10 months, in a local jail. This contributes to the overcrowding and generally deplorable state of those institutions. Lengthy exposure to these conditions "has a destructive effect on human character and makes the rehabilitation of the individual offender much more difficult." At times the result may even be violent rioting. Finally, lengthy pretrial detention is costly. The cost of maintaining a prisoner in jail varies from $3 to $9 per day, and this amounts to millions across the Nation. In addition, society loses wages which might have been earned, and it must often support families of incarcerated breadwinners.

A second difference between the right to speedy trial and the accused's other constitutional rights is that deprivation of the right may work to the accused's advantage. Delay is not an uncommon defense tactic. As the time between the commission of the crime and trial lengthens, witnesses may become unavailable or their memories may fade. If the witnesses support the prosecution, its case will be weakened, sometimes seriously so. And it is the prosecution which carries the burden of proof. Thus, unlike the right to counsel or the right to be free from compelled self-incrimination, deprivation of the right to speedy trial does not per se prejudice the accused's ability to defend himself.

Finally, and perhaps most importantly, the right to speedy trial is a more vague concept than other procedural rights. It is, for example, impossible to determine with precision when the right has been denied. We cannot definitely say how long is too long in a system where justice is supposed to be swift but deliberate. As a consequence, there is no fixed point in the criminal process when the State can put the defendant to the choice of either exercising or waiving the right to a speedy trial. * * *

The amorphous quality of the right also leads to the unsatisfactorily severe remedy of dismissal of the indictment when the right has been deprived. This is indeed a serious consequence because it means that a defendant who may be guilty of a serious crime will go free, without having been tried. Such a remedy is more serious than an exclusionary rule or a reversal for a new trial, but it is the only possible remedy.

Perhaps because the speedy trial right is so slippery, two rigid approaches are urged upon us as ways of eliminating some of the uncertainty which courts experience in protecting the right. The first suggestion is that we hold that the Constitution requires a criminal defendant to be offered a trial within a specified time period. The result of such a ruling would have the virtue of clarifying when the right is infringed and of simplifying courts' application of it. Recognizing this, some legislatures have enacted laws, and some courts have adopted procedural rules which more narrowly define the right. The United States Court of Appeals for the Second Circuit has promulgated rules for the district courts in that Circuit establishing that the government must be ready for trial within six months of the date of arrest, except in unusual circumstances, or the charge will be dismissed. This type of rule is also recommended by the American Bar Association.

But such a result would require this Court to engage in legislative or rulemaking activity, rather than in the adjudicative process to which we should confine our efforts. We do not establish procedural rules for the States, except when mandated by the Constitution. We find no constitutional basis for holding that the speedy trial right can be quantified into a specified number of days or months. The States, of course, are free to prescribe a reasonable period consistent with constitutional standards, but our approach must be less precise.

The second suggested alternative would restrict consideration of the right to those cases in which the accused has demanded a speedy trial. Most States have recognized what is loosely referred to as the "demand rule," although eight States reject it. It is not clear, however, precisely what is meant by that term. Although every federal court of appeals that has considered the question has endorsed some kind of demand rule, some have regarded the rule within the concept of waiver, whereas others have viewed it as a factor to be weighed in assessing whether there has been a deprivation of the speedy trial right. We shall refer to the former approach as the demand-waiver doctrine. The demand-waiver doctrine provides that a defendant waives any consideration of his right to speedy trial for any period prior to which he has not demanded a trial. Under this rigid approach, a prior demand is a necessary condition to the consideration of the speedy trial right. This essentially was the approach the Sixth Circuit took below.

Such an approach, by presuming waiver of a fundamental right from inaction, is inconsistent with this Court's pronouncements on waiver of constitutional rights. The Court has defined waiver as "an intentional relinquishment or abandonment of a known right or privilege." Courts should "indulge every reasonable presumption against waiver," and they should "not presume acquiescence in the loss of fundamental rights." * * *

In excepting the right to speedy trial from the rule of waiver we have applied to other fundamental rights, courts that have applied the demand-waiver rule have relied on the assumption that delay usually works for the benefit of the accused and on the absence of any readily ascertainable time in the criminal process for a defendant to be given the choice of exercising or waiving his right. But it is not necessarily true that delay benefits the defendant. There are cases in which delay appreciably harms the defendant's ability to defend himself. Moreover, a defendant confined to jail prior to trial is obviously disadvantaged by delay as is a defendant released on bail but unable to lead a normal life because of community suspicion and his own anxiety.

The nature of the speedy trial right does make it impossible to pinpoint a precise time in the process when the right must be asserted or waived, but that fact does not argue for placing the burden of protecting the right solely on defendants. A defendant has no duty to bring himself to trial; the State has that duty as well as the duty of insuring that the trial is consistent with due process. Moreover, for the reasons earlier expressed, society has a particular interest in bringing swift prosecutions, and society's representatives are the ones who should protect that interest.

It is also noteworthy that such a rigid view of the demand-waiver rule places defense counsel in an awkward position. Unless he demands a trial early and often, he is in danger of frustrating his client's right. If counsel is willing to tolerate some delay because he finds it reasonable and helpful in preparing his own case, he may be unable to obtain a speedy trial for his client at the end of that time. * * *

We reject, therefore, the rule that a defendant who fails to demand a speedy trial forever waives his right. This does not mean, however, that the defendant has no responsibility to assert his right. We think the better rule is that the defendant's assertion of or failure to assert his right to a speedy trial is one of the factors to be considered in an inquiry into the deprivation of the right. Such a formulation avoids the rigidities of the demand-waiver rule and the resulting possible unfairness in its application. It allows the trial court to exercise a judicial discretion based on the circumstances, including due consideration of any applicable formal procedural rule. It would permit, for example, a court to attach a different weight to a situation in which the defendant knowingly fails to object from a situation in which his attorney acquiesces in long delay without adequately informing his client, or from a situation in which no counsel is appointed. It would also allow a court to weigh the frequency and force of the objections as opposed to attaching significant weight to a purely pro forma objection.

In ruling that a defendant has some responsibility to assert a speedy trial claim, we do not depart from our holdings in other cases concerning the waiver of fundamental rights, in which we have placed the entire responsibility on the prosecution to show that the claimed waiver was knowingly and voluntarily made. * * * We have shown above that the right to a speedy trial is unique in its uncertainty as to when and under what circumstances it must be asserted or may be deemed waived. But the rule we announce today, which comports with constitutional principles, places the primary burden on the courts and the prosecutors to assure that cases are brought to trial. * * *

We, therefore, reject both of the inflexible approaches—the fixed-time period because it goes further than the Constitution requires; the demand-waiver rule because it is insensitive to a right which he have deemed fundamental. The approach we accept is a balancing test, in which the conduct of both the prosecution and the defendant are weighed.

A balancing test necessarily compels courts to approach speedy trial cases on an ad hoc basis. We can do little more than identify some of the factors which courts should assess in determining whether a particular defendant has been deprived of his right. Though some might express them in different ways, we identify four such factors: Length of delay, the reason for the delay, the defendant's assertion of his right, and prejudice to the defendant.

The length of the delay is to some extent a triggering mechanism. Until there is some delay which is presumptively prejudicial, there is no necessity for inquiry into the other factors that go into the balance. Nevertheless, because of the imprecision of the right to speedy trial, the length of delay that will provoke such an inquiry is necessarily dependent upon the peculiar circumstances of the case. To take but one example, the delay that can be tolerated for an ordinary street crime is considerably less than for a serious, complex conspiracy charge.

Closely related to length of delay is the reason the government assigns to justify the delay. Here, too, different weights should be assigned to different reasons. A deliberate attempt to delay the trial in order to hamper the defense should be weighted heavily against the government. A more neutral reason such as negligence or overcrowded courts should be weighted less heavily but nevertheless should be considered since the ultimate responsibility for such circumstances must rest with the government rather than with the defendant. Finally, a valid reason, such as a missing witness, should serve to justify appropriate delay.

We have already discussed the third factor, the defendant's responsibility to assert his right. Whether and how a defendant asserts his right is closely related to the other factors we have mentioned. The strength of his efforts will be affected by the length of the delay, to some extent by the reason for the delay, and most particularly by the personal prejudice, which is not always readily identifiable, that he experiences. The more serious the deprivation, the more likely a defendant is to complain. The defendant's assertion of his speedy trial right, then, is entitled to strong evidentiary weight in determining whether the defendant is being deprived of the right. We emphasize that failure to assert the right will make it difficult for a defendant to prove that he was denied a speedy trial.

A fourth factor is prejudice to the defendant. Prejudice, of course, should be assessed in the light of the interests of defendants which the speedy trial right was designed to protect. This Court has identified three such interests: (i) to prevent oppressive pretrial incarceration; (ii) to minimize anxiety and concern of the accused; and (iii) to limit the possibility that the defense will be impaired. Of these, the most serious is the last, because the inability of a defendant adequately to prepare his case skews the fairness of the entire system. If witnesses die or disappear during a delay, the prejudice is obvious.[a] There is also prejudice if defense

---

[a]   In a later case, the Court held that a showing of actual prejudice is not essential to a defendant's speedy trial claim. In *Doggett v. United States*, 505 U.S. 647 (1992), the Court held that a judge can find a violation of the Sixth Amendment right to a speedy trial based on

witnesses are unable to recall accurately events of the distant past. Loss of memory, however, is not always reflected in the record because what has been forgotten can rarely be shown.

We have discussed previously the societal disadvantages of lengthy pretrial incarceration, but obviously the disadvantages for the accused who cannot obtain his release are even more serious. The time spent in jail awaiting trial has a detrimental impact on the individual. It often means loss of a job; it disrupts family life; and it enforces idleness. Most jails offer little or no recreational or rehabilitative programs. The time spent in jail is simply dead time. Moreover, if a defendant is locked up, he is hindered in his ability to gather evidence, contact witnesses, or otherwise prepare his defense. Imposing those consequences on anyone who has not yet been convicted is serious. It is especially unfortunate to impose them on those persons who are ultimately found to be innocent. Finally, even if an accused is not incarcerated prior to trial, he is still disadvantaged by restraints on his liberty and by living under a cloud of anxiety, suspicion, and often hostility.

We regard none of the four factors identified above as either a necessary or sufficient condition to the finding of a deprivation of the right of speedy trial. Rather, they are related factors and must be considered together with such other circumstances as may be relevant. In sum, these factors have no talismanic qualities; courts must still engage in a difficult and sensitive balancing process. But, because we are dealing with a fundamental right of the accused, this process must be carried out with full recognition that the accused's interest in a speedy trial is specifically affirmed in the Constitution.

The difficulty of the task of balancing these factors is illustrated by this case, which we consider to be close. It is clear that the length of delay between arrest and trial—well over five years—was extraordinary. Only seven months of that period can be attributed to a strong excuse, the illness of the ex-sheriff who was in charge of the investigation. Perhaps some delay would have been permissible under ordinary circumstances, so that Manning could be utilized as a witness in Barker's trial, but more than four years was too long a period, particularly since a good part of that period was attributable to the Commonwealth's failure or inability to try Manning under circumstances that comported with due process.

Two counterbalancing factors, however, outweigh these deficiencies. The first is that prejudice was minimal. Of course, Barker was prejudiced to some extent by living for over four years under a cloud of suspicion and anxiety. Moreover, although he was released on bond for most of the period, he did spend 10 months in jail before trial. But there is no claim that any

---

presumptive prejudice since excessive delay may compromise the reliability of a trial in ways that the defendant cannot prove or identify.

of Barker's witnesses died or otherwise became unavailable owing to the delay. The trial transcript indicates only two very minor lapses of memory—one on the part of a prosecution witness—which were in no way significant to the outcome.

More important than the absence of serious prejudice, is the fact that Barker did not want a speedy trial. Counsel was appointed for Barker immediately after his indictment and represented him throughout the period. No question is raised as to the competency of such counsel. Despite the fact that counsel had notice of the motions for continuances, the record shows no action whatever taken between October 21, 1958, and February 12, 1962, that could be construed as the assertion of the speedy trial right. On the latter date, in response to another motion for continuance, Barker moved to dismiss the indictment. The record does not show on what ground this motion was based, although it is clear that no alternative motion was made for an immediate trial. Instead the record strongly suggests that while he hoped to take advantage of the delay in which he had acquiesced, and thereby obtain a dismissal of the charges, he definitely did not want to be tried. Counsel conceded as much at oral argument:

> Your honor, I would concede that Willie Mae Barker probably—I don't know this for a fact—probably did not want to be tried. I don't think any man wants to be tried. And I don't consider this a liability on his behalf. I don't blame him.

The probable reason for Barker's attitude was that he was gambling on Manning's acquittal. The evidence was not very strong against Manning, as the reversals and hung juries suggest, and Barker undoubtedly thought that if Manning were acquitted, he would never be tried. Counsel also conceded this:

> Now, it's true that the reason for this delay was the Commonwealth of Kentucky's desire to secure the testimony of the accomplice, Silas Manning. And it's true that if Silas Manning were never convicted, Willie Mae Barker would never have been convicted. We concede this.

That Barker was gambling on Manning's acquittal is also suggested by his failure, following the pro forma motion to dismiss filed in February 1962, to object to the Commonwealth's next two motions for continuances. Indeed, it was not until March 1963, after Manning's convictions were final, that Barker, having lost his gamble, began to object to further continuances. At that time, the Commonwealth's excuse was the illness of the ex-sheriff, which Barker has conceded justified the further delay.

We do not hold that there may never be a situation in which an indictment may be dismissed on speedy trial grounds where the defendant has failed to object to continuances. There may be a situation in which the defendant was represented by incompetent counsel, was severely prejudiced, or even cases in which the continuances were granted ex parte. But barring extraordinary circumstances, we would be reluctant indeed to rule that a defendant was denied this constitutional right on a record that strongly indicates, as does this one, that the defendant did not want a speedy trial. We hold, therefore, that Barker was not deprived of his * * * right to a speedy trial. * * *

[JUSTICE WHITE's concurring opinion has been omitted.]

## BETTERMAN V. MONTANA
Supreme Court of the United States
578 U.S. ___, 136 S.Ct. 1609, 194 L.Ed.2d 723 (2016)

JUSTICE GINSBURG, delivered the opinion of the Court.

The Sixth Amendment to the U.S. Constitution provides that "[i]n all criminal prosecutions, the accused shall enjoy the right to a speedy and public trial, by an impartial jury. . . ." Does the Sixth Amendment's speedy trial guarantee apply to the sentencing phase of a criminal prosecution? That is the sole question this case presents. * * *

Ordered to appear in court on domestic assault charges, Brandon Betterman failed to show up and was therefore charged with bail jumping. After pleading guilty to the bail-jumping charge, he was jailed for over 14 months awaiting sentence on that conviction. The holdup, in large part, was due to institutional delay: the presentence report took nearly five months to complete; the trial court took several months to deny two presentence motions (one seeking dismissal of the charge on the ground of delay); and the court was slow in setting a sentencing hearing. Betterman was eventually sentenced to seven years' imprisonment, with four of those years suspended.

Arguing that the 14-month gap between conviction and sentencing violated his speedy trial right, Betterman appealed. The Montana Supreme Court affirmed his conviction and sentence, ruling that the Sixth Amendment's Speedy Trial Clause does not apply to postconviction, presentencing delay.

We granted certiorari, to resolve a split among courts over whether the Speedy Trial Clause applies to such delay. Holding that the Clause does not apply to delayed sentencing, we affirm the Montana Supreme Court's judgment.

Criminal proceedings generally unfold in three discrete phases. First, the State investigates to determine whether to arrest and charge a suspect. Once charged, the suspect stands accused but is presumed innocent until conviction upon trial or guilty plea. After conviction, the court imposes sentence. There are checks against delay throughout this progression, each geared to its particular phase.

In the first stage—before arrest or indictment, when the suspect remains at liberty—statutes of limitations provide the primary protection against delay, with the Due Process Clause as a safeguard against fundamentally unfair prosecutorial conduct.

The Sixth Amendment's Speedy Trial Clause homes in on the second period: from arrest or indictment through conviction. The constitutional right, our precedent holds, does not attach until this phase begins, that is, when a defendant is arrested or formally accused. Today we hold that the right detaches upon conviction, when this second stage ends.

Prior to conviction, the accused is shielded by the presumption of innocence, the "bedrock[,] axiomatic and elementary principle whose enforcement lies at the foundation of the administration of our criminal law." The Speedy Trial Clause implements that presumption by "prevent[ing] undue and oppressive incarceration prior to trial, . . . minimiz[ing] anxiety and concern accompanying public accusation[,] and . . . limit[ing] the possibilities that long delay will impair the ability of an accused to defend himself." As a measure protecting the presumptively innocent, the speedy trial right—like other similarly aimed measures—loses force upon conviction. * * *

Reflecting the concern that a presumptively innocent person should not languish under an unresolved charge, the Speedy Trial Clause guarantees "the *accused*" "the right to a speedy . . . *trial*." At the founding, "accused" described a status preceding "convicted." And "trial" meant a discrete episode after which judgment (*i.e.,* sentencing) would follow.

This understanding of the Sixth Amendment language—"accused" as distinct from "convicted," and "trial" as separate from "sentencing"—endures today.

* * * [I]n *Marion*, addressing "the major evils protected against by the speedy trial guarantee," we observed: "Arrest is a public act that may seriously interfere with the defendant's liberty, whether he is free on bail or not, and that may disrupt his employment, drain his financial resources, curtail his associations, subject him to public obloquy, and create anxiety in him, his family and his friends." We acknowledged in *Marion* that even prearrest—a stage at which the right to a speedy trial does not arise—the passage of time "may impair memories, cause evidence to be lost, deprive the defendant of witnesses, and otherwise interfere with his ability to defend himself." Nevertheless, we determined, "this possibility of prejudice at trial is not itself sufficient reason to wrench the Sixth Amendment from its proper [arrest or charge triggered] context." Adverse consequences of postconviction delay, though subject to other checks, are similarly outside the purview of the Speedy Trial Clause.

The sole remedy for a violation of the speedy trial right—dismissal of the charges—fits the preconviction focus of the Clause. It would be an unjustified windfall, in most cases, to remedy sentencing delay by vacating validly obtained convictions. Betterman concedes that a dismissal remedy ordinarily would not be in order once a defendant has been convicted. * * *[6]

As we have explained, at the third phase of the criminal-justice process, *i.e.*, between conviction and sentencing, the Constitution's presumption-of-innocence protective speedy trial right is not engaged. That does not mean, however, that defendants lack any protection against undue delay at this stage. The primary safeguard comes from statutes and rules. The federal rule on point directs the court to "impose sentence without unnecessary delay." Many States have provisions to the same effect, and some States prescribe numerical time limits. Further, as at the prearrest stage, due process serves as a backstop against exorbitant delay. After conviction, a defendant's due process right to liberty, while diminished, is still present. He retains an interest in a sentencing proceeding that is fundamentally fair. But because Betterman advanced no due process claim here, we express no opinion on how he might fare under that more pliable standard.

The course of a criminal prosecution is composed of discrete segments. During the segment between accusation and conviction, the Sixth Amendment's Speedy Trial Clause protects the presumptively innocent from long enduring unresolved criminal charges. The Sixth Amendment speedy trial right, however, does not extend beyond conviction, which terminates the presumption of innocence. The judgment of the Supreme Court of Montana is therefore

*Affirmed.*

[JUSTICE THOMAS' and JUSTICE SOTOMAYOR'S concurring opinions have been omitted.][a]

## UNITED STATES V. LOVASCO

Supreme Court of the United States
431 U.S. 783, 97 S.Ct. 2044, 52 L.Ed.2d 752 (1977)

JUSTICE MARSHALL delivered the opinion of the Court.

We granted certiorari in this case to consider the circumstances in which the Constitution requires that an indictment be dismissed because of delay between the commission of an offense and the initiation of prosecution.

---

[6] Betterman suggests that an appropriate remedy for the delay in his case would be reduction of his sentence by 14 months—the time between his conviction and sentencing. See Tr. of Oral Arg. 6. We have not read the Speedy Trial Clause, however, to call for a flexible or tailored remedy. Instead, we have held that violation of the right demands termination of the prosecution.

[a] In her concurring opinion, Justice Sotomayor suggests that courts assessing whether a person's due process rights have been violated by a post-conviction presentencing delay should balance the four factors enunciated in *Barker v. Wingo*.

On March 6, 1975, respondent was indicted for possessing eight firearms stolen from the United States mails, and for dealing in firearms without a license. The offenses were alleged to have occurred between July 25 and August 31, 1973, more than 18 months before the indictment was filed. Respondent moved to dismiss the indictment due to the delay.

The District Court conducted a hearing on respondent's motion at which the respondent sought to prove that the delay was unnecessary and that it had prejudiced his defense. In an effort to establish the former proposition, respondent presented a Postal Inspector's report on his investigation that was prepared one month after the crimes were committed, and a stipulation concerning the post-report progress of the probe. The report stated, in brief, that within the first month of the investigation respondent had admitted to Government agents that he had possessed and then sold five of the stolen guns, and that the agents had developed strong evidence linking respondent to the remaining three weapons. The report also stated, however, that the agents had been unable to confirm or refute respondent's claim that he had found the guns in his car when he returned to it after visiting his son, a mail handler, at work. The stipulation into which the Assistant United States Attorney entered indicated that little additional information concerning the crimes was uncovered in the 17 months following the preparation of the Inspector's report.

To establish prejudice to the defense, respondent testified that he had lost the testimony of two material witnesses due to the delay. The first witness, Tom Stewart, died more than a year after the alleged crimes occurred. At the hearing respondent claimed that Stewart had been his source for two or three of the guns. The second witness, respondent's brother, died in April 1974, eight months after the crimes were completed. Respondent testified that his brother was present when respondent called Stewart to secure the guns, and witnessed all of respondent's sales. Respondent did not state how the witnesses would have aided the defense had they been willing to testify.

The Government made no systematic effort in the District Court to explain its long delay. The Assistant United States Attorney did expressly disagree, however, with defense counsel's suggestion that the investigation had ended after the Postal Inspector's report was prepared. The prosecutor also stated that it was the Government's theory that respondent's son, who had access to the mail at the railroad terminal from which the guns were "possibly stolen," was responsible for the thefts. * * *

Following the hearing, the District Court filed a brief opinion and order. The court found that by October 2, 1973, the date of the Postal Inspector's report, "the Government had all the information relating to defendant's alleged commission of the offenses charged against him," and that the 17-month delay before the case was presented to the grand jury "had not been explained or justified" and was "unnecessary and unreasonable." The court also found that "[a]s a result of the delay defendant has been prejudiced by reason of the death of Tom Stewart, a material witness on his behalf." Accordingly, the court dismissed the indictment.

The Government appealed to the United States Court of Appeals for the Eighth Circuit. In its brief the Government explained the months of inaction by stating:

> [T]here was a legitimate Government interest in keeping the investigation open in the instant case. The defendant's son worked for the Terminal Railroad and had access to mail. It was the Government's position that the son was responsible for the theft and therefore further investigation to establish this fact was important. * * *

The Court of Appeals accepted the Government's representation as to the motivation for the delay, but a majority of the court nevertheless affirmed the District Court's finding that the Government's actions were "unjustified, unnecessary, and unreasonable." The majority also found that respondent had established that his defense had been impaired by the loss of Stewart's testimony because it understood respondent to contend that "were Stewart's testimony available it would support (respondent's) claim that he did not know that the guns were stolen from the United States mails." The court therefore affirmed the District Court's dismissal of the three possession counts by a divided vote.

We granted certiorari and now reverse.

In *United States v. Marion*, this Court considered the significance, for constitutional purposes, of a lengthy preindictment delay. We held that as far as the Speedy Trial Clause of the Sixth Amendment is concerned, such delay is wholly irrelevant, since our analysis of the language, history, and purposes of the Clause persuaded us that only "a formal indictment or information or else the actual restraints imposed by arrest and holding to answer a criminal charge . . . engage the particular protections" of that provision. We went on to note that statutes of limitations, which provide predictable, legislatively enacted limits on prosecutorial delay, provide "the primary guarantee, against bringing overly stale criminal charges." But we did acknowledge that the "statute of limitations does not fully define (defendants') rights with respect to the events occurring prior to indictment," and that the Due Process Clause has a limited role to play in protecting against oppressive delay.

Respondent seems to argue that due process bars prosecution whenever a defendant suffers prejudice as a result of preindictment delay. To support that proposition respondent relies on the concluding sentence of the Court's opinion in *Marion* where, in remanding the case, we stated that "[e]vents of the trial may demonstrate actual prejudice, but at the present time appellees' due process claims are speculative and premature." But the quoted sentence establishes only that proof of actual prejudice makes a due process claim concrete and ripe for adjudication, not that it makes the claim automatically valid. Indeed, two pages earlier in the opinion we expressly rejected the argument respondent advances here:

> [W]e need not . . . determine when and in what circumstances actual prejudice resulting from preaccusation delays requires the dismissal of the prosecution. Actual prejudice to the defense of a criminal case may result from the shortest and most necessary delay; and no one suggests that every delay-caused detriment to a defendant's case should abort a criminal prosecution.

Thus *Marion* makes clear that proof of prejudice is generally a necessary but not sufficient element of a due process claim, and that the due process inquiry must consider the reasons for the delay as well as the prejudice to the accused.

The Court of Appeals found that the sole reason for the delay here was "a hope on the part of the Government that others might be discovered who may have participated in the theft. . . ." It concluded that this hope did not justify the delay, and therefore affirmed the dismissal of the indictment. But the Due Process Clause does not permit courts to abort criminal prosecutions simply because they disagree with a prosecutor's judgment as to when to seek an indictment. Judges are not free, in defining "due process," to impose on law enforcement officials our "personal and private notions" of fairness and to "disregard the limits that bind judges in their judicial function." Our task is more circumscribed. We are to determine only whether the action complained of here, compelling respondent to stand trial after the Government delayed indictment to investigate further, violates those "fundamental conceptions of justice which lie at the base of our civil and political institutions," and which define "the community's sense of fair play and decency,"

It requires no extended argument to establish that prosecutors do not deviate from "fundamental conceptions of justice" when they defer seeking indictments until they have probable cause to believe an accused is guilty; indeed it is unprofessional conduct for a prosecutor to recommend an indictment on less than probable cause. It should be equally obvious that prosecutors are under no duty to file charges as soon as probable cause exists but before they are satisfied they will be able to establish the suspect's guilt beyond a reasonable doubt. To impose such a duty "would have a deleterious effect both upon the rights of the accused and upon the ability of society to protect itself." From the perspective of potential defendants, requiring prosecutions to commence when probable cause is established is undesirable because it would increase the likelihood of unwarranted charges being filed, and would add to the time during which defendants stand accused but untried. These costs are by no means insubstantial since * * * a formal accusation may "interfere with the defendant's liberty, . . . disrupt his employment, drain his financial resources, curtail his associations, subject him to public obloquy, and create anxiety in him, his family and his friends." From the perspective of law enforcement officials, a requirement of immediate prosecution upon probable cause is equally unacceptable because it could make obtaining proof of guilt beyond a reasonable doubt impossible by causing potentially fruitful sources of information to evaporate before they are fully exploited. And from the standpoint of the courts, such a requirement is unwise because it would cause scarce resources to be consumed on cases that prove to be insubstantial, or that involve only some of the responsible parties or some of the criminal acts. Thus, no one's interests would be well served by compelling prosecutors to initiate prosecutions as soon as they are legally entitled to do so. * * *

We would be most reluctant to adopt a rule which would [require prosecutors to file charges as soon as they have probable cause or guilt beyond a reasonable doubt] absent a clear constitutional command to do so. We can find no such command in the Due Process Clause of the Fifth Amendment. In our view, investigative delay is fundamentally unlike delay undertaken by the Government solely "to gain tactical advantage over the accused," precisely because investigative delay is not so one-sided. Rather than deviating from elementary standards of "fair play and decency," a prosecutor abides by them if he refuses to seek indictments until he is completely satisfied that he should prosecute and will be able promptly to establish guilt beyond a reasonable doubt. Penalizing prosecutors who defer action for these reasons would subordinate the goal of "orderly expedition" to that of "mere speed." This the Due Process Clause does not require. We therefore hold that to prosecute a defendant following investigative delay does not deprive him of due process, even if his defense might have been somewhat prejudiced by the lapse of time. * * *

[JUSTICE STEVENS' dissenting opinion has been omitted.]

### NOTE

The Due Process Clause of the Fifth Amendment provides, "No person shall . . . be deprived of life, liberty, or property, without due process of law." *Lovasco* informs us that a defendant who claims a violation of due process stemming from preindictment delay must show: (1) actual prejudice, and (2) an unacceptable reason for the delay. Do you agree with the Supreme Court's assessment that the government's reason for the delay in filing an indictment against Lovasco was acceptable?

# CHAPTER 26

# DISCOVERY

■ ■ ■

Discovery is the process through which the parties in a case discover, usually before trial, what evidence the other party possesses. At common law, subject to a few limited exceptions, discovery was prohibited in criminal cases. Jerry E. Norton, *Discovery in the Criminal Process*, 81 J. CRIM. L. & CRIMINOLOGY 11, 12–13 (1970). Gradually, the common law prohibition on criminal discovery was replaced by rules permitting discovery.

Today, criminal discovery in federal court is governed by Rule 16 of the Federal Rules of Criminal Procedure. Rule 16 requires the government to permit the defendant to inspect and copy certain documents and tangible objects in the government's possession, custody, and control.[a] Each state has its own rules governing discovery in criminal cases in state court.[b]

Separate and apart from Rule 16 and state discovery rules, the U.S. Supreme Court has held that prosecutors have a constitutional obligation to provide the defendant with "evidence favorable to the accused" that is material to guilt or punishment. *Brady v. Maryland* leads off the chapter and is the seminal case articulating the rules governing prosecutorial disclosure of exculpatory evidence to the defense under the Due Process Clause. *United States v. Bagley* elaborates on the meaning of "materiality" for purposes of the *Brady* rule.

In addition to the constitutional duty to disclose exculpatory evidence under *Brady*, prosecutors also have an ethical obligation to disclose evidence favorable to the defendant under Model Rule 3.8(d) of the Model Rules of Professional Conduct, which is reprinted in this chapter. As you read Model Rule 3.8(d), think about how it differs from the *Brady* rule. In

---

[a]    Under Rule 16(a)(1)(E), the documents sought by the defendant must be (1) material to the preparation of the defense, (2) intended for use by the government in its case-in-chief, or (3) obtained from or belong to the defendant. *See* FED. R. CRIM. P. 16(a)(1)(E). If the defendant requests discovery under Rule 16, the government may, upon compliance with the defendant's discovery request, request documents and tangible objects that are in the possession, custody, or control of the defendant that the defendant intends to use at trial, excluding work product and any statements of the defendant or the defendant's witnesses. *See* FED. R. CRIM. P. 16(b).

[b]    Many states have expanded what the government is required to give the defense beyond what is specified in Rule 16. For example, some states require the government to disclose to the defense the names of the prosecution's prospective witnesses and any statements these witnesses have given to police. At least one state has an "open file" rule, requiring the government to give the defense access to "all the material and information within the prosecution's possession or control." WAYNE R. LAFAVE ET AL., CRIMINAL PROCEDURE 957 (5th ed. 2009).

the excerpt that follows, *Prosecutorial Discretion at the Core: The Good Prosecutor Meets Brady*, Janet Hoeffel explains why the prudent prosecutor will not disclose evidence favorable to the accused despite the duties to disclose outlined in *Brady v. Maryland* and Model Rule 3.8(d).

Finally, while for many years discovery in state court was a one-way street, permitting the defendant to obtain from the government evidence that the government planned to use against him at trial, but not permitting the government to obtain information about the defendant's case from the defense, today almost every state requires some sort of reciprocal discovery. The widespread acceptance of reciprocal discovery was likely encouraged by the Supreme Court's decision in *Williams v. Florida*, the last case in the chapter.

## BRADY V. MARYLAND

Supreme Court of the United States

373 U.S. 83, 83 S.Ct. 1194, 10 L.Ed.2d 215 (1963)

Opinion of the Court by JUSTICE DOUGLAS, announced by JUSTICE BRENNAN.

Petitioner and a companion, Boblit, were found guilty of murder in the first degree and were sentenced to death, their convictions being affirmed by the Court of Appeals of Maryland. Their trials were separate, petitioner being tried first. At his trial Brady took the stand and admitted his participation in the crime, but he claimed that Boblit did the actual killing. * * * Prior to the trial petitioner's counsel had requested the prosecution to allow him to examine Boblit's extrajudicial statements. Several of those statements were shown to him; but one dated July 9, 1958, in which Boblit admitted the actual homicide, was withheld by the prosecution and did not come to petitioner's notice until after he had been tried, convicted, and sentenced, and after his conviction had been affirmed.

Petitioner moved the trial court for a new trial based on the newly discovered evidence that had been suppressed by the prosecution. * * * [O]n appeal the Court of Appeals held that suppression of the evidence by the prosecution denied petitioner due process of law and remanded the case for a retrial of the question of punishment, not the question of guilt. The case is here on certiorari. * * *

We agree with the Court of Appeals that suppression of this confession was a violation of the Due Process Clause of the Fourteenth Amendment. * * * This ruling is an extension of *Mooney v. Holohan*, where the Court ruled on what nondisclosure by a prosecutor violates due process:

It is a requirement that cannot be deemed to be satisfied by mere notice and hearing if a state has contrived a conviction through the pretense of a trial which in truth is but used as a means of depriving a defendant of liberty through a deliberate deception of court and jury by the presentation of testimony known to be perjured. Such a contrivance by a state to procure the conviction and imprisonment of a defendant is as inconsistent with the rudimentary demands of justice as is the obtaining of a like result by intimidation. * * *

We now hold that the suppression by the prosecution of evidence favorable to an accused upon request violates due process where the evidence is material either to guilt or to punishment, irrespective of the good faith or bad faith of the prosecution.

The principle of *Mooney* is not punishment of society for misdeeds of a prosecutor but avoidance of an unfair trial to the accused. Society wins not only when the guilty are convicted but when criminal trials are fair; our system of the administration of justice suffers when any accused is treated unfairly. A prosecution that withholds evidence on demand of an accused which, if made available, would tend to exculpate him or reduce the penalty helps shape a trial that bears heavily on the defendant. That casts the prosecutor in the role of an architect of a proceeding that does not comport with standards of justice, even though, as in the present case, his action is not "the result of guile," to use the words of the Court of Appeals. * * *

Affirmed.

[The separate opinion of JUSTICE WHITE and JUSTICE HARLAN's dissenting opinion have been omitted.]

### NOTE

On remand, Brady's sentence was commuted to life and he was later released on parole. Stephanos Bibas, *Brady v. Maryland: From Adversarial Gamesmanship Toward the Search for Innocence?* in CRIMINAL PROCEDURE STORIES 137 (Steiker ed. 2006).

### UNITED STATES V. BAGLEY
Supreme Court of the United States
473 U.S. 667, 105 S.Ct. 3375, 87 L.E.2d 481 (1985)

JUSTICE BLACKMUN announced the judgment of the Court * * *.

In *Brady v. Maryland*, this Court held that "the suppression by the prosecution of evidence favorable to an accused upon request violates due process where the evidence is material either to guilt or punishment." The issue in the present case concerns the standard of materiality to be applied in determining whether a conviction should be reversed because the prosecutor failed to disclose requested evidence that could have been used to impeach Government witnesses.

In October 1977, respondent Hughes Anderson Bagley was indicted in the Western District of Washington on 15 charges of violating federal narcotics and firearms statutes. On November 18, 24 days before trial, respondent filed a discovery motion. The sixth paragraph of that motion requested:

> The names and addresses of witnesses that the government intends to call at trial. Also the prior criminal records of witnesses, and any deals, promises or inducements made to witnesses in exchange for their testimony.

The Government's two principal witnesses at the trial were James F. O'Connor and Donald E. Mitchell. O'Connor and Mitchell were state law-enforcement officers employed by the Milwaukee Railroad as private security guards. Between April and June 1977, they assisted the federal Bureau of Alcohol, Tobacco and Firearms (ATF) in conducting an undercover investigation of respondent.

The Government's response to the discovery motion did not disclose that any "deals, promises or inducements" had been made to O'Connor or Mitchell. In apparent reply to a request in the motion's ninth paragraph for "[c]opies of all Jencks Act material,"[a] the Government produced a series of affidavits that O'Connor and Mitchell had signed between April 12 and May 4, 1977, while the undercover investigation was in progress. These affidavits recounted in detail the undercover dealings that O'Connor and Mitchell were having at the time with respondent. Each affidavit concluded with the statement, "I made this statement freely and voluntarily without any threats or rewards, or promises of reward having been made to me in return for it."

\* \* \* At the trial, O'Connor and Mitchell testified about both the firearms and the narcotics charges. On December 23, the court found respondent guilty on the narcotics charges, but not guilty on the firearms charges.

In mid-1980, respondent filed requests for information pursuant to the Freedom of Information Act and to the Privacy Act of 1974. He received in response copies of ATF form contracts that O'Connor and Mitchell had signed on May 3, 1977. Each form was entitled "Contract for Purchase of Information and Payment of Lump Sum Therefor." The printed portion of the form stated that the vendor "will provide" information to ATF and that "upon receipt of such information by the Regional Director, Bureau of Alcohol, Tobacco and Firearms, or his representative, and upon the accomplishment of the objective sought to be obtained by the use of such

---

[a] Under the Jencks Act, after a witness for the government testifies at trial and upon defense request, the court must order the government to produce any statements of the witness in the government's possession that relate to the witness's testimony. *See* Note at the end of this chapter, *infra*.

information to the satisfaction of said Regional Director, the United States will pay to said vendor a sum commensurate with services and information rendered." Each form contained the following typewritten description of services:

> That he will provide information regarding T-I and other violations committed by Hughes A. Bagley, Jr.; that he will purchase evidence for ATF; that he will cut [sic] in an undercover capacity for ATF; that he will assist ATF in gathering of evidence and testify against the violator in federal court.

The figure "$300.00" was handwritten in each form on a line entitled "Sum to Be Paid to Vendor."

Because these contracts had not been disclosed to respondent in response to his pretrial discovery motion, respondent moved under 28 U.S.C. § 2255 to vacate his sentence. He alleged that the Government's failure to disclose the contracts, which he could have used to impeach O'Connor and Mitchell, violated his right to due process under *Brady v. Maryland*.

* * * [T]he [District] [C]ourt found that it was "probable" that O'Connor and Mitchell expected to receive compensation, in addition to their expenses, for their assistance * * *. The District Court found beyond a reasonable doubt, however, that had the existence of the agreements been disclosed to it during trial, the disclosure would have had no effect upon its finding that the Government had proved beyond a reasonable doubt that respondent was guilty of the offenses for which he had been convicted. The District Court reasoned: Almost all of the testimony of both witnesses was devoted to the firearms charges in the indictment. Respondent, however, was acquitted on those charges. The testimony of O'Connor and Mitchell concerning the narcotics charges was relatively very brief [and] tended to be favorable to respondent. Thus, the claimed impeachment evidence would not have been helpful to respondent and would not have affected the outcome of the trial. Accordingly, the District Court denied respondent's motion to vacate his sentence.

The United States Court of Appeals for the Ninth Circuit reversed. The Court of Appeals [distinguished between exculpatory evidence and impeachment evidence, treated the nondisclosure of impeachment evidence as more egregious than the nondisclosure of exculpatory evidence, and held that the Government's failure to disclose impeachment evidence required automatic reversal of the conviction.]

We granted certiorari, and we now reverse.

The holding in *Brady* requires disclosure only of evidence that is both favorable to the accused and "material either to guilt or to punishment." The Court explained in *United States v. Agurs*: "A fair analysis of the holding in *Brady* indicates that implicit in the requirement of materiality is a concern that the suppressed evidence might have affected the outcome of the trial." * * *

The *Brady* rule is based on the requirement of due process. * * * Thus, the prosecutor is not required to deliver his entire file to defense counsel, but only to disclose evidence favorable to the accused that, if suppressed, would deprive the defendant of a fair trial:

> * * * [T]he prosecutor will not have violated his constitutional duty of disclosure unless his omission is of sufficient significance to result in the denial of the defendant's right to a fair trial.

In *Brady* and *Agurs*, the prosecutor failed to disclose exculpatory evidence. In the present case, the prosecutor failed to disclose evidence that the defense might have used to impeach the Government's witnesses by showing bias or interest. Impeachment evidence * * * as well as exculpatory evidence, falls within the *Brady* rule. Such evidence is "evidence favorable to an accused," so that, if disclosed and used effectively, it may make the difference between conviction and acquittal. * * *

The Court of Appeals treated impeachment evidence as constitutionally different from exculpatory evidence. According to that court, failure to disclose impeachment evidence is "even more egregious" than failure to disclose exculpatory evidence "because it threatens the defendant's right to confront adverse witnesses." * * *

This Court has rejected any such distinction between impeachment evidence and exculpatory evidence. In *Giglio*, the Government failed to disclose impeachment evidence similar to the evidence at issue in the present case, that is, a promise made to the key Government witness that he would not be prosecuted if he testified for the Government. This Court said:

> When the "reliability of a given witness may well be determinative of guilt or innocence," nondisclosure of evidence affecting credibility falls within th[e] general rule [of *Brady*]. We do not, however, automatically require a new trial whenever "a combing of the prosecutors' files after the trial has disclosed evidence possibly useful to the defense but not likely to have changed the verdict. . . ." A finding of materiality of the evidence is required under *Brady*. . . . A new trial is required if "the false testimony could . . . in any reasonable likelihood have affected the judgment of the jury. . . ."

Thus, the Court of Appeals' holding is inconsistent with our precedents. * * *

It remains to determine the standard of materiality applicable to the nondisclosed evidence at issue in this case. Our starting point is the framework for evaluating the materiality of *Brady* evidence established in *United States v. Agurs*. The Court in *Agurs* distinguished three situations involving the discovery, after trial, of information favorable to the accused that had been known to the prosecution but unknown to the defense. The first situation was the prosecutor's knowing use of perjured testimony or, equivalently, the prosecutor's knowing failure to disclose that testimony used to convict the defendant was false. * * *

At the other extreme is the situation in *Agurs* itself, where the defendant does not make a *Brady* request and the prosecutor fails to disclose certain evidence favorable to the accused. * * *

The third situation identified by the Court in *Agurs* is where the defense makes a specific request and the prosecutor fails to disclose responsive evidence. * * * The Court did not define the standard of materiality applicable in this situation, but suggested that the standard might be more lenient to the defense than in the situation in which the defense makes no request or only a general request. The Court also noted: "When the prosecutor receives a specific and relevant request, the failure to make any response is seldom, if ever, excusable."

The Court has relied on and reformulated the *Agurs* standard for the materiality of undisclosed evidence in two subsequent cases arising outside the Brady context. In neither case did the Court's discussion * * * distinguish among the three situations described in *Agurs*. In *United States v. Valenzuela-Bernal*, the Court held that due process is violated when testimony is made unavailable to the defense by Government deportation of witnesses "only if there is a reasonable likelihood that the testimony could have affected the judgment of the trier of fact." And in *Strickland v. Washington*, the Court held that a new trial must be granted when evidence is not introduced because of the incompetence of counsel only if "there is a reasonable probability that, but for counsel's unprofessional errors, the result of the proceeding would have been different." The *Strickland* Court defined a "reasonable probability" as "a probability sufficient to undermine confidence in the outcome."

We find the *Strickland* formulation of the *Augurs* test for materiality sufficiently flexible to cover the "no request," "general request," and "specific request" cases of prosecutorial failure to disclose evidence favorable to the excused: The evidence is material only if there is a reasonable probability that, had the evidence been disclosed to the defense, the result of the proceeding would have been different. A "reasonable probability" is a probability sufficient to undermine confidence in the outcome. * * *

We agree that the prosecutor's failure to respond fully to a *Brady* request may impair the adversary process * * *. And the more specifically the defense requests certain evidence, thus putting the prosecutor on notice of its value, the more reasonable it is for the defense to assume from the nondisclosure that the evidence does not exist, and to make pretrial and trial decisions on the basis of this assumption. This possibility of impairment does not necessitate a different standard of materiality. * * * [T]he reviewing court may consider directly any adverse effect that the prosecutor's failure to respond might have had on the preparation or presentation of the defendant's case. The reviewing court should assess the possibility that such effect might have occurred in light of the totality of the circumstances and with an awareness of the difficulty of reconstructing in a post-trial proceeding the course that the defense and the trial would have taken had the defense not been misled by the prosecutor's incomplete response.

In the present case, we think that there is a significant likelihood that the prosecutor's response to respondent's discovery motion misleadingly induced defense counsel to believe that O'Connor and Mitchell could not be impeached on the basis of bias or interest arising from inducements offered by the Government. * * * Moreover, the prosecutor disclosed affidavits that stated that O'Connor and Mitchell received no promises of reward in return for providing information in the affidavits implicating respondent in criminal activity.

* * * Accordingly, we reverse the judgment of the Court of Appeals and remand the case to that court for a determination whether there is a reasonable probability that, had the inducement offered by the Government to O'Connor and Mitchell been disclosed to the defense, the result of the trial would have been different.

*It is so ordered.*

JUSTICE MARSHALL, with whom JUSTICE BRENNAN joins, dissenting.

When the Government withholds from a defendant evidence that might impeach the prosecution's only witnesses, that failure to disclose cannot be deemed harmless error. Because that is precisely the nature of the undisclosed evidence in this case, I would affirm the judgment of the Court of Appeals and would not remand for further proceedings.

* * * [W]itnesses O'Connor and Mitchell were crucial to the Government's case. * * * [T]heir personal credibility was potentially dispositive * * *. It simply cannot be denied that the existence of a contract signed by those witnesses, promising a reward whose size would depend "on the Government's satisfaction with the end result," might sway the trier of fact, or cast doubt on the truth of all that the witnesses allege. In such a case, the trier of fact is absolutely entitled to know of the contract, and the defense counsel is absolutely entitled to develop his case with an awareness of it. Whatever the applicable standard of materiality, in this instance it undoubtedly is well met. * * *

I begin from the fundamental premise, which hardly bears repeating, that "[t]he purpose of a trial is as much the acquittal of an innocent person as it is the conviction of a guilty one." When evidence favorable to the defendant is known to exist, disclosure only enhances the quest for truth; it takes no direct toll on that inquiry. Moreover, the existence of any small piece of evidence favorable to the defense may, in a particular case, create just the doubt that prevents the jury from returning a verdict of guilty. The private whys and wherefores of jury deliberations pose an impenetrable barrier to our ability to know just which piece of information might make, or might have made, a difference.

When the state does not disclose information in its possession that might reasonably be considered favorable to the defense, it precludes the trier of fact from gaining access to such information and thereby undermines the reliability of the verdict. Unlike a situation in which exculpatory evidence exists but neither the defense nor the prosecutor has uncovered it, in this situation the state already has, resting in its files, material that would be of assistance to the defendant. With a minimum of effort, the state could improve the real and apparent fairness of the trial enormously, by assuring that the defendant may place before the trier of fact favorable evidence known to the government.

* * * [F]requently considerable imbalance exists in resources between most criminal defendants and most prosecutors' offices. * * * [U]nlike the government, defense counsel is not in the position to make deals with witnesses to gain evidence. Thus, an inexperienced, unskilled, or unaggressive attorney often is unable to amass the factual support necessary to a reasonable defense. When favorable evidence is in the hands of the prosecutor but not disclosed, the result may well be that the defendant is deprived of a fair chance before the trier of fact, and the trier of fact is deprived of the ingredients necessary to a fair decision. * * *

My view is based in significant part on the reality of criminal practice and on the consequently inadequate protection to the defendant that a different rule would offer. * * * Our system of criminal justice is animated by two seemingly incompatible notions: the adversary model, and the state's primary concern with justice, not convictions. *Brady*, of course, reflects the latter goal of justice, and is in some ways at odds with the competing model of a sporting event. Our goal, then, must be to integrate the *Brady* right into the harsh, daily reality of this apparently discordant criminal process. * * *

[F]for purposes of *Brady*, the prosecutor must abandon his role as an advocate and pore through his files, as objectively as possible, to identify the material that could undermine his case. Given this obviously unharmonious role, it is not surprising that these advocates oftentimes overlook or downplay potentially favorable evidence. * * * One telling example, offered by Judge Newman when he was a United States Attorney, suffices:

> I recently had occasion to discuss [*Brady*] at a PLI Conference in New York City before a large group of State prosecutors. . . . I put to them this case: You are prosecuting a bank robbery. You have talked to two or three of the tellers and one or two of the customers at the time of the robbery. They have all taken a look at your defendant in a line-up, and they have said, 'This is the man.' In the course of your investigation you also have found another customer who was in the bank that day, who viewed the suspect, and came back and said, 'This is *not* the man.'

> The question I put to these prosecutors was, do you believe you should disclose to the defense the name of the witness who, when he viewed the suspect, said 'that is not the man'? In a room of prosecutors not quite as large as this group but almost as large, only two hands went up. There were only two prosecutors in that group who felt they should disclose or would disclose that information. Yet I was putting to them what I thought was the easiest case—the clearest case for disclosure of exculpatory information!"

While familiarity with *Brady* no doubt has increased since 1967, the dual role that the prosecutor must play, and the very real pressures that role creates, have not changed. * * *

Once the prosecutor suspects that certain information might have favorable implications for the defense, either because it is potentially exculpatory or relevant to credibility, I see no reason why he should not be required to disclose it. After all, favorable evidence indisputably enhances the truthseeking process at trial. And it is the job of the defense, not the prosecution, to decide whether and in what way to use arguably favorable evidence. In addition, to require disclosure of all evidence that might reasonably be considered favorable to the defendant would have the precautionary effect of assuring that no information of potential consequence is mistakenly overlooked. By requiring full disclosure of favorable evidence in this way, courts could begin to assure that a possibly dispositive piece of information is not withheld from the trier of fact by a prosecutor who is torn between the two roles he must play. A clear rule of this kind, coupled with a presumption in favor of disclosure, also would facilitate the prosecutor's admittedly difficult task by removing a substantial amount of unguided discretion.

The standard for disclosure that the Court articulates today enables prosecutors to avoid disclosing obviously exculpatory evidence while acting well within the bounds of their constitutional obligation. * * *

The Court's definition poses other, serious problems. Besides legitimizing the nondisclosure of clearly favorable evidence, the standard set out by the Court also asks the prosecutor to predict what effect various pieces of evidence will have on the trial. He must evaluate his case and the case of the defendant—of which he presumably knows very little—and perform the impossible task of deciding whether a certain piece of information will have a significant impact on the trial, bearing in mind that a defendant will later shoulder the heavy burden of proving how it would have affected the outcome. At best, this standard places on the prosecutor a responsibility to speculate, at times without foundation, since the prosecutor will not normally know what strategy the defense will pursue or what evidence the defense will find useful. At worst, the standard invites a prosecutor, whose interests are conflicting, to gamble, to play the odds, and to take a chance that evidence will later turn out not to have been potentially dispositive. * * *

JUSTICE POWELL took no part in the decision of this case.

[JUSTICE WHITE's concurring opinion and JUSTICE STEVENS' dissenting opinion have been omitted.]

## NOTE

In a later case, the Court elaborated on the proof required for the showing of materiality, noting that "a showing of materiality does not require demonstration by a preponderance that disclosure of the suppressed evidence would have resulted ultimately in the defendant's acquittal." *Kyles v. Whitley*, 514 U.S. 419, 434 (1995). The Court explained:

> *Bagley*'s touchstone of materiality is a "reasonable probability" of a different result, and the adjective is important. The question is not whether the defendant would more likely than not have received a different verdict with the evidence, but whether in its absence he received a fair trial, understood as a trial resulting in a verdict worthy of confidence. A "reasonable probability" of a different result is accordingly shown when the government's evidentiary suppression "undermines confidence in the outcome of the trial."

*Id.* The Court also noted that "the individual prosecutor has a duty to learn of any favorable evidence known to the others acting on the government's behalf in the case, including the police." *Id.* at 437.

# RULE 3.8: SPECIAL RESPONSIBILITIES OF A PROSECUTOR

MODEL RULES OF PROFESSIONAL CONDUCT AMERICAN BAR ASSOCIATION
CENTER FOR PROFESSIONAL RESPONSIBILITY (2015)

The prosecutor in a criminal case shall: * * *

(d) make timely disclosure to the defense of all evidence or information known to the prosecutor that tends to negate the guilt of the accused or mitigates the offense, and, in connection with sentencing, disclose to the defense and to the tribunal all unprivileged mitigating information known to the prosecutor, except when the prosecutor is relieved of this responsibility by a protective order of the tribunal.

* * *

(g) When a prosecutor knows of new, credible, and material evidence creating a reasonable likelihood that a convicted defendant did not commit an offense of which the defendant was convicted, the prosecutor shall:

    1) Promptly disclose that evidence to an appropriate court or authority, and

    2) If the conviction was obtained in the prosecutor's jurisdiction,

        i) promptly disclose that evidence to the defendant unless a court authorizes delay, and

        ii) undertake further investigation, or make reasonable efforts to cause an investigation, to determine whether the defendant was convicted of an offense that the defendant did not commit.

(h) When a prosecutor knows of clear and convincing evidence establishing that a defendant in the prosecutor's jurisdiction was convicted of an offense that the defendant did not commit, the prosecutor shall seek to remedy the conviction.

## NOTE

One of the biggest challenges of both the *Brady* rule and Model Rule 3.8(d) lies in identifying violations. Because violations of the *Brady* rule and Model Rule 3.8(d) can occur without the defendant ever knowing that evidence that should have been disclosed was not disclosed, it is the rare case when a violation is identified and an even rarer case when a prosecutor is punished for that violation. Studies conducted by the Center for Prosecutor Integrity reveal that courts punish prosecutorial misconduct in less than 2 percent of the cases in which such misconduct is identified. Editorial, *Rampant Prosecutorial Misconduct*, N.Y. Times, Jan. 4, 2014, http://www.nytimes.com/2014/01/05/opinion/sunday/rampant-prosecutorial-misconduct.html?_r=0. *Also available at* https://perma.cc/TB5R-ZZN6.

Chief Judge Kozinski of the Ninth Circuit Court of Appeals commented upon the difficulty of identifying violations of the *Brady* rule in a recent dissenting opinion:

> Due to the nature of a *Brady* violation, it's highly unlikely wrongdoing will ever come to light in the first place. This creates a serious moral hazard for * * * prosecutors * * *. In the rare event that the suppressed evidence does surface, the consequences usually leave the prosecution no worse than had it complied with *Brady* from the outset. Professional discipline is rare, and violations seldom give rise to liability.

*United States v. Olsen*, 737 F.3d 625, 630 (9th Cir. 2013) (Kozinski, C.J., dissenting).

While violations of the *Brady* rule usually go unnoticed, a few notable cases show what can happen to a prosecutor who is caught failing to disclose exculpatory evidence to the defense. First, a prosecutor who fails to disclose such evidence risks losing the right to practice law. The Duke Lacrosse case, in which North Carolina Durham County's District Attorney Mike Nifong failed to disclose exculpatory evidence to the defense in a rape prosecution, provides one example of a case in which the failure to disclose resulted in the prosecutor being disbarred. *See* Duke Office of News & Commc'n, *Looking Back at the Duke Lacrosse Case*, http://today.duke.edu/showcase/lacrosseincident/ or https://perma.cc/NQ8V-Y24U (last visited September 17, 2017).

In March 2006, a female victim alleged that multiple members of Duke University's LaCrosse team raped her. In response to these allegations, the members of the team were suspended, the coach was forced to resign, and the entire season was canceled. District Attorney Mike Nifong filed sexual assault charges against three members of the team. As part of the criminal investigation, Nifong's office arranged for a private lab to conduct DNA testing. The DNA testing uncovered genetic material from several men—but no matches to members of the Lacrosse team. Nifong failed to disclose the results of the DNA testing notwithstanding defense counsel's repeated requests for the DNA results. Instead Nifong denied that these tests had been conducted and continued to pursue the rape prosecution. Some speculated that Nifong was motivated to get a conviction in this high-profile case because it was an election year. *McFadyen v. Duke Univ.*, 786 F. Supp. 2d 887, 908 (M.D.N.C. 2011) (alleging that Nifong intended to use the media interest in the case to aid his election campaign).

Nifong's failure to disclose the DNA test results was revealed when the prosecution's forensic expert testified that DNA tests were conducted and that the test results contained no matches between the victim and the accused defendants. The North Carolina State Bar charged Nifong with multiple ethics violations including "lying to the court about his compliance with discovery requests (in violation of N.C. Rule 3.3(a))." R. Michael Cassidy, *The Prosecutor and the Press: Lesson (Not) Learned from the Mike Nifong Debacle*, 71 LAW AND CONTEMP. PROB. 67, 68 (2008). On June 16, 2007, Nifong was disbarred. Duff

Wilson, *Prosecutor in Duke Case is Disbarred for Ethics Breaches*, N.Y. TIMES, June 16, 2007, http://www.nytimes.com/2007/06/16/us/16cnd-nifong.html?_r= 0. The Attorney General of North Carolina later dropped the criminal charges against the defendants. If convicted, the players could have received up to 30 years in prison. Susannah Meadows, *What Really Happened That Night at Duke*, NEWSWEEK, Apr. 22, 2007, http://www.newsweek.com/what-really-happened-night-duke-97835 or https://perma.cc/R2DZ-6SBD.

Second, a prosecutor can face criminal contempt charges for failing to disclose exculpatory evidence to the defense. In one case out of Texas, for example, a prosecutor who failed to disclose exculpatory evidence after being ordered by a judge to do so was held in contempt of court and ordered to serve 10 days in jail, pay a $500 fine, perform 500 hours community service, and surrender his license to practice law. Paul Cates, *Former Williamson County Prosecutor Ken Anderson Enters Plea to Contempt for Misconduct in Michael Morton's Wrongful Murder Conviction*, Innocence Project.org (Nov. 8, 2013, 12:00 AM), https://www.innocenceproject.org/former-williamson-county-prosecutor-ken-anderson-enters-plea-to-contempt-for-misconduct-in-michael-mortonaes-wrongful-murder-conviction/ or https://perma.cc/2MYN-LXBR.

### PROSECUTORIAL DISCRETION AT THE CORE: THE GOOD PROSECUTOR MEETS BRADY

Janet C. Hoeffel
109 Penn. St. L. Rev. 1133 (2005)

If the good prosecutor were the ethical prosecutor, he would disclose to the defense all information favorable to the defense, without hesitation. He would seek such information from any government official who touched the case. If in doubt, he would err on the side of disclosure. Consistent with "doing justice," such disclosure ensures that the adversarial process is fair. In reality, however, the good prosecutor must do none of these things to be a worthy adversary, according to the Supreme Court of the United States.

It may be that the Warren Court originally intended to place the prosecutor in the ethical role. In *Brady v. Maryland*, the Court broke new ground by holding that "the suppression by the prosecution of evidence favorable to an accused upon request violates due process where the evidence is material either to guilt or to punishment, irrespective of the good faith or the bad faith of the prosecution." * * * The Court emphasized the role of the ethical prosecutor, saying that "[a] prosecution that withholds evidence on demand of an accused which, if made available, would tend to exculpate him or reduce the penalty . . . casts the prosecutor in the role of an architect of a proceeding that does not comport with standards of justice[.]" Hence "[s]ociety wins not only when the guilty are convicted but when criminal trials are fair [.]"

In any event, this view of the good prosecutor as the ethical prosecutor was undone by the march of [several cases.] In [*United States v.*] *Bagley*, the Court held that favorable evidence is "material," and constitutional error results from its suppression, "if there is a reasonable probability that, had the evidence been disclosed to the defense, the result of the proceeding would have been different."

* * * *Bagley* directly places the prosecutor in the role of the architect of the proceeding. The prosecutor can withhold the evidence if he or she believes there would not be a reasonable probability that the disclosure would have affected the jury's verdict. * * *

The Court's admonishments that "the prudent prosecutor will resolve doubtful questions in favor of disclosure" and that "a prosecutor anxious about tacking too close to the wind will disclose a favorable piece of evidence" are either ignorant or disingenuous. The prudent prosecutor will do no such thing. * * *

For example, imagine that the prudent prosecutor is in possession of information that one of the two eyewitnesses to a robbery initially gave the police a description of the perpetrator of the crime that was inconsistent with the appearance of the defendant. The eyewitness described the person as 5'8" tall, with a medium build. The defendant is 5'11" tall and thin. That same eyewitness, however, picked the defendant out of a lineup and indicated she was sure that the defendant was the robber. The other eyewitness gave a general description that fit the defendant and also picked the defendant out of a lineup. The prudent prosecutor, convinced of the defendant's guilt, will not disclose that information.

Several rational reasons explain this decision. First, he is convinced of the defendant's guilt and he is certain that a defense attorney will use this information to attempt to create reasonable doubt where none exists. The prudent prosecutor believes people misgauge the actual height and weight of a person for many reasons, and a minor discrepancy should not derail the prosecution. Second, the prudent prosecutor has read *Bagley* * * * and realizes he has discretion to wait to disclose until he feels a reasonable probability exists that the information would change the outcome of the case. He does not believe this inconsistency creates a reasonable probability, and who is to fault his discretion?

Third, the prudent prosecutor also knows that, because he has no obligation to disclose this evidence, it may never be discovered and, therefore, will never make its way into an appeal of the conviction. Fourth, he knows that even if it is discovered post-trial, an appellate court is likely to view this evidence as harmless in hindsight. The burden will be on the defendant and appellate courts have shown themselves to be predisposed to upholding convictions. The remote prospect of a reversal at some point in the future is hardly a deterrent now, when faced with a discretionary decision which will help him get a conviction. In any case, a reversal simply calls for a retrial, so that the prosecutor is put in essentially the same position he was in prior to the error.

Fifth, the prudent prosecutor is unconcerned about an ethical violation. Even assuming the prosecutor is aware of his duty to disclose favorable evidence under the professional codes (which may be a stretch), he has never heard of a prosecutor being disciplined for his exercise of discretion in withholding evidence. In 1987, Richard Rosen combed the universe of written disciplinary decisions and found only nine which even involved a referral of a prosecutor for withholding exculpatory evidence. In only one of those was the prosecutor given a major sanction, and then, only a suspension. The message sent is that, although it is a rule on the books, the disciplinary authorities do not believe its violation worthy of condemnation.

The barriers to enforcement of the ethical rule are enormous. First, a third party must have the time, wherewithal, and inclination to refer the prosecutor. The only third party who might have an interest is a defendant, who likely is focused on reversing his conviction and does not have the resources to engage an attorney to handle the ethical claim. Even if referred, all incentives point in favor of letting the prosecutor off the hook. If the appellate courts have already determined that the nondisclosure did not amount to a constitutional violation, it is unlikely that the ethical board or the overseeing court will find fault with the prosecutor, despite a technical violation of the rules. Politics, separation of powers, and judicial restraint all play a role. * * *

Withholding favorable evidence, however, seems to be the norm. One recent study reported that convictions in 381 homicide cases nationwide had been reversed because prosecutors concealed evidence suggesting the defendants' innocence or presented evidence they knew to be false. Of the first seventy exonerations of prisoners through DNA testing nationwide, 34% involved prosecutorial misconduct; and of the instances of prosecutorial misconduct in the 152 exonerations occurring between 1989 and 2004, 37% were due to the suppression of exculpatory evidence. These, of course, are only the cases where somehow the nondisclosure came to light. Most cases of nondisclosure likely go undiscovered.

Therefore, we have a criminal justice system which encourages adversarial zeal in its prosecutors to the tune of withholding favorable evidence. To hold our noses at such conduct on the part of prosecutors is unrealistic. To blame the prosecutor ignores fundamental problems inherent in our adversarial system of justice that assumes the average criminal defendant is guilty and encourages prosecutors to pursue convictions in the name of justice. * * *

## WILLIAMS V. FLORIDA
Supreme Court of the United States
399 U.S. 78, 90 S.Ct. 1893, 26 L.E.2d 446 (1970)

JUSTICE WHITE delivered the opinion of the Court.

Prior to his trial for robbery in the State of Florida, petitioner filed a "Motion for a Protective Order," seeking to be excused from the requirements of Rule 1.200 of the Florida Rules of Criminal Procedure. That rule requires a defendant, on written demand of the prosecuting attorney, to give notice in advance of trial if the defendant intends to claim an alibi, and to furnish the prosecuting attorney with information as to the place where he claims to have been and with the names and addresses of the alibi witnesses he intends to use.[a] In his motion petitioner openly declared his intent to claim an alibi, but objected to the further disclosure requirements on the ground that the rule "compels the Defendant in a criminal case to be a witness against himself" in violation of his Fifth and Fourteenth Amendment rights. The motion was denied. * * *

Florida's notice-of-alibi rule is in essence a requirement that a defendant submit to a limited form of pretrial discovery by the State whenever he intends to rely at trial on the defense of alibi. In exchange for the defendant's disclosure of the witnesses he proposes to use to establish that defense, the State in turn is required to notify the defendant of any witnesses it proposes to offer in rebuttal to that defense. Both sides are under a continuing duty promptly to disclose the names and addresses of additional witnesses bearing on the alibi as they become available. The threatened sanction for failure to comply is the exclusion at trial of the defendant's alibi evidence—except for his own testimony—or, in the case of the State, the exclusion of the State's evidence offered in rebuttal of the alibi.

In this case, following the denial of his Motion for a Protective Order, petitioner complied with the alibi rule and gave the State the name and address of one Mary Scotty. Mrs. Scotty was summoned to the office of the State Attorney on the morning of the trial, where she gave pretrial testimony. At the trial itself, Mrs. Scotty, petitioner, and petitioner's wife all testified that the three of them had been in Mrs. Scotty's apartment during the time of the robbery. On two occasions during cross-examination of Mrs. Scotty, the prosecuting attorney confronted her with her earlier deposition in which she had given dates and times that in some respects did not correspond with the dates and times given at trial. Mrs. Scotty

---

    [a]   Similarly, Rule 12.1 of the Federal Rules of Criminal Procedure, reprinted in the Appendix, requires the defendant in a federal case, within 14 days of receiving a written request from an attorney for the government, to provide written notice of any intended alibi defense. That notice must state "each specific place where the defendant claims to have been at the time of the alleged offense" and "the name, address, and telephone number of each alibi witness on whom the defendant intends to rely." FED. R. CRIM. P. 12.1.

adhered to her trial story, insisting that she had been mistaken in her earlier testimony. The State also offered in rebuttal the testimony of one of the officers investigating the robbery who claimed that Mrs. Scotty had asked him for directions on the afternoon in question during the time when she claimed to have been in her apartment with petitioner and his wife.

* * * Given the ease with which an alibi can be fabricated, the State's interest in protecting itself against an eleventh-hour defense is both obvious and legitimate. Reflecting this interest, notice-of-alibi provisions, dating at least from 1927, are now in existence in a substantial number of States. The adversary system of trial * * * is not yet a poker game in which players enjoy an absolute right always to conceal their cards until played. We find ample room in that system, at least as far as "due process" is concerned, for the instant Florida rule, which is designed to enhance the search for truth in the criminal trial by insuring both the defendant and the State ample opportunity to investigate certain facts crucial to the determination of guilt or innocence.

Petitioner's major contention is that he was "compelled * * * to be a witness against himself" contrary to the commands of the Fifth and Fourteenth Amendments because the notice-of-alibi rule required him to give the State the name and address of Mrs. Scotty in advance of trial and thus to furnish the State with information useful in convicting him. No pretrial statement of petitioner was introduced at trial; but armed with Mrs. Scotty's name and address and the knowledge that she was to be petitioner's alibi witness, the State was able to take her deposition in advance of trial and to find rebuttal testimony. Also, requiring him to reveal the elements of his defense is claimed to have interfered with his right to wait until after the State had presented its case to decide how to defend against it. We conclude, however, as has apparently every other court that has considered the issue, that the privilege against self-incrimination is not violated by a requirement that the defendant give notice of an alibi defense and disclose his alibi witnesses.

The defendant in a criminal trial is frequently forced to testify himself and to call other witnesses in an effort to reduce the risk of conviction. When he presents his witnesses, he must reveal their identity and submit them to cross-examination which in itself may prove incriminating or which may furnish the State with leads to incriminating rebuttal evidence. That the defendant faces such a dilemma demanding a choice between complete silence and presenting a defense has never been thought an invasion of the privilege against compelled self-incrimination. The pressures generated by the State's evidence may be severe but they do not vitiate the defendant's choice to present an alibi defense and witnesses to prove it, even though the attempted defense ends in catastrophe for the defendant. However "testimonial" or "incriminating" the alibi defense proves to be, it cannot be considered "compelled" within the meaning of the Fifth and Fourteenth Amendments.

Very similar constraints operate on the defendant when the State requires pretrial notice of alibi and the naming of alibi witnesses. Nothing in such a rule requires the defendant to rely on an alibi or prevents him from abandoning the defense; these matters are left to his unfettered choice. That choice must be made, but the pressures that bear on his pretrial decision are of the same nature as those that would induce him to call alibi witnesses at the trial: the force of historical fact beyond both his and the State's control and the strength of the State's case built on these facts. Response to that kind of pressure by offering evidence or testimony is not compelled self-incrimination transgressing the Fifth and Fourteenth Amendments.

In the case before us, the notice-of-alibi rule by itself in no way affected petitioner's crucial decision to call alibi witnesses or added to the legitimate pressures leading to that course of action. At most, the rule only compelled petitioner to accelerate the timing of his disclosure, forcing him to divulge at an earlier date information that the petitioner from the beginning planned to divulge at trial. Nothing in the Fifth Amendment privilege entitles a defendant as a matter of constitutional right to await the end of the State's case before announcing the nature of his defense, any more than it entitles him to await the jury's verdict on the State's case-in-chief before deciding whether or not to take the stand himself.

Petitioner concedes that absent the notice-of-alibi rule the Constitution would raise no bar to the court's granting the State a continuance at trial on the ground of surprise as soon as the alibi witness is called. Nor would there be self-incrimination problems if, during that continuance, the State was permitted to do precisely what it did here prior to trial: take the deposition of the witness and find rebuttal evidence. But if so utilizing a continuance is permissible under the Fifth and Fourteenth Amendments, then surely the same result may be accomplished through pretrial discovery, as it was here, avoiding the necessity of a disrupted trial. We decline to hold that the privilege against compulsory self-incrimination guarantees the defendant the right to surprise the State with an alibi defense. * * *

CHIEF JUSTICE BURGER, concurring.

I join fully in Mr. Justice WHITE's opinion for the Court. I see an added benefit to the notice-of-alibi rule in that it will serve important functions by way of disposing of cases without trial in appropriate circumstances—a matter of considerable importance when courts, prosecution offices, and legal aid and defender agencies are vastly overworked. The prosecutor upon receiving notice will, of course, investigate prospective alibi witnesses. If he finds them reliable and unimpeachable he will doubtless re-examine his entire case and this process would very likely lead to dismissal of the charges. In turn he might be obliged to determine why false charges were instituted and where the breakdown occurred in the examination of evidence that led to a charge.

On the other hand, inquiry into a claimed alibi defense may reveal it to be contrived and fabricated and the witnesses accordingly subject to impeachment or other attack. In this situation defense counsel would be obliged to re-examine his case and, if he found his client has proposed the use of false testimony, either seek to withdraw from the case or try to persuade his client to enter a plea of guilty, possibly by plea discussions which could lead to disposition on a lesser charge.

In either case the ends of justice will have been served and the processes expedited. These are the likely consequences of an enlarged and truly reciprocal pretrial disclosure of evidence and the move away from the "sporting contest" idea of criminal justice.

JUSTICE BLACK, with whom JUSTICE DOUGLAS joins, concurring in part and dissenting in part.

The Court [today] holds that a State can require a defendant in a criminal case to disclose in advance of trial the nature of his alibi defense and give the names and addresses of witnesses he will call to support that defense. This requirement, the majority says, does not violate the Fifth Amendment prohibition against compelling a criminal defendant to be a witness against himself. Although this case itself involves only a notice-of-alibi provision, it is clear that the decision means that a State can require a defendant to disclose in advance of trial any and all information he might possibly use to defend himself at trial. This decision, in my view, is a radical and dangerous departure from the historical and constitutionally guaranteed right of a defendant in a criminal case to remain completely silent, requiring the State to prove its case without any assistance of any kind from the defendant himself.

The core of the majority's decision is an assumption that compelling a defendant to give notice of an alibi defense before a trial is no different from requiring a defendant, after the State has produced the evidence against him at trial, to plead alibi before the jury retires to consider the case. This assumption is clearly revealed by the statement that "the pressures that bear on (a defendant's) pre-trial decision are of the same nature as those that would induce him to call alibi witnesses at the trial." * * * That statement is plainly and simply wrong as a matter of fact and law, and the Court's holding based on that statement is a complete misunderstanding of the protections provided for criminal defendants by the Fifth Amendment and other provisions of the Bill of Rights.

When a defendant is required to indicate whether he might plead alibi in advance of trial, he faces a vastly different decision from that faced by one who can wait until the State has presented the case against him before making up his mind. Before trial the defendant knows only what the State's case might be. Before trial there is no such thing as the "strength of the State's case"; there is only a range of possible cases. At that time there is no certainty as to what kind of case the State will ultimately be able to prove at trial. Therefore any appraisal of the desirability of pleading alibi will be beset with guesswork and gambling far greater than that accompanying the decision at the trial itself. Any lawyer who has actually tried a case knows that, regardless of the amount of pretrial preparation, a case looks far different when it is actually being tried than when it is only being thought about.

The Florida system, as interpreted by the majority, plays upon this inherent uncertainty in predicting the possible strength of the State's case in order effectively to coerce defendants into disclosing an alibi defense that may never be actually used. Under the Florida rule, a defendant who might plead alibi must, at least 10 days before the date of trial, tell the prosecuting attorney that he might claim an alibi or else the defendant faces the real threat that he may be completely barred from presenting witnesses in support of his alibi. * * * Thus in most situations defendants with any possible thought of pleading alibi are in effect compelled to disclose their intentions in order to preserve the possibility of later raising the defense at trial. Necessarily few defendants and their lawyers will be willing to risk the loss of that possibility by not disclosing the alibi. Clearly the pressures on defendants to plead an alibi created by this procedure are not only quite different from the pressures operating at the trial itself, but are in fact significantly greater. Contrary to the majority's assertion, the pretrial decision cannot be analyzed as simply a matter of "timing," influenced by the same factors operating at the trial itself.

The Court apparently also assumes that a defendant who has given the required notice can abandon his alibi without hurting himself. Such an assumption is implicit in and necessary for the majority's argument that the pretrial decision is no different from that at the trial itself. I, however, cannot so lightly assume that pretrial notice will have no adverse effects on a defendant who later decides to forgo such a defense. Necessarily the defendant will have given the prosecutor the names of persons who may have some knowledge about the defendant himself or his activities. Necessarily the prosecutor will have every incentive to question these persons fully, and in doing so he may discover new leads or evidence. Undoubtedly there will be situations in which the State will seek to use such information—information it would probably never have obtained but for the defendant's coerced cooperation.

It is unnecessary for me, however, to engage in any such intellectual gymnastics concerning the practical effects of the notice-of-alibi procedure, because the Fifth Amendment itself clearly provides that "[n]o person * * * shall be compelled in any criminal case to be a witness against himself." If words are to be given their plain and obvious meaning, that provision, in my opinion, states that a criminal defendant cannot be required to give evidence, testimony, or any other assistance to the State to aid it in convicting him of crime. The Florida notice-of-alibi rule in my opinion is a patent violation of [the Fifth Amendment's] constitutional provision because it requires a defendant to disclose information to the State so that the State can use that information to destroy him. It seems to me at least slightly incredible to suggest that this procedure may have some beneficial effects for defendants. There is no need to encourage defendants to take actions they think will help them. The fear of conviction and the substantial cost or inconvenience resulting from criminal prosecutions are more than sufficient incentives to make defendants want to help themselves. If a defendant thinks that making disclosure of an alibi before trial is in his best interest, he will obviously do so. And the only time the State needs the compulsion provided by this procedure is when the defendant has decided that such disclosure is likely to hurt his case.

It is no answer to this argument to suggest that the Fifth Amendment as so interpreted would give the defendant an unfair element of surprise, turning a trial into a "poker game" or "sporting contest," for that tactical advantage to the defendant is inherent in the type of trial required by our Bill of Rights. The Framers were well aware of the awesome investigative and prosecutorial powers of government and it was in order to limit those powers that they spelled out in detail in the Constitution the procedure to be followed in criminal trials. A defendant, they said, is entitled to notice of the charges against him, trial by jury, the right to counsel for his defense, the right to confront and cross-examine witnesses, the right to call witnesses in his own behalf, and the right not to be a witness against himself. All of these rights are designed to shield the defendant against state power. None are designed to make convictions easier and taken together they clearly indicate that in our system the entire burden of proving criminal activity rests on the State. The defendant, under our Constitution, need not do anything at all to defend himself, and certainly he cannot be required to help convict himself. Rather he has an absolute, unqualified right to compel the State to investigate its own case, find its own witnesses, prove its own facts, and convince the jury through its own resources. Throughout the process the defendant has a fundamental right to remain silent, in effect challenging the State at every point to: "Prove it!" * * *

On the surface this case involves only a notice-of-alibi provisions, but in effect the decision opens the way for a profound change in one of the most important traditional safeguards of a criminal defendant. The rationale of today's decision is in no way limited to alibi defenses, or any other type or classification of evidence. The theory advanced goes at least so far as to permit the State to obtain under threat of sanction complete disclosure by the defendant in advance of trial of all evidence, testimony, and tactics he plans to use at that trial. In each case the justification will be that the rule affects only the "timing" of the disclosure, and not the substantive decision itself.

\* \* \* [T]he rationale of today's decision can be used to transform radically our system of criminal justice into a process requiring the defendant to assist the State in convicting him, or be punished for failing to do so. \* \* \*

[JUSTICE MARSHALL's opinion, dissenting in part, has been omitted.]

## *NOTE*

In 1957, the Supreme Court held in *Jencks v. United States*, 353 U.S. 657 (1957), that the government is required to give statements of its witnesses to the defense. In response, Congress passed the Jencks Act, 18 U.S.C. § 3500(b), *see* Appendix, limiting this rule such that the government need not turn over prosecution witness statements to the defense until after the witness testifies on direct examination at trial. After the government's witness testifies and upon the defendant's request, the court shall order the government to deliver any statements of the witness in the government's possession that relate to the subject matter upon which the witness has testified. Federal Rule of Criminal Procedure 26.2(a) codified the Jencks Act and made the disclosure obligation reciprocal, requiring the defense, upon prosecution request, to deliver the statements of its witnesses to the prosecution after those witnesses testify. Rule 26.2(a) does not require the production of a testifying defendant's statements.

# CHAPTER 27

# PLEA BARGAINING

■ ■ ■

Although a criminal defendant has a constitutional right to a jury trial, a defendant may choose to waive this right and enter a guilty plea. When the defendant does so as the result of a plea bargain with the government, he foregoes his right to a trial usually in exchange for a lesser charge or a favorable sentencing recommendation. The Supreme Court has noted that "[p]lea bargaining flows from 'the mutuality of advantage' to defendants and prosecutors, each with his own reason for wanting to avoid trial." *Bordenkircher v. Hayes, infra.* This chapter examines the constitutional requirements surrounding plea bargaining.

Plea bargaining is an extremely common practice. It has become such a dominant force in the criminal justice process that very few criminal cases go to trial today. Indeed "[n]inety-seven percent of all federal convictions and ninety-four percent of all state convictions are the result of guilty pleas." *Missouri v. Frye,* 566 U.S. 134, 143 (2012). As one judge has noted, "our entire criminal justice system has shifted far away from trials and juries and adjudication to a massive system of [plea] bargaining that is heavily rigged against the accused citizen."

In the plea bargaining process, the prosecutor holds most of the cards. The prosecutor can reduce or dismiss some or all of the charges in exchange for the defendant's guilty plea. Since there is no constitutional right to a plea bargain, the prosecutor can even refuse to plea bargain with the defendant. What if the prosecutor threatens to add a charge that will subject the defendant to a mandatory sentence of life imprisonment if the defendant does not plead guilty to the offense with which he was originally charged? The first case in this chapter, *Bordenkircher v. Hayes,* considers whether such conduct violates the Due Process Clause of the Fourteenth Amendment.

The plea agreement is often viewed as a contract that binds the prosecutor as well as the defendant. When the prosecutor breaches the plea agreement, what is the defendant's remedy? In *Santobello v. New York,* the Court considers the various ways a defendant can be made whole when the government breaches its half of the plea bargain. In *Mabry v. Johnson,* the Court considers whether the defendant's acceptance of a prosecutor's proposed plea agreement creates an enforceable agreement. If one views plea bargaining as a contractual arrangement between the prosecutor and the defendant, one may be surprised at the Court's answer to this question.

In the chapter on discovery, we learned that the prosecutor has an ethical and constitutional duty to provide exculpatory evidence to the defense. Given this duty, can prosecutors insist that defendants waive their right to such evidence as part of a plea bargain? For many years, federal prosecutors routinely conditioned their plea agreements on defendants waiving their right to receive impeachment evidence relating to the government's informants and witnesses. In *United States v. Ruiz*, the Court considers whether this practice comports with due process.

In *Boykin v. Alabama* and *Henderson v. Morgan*, the Court outlines the requirements for a constitutionally valid guilty plea. In the last case in this chapter, *North Carolina v. Alford*, the Court considers whether a judge can accept a guilty plea from a defendant who claims he is innocent of the charge to which he is pleading guilty and what procedural safeguards are needed in this type of situation. The chapter ends with an article by John Keker, lamenting the fact that so many cases today never go to trial.

## BORDENKIRCHER V. HAYES

Supreme Court of the United States
434 U.S. 357, 98 S.Ct. 663, 54 L.Ed.2d 604 (1978)

JUSTICE STEWART delivered the opinion of the Court.

The question in this case is whether the Due Process Clause of the Fourteenth Amendment is violated when a state prosecutor carries out a threat made during plea negotiations to reindict the accused on more serious charges if he does not plead guilty to the offense with which he was originally charged.

The respondent, Paul Lewis Hayes, was indicted by a Fayette County, Ky., grand jury on a charge of uttering a forged instrument in the amount of $88.30, an offense then punishable by a term of 2 to 10 years in prison. After arraignment, Hayes, his retained counsel, and the Commonwealth's Attorney met in the presence of the Clerk of the Court to discuss a possible plea agreement. During these conferences the prosecutor offered to recommend a sentence of five years in prison if Hayes would plead guilty to the indictment. He also said that if Hayes did not plead guilty and "save the court the inconvenience and necessity of a trial," he would return to the grand jury to seek an indictment under the Kentucky Habitual Criminal Act, which would subject Hayes to a mandatory sentence of life imprisonment by reason of his two prior felony convictions. Hayes chose not to plead guilty, and the prosecutor did obtain an indictment charging him under the Habitual Criminal Act. * * *

A jury found Hayes guilty on the principal charge of uttering a forged instrument and, in a separate proceeding, further found that he had twice before been convicted of felonies. As required by the habitual offender statute, he was sentenced to a life term in the penitentiary. * * * We granted certiorari to consider a constitutional question of importance in the administration of criminal justice.

It may be helpful to clarify at the outset the nature of the issue in this case. While the prosecutor did not actually obtain the recidivist indictment until after the plea conferences had ended, his intention to do so was clearly expressed at the outset of the plea negotiations. Hayes was thus fully informed of the true terms of the offer when he made his decision to plead not guilty. This is not a situation, therefore, where the prosecutor without notice brought an additional and more serious charge after plea negotiations relating only to the original indictment had ended with the defendant's insistence on pleading not guilty. As a practical matter, in short, this case would be no different if the grand jury had indicted Hayes as a recidivist from the outset, and the prosecutor had offered to drop that charge as part of the plea bargain.

The Court of Appeals nonetheless drew a distinction between "concessions relating to prosecution under an existing indictment," and threats to bring more severe charges not contained in the original indictment—a line it thought necessary in order to establish a prophylactic rule to guard against the evil of prosecutorial vindictiveness. Quite apart from this chronological distinction, however, the Court of Appeals found that the prosecutor had acted vindictively in the present case since he had conceded that the indictment was influenced by his desire to induce a guilty plea.

We have recently had occasion to observe: "[W]hatever might be the situation in an ideal world, the fact is that the guilty plea and the often concomitant plea bargain are important components of this country's criminal justice system. Properly administered, they can benefit all concerned." The open acknowledgment of this previously clandestine practice has led this Court to recognize the importance of counsel during plea negotiations, the need for a public record indicating that a plea was knowingly and voluntarily made and the requirement that a prosecutor's plea-bargaining promise must be kept. The decision of the Court of Appeals in the present case, however, did not deal with considerations such as these, but held that the substance of the plea offer itself violated the limitations imposed by the Due Process Clause of the Fourteenth Amendment. For the reasons that follow, we have concluded that the Court of Appeals was mistaken in so ruling.

This Court held in *North Carolina v. Pearce*, that the Due Process Clause of the Fourteenth Amendment "requires that vindictiveness against a defendant for having successfully attacked his first conviction must play no part in the sentence he receives after a new trial." The same principle was later applied [in *Blackledge v. Perry*] to prohibit a prosecutor from reindicting a convicted misdemeanant on a felony charge after the defendant had invoked an appellate remedy, since in this situation there was also a "realistic likelihood of 'vindictiveness.'"

In those cases the Court was dealing with the State's unilateral imposition of a penalty upon a defendant who had chosen to exercise a legal right to attack his original conviction—a situation "very different from the give-and-take negotiation common in plea bargaining between the prosecution and defense, which arguably possess relatively equal bargaining power." The Court has emphasized that the due process violation in cases such as *Pearce* and *Perry* lay not in the possibility that a defendant might be deterred from the exercise of a legal right, but rather in the danger that the State might be retaliating against the accused for lawfully attacking his conviction.

To punish a person because he has done what the law plainly allows him to do is a due process violation of the most basic sort, and for an agent of the State to pursue a course of action whose objective is to penalize a person's reliance on his legal rights is "patently unconstitutional." But in the "give-and-take" of plea bargaining, there is no such element of punishment or retaliation so long as the accused is free to accept or reject the prosecution's offer.

Plea bargaining flows from "the mutuality of advantage" to defendants and prosecutors, each with his own reasons for wanting to avoid trial. Defendants advised by competent counsel and protected by other procedural safeguards are presumptively capable of intelligent choice in response to prosecutorial persuasion, and unlikely to be driven to false self-condemnation. Indeed, acceptance of the basic legitimacy of plea bargaining necessarily implies rejection of any notion that a guilty plea is involuntary in a constitutional sense simply because it is the end result of the bargaining process. By hypothesis, the plea may have been induced by promises of a recommendation of a lenient sentence or a reduction of charges, and thus by fear of the possibility of a greater penalty upon conviction after a trial.

While confronting a defendant with the risk of more severe punishment clearly may have a "discouraging effect on the defendant's assertion of his trial rights, the imposition of these difficult choices [is] an inevitable"—and permissible—"attribute of any legitimate system which tolerates and encourages the negotiation of pleas." It follows that, by tolerating and encouraging the negotiation of pleas, this Court has necessarily accepted as constitutionally legitimate the simple reality that the prosecutor's interest at the bargaining table is to persuade the defendant to forgo his right to plead not guilty.

It is not disputed here that Hayes was properly chargeable under the recidivist statute, since he had in fact been convicted of two previous felonies. In our system, so long as the prosecutor has probable cause to believe that the accused committed an offense defined by statute, the decision whether or not to prosecute, and what charge to file or bring before a grand jury, generally rests entirely in his discretion.[8] Within the limits set by the legislature's constitutionally valid definition of chargeable offenses, "the conscious exercise of some selectivity in enforcement is not in itself a federal constitutional violation" so long as "the selection was [not] deliberately based upon an unjustifiable standard such as race, religion, or other arbitrary classification." To hold that the prosecutor's desire to induce a guilty plea is an "unjustifiable standard," which, like race or religion, may play no part in his charging decision, would contradict the very premises that underlie the concept of plea bargaining itself. Moreover, a rigid constitutional rule that would prohibit a prosecutor from acting forthrightly in his dealings with the defense could only invite unhealthy subterfuge that would drive the practice of plea bargaining back into the shadows from which it has so recently emerged.

There is no doubt that the breadth of discretion that our country's legal system vests in prosecuting attorneys carries with it the potential for both individual and institutional abuse. And broad though that discretion may be, there are undoubtedly constitutional limits upon its exercise. We hold only that the course of conduct engaged in by the prosecutor in this case, which no more than openly presented the defendant with the unpleasant alternatives of forgoing trial or facing charges on which he was plainly subject to prosecution, did not violate the Due Process Clause of the Fourteenth Amendment.

Accordingly, the judgment of the Court of Appeals is

*Reversed.*

JUSTICE BLACKMUN, with whom JUSTICE BRENNAN and JUSTICE MARSHALL join, dissenting. * * *

Prosecutorial vindictiveness, it seems to me, in the present narrow context, is the fact against which the Due Process Clause ought to protect. I perceive little difference between vindictiveness after what the Court describes as the exercise of a "legal right to attack his original conviction," and vindictiveness in the "give-and-take negotiation common in plea bargaining." Prosecutorial vindictiveness in any context is still

---

[8] This case does not involve the constitutional implications of a prosecutor's offer during plea bargaining of adverse or lenient treatment for some person other than the accused, which might pose a greater danger of inducing a false guilty plea by skewing the assessment of the risks a defendant must consider.

prosecutorial vindictiveness. The Due Process Clause should protect an accused against it, however it asserts itself. The Court of Appeals rightly so held, and I would affirm the judgment. * * *

It might be argued that it really makes little difference how this case, now that it is here, is decided. The Court's holding gives plea bargaining full sway despite vindictiveness. A contrary result, however, merely would prompt the aggressive prosecutor to bring the greater charge initially in every case, and only thereafter to bargain. The consequences to the accused would still be adverse, for then he would bargain against a greater charge, face the likelihood of increased bail, and run the risk that the court would be less inclined to accept a bargained plea. Nonetheless, it is far preferable to hold the prosecution to the charge it was originally content to bring and to justify in the eyes of its public.

JUSTICE POWELL, dissenting.

Although I agree with much of the Court's opinion, I am not satisfied that the result in this case is just or that the conduct of the plea bargaining met the requirements of due process. * * *

The prosecutor's initial assessment of respondent's case led him to forgo an indictment under the habitual criminal statute. The circumstances of respondent's prior convictions are relevant to this assessment and to my view of the case. Respondent was 17 years old when he committed his first offense. He was charged with rape but pleaded guilty to the lesser included offense of "detaining a female." One of the other participants in the incident was sentenced to life imprisonment. Respondent was sent not to prison but to a reformatory where he served five years. Respondent's second offense was robbery. This time he was found guilty by a jury and was sentenced to five years in prison, but he was placed on probation and served no time. Although respondent's prior convictions brought him within the terms of the Habitual Criminal Act, the offenses themselves did not result in imprisonment; yet the addition of a conviction on a charge involving $88.30 subjected respondent to a mandatory sentence of imprisonment for life. Persons convicted of rape and murder often are not punished so severely. * * *

It seems to me that the question to be asked under the circumstances is whether the prosecutor reasonably might have charged respondent under the Habitual Criminal Act in the first place. The deference that courts properly accord the exercise of a prosecutor's discretion perhaps would foreclose judicial criticism if the prosecutor originally had sought an indictment under that Act, as unreasonable as it would have seemed. But here the prosecutor evidently made a reasonable, responsible judgment not to subject an individual to a mandatory life sentence when his only new offense had societal implications as limited as those accompanying the uttering of a single $88 forged check and when the circumstances of his prior convictions confirmed the inappropriateness of applying the habitual criminal statute. I think it may be inferred that the prosecutor himself deemed it unreasonable and not in the public interest to put this defendant in jeopardy of a sentence of life imprisonment. * * *

The plea bargaining process, as recognized by this Court, is essential to the functioning of the criminal-justice system. It normally affords genuine benefits to defendants as well as to society. And if the system is to work effectively, prosecutors must be accorded the widest discretion, within constitutional limits, in conducting bargaining. This is especially true when a defendant is represented by counsel and presumably is fully advised of his rights. Only in the most exceptional case should a court conclude that the scales of the bargaining are so unevenly balanced as to arouse suspicion. In this case, the prosecutor's actions denied respondent due process because their admitted purpose was to discourage and then to penalize with unique severity his exercise of constitutional rights. Implementation of a strategy calculated solely to deter the exercise of constitutional rights is not a constitutionally permissible exercise of discretion. I would affirm the opinion of the Court of Appeals on the facts of this case.

## SANTOBELLO V. NEW YORK

Supreme Court of the United States
404 U.S. 257, 92 S.Ct. 495, 30 L.Ed.2d 427 (1971)

CHIEF JUSTICE BURGER delivered the opinion of the Court.

We granted certiorari in this case to determine whether the State's failure to keep a commitment concerning the sentence recommendation on a guilty plea required a new trial.

The facts are not in dispute. The State of New York indicted petitioner in 1969 on two felony counts, Promoting Gambling in the First Degree, and Possession of Gambling Records in the First Degree. Petitioner first entered a plea of not guilty to both counts. After negotiations, the Assistant District Attorney in charge of the case agreed to permit petitioner to plead guilty to a lesser-included offense, Possession of Gambling Records in the Second Degree, conviction of which would carry a maximum prison sentence of one year. The prosecutor agreed to make no recommendation as to the sentence.

On June 16, 1969, petitioner accordingly withdrew his plea of not guilty and entered a plea of guilty to the lesser charge. Petitioner represented to the sentencing judge that the plea was voluntary and that the facts of the case, as described by the Assistant District Attorney, were true. The court accepted the plea and set a date for sentencing. * * *

At [sentencing], another prosecutor had replaced the prosecutor who had negotiated the plea. The new prosecutor recommended the maximum one-year sentence. In making this recommendation, he cited petitioner's criminal record and alleged links with organized crime. Defense counsel immediately objected on the ground that the State had promised petitioner before the plea was entered that there would be no sentence recommendation by the prosecution. He sought to adjourn the sentence hearing in order to have time to prepare proof of the first prosecutor's promise. The second prosecutor, apparently ignorant of his colleague's commitment, argued that there was nothing in the record to support petitioner's claim of a promise, but the State, in subsequent proceedings, has not contested that such a promise was made.

The sentencing judge ended discussion, with the following statement, quoting extensively from the pre-sentence report:

> Mr. Aronstein (Defense Counsel), I am not at all influenced by what the District Attorney says, so that there is no need to adjourn the sentence, and there is no need to have any testimony. It doesn't make a particle of difference what the District Attorney says he will do, or what he [won't] do.

> I have here, Mr. Aronstein, a probation report. I have here a history of a long, long serious criminal record. I have here a picture of the life history of this man. . . .

> "He is unamenable to supervision in the community. He is a professional criminal." This is in quotes. "And a recidivist. Institutionalization—"; that means, in plain language, just putting him away, "is the only means of halting his anti-social activities," and protecting you, your family, me, my family, protecting society. "Institutionalization." Plain language, put him behind bars.

> Under the plea, I can only send him to the New York City Correctional Institution for men for one year, which I am hereby doing.

The judge then imposed the maximum sentence of one year. * * *

This record represents another example of an unfortunate lapse in orderly prosecutorial procedures, in part, no doubt, because of the enormous increase in the workload of the often understaffed prosecutor's offices. The heavy workload may well explain these episodes, but it does not excuse them. The disposition of criminal charges by agreement between the prosecutor and the accused, sometimes loosely called "plea bargaining," is an essential component of the administration of justice. Properly administered, it is to be encouraged. If every criminal charge were subjected to a full-scale trial, the States and the Federal Government would need to multiply by many times the number of judges and court facilities.

Disposition of charges after plea discussions is not only an essential part of the process but a highly desirable part for many reasons. It leads to prompt and largely final disposition of most criminal cases; it avoids much of the corrosive impact of enforced idleness during pre-trial confinement for those who are denied release pending trial; it protects the public from those accused persons who are prone to continue criminal conduct even while on pretrial release; and, by shortening the time between charge and disposition, it enhances whatever may be the rehabilitative prospects of the guilty when they are ultimately imprisoned.

However, all of these considerations presuppose fairness in securing agreement between an accused and a prosecutor. * * * [A] constant factor is that when a plea rests in any significant degree on a promise or agreement of the prosecutor, so that it can be said to be part of the inducement or consideration, such promise must be fulfilled.

On this record, petitioner "bargained" and negotiated for a particular plea in order to secure dismissal of more serious charges, but also on condition that no sentence recommendation would be made by the prosecutor. It is now conceded that the promise to abstain from a recommendation was made, and at this stage the prosecution is not in a good position to argue that its inadvertent breach of agreement is immaterial. The staff lawyers in a prosecutor's office have the burden of "letting the left hand know what the right hand is doing" or has done. That the breach of agreement was inadvertent does not lessen its impact.

* * * [W]e conclude that the interests of justice and appropriate recognition of the duties of the prosecution in relation to promises made in the negotiation of pleas of guilty will be best served by remanding the case to the state courts for further consideration. The ultimate relief to which petitioner is entitled we leave to the discretion of the state court, which is in a better position to decide whether the circumstances of this case require only that there be specific performance of the agreement on the plea, in which case petitioner should be resentenced by a different judge, or whether, in the view of the state court, the circumstances require granting the relief sought by petitioner, i.e., the opportunity to withdraw his plea of guilty. * * *

The judgment is vacated and the case is remanded for reconsideration not inconsistent with this opinion.

Justice Douglas, concurring.

* * * [I]t is * * * clear that a prosecutor's promise may deprive a guilty plea of the "character of a voluntary act." The decisions of this Court have not spelled out what sorts of promises by prosecutors tend to be coercive,

but in order to assist appellate review in weighing promises in light of all the circumstances, all trial courts are now required to interrogate the defendants who enter guilty pleas so that the waiver of these fundamental rights will affirmatively appear in the record. The lower courts, however, have uniformly held that a prisoner is entitled to some form of relief when he shows that the prosecutor reneged on his sentencing agreement made in connection with a plea bargain, most jurisdictions preferring vacation of the plea on the ground of "involuntariness," while a few permit only specific enforcement.

* * * In choosing a remedy, however, a court ought to accord a defendant's preference considerable, if not controlling, weight inasmuch as the fundamental rights flouted by a prosecutor's breach of a plea bargain are those of the defendant, not of the State.

JUSTICE MARSHALL, with whom JUSTICE BRENNAN and JUSTICE STEWART join, concurring in part and dissenting in part.

I agree with much of the majority's opinion, but conclude that petitioner must be permitted to withdraw his guilty plea. This is the relief petitioner requested and, on the facts set out by the majority, it is a form of relief to which he is entitled.

* * * When a prosecutor breaks [a plea] bargain, he undercuts the basis for the waiver of constitutional rights implicit in the plea. This, it seems to me, provides the defendant ample justification for rescinding the plea. Where a promise is "unfulfilled," *Brady v. United States* specifically denies that the plea "must stand." Of course, where the prosecutor has broken the plea agreement, it may be appropriate to permit the defendant to enforce the plea bargain. But that is not the remedy sought here. Rather, it seems to me that a breach of the plea bargain provides ample reason to permit the plea to be vacated. * * *

## MABRY V. JOHNSON

Supreme Court of the United States
467 U.S. 504, 104 S.Ct. 2543, 81 L.Ed.2d 437 (1984)

JUSTICE STEVENS delivered the opinion of the Court.

The question presented is whether a defendant's acceptance of a prosecutor's proposed plea bargain creates a constitutional right to have the bargain specifically enforced.

In the late evening of May 22, 1970, three members of a family returned home to find a burglary in progress. Shots were exchanged resulting in the daughter's death and the wounding of the father and respondent—one of the burglars. Respondent was tried and convicted on three charges: burglary, assault, and murder. The murder conviction was set aside by the Arkansas Supreme Court. Thereafter, plea negotiations ensued.

At the time of the negotiations respondent was serving his concurrent 21- and 12-year sentences on the burglary and assault convictions. On Friday, October 27, 1972, a deputy prosecutor proposed to respondent's attorney that in exchange for a plea of guilty to the charge of accessory after a felony murder, the prosecutor would recommend a sentence of 21 years to be served concurrently with the burglary and assault sentences. On the following day, counsel communicated the offer to respondent who agreed to accept it. On the next Monday the lawyer called the prosecutor "and communicated [respondent's] acceptance of the offer." The prosecutor then told counsel that a mistake had been made and withdrew the offer. He proposed instead that in exchange for a guilty plea he would recommend a sentence of 21 years to be served consecutively to respondent's other sentences.

Respondent rejected the new offer and elected to stand trial. On the second day of trial, the judge declared a mistrial and plea negotiations resumed, ultimately resulting in respondent's acceptance of the prosecutor's second offer. In accordance with the plea bargain, the state trial judge imposed a 21-year sentence to be served consecutively to the previous sentences.

After exhausting his state remedies, respondent filed a petition for a writ of habeas corpus * * *. The District Court dismissed the petition, finding that respondent had understood the consequences of his guilty plea, that he had received the effective assistance of counsel, and that because the evidence did not establish that respondent had detrimentally relied on the prosecutor's first proposed plea agreement, respondent had no right to enforce it. The Court of Appeals reversed * * *. The majority concluded that "fairness" precluded the prosecution's withdrawal of a plea proposal once accepted by respondent. * * * [W]e granted certiorari. We now reverse. * * *

It is well settled that a voluntary and intelligent plea of guilty made by an accused person, who has been advised by competent counsel, may not be collaterally attacked. It is also well settled that plea agreements are consistent with the requirements of voluntariness and intelligence—because each side may obtain advantages when a guilty plea is exchanged for sentencing concessions, the agreement is no less voluntary than any other bargained-for exchange. It is only when the consensual character of the plea is called into question that the validity of a guilty plea may be impaired. In *Brady v. United States*, we stated the applicable standard:

> [A] plea of guilty entered by one fully aware of the direct consequences, including the actual value of any commitments made to him by the court, prosecutor, or his own counsel, must stand unless induced by threats (or promises to discontinue

improper harassment), misrepresentation (including unfulfilled or unfulfillable promises), or perhaps by promises that are by their nature improper as having no proper relationship to the prosecutor's business (e.g. bribes).

Thus, only when it develops that the defendant was not fairly apprised of its consequences can his plea be challenged under the Due Process Clause. * * * [T]he conditions for a valid plea "presuppose fairness in securing agreement between an accused and a prosecutor. . . . The plea must, of course, be voluntary and knowing and if it was induced by promises, the essence of those promises must in some way be made known." It follows that when the prosecution breaches its promise with respect to an executed plea agreement, the defendant pleads guilty on a false premise, and hence his conviction cannot stand.

* * * Respondent's plea was in no sense induced by the prosecutor's withdrawn offer. * * * [A]t the time respondent pleaded guilty he knew the prosecution would recommend a 21-year consecutive sentence. Respondent * * * pleaded guilty with the advice of competent counsel and with full awareness of the consequences—he knew that the prosecutor would recommend and that the judge could impose the sentence now under attack. Respondent's plea was thus in no sense the product of governmental deception; it rested on no "unfulfilled promise" and fully satisfied the test for voluntariness and intelligence.

Thus, because it did not impair the voluntariness or intelligence of his guilty plea, respondent's inability to enforce the prosecutor's offer is without constitutional significance. Neither is the question whether the prosecutor was negligent or otherwise culpable in first making and then withdrawing his offer relevant. The Due Process Clause is not a code of ethics for prosecutors; its concern is with the manner in which persons are deprived of their liberty. Here respondent was not deprived of his liberty in any fundamentally unfair way. Respondent was fully aware of the likely consequences when he pleaded guilty; it is not unfair to expect him to live with those consequences now.

The judgment of the Court of Appeals is

*Reversed.*

## UNITED STATES V. RUIZ

Supreme Court of the United States
536 U.S. 622, 122 S.Ct. 2450, 153 L.Ed.2d 586 (2002)

JUSTICE BREYER delivered the opinion of the Court. * * *

After immigration agents found 30 kilograms of marijuana in Angela Ruiz's luggage, federal prosecutors offered her what is known in the Southern District of California as a "fast track" plea bargain. That bargain—standard in that district—asks a defendant to waive indictment, trial, and an appeal. In return, the Government agrees to recommend to the sentencing judge a two-level departure downward from the otherwise applicable United States Sentencing Guidelines sentence. In Ruiz's case, a two-level departure downward would have shortened the ordinary Guidelines-specified 18-to-24-month sentencing range by 6 months, to 12-to-18 months.

The prosecutors' proposed plea agreement * * * specifies that "any [known] information establishing the factual innocence of the defendant" "has been turned over to the defendant" and it acknowledges the Government's "continuing duty to provide such information." At the same time it require[s] that the defendant "waiv[e] the right" to receive "impeachment information relating to any informants or other witnesses" as well as the right to receive information supporting any affirmative defense the defendant raises if the case goes to trial. Because Ruiz would not agree to this last-mentioned waiver, the prosecutors withdrew their bargaining offer. The Government then indicted Ruiz for unlawful drug possession. And despite the absence of any agreement, Ruiz ultimately pleaded guilty.

At sentencing, Ruiz asked the judge to grant her the same two-level downward departure that the Government would have recommended had she accepted the "fast track" agreement. The Government opposed her request, and the District Court denied it, imposing a standard Guideline sentence instead.

* * * Ruiz appealed her sentence to the United States Court of Appeals for the Ninth Circuit. The Ninth Circuit vacated the District Court's sentencing determination. The Ninth Circuit pointed out that the Constitution requires prosecutors to make certain impeachment information available to a defendant before trial. It decided that this obligation entitles defendants to receive that same information before they enter into a plea agreement. The Ninth Circuit also decided that the Constitution prohibits defendants from waiving their right to that information. And it held that the prosecutors' standard "fast track" plea agreement was unlawful because it insisted upon that waiver. * * *

When a defendant pleads guilty he or she, of course, forgoes not only a fair trial, but also other accompanying constitutional guarantees. Given the seriousness of the matter, the Constitution insists, among other things, that the defendant enter a guilty plea that is "voluntary" and that the defendant must make related waivers "knowing[ly], intelligent[ly], [and] with sufficient awareness of the relevant circumstances and likely consequences."

In this case, the Ninth Circuit in effect held that a guilty plea is not "voluntary" (and that the defendant could not, by pleading guilty, waive her right to a fair trial) unless the prosecutors first made the same disclosure of material impeachment information that the prosecutors would have had to make had the defendant insisted upon a trial. We must decide whether the Constitution requires that preguilty plea disclosure of impeachment information. We conclude that it does not.

First, impeachment information is special in relation to the fairness of a trial, not in respect to whether a plea is voluntary ("knowing," "intelligent," and "sufficient[ly] aware"). Of course, the more information the defendant has, the more aware he is of the likely consequences of a plea, waiver, or decision, and the wiser that decision will likely be. But the Constitution does not require the prosecutor to share all useful information with the defendant. And the law ordinarily considers a waiver knowing, intelligent, and sufficiently aware if the defendant fully understands the nature of the right and how it would likely apply in general in the circumstances—even though the defendant may not know the specific detailed consequences of invoking it. A defendant, for example, may waive his right to remain silent, his right to a jury trial, or his right to counsel even if the defendant does not know the specific questions the authorities intend to ask, who will likely serve on the jury, or the particular lawyer the State might otherwise provide. * * *

Second, we have found no legal authority embodied either in this Court's past cases or in cases from other circuits that provides significant support for the Ninth Circuit's decision. To the contrary, this Court has found that the Constitution, in respect to a defendant's awareness of relevant circumstances, does not require complete knowledge of the relevant circumstances, but permits a court to accept a guilty plea, with its accompanying waiver of various constitutional rights, despite various forms of misapprehension under which a defendant might labor. * * *

Third, due process considerations, the very considerations that led this Court to find trial-related rights to exculpatory and impeachment information in *Brady* and *Giglio*, argue against the existence of the "right" that the Ninth Circuit found here. This Court has said that due process considerations include not only (1) the nature of the private interest at stake, but also (2) the value of the additional safeguard, and (3) the adverse impact of the requirement upon the Government's interests. Here, * * * the added value of the Ninth Circuit's "right" to a defendant is often limited, for it depends upon the defendant's independent awareness of the details of the Government's case. And in any case, as the proposed plea agreement at issue here specifies, the Government will provide "any information establishing the factual innocence of the defendant" regardless. That fact, along with other guilty-plea safeguards, * * * diminishes the force of Ruiz's concern that, in the absence of impeachment information, innocent individuals, accused of crimes, will plead guilty. * * *

At the same time, a constitutional obligation to provide impeachment information during plea bargaining, prior to entry of a guilty plea, could seriously interfere with the Government's interest in securing those guilty pleas that are factually justified, desired by defendants, and help to secure the efficient administration of justice. The Ninth Circuit's rule risks premature disclosure of Government witness information, which, the Government tells us, could "disrupt ongoing investigations" and expose prospective witnesses to serious harm. * * *

Consequently, the Ninth Circuit's requirement could force the Government to abandon its "general practice" of not "disclos[ing] to a defendant pleading guilty information that would reveal the identities of cooperating informants, undercover investigators, or other prospective witnesses." It could require the Government to devote substantially more resources to trial preparation prior to plea bargaining, thereby depriving the plea-bargaining process of its main resource-saving advantages. Or it could lead the Government instead to abandon its heavy reliance upon plea bargaining in a vast number—90% or more—of federal criminal cases. We cannot say that the Constitution's due process requirement demands so radical a change in the criminal justice process in order to achieve so comparatively small a constitutional benefit.

These considerations, taken together, lead us to conclude that the Constitution does not require the Government to disclose material impeachment evidence prior to entering a plea agreement with a criminal defendant.

For these reasons the judgment of the Court of Appeals for the Ninth Circuit is

*Reversed.*

[JUSTICE THOMAS' concurring opinion has been omitted.]

## BOYKIN V. ALABAMA

Supreme Court of the United States
395 U.S. 238, 89 S.Ct. 1709, 23 L.Ed.2d 274 (1969)

JUSTICE DOUGLAS delivered the opinion of the Court.

In the spring of 1966, within the period of a fortnight, a series of armed robberies occurred in Mobile, Alabama. The victims, in each case, were local shopkeepers open at night who were forced by a gunman to hand over money. While robbing one grocery store, the assailant fired his gun once, sending a bullet through a door into the ceiling. A few days earlier in a drugstore, the robber had allowed his gun to discharge in such a way that the bullet, on ricochet from the floor, struck a customer in the leg. Shortly thereafter, a local grand jury returned five indictments against petitioner, a 27-year-old Negro, for commonlaw robbery—an offense punishable in Alabama by death.[a]

Before the matter came to trial, the court determined that petitioner was indigent and appointed counsel to represent him. Three days later, at his arraignment, petitioner pleaded guilty to all five indictments. So far as the record shows, the judge asked no questions of petitioner concerning his plea, and petitioner did not address the court.

Trial strategy may of course make a plea of guilty seem the desirable course. But the record is wholly silent on that point and throws no light on it.

Alabama provides that when a defendant pleads guilty, "the court must cause the punishment to be determined by a jury" (except where it is required to be fixed by the court) and may "cause witnesses to be examined, to ascertain the character of the offense." In the present case a trial of that dimension was held, the prosecution presenting its case largely through eyewitness testimony. Although counsel for petitioner engaged in cursory cross-examination, petitioner neither testified himself nor presented testimony concerning his character and background. There was nothing to indicate that he had a prior criminal record.

In instructing the jury, the judge stressed that petitioner had pleaded guilty in five cases of robbery, defined as "the felonious taking of money * * * from another against his will * * * by violence or by putting him in fear * * * (carrying) from ten years minimum in the penitentiary to the supreme penalty of death by electrocution." The jury, upon deliberation, found petitioner guilty and sentenced him severally to die on each of the five indictments.

It was error, plain on the face of the record, for the trial judge to accept petitioner's guilty plea without an affirmative showing that it was intelligent and voluntary.

A plea of guilty is more than a confession which admits that the accused did various acts; it is itself a conviction; nothing remains but to give judgment and determine punishment. Admissibility of a confession must be based on a "reliable determination on the voluntariness issue which satisfies the constitutional rights of the defendant." The requirement that the prosecution spread on the record the prerequisites of a valid waiver is no constitutional innovation. In *Carnley v. Cochran*, we dealt with a problem of waiver of the right to counsel, a Sixth Amendment right. We held: "Presuming waiver from a silent record is impermissible. The record must show, or there must be an allegation and evidence which show, that

---

[a] At the time this case was decided, robbery was a capital crime in Alabama. Leonard D. Savitz, *Capital Crimes as Defined in American Statutory Law*, 46 J. CRIM. L. & CRIMINOLOGY 355, 358–59 (1955). Today, robbery is no longer a capital offense in Alabama. *See* ALA. CODE § 13A–5–40 (listing only murder under various aggravating circumstances as a capital offense in Alabama).

an accused was offered counsel but intelligently and understandingly rejected the offer. Anything less is not waiver."

We think that the same standard must be applied to determining whether a guilty plea is voluntarily made. For, as we have said, a plea of guilty is more than an admission of conduct; it is a conviction. Ignorance, incomprehension, coercion, terror, inducements, subtle or blatant threats might be a perfect cover-up of unconstitutionality. * * *

Several federal constitutional rights are involved in a waiver that takes place when a plea of guilty is entered in a state criminal trial. First, is the privilege against compulsory self-incrimination guaranteed by the Fifth Amendment and applicable to the States by reason of the Fourteenth. Second, is the right to trial by jury. Third, is the right to confront one's accusers. We cannot presume a waiver of these three important federal rights from a silent record.

What is at stake for an accused facing death or imprisonment demands the utmost solicitude of which courts are capable in canvassing the matter with the accused to make sure he has a full understanding of what the plea connotes and of its consequence. When the judge discharges that function, he leaves a record adequate for any review that may be later sought, and forestalls the spin-off of collateral proceedings that seek to probe murky memories.

The three dissenting justices in the Alabama Supreme Court stated the law accurately when they concluded that there was reversible error "because the record does not disclose that the defendant voluntarily and understandingly entered his pleas of guilty."

Reversed.

JUSTICE HARLAN, whom JUSTICE BLACK joins, dissenting.

The Court today holds that petitioner Boykin was denied due process of law, and that his robbery convictions must be reversed outright, solely because "the record (is) inadequate to show that petitioner * * * intelligently and knowingly pleaded guilty." * * * [T]he Court does all this at the behest of a petitioner who has never at any time alleged that his guilty plea was involuntary or made without knowledge of the consequences. I cannot possibly subscribe to so bizarre a result. * * *

## HENDERSON V. MORGAN

Supreme Court of the United States
426 U.S. 637, 96 S.Ct. 2253, 49 L.Ed.2d 108 (1976)

JUSTICE STEVENS delivered the opinion of the Court.

The question presented is whether a defendant may enter a voluntary plea of guilty to a charge of second-degree murder without being informed that intent to cause the death of the victim was an element of the offense.

* * * Respondent, having been indicted on a charge of first-degree murder, pleaded guilty to second-degree murder and [in 1965] was sentenced to an indeterminate term of imprisonment of 25 years to life. * * *

In 1970, respondent initiated proceedings * * * seeking to have his conviction vacated on the ground that his plea of guilty was involuntary. * * * He alleged that his guilty plea was involuntary because [among other things] he was not aware * * * that intent to cause death was an element of the offense. * * * [T]he Federal District Court denied relief. The Court of Appeals reversed summarily and directed the District Court "to conduct an evidentiary hearing on the issues raised by petitioner, including whether, at the time of his entry of his guilty plea, he was aware that intent was an essential element of the crime and was advised of the scope of the punishment that might be imposed." * * *

At the conclusion of the hearing, the District Court * * * found that respondent "was not advised by counsel or court, at any time, that an intent to cause the death or a design to effect the death of the victim was an essential element of Murder 2nd degree." On the basis of the latter finding, the District Court held "as a matter of law" that the plea of guilty was involuntary and had to be set aside. This holding was affirmed, without opinion, by the Court of Appeals.

Before addressing the question whether the District Court correctly held the plea invalid as a matter of law, we review some of the facts developed at the evidentiary hearing.

On April 6, 1965, respondent killed Mrs. Ada Francisco in her home. When he was in seventh grade, respondent was committed to the Rome State School for Mental Defectives where he was classified as "retarded." He was released to become a farm laborer and ultimately went to work on Mrs. Francisco's farm. Following an argument, she threatened to return him to state custody. He then decided to abscond. During the night he entered Mrs. Francisco's bedroom with a knife, intending to collect his earned wages before leaving; she awoke, began to scream, and he stabbed her. He took a small amount of money, fled in her car, and became involved in an accident about 80 miles away. The knife was found in the glove compartment of her car. He was promptly arrested and made a statement to the police. He was then 19 years old and substantially below average intelligence.

Respondent was indicted for first-degree murder and arraigned on April 15, 1965. Two concededly competent attorneys were appointed to represent him. The indictment, which charged that he "willfully" stabbed his victim, was read in open court. * * *

Respondent was found competent to stand trial. Defense counsel held a series of conferences with the prosecutors, with the respondent, and with members of his family. The lawyers "thought manslaughter first would satisfy the needs of justice." They therefore endeavored to have the charge reduced to manslaughter, but the prosecution would agree to nothing less than second-degree murder and a minimum sentence of 25 years. The lawyers gave respondent advice about the different sentences which could be imposed for the different offenses, but, as the District Court found, did not explain the required element of intent.

On June 8, 1965, respondent appeared in court with his attorneys and entered a plea of guilty to murder in the second degree in full satisfaction of the first-degree murder charge made in the indictment. In direct colloquy with the trial judge respondent stated that his plea was based on the advice of his attorneys, that he understood he was accused of killing Mrs. Francisco in Fulton County, that he was waiving his right to a jury trial, and that he would be sent to prison. There was no discussion of the elements of the offense of second-degree murder, no indication that the nature of the offense had ever been discussed with respondent, and no reference of any kind to the requirement of intent to cause the death of the victim.

At the sentencing hearing a week later his lawyers made a statement explaining his version of the offense, particularly noting that respondent "meant no harm to that lady" when he entered her room with the knife. The prosecutor disputed defense counsel's version of the matter, but did not discuss it in detail. After studying the probation officer's report, the trial judge pronounced sentence.

At the evidentiary hearing in the Federal District Court, respondent testified that he would not have pleaded guilty if he had known that an intent to cause the death of his victim was an element of the offense of second-degree murder.

* * * [A] plea cannot support a judgment of guilt unless it was voluntary in a constitutional sense. And clearly the plea could not be voluntary in the sense that it constituted an intelligent admission that he committed the offense unless the defendant received "real notice of the true nature of the charge against him, the first and most universally recognized requirement of due process."

The charge of second-degree murder was never formally made. Had it been made, it necessarily would have included a charge that respondent's assault was "committed with a design to effect the death of the person killed." * * * [A]n admission by respondent that he killed Mrs. Francisco does not necessarily also admit that he was guilty of second-degree murder.

There is nothing in this record that can serve as a substitute for either a finding after trial, or a voluntary admission, that respondent had the requisite intent. Defense counsel did not purport to stipulate to that fact; they did not explain to him that his plea would be an admission of that fact; and he made no factual statement or admission necessarily implying that he had such intent. In these circumstances it is impossible to conclude that his plea to the unexplained charge of second-degree murder was voluntary.

Petitioner argues that affirmance of the Court of Appeals will invite countless collateral attacks on judgments entered on pleas of guilty, since frequently the record will not contain a complete enumeration of the elements of the offense to which an accused person pleads guilty.[18] We think petitioner's fears are exaggerated.

Normally the record contains either an explanation of the charge by the trial judge, or at least a representation by defense counsel that the nature of the offense has been explained to the accused. Moreover, even without such an express representation, it may be appropriate to presume that in most cases defense counsel routinely explain the nature of the offense in sufficient detail to give the accused notice of what he is being asked to admit. This case is unique because the trial judge found as a fact that the element of intent was not explained to respondent. Moreover, respondent's unusually low mental capacity provides a reasonable explanation for counsel's oversight; it also forecloses the conclusion that the error was harmless beyond a reasonable doubt, for it lends at least a modicum of credibility to defense counsel's appraisal of the homicide as a manslaughter rather than a murder.

Since respondent did not receive adequate notice of the offense to which he pleaded guilty, his plea was involuntary and the judgment of conviction was entered without due process of law.

*Affirmed.*

JUSTICE REHNQUIST, with whom THE CHIEF JUSTICE joins, dissenting. * * *

Respondent was originally indicted for the crime of first-degree murder, and that indictment charged that in April 1965, he had "willfully,

---

[18] There is no need in this case to decide whether notice of the true nature, or substance, of a charge always requires a description of every element of the offense; we assume it does not. Nevertheless, intent is such a critical element of the offense of second-degree murder that notice of that element is required.

feloniously and of malice aforethought, stabbed and cut Ada Francisco with a dangerous knife . . . and that thereafter . . . the said Ada Francisco died of said wounds and injuries, said killing being inexcusable and unjustifiable." Respondent's attorney at the habeas hearing testified that respondent had stabbed his victim "many times" which suggests that experienced counsel would not consider the "design to effect death" issue to be in serious dispute. The habeas judge, in deciding that there was a factual basis for the entry of the plea, took much the same approach when he observed:

> The Court: Well the intent, I think there is a factual basis from the evidence where it, that is the jury would have a right to infer on the mere fact, I think when he hit her first and then used the knife, that there were multiple knife wounds, that the jury could infer, and as a matter of fact, I think from those same facts the Judge would have to permit the jury to decide as a question of fact whether there was premeditation on first degree murder, so that this man was a long way short of being out of the woods.

> So I am satisfied that there was a factual basis for the entry of the plea.

I do not see how this Court, or any court, could conclude on this state of the record that respondent was not "properly advised" at the time he entered his plea of guilty to the charge of second-degree murder.

His attorneys were motivated by the eminently reasonable tactical judgment on their part that he should plead guilty to second-degree murder in order to avoid the possibility of conviction for first-degree murder with its more serious attendant penalties. Since the Court concedes both the competence of respondent's counsel and the wisdom of their advice, that should be the end of the matter. * * *

[JUSTICE WHITE's concurring opinion has been omitted.]

## NORTH CAROLINA V. ALFORD

Supreme Court of the United States
400 U.S. 25, 91 S.Ct. 160, 27 L.Ed.2d 162 (1970)

JUSTICE WHITE delivered the opinion of the Court.

On December 2, 1963, Alford was indicted for first-degree murder, a capital offense under North Carolina law. The court appointed an attorney to represent him, and this attorney questioned all but one of the various witnesses who appellee said would substantiate his claim of innocence. The witnesses, however, did not support Alford's story but gave statements that strongly indicated his guilt. Faced with strong evidence of guilt and no substantial evidentiary support for the claim of innocence. Alford's attorney recommended that he plead guilty, but left the ultimate decision to Alford himself. The prosecutor agreed to accept a plea of guilty to a charge of second-degree murder, and on December 10, 1963, Alford pleaded guilty to the reduced charge.

Before the plea was finally accepted by the trial court, the court heard the sworn testimony of a police officer who summarized the State's case. Two other witnesses besides Alford were also heard. Although there was no eyewitness to the crime, the testimony indicated that shortly before the killing Alford took his gun from his house, stated his intention to kill the victim, and returned home with the declaration that he had carried out the killing. After the summary presentation of the State's case, Alford took the stand and testified that he had not committed the murder but that he was pleading guilty because he faced the threat of the death penalty if he did not do so.[1] In response to the questions of his counsel, he acknowledged that his counsel had informed him of the difference between second-and first-degree murder and of his rights in case he chose to go to trial. The trial court then asked appellee if, in light of his denial of guilt, he still desired to plead guilty to second-degree murder and appellee answered, "Yes, sir. I plead guilty on—from the circumstances that he (Alford's attorney) told me." After eliciting information about Alford's prior criminal record, which was a long one, the trial court sentenced him to 30 years' imprisonment, the maximum penalty for second-degree murder.

Alford sought post-conviction relief in the state court. Among the claims raised was the claim that his plea of guilty was invalid because it was the product of fear and coercion. After a hearing, the state court in 1965 found that the plea was "willingly, knowingly, and understandingly" made on the advice of competent counsel and in the face of a strong prosecution case. * * * On appeal, a divided panel of the Court of Appeals for the Fourth Circuit reversed on the ground that Alford's guilty plea was made involuntarily. * * * [T]he Court of Appeals ruled that Alford's guilty

---

[1]   After giving his version of the events of the night of the murder, Alford stated:

I pleaded guilty on second degree murder because they said there is too much evidence, but I ain't shot no man, but I take the fault for the other man. We never had an argument in our life and I just pleaded guilty because they said if I didn't they would gas me for it, and that is all.

In response to questions from his attorney, Alford affirmed that he had consulted several times with his attorney and with members of his family and had been informed of his rights if he chose to plead not guilty. Alford then reaffirmed his decision to plead guilty to second-degree murder:

Q. (by Alford's attorney). And you authorized me to tender a plea of guilty to second degree murder before the court?

A. Yes, sir.

Q. And in doing that, that you have again affirmed your decision on that point?

A. Well, I'm still pleading that you all got me to plead guilty. I plead the other way, circumstantial evidence; that the jury will prosecute me on—on the second. You told me to plead guilty, right. I don't—I'm not guilty but I plead guilty.

plea was involuntary because its principal motivation was fear of the death penalty. * * *

We held in *Brady v. United States*, that a plea of guilty which would not have been entered except for the defendant's desire to avoid a possible death penalty and to limit the maximum penalty to life imprisonment or a term of years was not for that reason compelled. * * * The standard was and remains whether the plea represents a voluntary and intelligent choice among the alternative courses of action open to the defendant. That he would not have pleaded except for the opportunity to limit the possible penalty does not necessarily demonstrate that the plea of guilty was not the product of a free and rational choice, especially where the defendant was represented by competent counsel whose advice was that the plea would be to the defendant's advantage. The standard fashioned and applied by the Court of Appeals was therefore erroneous and we would, without more, vacate and remand the case for further proceedings with respect to any other claims of Alford which are properly before that court, if it were not for other circumstances appearing in the record which might seem to warrant an affirmance of the Court of Appeals.

As previously recounted, after Alford's plea of guilty was offered and the State's case was placed before the judge, Alford denied that he had committed the murder but reaffirmed his desire to plead guilty to avoid a possible death sentence and to limit the penalty to the 30-year maximum provided for second-degree murder. Ordinarily, a judgment of conviction resting on a plea of guilty is justified by the defendant's admission that he committed the crime charged against him and his consent that judgment be entered without a trial of any kind. The plea usually subsumes both elements, and justifiably so, even though there is no separate, express admission by the defendant that he committed the particular acts claimed to constitute the crime charged in the indictment. Here Alford entered his plea but accompanied it with the statement that he had not shot the victim.

If Alford's statements were to be credited as sincere assertions of his innocence, there obviously existed a factual and legal dispute between him and the State. Without more, it might be argued that the conviction entered on his guilty plea was invalid, since his assertion of innocence negatived any admission of guilt, which, as we observed last Term in *Brady*, is normally "[c]entral to the plea and the foundation for entering judgment against the defendant." * * *

State and lower federal courts are divided upon whether a guilty plea can be accepted when it is accompanied by protestations of innocence and hence contains only a waiver of trial but no admission of guilt. Some courts, giving expression to the principle that "[o]ur law only authorizes a conviction where guilt is shown," require that trial judges reject such pleas. But others have concluded that * * * "[a]n accused, though believing in or entertaining doubts respecting his innocence, might reasonably conclude a jury would be convinced of his guilt and that he would fare better in the sentence by pleading guilty."

* * * The fact that [Alford's] plea was denominated a plea of guilty rather than a plea of nolo contendere is of no constitutional significance with respect to the issue now before us, for the Constitution is concerned with the practical consequences, not the formal categorizations, of state law. Thus, while most pleas of guilty consist of both a waiver of trial and an express admission of guilt, the latter element is not a constitutional requisite to the imposition of criminal penalty. An individual accused of crime may voluntarily, knowingly, and understandingly consent to the imposition of a prison sentence even if he is unwilling or unable to admit his participation in the acts constituting the crime.

Nor can we perceive any material difference between a plea that refuses to admit commission of the criminal act and a plea containing a protestation of innocence when, as in the instant case, a defendant intelligently concludes that his interests require entry of a guilty plea and the record before the judge contains strong evidence of actual guilt. Here the State had a strong case of first-degree murder against Alford. Whether he realized or disbelieved his guilt, he insisted on his plea because in his view he had absolutely nothing to gain by a trial and much to gain by pleading. Because of the overwhelming evidence against him, a trial was precisely what neither Alford nor his attorney desired. Confronted with the choice between a trial for first-degree murder, on the one hand, and a plea of guilty to second-degree murder, on the other, Alford quite reasonably chose the latter and thereby limited the maximum penalty to a 30-year term. When his plea is viewed in light of the evidence against him, which substantially negated his claim of innocence and which further provided a means by which the judge could test whether the plea was being intelligently entered, its validity cannot be seriously questioned. In view of the strong factual basis for the plea demonstrated by the State and Alford's clearly expressed desire to enter it despite his professed belief in his innocence, we hold that the trial judge did not commit constitutional error in accepting it. * * *

The Court of Appeals for the Fourth Circuit was in error to find Alford's plea of guilty invalid because it was made to avoid the possibility of the death penalty. That court's judgment directing the issuance of the writ of habeas corpus is vacated and the case is remanded to the Court of Appeals for further proceedings consistent with this opinion.

It is so ordered.

Vacated and remanded.

JUSTICE BRENNAN, with whom JUSTICE DOUGLAS and JUSTICE MARSHALL join, dissenting.

Last Term, this Court held, over my dissent, that a plea of guilty may validly be induced by an unconstitutional threat to subject the defendant to the risk to death, so long as the plea is entered in open court and the defendant is represented by competent counsel who is aware of the threat, albeit not of its unconstitutionality. Today the Court makes clear that its previous holding was intended to apply even when the record demonstrates that the actual effect of the unconstitutional threat was to induce a guilty plea from a defendant who was unwilling to admit his guilt.

I adhere to the view that, in any given case, the influence of such an unconstitutional threat "must necessarily be given weight in determining the voluntariness of a plea." And, without reaching the question whether due process permits the entry of judgment upon a plea of guilty accompanied by a contemporaneous denial of acts constituting the crime, I believe that at the very least such a denial of guilt is also a relevant factor in determining whether the plea was voluntarily and intelligently made. With these factors in mind, it is sufficient in my view to state that the facts set out in the majority opinion demonstrate that Alford was "so gripped by fear of the death penalty" that his decision to plead guilty was not voluntary but was "the product of duress as much so as choice reflecting physical constraint." Accordingly, I would affirm the judgment of the Court of Appeals.

[JUSTICE BLACK's concurring opinion has been omitted.]

## NOTE

*North Carolina v. Alford* illustrates the dilemma that a trial court judge faces when a defendant pleads guilty while protesting his innocence. Such pleas are called *Alford* pleas. The ruling in *Alford* has been understood to require a strong factual basis supporting the entry of a judgment of conviction whenever a defendant claims to be innocent of the crime to which he is pleading guilty. In such cases, the record before the judge must contain "strong evidence of actual guilt" demonstrated by the State.

Apart from the unique circumstances of an *Alford* plea, a factual basis for a guilty plea is not constitutionally required even though it may be required as a matter of statute or rule of criminal procedure. *See, e.g.,* Rule 11(b)(3) of the Federal Rule of Criminal Procedure (requiring federal trial judges to satisfy themselves that there is a factual basis for a defendant's guilty plea before accepting defendant's plea and entering judgment).

### THE ADVENT OF THE "VANISHING TRIAL": WHY TRIALS MATTER

John W. Keker
29–Oct Champion 32 (2005)

"The Vanishing Trial" has everyone's attention. That trials are increasingly an oddity is certain. One study found that in 2002, only 0.6 percent of civil cases filed went to trial, down from 1.8 percent in 1976. Data for criminal jury trials is just as extreme.

* * * Sustained now by the two most powerful courtroom patrons, [*i.e.*, judges and prosecutors], plea bargaining [has become] the dominant force in criminal procedure. * * *

No one puts it more bluntly than Chief Judge Young of Boston in *United States v. Green*:

> The Department [of Justice] is so addicted to plea bargaining to leverage its law enforcement resources to an overwhelming conviction rate that the focus of our entire criminal justice system has shifted far away from trials and juries and adjudication to a massive system of sentence bargaining that is heavily rigged against the accused citizen. * * *

So who cares if we are trying fewer cases? * * *

The first reason why trials matter is that more defendants would get off, which after all is our job. Try more cases, win more cases. Most acquittals occur because the prosecution makes a mistake, either in bringing the case or during trial of the case. Taking even "unwinnable" cases to trial often leads to surprising results. * * *

But * * * there are other equally important reasons we should try more cases, and challenge the government more. Probably the most obvious reason why trials matter is that without trials the law will not develop: trials provide the meat for appellate decisions. * * *

Judge Patrick Higginbotham gave a speech entitled "So Why Do We Still Call Them Trial Courts?" It is a good question. He concluded:

> Ultimately, law unenforced by courts is no law. We need trials, and a steady stream of them, to ground our normative standards—to make them sufficiently clear that persons can abide by them in planning their affairs—and never face the courthouse—the ultimate settlement. Trials reduce disputes, and it is a profound mistake to view a trial as a failure of the system. A well conducted trial is its crowning achievement.

Guilty pleas, on the other hand, create either no law, or bad law. * * * We have people pleading guilty to crimes they weren't aware they committed, in order to avoid the draconian penalty for going to trial. * * *

Our system of justice demands trials to work. We have a "battle model" of justice. Sometimes it leans towards "due process," as in the Warren Court years, and at other times it leans towards "efficiency," as it has under Chief Justices Burger and Rehnquist. But at heart the system is based on battle, usually called, in the quaint way of the English, "the adversarial system." It works on the premise that conflict and contradiction is the way to truth. * * *

Our prosecutors are trained to represent the state in the battle model. In our system, they need resisting, they need to be kept honest—indeed, in my opinion, they need to be kept humble. The only thing defense lawyers have to keep prosecutors in check is the threat that we will embarrass them by winning at trial. If they know we won't go to trial, we have nothing. One SEC lawyer told a colleague that the SEC in the old days would not bring a case unless it had at least a 70 percent chance of winning. Now, he said, SEC lawyers bring marginal cases if they think they have a 30 percent chance of winning, because they know their cases will settle without a trial.

Without trials, the jury system will atrophy; citizens will forget how to be jurors, forget that the government can be wrong. Jurors are already showing signs of forgetting. After several recent high profile white collar cases, jurors explained their guilty verdicts not with evidence or by the burden of proof but with speculation about what the defendant "must have known." Prosecutors urge them to substitute "common sense" for proof. This development, if it continues, is serious, not just to the legal system, but to democracy itself. * * *

Other countries find it simply astonishing that citizen jurors, not judges, decide who is guilty and who is not guilty. What they don't get is that it is not so much that jurors make great decisions, rather it is that they are not judges. Judges are bureaucrats, part of the system. As G. K. Chesterton said:

> The horrible thing about all legal officials, even the best . . . is not that they are wicked . . . not that they are stupid . . . it is simply that they have got used to it.

A little appreciated aspect of the Supreme Court's *Booker* decision is that it and its predecessors *Blakely*, *Apprendi* and *Ring* represent an increasingly loud endorsement by at least the conservative block of the importance of jury trials. For example, in *Blakely v. Washington*, the Court said the right to trial by jury "is no mere procedural formality, but a fundamental reservation of power in our constitutional structure. Just as suffrage ensures the people's ultimate control in the legislative and executive branches, jury trial is meant to ensure their control in the judiciary." * * *

Another virtue of trials over pleas is that trials are public, while most of what goes into a plea is not. The Rule 11 recital is ritual, not substance.

Someday during a plea I will do something I have always wanted to do. When the judge asks, "Have any promises or threats been made to you other than those recited here?" I will burst out laughing when the defendant answers as instructed. The honest answer is always "I am pleading guilty because I understand if I go to trial and lose you will give me four times the sentence, and that scares the [expletive] out of me."

Trials let light into the process, helping keep prosecutors honest, cops more honest, judges in check. Guilty pleas and deals occur behind closed doors, away from public scrutiny, where, as Lord Acton warned: "Everything secret degenerates, even the administration of justice." * * *

The last reason why trials matter, the one most dear to me, is that only frequent trials will guarantee the survival of the warrior class: defense counsel. Being a real, *i.e.*, adversarial, defense lawyer is hard. Fear stalks you. Before the trial starts in a tough case, we all feel like the guy who whines "Mom, I don't want to go to school today." His mother asks him "Why?" "The kids aren't nice to me and they all hate me." His mother says, "Well, you have to go to school." He says "Why?" She says, "Because you are 45 years old and the principal."

Trials are nasty and, yes, confrontational. You cannot try a case without suspecting the motives, even the integrity, of your opponent. The horror of defeat looms large. Opposing the government can be terrifying, particularly when you are friendly with, and probably belong to, the same associations as the prosecutors and the judges. Many of us can confront our enemies; few can stand the obloquy of friends. * * *

It takes courage to try difficult cases, ones we will probably lose. Recently in San Francisco two terrific young federal public defenders, Shawn Halbert and Rebecca Sullivan, tried a case I admired greatly. Their client was charged with illegal entry into the United States from Mexico. He had already pleaded guilty to the same offense twice before. It was a tough case, with a guideline range of 120–150 months. After some digging, Shawn and Rebecca figured out that their client had no idea where he was born (isn't our birth always a matter of hearsay) but that family members in Mexico believed it possible that the defendant's mother had been in the United States (illegally) at the time he was born. If that were true, he would be innocent. If there were a reasonable doubt about that, he deserved an acquittal. Unfortunately the jury found it less compelling than I did, and he was convicted. But the point is they tried the case, and made a real run of it.

Another personal example of why trials matter, and why defense lawyers should try more cases, arises out of the prosecution of my friend Patrick Hallinan. Patrick is a noted defense lawyer in San Francisco who my partner Jan Little and I defended on RICO, conspiracy and obstruction charges in federal court in Reno, Nevada. A Federal Drug task force there had been rolling up drug smugglers by means of "we will go light on you if you give us the next guy" for years. Scores of people had pled guilty. Hallinan represented one of the kingpins for a while, finally made a deal for him, and turned him over to the task force. The drug kingpin, having nowhere up to point, decided to offer the task force his defense lawyer and Patrick was indicted. These prosecutors had not tried a real case for years. They had forgotten how to evaluate a witness, they had forgotten what juries thought of the deals they made, and they had forgotten how offensive their tactics were. Patrick's trial, closely watched by the press, monitored by a stern, even-handed judge, was a debacle for prosecutors, as one witness after another was exposed as a lying dog. It took the jury just a few hours to acquit Patrick. But on paper, *i.e.*, reading the DEA's 6 reports, he never had a chance. * * *

# CHAPTER 28

# THE RIGHT TO TRIAL BY JURY

■ ■ ■

The Sixth Amendment to the U.S. Constitution provides in relevant part:

> In all criminal prosecutions, the accused shall enjoy the right to a speedy and public trial, by an impartial jury of the State and district wherein the crime shall have been committed. . . .

In *Duncan v. Louisiana*, 391 U.S. 145 (1968), the Court held that the Sixth Amendment right to trial by jury in criminal cases is "fundamental to the American scheme of justice" and thus is applicable to the states through the Due Process Clause of the Fourteenth Amendment. This means there is a right to a jury trial in both federal and state court. *Blanton v. City of North Las Vegas* examines whether this right to a jury trial applies to all criminal defendants. *Burch v. Louisiana* focuses on the number of persons who must serve on a criminal jury and whether and when a unanimous jury verdict is required. To help you think about the pros and cons of unanimous verdicts, this chapter includes an excerpt from Kim Taylor Thompson's law review article, *Empty Votes in Jury Deliberation*, which suggests ways in which unanimous verdicts help protect the voices of racial minority and female jurors. *Singer v. United States* examines whether federal criminal defendants can unilaterally waive their right to a jury trial.

The remaining cases in this chapter explore race and gender considerations in the selection of jurors. In *Taylor v. Louisiana*, the Court examines the constitutionality of systematically excluding women from jury service. *Turner v. Murray* focuses on whether and when a criminal defendant has the right to question prospective jurors on racial bias. *Batson v. Kentucky* and *J.E.B. v. Alabama* address race and gender discrimination in the selection of the petit jury.

## BLANTON V. CITY OF NORTH LAS VEGAS

Supreme Court of the United States
489 U.S. 538, 109 S.Ct. 1289, 103 L.Ed.2d 550 (1989)

JUSTICE MARSHALL delivered the opinion of the Court.

The issue in this case is whether there is a constitutional right to a trial by jury for persons charged under Nevada law with driving under the influence of alcohol (DUI). We hold that there is not.

DUI is punishable by a minimum term of two days' imprisonment and a maximum term of six months' imprisonment. Alternatively, a trial court may order the defendant "to perform 48 hours of work for the community while dressed in distinctive garb which identifies him as [a DUI offender]." The defendant also must pay a fine ranging from $200 to $1,000. In addition, the defendant automatically loses his driver's license for 90 days, and he must attend, at his own expense, an alcohol abuse education course. Repeat DUI offenders are subject to increased penalties.

Petitioners Melvin R. Blanton and Mark D. Fraley were charged with DUI in separate incidents. Neither petitioner had a prior DUI conviction. The North Las Vegas, Nevada, Municipal Court denied their respective pretrial demands for a jury trial. * * * We granted certiorari to consider whether petitioners were entitled to a jury trial, and now affirm.

It has long been settled that "there is a category of petty crimes or offenses which is not subject to the Sixth Amendment jury trial provision." In determining whether a particular offense should be categorized as "petty," our early decisions focused on the nature of the offense and on whether it was triable by a jury at common law. In recent years, however, we have sought more "objective indications of the seriousness with which society regards the offense." "[W]e have found the most relevant such criteria in the severity of the maximum authorized penalty." In fixing the maximum penalty for a crime, a legislature "include[s] within the definition of the crime itself a judgment about the seriousness of the offense." The judiciary should not substitute its judgment as to seriousness for that of a legislature, which is "far better equipped to perform the task, and [is] likewise more responsive to changes in attitude and more amenable to the recognition and correction of their misperceptions in this respect." In using the word "penalty," we do not refer solely to the maximum prison term authorized for a particular offense. A legislature's view of the seriousness of an offense also is reflected in the other penalties that it attaches to the offense. We thus examine "whether the length of the authorized prison term *or the seriousness of other punishment* is enough in itself to require a jury trial." Primary emphasis, however, must be placed on the maximum authorized period of incarceration. Penalties such as probation or a fine may engender "a significant infringement of personal freedom," but they cannot approximate in severity the loss of liberty that a prison term entails. Indeed, because incarceration is an "intrinsically different" form of punishment, it is the most powerful indication whether an offense is "serious."

Following this approach, our decision in *Baldwin* established that a defendant is entitled to a jury trial whenever the offense for which he is charged carries a maximum authorized prison term of greater than six months. The possibility of a sentence exceeding six months, we determined, is "sufficiently severe by itself" to require the opportunity for a jury trial. As for a prison term of six months or less, we recognized that it will seldom be viewed by the defendant as "trivial or petty." But we found that the disadvantages of such a sentence, "onerous though they may be, may be outweighed by the benefits that result from speedy and inexpensive nonjury adjudications."

Although we did not hold in *Baldwin* that an offense carrying a maximum prison term of six months or less automatically qualifies as a "petty" offense, and decline to do so today, we do find it appropriate to presume for purposes of the Sixth Amendment that society views such an offense as "petty." A defendant is entitled to a jury trial in such circumstances only if he can demonstrate that any additional statutory penalties, viewed in conjunction with the maximum authorized period of incarceration, are so severe that they clearly reflect a legislative determination that the offense in question is a "serious" one. This standard, albeit somewhat imprecise, should ensure the availability of a jury trial in the rare situation where a legislature packs an offense it deems "serious" with onerous penalties that nonetheless "do not puncture the 6-month incarceration line."

Applying these principles here, it is apparent that petitioners are not entitled to a jury trial. The maximum authorized prison sentence for first-time DUI offenders does not exceed six months. A presumption therefore exists that the Nevada Legislature views DUI as a "petty" offense for purposes of the Sixth Amendment. Considering the additional statutory penalties as well, we do not believe that the Nevada Legislature has clearly indicated that DUI is a "serious" offense.

In the first place, it is immaterial that a first-time DUI offender may face a minimum term of imprisonment. In settling on six months' imprisonment as the constitutional demarcation point, we have assumed that a defendant convicted of the offense in question would receive the *maximum* authorized prison sentence. It is not constitutionally determinative, therefore, that a particular defendant may be required to serve some amount of jail time *less* than six months. Likewise, it is of little moment that a defendant may receive the maximum prison term because of the prohibitions on plea bargaining and probation. As for the 90-day license suspension, it, too, will be irrelevant if it runs concurrently with the prison sentence, which we assume for present purposes to be the maximum of six months.

We are also unpersuaded by the fact that, instead of a prison sentence, a DUI offender may be ordered to perform 48 hours of community service dressed in clothing identifying him as a DUI offender. Even assuming the outfit is the source of some embarrassment during the 48-hour period, such a penalty will be less embarrassing and less onerous than six months in jail. As for the possible $1,000 fine, it is well below the $5,000 level set by Congress in its most recent definition of a "petty" offense, and petitioners do not suggest that this congressional figure is out of step with state practice for offenses carrying prison sentences of six months or less. Finally, we ascribe little significance to the fact that a DUI offender faces increased penalties for repeat offenses. Recidivist penalties of the magnitude imposed for DUI are commonplace and, in any event, petitioners do not face such penalties here.

Viewed together, the statutory penalties are not so severe that DUI must be deemed a "serious" offense for purposes of the Sixth Amendment. It was not error, therefore, to deny petitioners jury trials. Accordingly, the judgment of the Supreme Court of Nevada is

*Affirmed.*

### NOTE

What if a defendant is charged with multiple petty offenses and the maximum authorized penalty for all of the offenses added together would exceed 6 months if served consecutively? Would such a defendant have a right to a jury trial? In *Lewis v. United States*, 518 U.S. 322 (1996), the Supreme Court answered this question in the negative, holding there is no Sixth Amendment right to a trial by jury unless the defendant is charged with at least one non-petty offense.

### BURCH V. LOUISIANA
Supreme Court of the United States
441 U.S. 130, 99 S.Ct. 1623, 60 L.Ed.2d 96 (1979)

JUSTICE REHNQUIST delivered the opinion of the Court.

The Louisiana Constitution and Code of Criminal Procedure provide that criminal cases in which the punishment imposed may be confinement for a period in excess of six months "shall be tried before a jury of six persons, five of whom must concur to render a verdict." We granted certiorari to decide whether conviction by a nonunanimous six-person jury in a state criminal trial for a nonpetty offense as contemplated by these provisions of Louisiana law violates the rights of an accused to trial by jury guaranteed by the Sixth and Fourteenth Amendments.

Petitioners, an individual and a Louisiana corporation, were jointly charged in two counts with the exhibition of two obscene motion pictures. Pursuant to Louisiana law, they were tried before a six-person jury, which found both petitioners guilty as charged. A poll of the jury after verdict indicated that the jury had voted unanimously to convict petitioner Wrestle, Inc., and had voted 5–1 to convict petitioner Burch. Burch was sentenced to two consecutive 7-month prison terms, which were suspended, and fined $1,000; Wrestle, Inc., was fined $600 on each count.

Petitioners appealed their convictions to the Supreme Court of Louisiana, where they argued that the provisions of Louisiana law permitting conviction by a nonunanimous six-member jury violated the rights of persons accused of nonpetty criminal offenses to trial by jury guaranteed by the Sixth and Fourteenth Amendments. Though acknowledging that the issue was "close," the court held that conviction by a nonunanimous six-person jury did not offend the Constitution. * * *

We agree with the Louisiana Supreme Court that the question presented is a "close" one. Nonetheless, we believe that conviction by a nonunanimous six-member jury in a state criminal trial for a nonpetty offense deprives an accused of his constitutional right to trial by jury. Only in relatively recent years has this Court had to consider the practices of the several States relating to jury size and unanimity. *Duncan v. Louisiana* marked the beginning of our involvement with such questions. The Court in *Duncan* held that because trial by jury in "serious" criminal cases is "fundamental to the American scheme of justice" and essential to due process of law, the Fourteenth Amendment guarantees a state criminal defendant the right to a jury trial in any case which, if tried in a federal court, would require a jury under the Sixth Amendment.

Two Terms later in *Williams v. Florida*, the Court held that this constitutional guarantee of trial by jury did not require a State to provide an accused with a jury of 12 members and that Florida did not violate the jury trial rights of criminal defendants charged with nonpetty offenses by affording them jury panels comprised of only 6 persons. After canvassing the common-law development of the jury and the constitutional history of the jury trial right, the Court concluded that the 12-person requirement was "a historical accident" and that there was no indication that the Framers intended to preserve in the Constitution the features of the jury system as it existed at common law. Thus freed from strictly historical considerations, the Court turned to examine the function that this particular feature performs and its relation to the purposes of jury trial. The purpose of trial by jury, as noted in *Duncan*, is to prevent government oppression by providing a "safeguard against the corrupt or overzealous prosecutor and against the compliant, biased, or eccentric judge." Given this purpose, the *Williams* Court observed that the jury's essential feature lies in the "interposition between the accused and his accuser of the commonsense judgment of a group of laymen, and in the community participation and shared responsibility that results from that group's determination of guilt or innocence." These purposes could be fulfilled, the Court believed, so long as the jury was of a sufficient size to promote group deliberation, free from outside intimidation, and to provide a fair possibility that a cross section of the community would be represented on it. The Court concluded, however, that there is "little reason to think that these goals are in any meaningful sense less likely to be achieved when the jury numbers six, than when it numbers 12—particularly if the requirement of unanimity is retained."

A similar analysis led us to conclude in 1972 that a jury's verdict need not be unanimous to satisfy constitutional requirements, even though unanimity had been the rule at common law. Thus, in *Apodaca v. Oregon*, we upheld a state statute providing that only 10 members of a 12-person jury need concur to render a verdict in certain noncapital cases. In terms of the role of the jury as a safeguard against oppression, the plurality opinion perceived no difference between those juries required to act unanimously and those permitted to act by votes of 10 to 2. Nor was unanimity viewed by the plurality as contributing materially to the exercise of the jury's common-sense judgment or as a necessary precondition to effective application of the requirement that jury panels represent a fair cross section of the community.

Last Term, in *Ballew v. Georgia*, we considered whether a jury of less than six members passes constitutional scrutiny, a question that was explicitly reserved in *Williams v. Florida*. The Court, in separate opinions, held that conviction by a unanimous five-person jury in a trial for a nonpetty offense deprives an accused of his right to trial by jury. While readily admitting that the line between six members and five was not altogether easy to justify, at least five Members of the Court believed that reducing a jury to five persons in nonpetty cases raised sufficiently substantial doubts as to the fairness of the proceeding and proper functioning of the jury to warrant drawing the line at six.

We thus have held that the Constitution permits juries of less than 12 members, but that it requires at least 6. And we have approved the use of certain nonunanimous verdicts in cases involving 12-person juries. These principles are not questioned here. Rather, this case lies at the intersection of our decisions concerning jury size and unanimity. * * * [W]e do not pretend the ability to discern a priori a bright line below which the number of jurors participating in the trial or in the verdict would not permit the jury to function in the manner required by our prior cases. But having already departed from the strictly historical requirements of jury trial, it is inevitable that lines must be drawn somewhere if the substance of the jury trial right is to be preserved. * * * [M]uch the same reasons that led us in *Ballew* to decide that use of a five-member jury threatened the fairness of the proceeding and the proper role of the jury, lead us to conclude now that conviction for a nonpetty offense by only five members of a six-person jury presents a similar threat to preservation of the substance of the jury trial guarantee and justifies our requiring verdicts rendered by six-person juries to be unanimous. We are buttressed in this view by the current jury practices of the several States. It appears that of those States that utilize six-member juries in trials of nonpetty offenses, only two, including Louisiana, also allow nonunanimous verdicts. We think that this near-uniform judgment of the Nation provides a useful guide in delimiting the line between those jury practices that are constitutionally permissible and those that are not.

The State seeks to justify its use of nonunanimous six-person juries on the basis of the "considerable time" savings that it claims results from trying cases in this manner. It asserts that under its system, juror deliberation time is shortened and the number of hung juries is reduced. Undoubtedly, the State has a substantial interest in reducing the time and expense associated with the administration of its system of criminal justice. But that interest cannot prevail here. First, on this record, any benefits that might accrue by allowing five members of a six-person jury to render a verdict, as compared with requiring unanimity of a six-member jury, are speculative, at best. More importantly, we think that when a State has reduced the size of its juries to the minimum number of jurors permitted by the Constitution, the additional authorization of nonunanimous verdicts by such juries sufficiently threatens the constitutional principles that led to the establishment of the size threshold that any countervailing interest of the State should yield.

The judgment of the Louisiana Supreme Court affirming the conviction of petitioner Burch is, therefore, reversed, and its judgment affirming the conviction of petitioner Wrestle, Inc., is affirmed. The case is remanded to the Louisiana Supreme Court for proceedings not inconsistent with this opinion.

*It is so ordered.*

[JUSTICE STEVENS' concurring opinion and JUSTICE BRENNAN's opinion, concurring in part and dissenting in part, have been omitted.]

## *NOTE*

Despite the fact that non-unanimous verdicts and 6 person juries are permitted in state court, criminal defendants in federal court must be tried before a 12 person jury and the criminal jury's verdict must be unanimous. *See* FED. R. OF CRIM. P. 23, 31.

## EMPTY VOTES IN JURY DELIBERATIONS

Kim Taylor-Thompson
113 Harv. L. Rev. 1261 (2000)

For much of the past quarter-century, courts and legal scholars have devised various strategies to combat the exclusion of people of color and women from juries. Animating this effort has been the belief that to deny access to jury service based on an individual's heritage or gender offends core democratic principles. The Supreme Court has outlawed the wholesale exclusion of members of protected groups and has similarly disapproved procedural devices that function as barriers to full participation of members of these groups. For the most part, courts and litigants have tried to follow these rules. Yet the complexion and composition of juries have barely changed. Juries remain overwhelmingly white and male.

Scholars have clashed over the causes of this lack of diversity. Some blame race-and gender-based peremptory strikes exercised during voir dire. Many of these scholars applaud the Supreme Court's requirements of closer scrutiny of peremptory challenges excluding people of color and women. Others dispute the efficacy of prohibiting such strikes, observing that courts routinely accept lawyers' pretextual reasons for removing members of commonly targeted groups. * * *

But the picture is incomplete. Peremptory challenges may not be the only cause for concern. Another phenomenon within the jury box threatens quietly—but effectively—to deprive individuals with diverse views who actually serve on juries from exercising any real voting power. This phenomenon is the emerging acceptance of nonunanimous verdicts in criminal cases, in which ten or sometimes nine of twelve jurors are permitted to issue the verdict. The picture becomes all the more complex because, on the surface, majority rule voting seems innocuous enough. Advocates of nonunanimous voting almost reflexively equate majority rule with democracy. But for all its appearance of fairness, nonunanimous voting in this setting tends to inhibit inclusion. Jury research conducted in the past two decades reveals that eliminating the obligation to secure each person's agreement on the verdict can result in truncating or even eliminating jury deliberations. By discouraging meaningful examination of opposing viewpoints, majority rule decisionmaking impoverishes deliberations.

But an even more basic and fractious consequence looms. Nonunanimous decisionmaking in criminal trials could jeopardize the limited victories that historically excluded groups have won in cases challenging barriers to jury service. If—as is often true—the views of jurors of color and female jurors diverge from the mainstream, nonunanimous decisionmaking rules can operate to eliminate the voice of difference on the jury. Given that people of color tend to form the numerical minority on juries, the majority could ignore minority views by simply outvoting dissenters. Equally troubling is the fact that studies examining the participation rates of women in a group setting, coupled with jury research on the impact of nonunanimous voting, suggest that a majority of jurors could reach a verdict without ever hearing from women on the jury. Thus, despite the simplistic appeal of making the jury system more "democratic," nonunanimity threatens to eliminate the voices of those who have only recently secured the right to participate in the democratic process.

* * * An examination of psychological and social science research suggests that personal background and experience define and in very real ways limit individual perception. An individual's experiences influence her capacity to interpret and evaluate facts and then to make judgments about justice. More particularly, race and gender inform the processes by which individuals make decisions, especially about social justice. Until now the requirement to reach complete consensus has at least provided an impetus to stretch beyond group experiences and loyalties. But the race and gender unconsciousness inherent in majority rule would permit a jury to return a verdict without ever acknowledging or confronting gaps in its interpretation of evidence.

The United States Supreme Court [has] played a role in creating this dilemma. Over two decades ago, the Court issued a pair of decisions holding that the Constitution does not mandate jury-verdict unanimity in state criminal trials.[a] The Court's review of the constitutionality of majority rule showed little appreciation of a possible relationship between this practice and the Court's long history of battling exclusions of groups from the jury process. The Court perceived no dissonance between nonunanimous decisionmaking and the democratic aspirations it had consistently embraced. * * * All of the Justices agreed on the importance of the deliberative process, but they disagreed on the likely impact of an alteration in the voting rule, and particularly the extent to which a minority of jurors can still influence the ultimate decision. Against that backdrop, the Court granted states the opportunity to experiment with majority rule. * * *

In the wake of the Supreme Court's decisions in *Johnson* and *Apodaca*, researchers began to experiment with nonunanimous decision rules. They constructed jury studies to test the assumptions of both the majority and dissenting opinions. Although jury research should perhaps be viewed with some caution, its findings provide necessary insight into the operation of such rules. Indeed, the evidence that jury researchers have amassed directly contravenes the majority opinions' contentions that these decision

---

[a] The author is referring to *Apodaca v. Oregon*, 406 U.S. 404 (1972) (upholding state rule allowing non-unanimous jury verdicts in which 10 out of 12 jurors vote to convict) and *Johnson v. Louisiana*, 406 U.S. 356 (1972) (upholding state rule allowing non-unanimous jury verdicts in which 9 out of 12 jurors vote to convict).

rules have no effect on the reliability of jury decisions. A shift to majority rule appears to alter both the quality of the deliberative process and the accuracy of the jury's judgment. In the end, the data indicates that unanimity assures viewpoint diversity better than majority rule.

The heart of the problem is that nonunanimous decisionmaking constricts the flow of information. Researchers have discovered that once a vote indicates that the required majority has formed, deliberations halt in a matter of minutes. Jury research reveals how rarely juries deliberating under majority rule attain full consensus. In more than seventy percent of the cases in which a majority develops, the jury does not bother reaching consensus. This behavior reduces the amount of information considered by jurors.

* * * Jury research [also] indicates that shorter deliberation leads to less accurate judgments. At first blush, to question the accuracy of the jury's decision in a criminal trial may seem odd. The justice system tends not to expect the jury to discern the objective "truth" about the events at issue. Instead the jury must deliver its evaluation of whether the government has met its burden of proof. Still, empirical research alerts us to the fact that majority rule discourages painstaking analyses of the evidence and steers jurors toward swift judgments that too often are erroneous or at least highly questionable.

In one study individuals called for jury duty were given the opportunity to volunteer to serve on a mock jury. Researchers conducted a mock voir dire, showed participants a film re-enactment of a murder trial, and then divided jurors into groups governed by either unanimity or majority rule. Legal experts evaluating the murder case considered first-degree murder an untenable verdict given the evidence. According to pre-deliberation questionnaires, many individual jurors initially preferred the higher charge. Following deliberations, however, not one unanimous jury returned a first-degree murder verdict—the arguably "incorrect" choice. By contrast, twelve percent of the majority-rule juries reached this result. * * *

These findings should not be surprising. Because the jury's work largely depends on subjective interpretations of evidence, a variety of perspectives will enrich jury discussions. It is true that many facts will be readily apparent to all jurors. For example, in a homicide case, jurors may easily accept medical evidence establishing that the victim sustained a fatal injury on the day in question. But significant questions of guilt or innocence and the degrees of responsibility for conduct often hinge on a juror's personal interpretation of behavior—which other jurors may or may not share. When deciding whether the government has established the requisite mental state for the offense, for instance, the juror often must infer the actor's state of mind from conduct open to numerous interpretations. The juror must also determine whether the actor's conduct is culpable or can instead be justified or excused. And in all cases the juror must determine whether the witnesses are sufficiently credible. Like other members of society, jurors approach these responsibilities with the imperfect yet well-worn assumptions and expectations that guide their everyday evaluations of events. They often have a wide range of views regarding whose word merits trust or distrust.

So open discussion is critical. An individual juror's experience can affect her perception of and reaction to the evidence. As knowledge and expertise may be distributed unequally within any given jury, interaction among jurors will expand the range of issues to be discussed and broaden the scope of information shared by the group. * * * In the end, a deliberative process that emphasizes and maximizes consultation among individual jurors with diverse backgrounds broadens the overall perspective of the jury.

* * * Perhaps more than anywhere else in the legal system, race plays a significant role in the administration of criminal justice. * * * Although the juror of color will not necessarily sympathize with or support the accused, her presence offers the accused the best possible chance that someone in the jury room will understand the accused's world and world views. Because of the pervasiveness of racism, jurors of color, regardless of their socioeconomic position, are likely to have experienced some form of racial subordination that may provide them with a broader conceptual framework for the ensuing discussion in the deliberation room. * * *

Similar concerns arise when one considers the impact of majority rule upon the participation of women on juries. * * *

In mock-jury studies, researchers have observed that women generally speak less frequently than men in the deliberation process. When women offer comments in the course of mock deliberations, men often interrupt them or ignore their statements. This process of dismissing women's contributions frequently results in a progressive diminution of remarks from women as time passes. Women also tend to take longer than men to enter a discussion and to voice their views. In a decision scheme that demands full jury consensus, jurors may at least recognize the need to draw out the views of those who do not contribute as readily or as frequently. But under majority rule, decisions tend to be reached faster, leaving jurors without an incentive to encourage full participation in the deliberations. * * * This would be of little practical consequence if women's perspectives were not unique. Both feminist theory and jury research suggest that gender matters in moral decisionmaking. * * *

In addition to its practical role as factfinder, the jury serves an important symbolic function: it adds legitimacy to the justice system by providing citizens with the "security . . . that they, as jurors, actual or possible, being part of the judicial system of the country can prevent its

THE RIGHT TO TRIAL BY JURY

arbitrary use or abuse." * * * The operation of majority rule does interfere with the participation of people of color and women. Its adoption should trigger the same concerns that prompted the Court to outlaw the wholesale exclusion of jurors who happen to be members of these groups. The jury system must find ways to build consensus and to encourage expression of and debate about divergent views. Deliberation and group agreement help to ferret out extreme views and to ensure that all jurors are engaged. By contrast, the growing disenchantment with the justice system will only become more pronounced if it adopts a decisionmaking rule that in essence excludes segments of the jury and, by extension, segments of the community.

## SINGER V. UNITED STATES

Supreme Court of the United States
380 U.S. 24, 85 S.Ct. 783, 13 L.Ed.2d 630 (1965)

CHIEF JUSTICE WARREN delivered the opinion of the Court.

Rule 23(a) of the Federal Rules of Criminal Procedure provides:

Cases required to be tried by jury shall be so tried unless the defendant waives a jury trial in writing with the approval of the court and the consent of the government.

Petitioner challenges the permissibility of this rule, arguing that the Constitution gives a defendant in a federal criminal case the right to waive a jury trial whenever he believes such action to be in his best interest, regardless of whether the prosecution and the court are willing to acquiesce in the waiver.

Petitioner was charged in a federal district court with 30 infractions of the mail fraud statute. The gist of the indictment was that he used the mails to dupe amateur songwriters into sending him money for the marketing of their songs. On the opening day of trial petitioner offered in writing to waive a trial by jury "[f]or the purpose of shortening the trial." The trial court was willing to approve the waiver, but the Government refused to give its consent. Petitioner was subsequently convicted by a jury on 29 of the 30 counts and the Court of Appeals for the Ninth Circuit affirmed. We granted certiorari.

Petitioner's argument is that a defendant in a federal criminal case has not only an unconditional constitutional right * * * to a trial by jury, but also a correlative right to have his case decided by a judge alone if he considers such a trial to be to his advantage. * * * [P]etitioner argues that the provisions relating to jury trial are for the protection of the accused. Petitioner further urges that since a defendant can waive other constitutional rights without the consent of the Government, he must necessarily have a similar right to waive a jury trial and that the

Constitution's guarantee of a fair trial gives defendants the right to safeguard themselves against possible jury prejudice by insisting on a trial before a judge alone. * * *

The issue whether a defendant could waive a jury trial in federal criminal cases was * * * presented to this Court in *Patton v. United States*. The *Patton* case came before the Court on a certified question from the Eighth Circuit. The wording of the question is significant:

> After the commencement of a trial in a federal court before a jury of twelve men upon an indictment charging a crime, punishment for which may involve a penitentiary sentence, if one juror becomes incapacitated and unable to further proceed with his work as a juror, can defendant or defendants and the government through its official representative in charge of the case consent to the trial proceeding to a finality with 11 jurors, and can defendant or defendants thus waive the right to a trial and verdict by a constitutional jury of 12 men?

The question explicitly stated that the Government had agreed with the defendant that his trial should proceed with 11 jurors. The case did not involve trial before a judge alone, but the Court believed that trial before 11 jurors was as foreign to the common law as was trial before a judge alone, and therefore, both forms of waiver "in substance amount(ed) to the same thing." The Court * * * concluded that a jury trial was a right which the accused might "forego at his election." The Court also spoke of jury trial as a "privilege," not an "imperative requirement," and remarked that jury trial was principally for the benefit of the accused. Nevertheless, the Court was conscious of the precise question that was presented by the Eighth Circuit, and concluded its opinion with carefully chosen language that dispelled any notion that the defendant had an absolute right to demand trial before a judge sitting alone:

> Not only must the right of the accused to a trial by a constitutional jury be jealously preserved, but the maintenance of the jury as a factfinding body in criminal cases is of such importance and has such a place in our traditions, that, before any waiver can become effective, the consent of government counsel and the sanction of the court must be had, in addition to the express and intelligent consent of the defendant. * * *

In *Adams v. United States ex rel. McCann*, this Court reaffirmed the position taken in *Patton* that "one charged with a serious federal crime may dispense with his Constitutional right to jury trial, where this action is taken with his express, intelligent consent, where the Government also consents, and where such action is approved by the responsible judgment of the trial court."

Thus, there is no federally recognized right to a criminal trial before a judge sitting alone, but a defendant can, as was held in *Patton*, in some instances waive his right to a trial by jury. The question remains whether the effectiveness of this waiver can be conditioned upon the consent of the prosecuting attorney and the trial judge.

The ability to waive a constitutional right does not ordinarily carry with it the right to insist upon the opposite of that right. For example, although a defendant can, under some circumstances, waive his constitutional right to a public trial, he has no absolute right to compel a private trial, although he can waive his right to be tried in the State and district where the crime was committed, he cannot in all cases compel transfer of the case to another district, and although he can waive his right to be confronted by the witnesses against him, it has never been seriously suggested that he can thereby compel the Government to try the case by stipulation. Moreover, it has long been accepted that the waiver of constitutional rights can be subjected to reasonable procedural regulations * * *.

Trial by jury has been established by the Constitution as the "normal and * * * preferable mode of disposing of issues of fact in criminal cases." As with any mode that might be devised to determine guilt, trial by jury has its weaknesses and the potential for misuse. However, the mode itself has been surrounded with safeguards to make it as fair as possible * * *.

In light of the Constitution's emphasis on jury trial, we find it difficult to understand how the petitioner can submit the bald proposition that to compel a defendant in a criminal case to undergo a jury trial against his will is contrary to his right to a fair trial or to due process. A defendant's only constitutional right concerning the method of trial is to an impartial trial by jury. We find no constitutional impediment to conditioning a waiver of this right on the consent of the prosecuting attorney and the trial judge when, if either refuses to consent, the result is simply that the defendant is subject to an impartial trial by jury—the very thing that the Constitution guarantees him. The Constitution recognizes an adversary system as the proper method of determining guilt, and the Government, as a litigant, has a legitimate interest in seeing that cases in which it believes a conviction is warranted are tried before the tribunal which the Constitution regards as most likely to produce a fair result. * * *

In upholding the validity of Rule 23(a), we reiterate the sentiment expressed in *Berger v. United States* that the government attorney in a criminal prosecution is not an ordinary party to a controversy, but a "servant of the law" with a "twofold aim . . . that guilt shall not escape or innocence suffer." It was in light of this concept of the role of prosecutor that Rule 23(a) was framed, and we are confident that it is in this light that it will continue to be invoked by government attorneys. Because of this confidence in the integrity of the federal prosecutor, Rule 23(a) does not require that the Government articulate its reasons for demanding a jury trial at the time it refuses to consent to a defendant's proffered waiver. Nor should we assume that federal prosecutors would demand a jury trial for an ignoble purpose. We need not determine in this case whether there might be some circumstances where a defendant's reasons for wanting to be tried by a judge alone are so compelling that the Government's insistence on trial by jury would result in the denial to a defendant of an impartial trial. Petitioner argues that there might arise situations where "passion, prejudice . . . public feeling" or some other factor may render impossible or unlikely an impartial trial by jury. However, since petitioner gave no reason for wanting to forgo jury trial other than to save time, this is not such a case, and petitioner does not claim that it is. * * *

The judgment of the Court of Appeals is affirmed. * * *

## TAYLOR V. LOUISIANA

Supreme Court of the United States
419 U.S. 522, 95 S.Ct. 692, 42 L.Ed.2d 690 (1975)

JUSTICE WHITE delivered the opinion of the Court.

When this case was tried, Art. VII, § 41, of the Louisiana Constitution, and Art. 402 of the Louisiana Code of Criminal Procedure provided that a woman should not be selected for jury service unless she had previously filed a written declaration of her desire to be subject to jury service. The constitutionality of these provisions is the issue in this case.

Appellant, Billy J. Taylor, was indicted by the grand jury * * * for aggravated kidnaping. On April 12, 1972, appellant moved the trial court to quash the petit jury venire drawn for the special criminal term beginning with his trial the following day. Appellant alleged that women were systematically excluded from the venire and that he would therefore be deprived of what he claimed to be his federal constitutional right to "a fair trial by jury of a representative segment of the community. . . ."

* * * The appellee has stipulated that 53% of the persons eligible for jury service * * * were female, and that no more than 10% of the persons on the jury wheel in St. Tammany Parish were women. During the period from December 8, 1971, to November 3, 1972, 12 females were among the 1,800 persons drawn to fill petit jury venires in St. Tammany Parish. * * * In the present case, a venire totaling 175 persons was drawn for jury service beginning April 13, 1972. There were no females on the venire.

Appellant's motion to quash the venire was denied that same day. After being tried, convicted, and sentenced to death, appellant sought review in the Supreme Court of Louisiana, where he renewed his claim that the petit jury venire should have been quashed. The Supreme Court of

Louisiana * * * held, one justice dissenting, that these provisions were valid and not unconstitutional under federal law.

Appellant appealed from that decision to this Court. We noted probable jurisdiction to consider whether the Louisiana jury-selection system deprived appellant of his Sixth and Fourteenth Amendment right to an impartial jury trial. * * *

The Louisiana jury-selection system does not disqualify women from jury service, but in operation its conceded systematic impact is that only a very few women, grossly disproportionate to the number of eligible women in the community, are called for jury service. In this case, no women were on the venire from which the petit jury was drawn. The issue we have, therefore, is whether a jury-selection system which operates to exclude from jury service an identifiable class of citizens constituting 53% of eligible jurors in the community comports with the Sixth and Fourteenth Amendments.

The State first insists that Taylor, a male, has no standing to object to the exclusion of women from his jury. * * * Taylor was not a member of the excluded class; but there is no rule that claims such as Taylor presents may be made only by those defendants who are members of the group excluded from jury service. In *Peters v. Kiff*, the defendant, a white man, challenged his conviction on the ground that Negroes had been systematically excluded from jury service. Six Members of the Court agreed that petitioner was entitled to present the issue and concluded that he had been deprived of his federal rights. * * * Our inquiry is whether the presence of a fair cross section of the community on venires, panels, of lists from which petit juries are drawn is essential to the fulfillment of the Sixth Amendment's guarantee of an impartial jury trial in criminal prosecutions. * * *

We accept the fair-cross-section requirement as fundamental to the jury trial guaranteed by the Sixth Amendment and are convinced that the requirement has solid foundation. The purpose of a jury is to guard against the exercise of arbitrary power—to make available the commonsense judgment of the community as a hedge against the overzealous or mistaken prosecutor and in preference to the professional or perhaps overconditioned or biased response of a judge. This prophylactic vehicle is not provided if the jury pool is made up of only special segments of the populace or if large, distinctive groups are excluded from the pool. Community participation in the administration of the criminal law, moreover, is not only consistent with our democratic heritage but is also critical to public confidence in the fairness of the criminal justice system. * * *

We are also persuaded that the fair-cross-section requirement is violated by the systematic exclusion of women, who in the judicial district involved here amounted to 53% of the citizens eligible for jury service. This conclusion necessarily entails the judgment that women are sufficiently numerous and distinct from men and that if they are systematically eliminated from jury panels, the Sixth Amendment's fair-cross-section requirement cannot be satisfied.

* * * If the fair-cross-section rule is to govern the selection of juries, as we have concluded it must, women cannot be systematically excluded from jury panels from which petit juries are drawn. This conclusion is consistent with the current judgment of the country, now evidenced by legislative or constitutional provisions in every State and at the federal level qualifying women for jury service.

There remains the argument that women as a class serve a distinctive role in society and that jury service would so substantially interfere with that function that the State has ample justification for excluding women from service unless they volunteer, even though the result is that almost all jurors are men. * * * The right to a proper jury cannot be overcome on merely rational grounds. There must be weightier reasons if a distinctive class representing 53% of the eligible jurors is for all practical purposes to be excluded from jury service. No such basis has been tendered here.

The States are free to grant exemptions from jury service to individuals in case of special hardship or incapacity and to those engaged in particular occupations the uninterrupted performance of which is critical to the community's welfare. It would not appear that such exemptions would pose substantial threats that the remaining pool of jurors would not be representative of the community. A system excluding all women, however, is a wholly different matter. It is untenable to suggest these days that it would be a special hardship for each and every woman to perform jury service or that society cannot spare any women from their present duties. This may be the case with many, and it may be burdensome to sort out those who should be exempted from those who should serve. But that task is performed in the case of men, and the administrative convenience in dealing with women as a class is insufficient justification for diluting the quality of community judgment represented by the jury in criminal trials. * * *

Accepting as we do, * * * the view that the Sixth Amendment affords the defendant in a criminal trial the opportunity to have the jury drawn from venires representative of the community, we think it is no longer tenable to hold that women as a class may be excluded to given automatic exemptions based solely on sex if the consequence is that criminal jury venires are almost totally male. * * * If it was ever the case that women were unqualified to sit on juries or were so situated that none of them should be required to perform jury service, that time has long since passed. If at one time it could be held that Sixth Amendment juries must be drawn from a fair cross section of the community but that this requirement permitted the almost total exclusion of women, this is not the case today.

Communities differ at different times and places. What is a fair cross section at one time or place is not necessarily a fair cross section at another time or a different place. Nothing persuasive has been presented to us in this case suggesting that all-male venires in the parishes involved here are fairly representative of the local population otherwise eligible for jury service.

* * * The fair-cross-section principle must have much leeway in application. The States remain free to prescribe relevant qualifications for their jurors and to provide reasonable exemptions so long as it may be fairly said that the jury lists or panels are representative of the community. * * *

It should also be emphasized that in holding that petit juries must be drawn from a source fairly representative of the community we impose no requirement that petit juries actually chosen must mirror the community and reflect the various distinctive groups in the population. Defendants are not entitled to a jury of any particular composition, but the jury wheels, pools of names, panels, or venires from which juries are drawn must not systematically exclude distinctive groups in the community and thereby fail to be reasonably representative thereof.

The judgment of the Louisiana Supreme Court is reversed and the case remanded to that court for further proceedings not inconsistent with this opinion.

So ordered.

Reversed and remanded.

CHIEF JUSTICE BURGER concurs in the result.

JUSTICE REHNQUIST, dissenting.

The Court's opinion reverses a conviction without a suggestion, much less a showing, that the appellant has been unfairly treated or prejudiced in any way by the manner in which his jury was selected. * * * I disagree with the Court and would affirm the judgment of the Supreme Court of Louisiana. * * *

I cannot conceive that today's decision is necessary to guard against oppressive or arbitrary law enforcement, or to prevent miscarriages of justice and to assure fair trials. Especially is this so when the criminal defendant involved makes no claims of prejudice or bias. The Court does accord some slight attention to justifying its ruling in terms of the basis on which the right to jury trial was read into the Fourteenth Amendment. It concludes that the jury is not effective, as a prophylaxis against arbitrary prosecutorial and judicial power, if the "jury pool is made up of only special segments of the populace or if large, distinctive groups are excluded from the pool." It fails, however, to provide any satisfactory explanation of the mechanism by which the Louisiana system undermines the prophylactic role of the jury, either in general or in this case. The best it can do is to posit "a flavor, a distinct quality," which allegedly is lost if either sex is excluded. * * *

[One change] that appears to undergird the Court's turnabout is societal in nature, encompassing both our higher degree of sensitivity to distinctions based on sex, and the "evolving nature of the structure of the family unit in American society." * * * [I]t may be fair to conclude that the Louisiana system is in fact an anachronism, inappropriate at this "time or place." But surely constitutional adjudication is a more canalized function than enforcing as against the States this Court's perception of modern life.

Absent any suggestion that appellant's trial was unfairly conducted, or its result was unreliable, I would not require Louisiana to retry him (assuming the State can once again produce its evidence and witnesses) in order to impose on him the sanctions which its laws provide.

### NOTE

The Supreme Court has addressed whether a criminal defendant has a right to question prospective jurors on the issue of racial bias in only a handful of cases. Initially, the Court was fairly sympathetic to the idea that a criminal defendant has a constitutional right to question prospective jurors about racial bias. In *Aldridge v. United States*, 283 U.S. 308 (1931), the Court reversed a Black defendant's murder conviction where the trial judge had refused a defense request to interrogate the venire on racial prejudice, explaining that fairness demands that inquiries into racial prejudice be allowed. In *Ham v. South Carolina*, 409 U.S. 524, 529 (1973), a case involving a Black civil rights activist charged with possession of marijuana, the Court again sided with the defendant, holding that a trial judge's refusal to question prospective jurors as to possible racial prejudice violated the defendant's constitutional rights. This time, the Court went further than it had in *Aldridge* and expressly grounded its decision in due process, holding that "the Due Process Clause of the Fourteenth Amendment requires that . . . the [defendant] be permitted to have the jurors interrogated on the issue of racial bias."

Three years later, the Court started retreating from its support for *voir dire* into racial bias. In *Ristaino v. Ross*, 424 U.S. 589, 597 (1976), the Court held that the mere fact that the defendant is Black and the victim is White is not enough to trigger the constitutional requirement that the trial court question prospective jurors about racial prejudice. The defendants in *Ristaino* were three Black men on trial for armed robbery, assault and battery by means of a dangerous weapon, and assault with intent to murder two White security guards. In holding that the trial court did not err in refusing to question the venire on racial bias, the Court established what some have called a "special circumstances" rule: a defendant has a constitutional right to have prospective jurors questioned on racial bias only if the circumstances of the case suggest a "significant likelihood" of prejudice by the jurors.

In the next case, *Turner v. Murray*, the Court once again addresses the issue of a defendant's right to have perspective jurors questioned on racial prejudice.[a]

# TURNER V. MURRAY

Supreme Court of the United States
476 U.S. 28, 106 S.Ct. 1683, 90 L.Ed.2d 27 (1986)

JUSTICE WHITE announced the judgment of the Court and delivered the opinion of the Court. * * *

Petitioner is a black man sentenced to death for the murder of a white storekeeper. The question presented is whether the trial judge committed reversible error at *voir dire* by refusing petitioner's request to question prospective jurors on racial prejudice.

On July 12, 1978, petitioner entered a jewelry store in Franklin, Virginia, armed with a sawed-off shotgun. He demanded that the proprietor, W. Jack Smith, Jr., put jewelry and money from the cash register into some jewelry bags. Smith complied with petitioner's demand, but triggered a silent alarm, alerting the Police Department. When Alan Bain, a police officer, arrived to inquire about the alarm, petitioner surprised him and forced him to surrender his revolver.

Having learned that Smith had triggered a silent alarm, petitioner became agitated. He fired toward the rear wall of the store and stated that if he saw or heard any more police officers, he was going to start killing those in the store. When a police siren sounded, petitioner walked to where Smith was stationed behind a counter and without warning shot him in the head with Bain's pistol, wounding Smith and causing him to slump incapacitated to the floor.

Officer Bain attempted to calm petitioner, promising to take him anywhere he wanted to go and asking him not to shoot again. Petitioner angrily replied that he was going to kill Smith for "snitching," and fired two pistol shots into Smith's chest, fatally wounding him. As petitioner turned away from shooting Smith, Bain was able to disarm him and place him under arrest.

A Southampton County, Virginia, grand jury indicted petitioner on charges of capital murder, use of a firearm in the commission of a murder, and possession of a sawed-off shotgun in the commission of a robbery. Petitioner requested and was granted a change of venue to Northampton County, Virginia, a rural county some 80 miles from the location of the murder.

---

[a] For more information on the Supreme Court's jurisprudence on *voir dire* into racial bias, *see* Cynthia Lee, *A New Approach to Voir Dire on Racial Bias*, 5 UC IRVINE L. REV. 843 (2015).

Prior to the commencement of *voir dire,* petitioner's counsel submitted to the trial judge a list of proposed questions, including the following:

> The defendant, Willie Lloyd Turner, is a member of the Negro race. The victim, W. Jack Smith, Jr., was a white Caucasian. Will these facts prejudice you against Willie Lloyd Turner or affect your ability to render a fair and impartial verdict based solely on the evidence?

The judge declined to ask this question, stating that it "has been ruled on by the Supreme Court." The judge did ask the venire, who were questioned in groups of five in petitioner's presence, whether any person was aware of any reason why he could not render a fair and impartial verdict, to which all answered "no." At the time the question was asked, the prospective jurors had no way of knowing that the murder victim was white.

The jury that was empaneled, which consisted of eight whites and four blacks, convicted petitioner on all of the charges against him. After a separate sentencing hearing on the capital charge, the jury recommended that petitioner be sentenced to death, a recommendation the trial judge accepted.

Petitioner appealed his death sentence to the Virginia Supreme Court. * * * The court held that "[t]he mere fact that a defendant is black and that a victim is white does not constitutionally mandate . . . an inquiry [into racial prejudice]."

Having failed in his direct appeal, petitioner sought habeas corpus relief. * * * The United States Court of Appeals for the Fourth Circuit * * * found no special circumstance in the fact that petitioner is black and his victim white.

We granted certiorari to review the Fourth Circuit's decision that petitioner was not constitutionally entitled to have potential jurors questioned concerning racial prejudice. We reverse. * * *

The Fourth Circuit's opinion correctly states the analytical framework for evaluating petitioner's argument: "The broad inquiry in each case must be . . . whether under all of the circumstances presented there was a constitutionally significant likelihood that, absent questioning about racial prejudice, the jurors would not be indifferent as [they stand] unsworn." The Fourth Circuit was correct, too, in holding that under *Ristaino* the mere fact that petitioner is black and his victim white does not constitute a "special circumstance" of constitutional proportions. What sets this case apart from *Ristaino*, however, is that in addition to petitioner's being accused of a crime against a white victim, the crime charged was a capital offense.

In a capital sentencing proceeding before a jury, the jury is called upon to make a "highly subjective, unique, individualized judgment regarding the punishment that a particular person deserves." The Virginia statute under which petitioner was sentenced is instructive of the kinds of judgments a capital sentencing jury must make. First, in order to consider the death penalty, a Virginia jury must find either that the defendant is likely to commit future violent crimes or that his crime was "outrageously or wantonly vile, horrible or inhuman in that it involved torture, depravity of mind or an aggravated battery to the victim." Second, the jury must consider any mitigating evidence offered by the defendant. Mitigating evidence may include, but is not limited to, facts tending to show that the defendant acted under the influence of extreme emotional or mental disturbance, or that at the time of the crime the defendant's capacity "to appreciate the criminality of his conduct or to conform his conduct to the requirements of law was significantly impaired." Finally, even if the jury has found an aggravating factor, and irrespective of whether mitigating evidence has been offered, the jury has discretion not to recommend the death sentence, in which case it may not be imposed. * * *

Because of the range of discretion entrusted to a jury in a capital sentencing hearing, there is a unique opportunity for racial prejudice to operate but remain undetected. On the facts of this case, a juror who believes that blacks are violence prone or morally inferior might well be influenced by that belief in deciding whether petitioner's crime involved the aggravating factors specified under Virginia law. Such a juror might also be less favorably inclined toward petitioner's evidence of mental disturbance as a mitigating circumstance. More subtle, less consciously held racial attitudes could also influence a juror's decision in this case. Fear of blacks, which could easily be stirred up by the violent facts of petitioner's crime, might incline a juror to favor the death penalty.

The risk of racial prejudice infecting a capital sentencing proceeding is especially serious in light of the complete finality of the death sentence. * * * In the present case, we find the risk that racial prejudice may have infected petitioner's capital sentencing unacceptable in light of the ease with which that risk could have been minimized. By refusing to question prospective jurors on racial prejudice, the trial judge failed to adequately protect petitioner's constitutional right to an impartial jury.

We hold that a capital defendant accused of an interracial crime is entitled to have prospective jurors informed of the race of the victim and questioned on the issue of racial bias. The rule we propose is minimally intrusive; as in other cases involving "special circumstances," the trial judge retains discretion as to the form and number of questions on the subject, including the decision whether to question the venire individually or collectively. Also, a defendant cannot complain of a judge's failure to question the venire on racial prejudice unless the defendant has specifically requested such an inquiry.

The inadequacy of *voir dire* in this case requires that petitioner's death sentence be vacated. It is not necessary, however, that he be retried on the issue of guilt. Our judgment in this case is that there was an unacceptable risk of racial prejudice infecting the *capital sentencing proceeding*. This judgment is based on a conjunction of three factors: the fact that the crime charged involved interracial violence, the broad discretion given the jury at the death-penalty hearing, and the special seriousness of the risk of improper sentencing in a capital case. At the guilt phase of petitioner's trial, the jury had no greater discretion than it would have had if the crime charged had been noncapital murder. * * *

The judgment of the Court of Appeals is reversed, and the case is remanded for further proceedings consistent with this opinion.

*It is so ordered.*

THE CHIEF JUSTICE concurs in the judgment.

JUSTICE BRENNAN, concurring in part and dissenting in part.

* * * [I]n my view, the decision in this case, although clearly half right, is even more clearly half wrong. After recognizing that the constitutional guarantee of an impartial jury entitles a defendant in a capital case involving interracial violence to have prospective jurors questioned on the issue of racial bias—a holding which requires that this case be reversed and remanded for new sentencing—the Court disavows the logic of its own reasoning in denying petitioner Turner a new trial on the issue of his guilt. It accomplishes this by postulating a jury role at the sentencing phase of a capital trial fundamentally different from the jury function at the guilt phase and by concluding that the former gives rise to a significantly greater risk of a verdict tainted by racism. * * * I join only that portion of the Court's judgment granting petitioner a new sentencing proceeding, but dissent from that portion of the judgment refusing to vacate the conviction. * * *

The Court's argument is simply untenable on its face. As best I can understand it, the thesis is that since there is greater discretion entrusted to a capital jury in the sentencing phase than in the guilt phase, "there is [in the sentencing hearing] a unique opportunity for racial prejudice to operate but remain undetected." However, the Court's own discussion of the issues demonstrates that the opportunity for racial bias to taint the jury process is not "uniquely" present at a sentencing hearing, but is equally a factor at the guilt phase of a bifurcated capital trial.

* * * [I]t is certainly true, as the Court maintains, that racial bias inclines one to disbelieve and disfavor the object of the prejudice, and it is similarly incontestable that subconscious, as well as express, racial fears

and hatreds operate to deny fairness to the person despised; that is why we seek to insure that the right to an impartial jury is a meaningful right by providing the defense with the opportunity to ask prospective jurors questions designed to expose even hidden prejudices. But the Court never explains why these biases should be of less concern at the guilt phase than at the sentencing phase. The majority asserts that "a juror who believes that blacks are violence prone or morally inferior might well be influenced by that belief in deciding whether petitioner's crime involved the aggravating factors specified under Virginia law." But might not that same juror be influenced by those same prejudices in deciding whether, for example, to credit or discredit white witnesses as opposed to black witnesses at the guilt phase? Might not those same racial fears that would incline a juror to favor death not also incline a juror to favor conviction?

A trial to determine guilt or innocence is, at bottom, nothing more than the sum total of a countless number of small discretionary decisions made by each individual who sits in the jury box. The difference between conviction and acquittal turns on whether key testimony is believed or rejected; on whether an alibi sounds plausible or dubious; on whether a character witness appears trustworthy or unsavory; and on whether the jury concludes that the defendant had a motive, the inclination, or the means available to commit the crime charged. A racially biased juror sits with blurred vision and impaired sensibilities and is incapable of fairly making the myriad decisions that each juror is called upon to make in the course of a trial. To put it simply, he cannot judge because he has prejudged. This is equally true at the trial on guilt as at the hearing on sentencing. * * *

The Court may believe that it is being Solomonic in "splitting the difference" in this case and granting petitioner a new sentencing hearing while denying him the other "half" of the relief demanded. Starkly put, petitioner "wins" in that he gets to be resentenced, while the State "wins" in that it does not lose its conviction. But King Solomon did not, in fact, split the baby in two, and had he done so, I suspect that he would be remembered less for his wisdom than for his hardheartedness. Justice is not served by compromising principles in this way. I would reverse the conviction as well as the sentence in this case to insure compliance with the constitutional guarantee of an impartial jury.

JUSTICE POWELL, with whom JUSTICE REHNQUIST joins, dissenting.

The Court today adopts a *per se* rule applicable in capital cases, under which "a capital defendant accused of an interracial crime is entitled to have prospective jurors informed of the race of the victim and questioned on the issue of racial bias." * * *

In effect, the Court recognizes a presumption that jurors who have sworn to decide the case impartially nevertheless are racially biased. * * *

[I]t is unnecessary and unwise for this Court to rule, as a matter of constitutional law, that a trial judge *always* must inquire into racial bias in a capital case involving an interracial murder, rather than leaving that decision to be made on a case-by-case basis. * * *

Nothing in this record suggests that racial bias played any role in the jurors' deliberations. * * * The prosecutor pointed out that the case presented no racial issues beyond the fact that petitioner and his victim were of different races. * * *

There is nothing in the record of this trial that reflects racial overtones of any kind. * * * The Court does not purport to identify any such circumstance, or to explain why the facts that a capital defendant is of one race and his victim of another now create a significant likelihood that racial issues will distort the jurors' consideration of the issues in the trial. This case illustrates that it is unnecessary for the Court to adopt a *per se* rule that constitutionalizes the unjustifiable presumption that jurors are racially biased. * * *

The *per se* rule announced today may appear innocuous. But the rule is based on what amounts to a constitutional presumption that jurors in capital cases are racially biased. Such presumption unjustifiably suggests that criminal justice in our courts of law is meted out on racial grounds. * * * The manner in which petitioner was tried and sentenced, and particularly the jurors who fulfilled their civic duty to sit in his case, reflected not a trace of the racial prejudice that the Court's new rule now presumes. * * *

[JUSTICE MARSHALL's opinion, concurring in part and dissenting in part, has been omitted.]

## BATSON V. KENTUCKY

Supreme Court of the United States
476 U.S. 79, 106 S.Ct. 1712, 90 L.Ed.2d 69 (1986)

JUSTICE POWELL delivered the opinion of the Court. * * *

Petitioner, a black man, was indicted in Kentucky on charges of second-degree burglary and receipt of stolen goods. On the first day of trial in Jefferson Circuit Court, the judge conducted *voir dire* examination of the venire, excused certain jurors for cause, and permitted the parties to exercise peremptory challenges. The prosecutor used his peremptory challenges to strike all four black persons on the venire, and a jury composed only of white persons was selected. Defense counsel moved to discharge the jury before it was sworn on the ground that the prosecutor's removal of the black veniremen violated petitioner's rights * * * under the Fourteenth Amendment to equal protection of the laws. Counsel requested a hearing on his motion. Without expressly ruling on the request for a hearing, the trial judge observed that the parties were entitled to use their peremptory challenges to "strike anybody they want to." The judge then denied petitioner's motion. * * *

The jury convicted petitioner on both counts. On appeal to the Supreme Court of Kentucky, petitioner pressed, among other claims, the argument concerning the prosecutor's use of peremptory challenges. * * * The Supreme Court of Kentucky affirmed [petitioner's conviction]. * * * We granted certiorari, and now reverse. * * *

In *Swain v. Alabama*, this Court recognized that a "State's purposeful or deliberate denial to Negroes on account of race of participation as jurors in the administration of justice violates the Equal Protection Clause." This principle has been "consistently and repeatedly" reaffirmed, in numerous decisions of this Court both preceding and following *Swain*. We reaffirm the principle today. * * *

Purposeful racial discrimination in selection of the venire violates a defendant's right to equal protection because it denies him the protection that a trial by jury is intended to secure. "The very idea of a jury is a body . . . composed of the peers or equals of the person whose rights it is selected or summoned to determine; that is, of his neighbors, fellows, associates, persons having the same legal status in society as that which he holds." The petit jury has occupied a central position in our system of justice by safeguarding a person accused of crime against the arbitrary exercise of power by prosecutor or judge. Those on the venire must be "indifferently chosen," to secure the defendant's right under the Fourteenth Amendment to "protection of life and liberty against race or color prejudice."

Racial discrimination in selection of jurors harms not only the accused whose life or liberty they are summoned to try. Competence to serve as a juror ultimately depends on an assessment of individual qualifications and ability impartially to consider evidence presented at a trial. A person's race simply "is unrelated to his fitness as a juror." * * *

The harm from discriminatory jury selection extends beyond that inflicted on the defendant and the excluded juror to touch the entire community. Selection procedures that purposefully exclude black persons from juries undermine public confidence in the fairness of our system of justice. * * *

Accordingly, the component of the jury selection process at issue here, the State's privilege to strike individual jurors through peremptory challenges, is subject to the commands of the Equal Protection Clause. Although a prosecutor ordinarily is entitled to exercise permitted peremptory challenges "for any reason at all, as long as that reason is related to his view concerning the outcome" of the case to be tried, the Equal Protection Clause forbids the prosecutor to challenge potential jurors solely on account of their race or on the assumption that black jurors as a group will be unable impartially to consider the State's case against a black defendant.

* * * [In] *Swain v. Alabama,* [we also held that] a black defendant could make out a prima facie case of purposeful discrimination * * * on evidence that a prosecutor, "in case after case, whatever the circumstances, whatever the crime and whoever the defendant or the victim may be, is responsible for the removal of Negroes who have been selected as qualified jurors by the jury commissioners and who have survived challenges for cause, with the result that no Negroes ever serve on petit juries." Evidence offered by the defendant in *Swain* did not meet that standard. While the defendant showed that prosecutors in the jurisdiction had exercised their strikes to exclude blacks from the jury, he offered no proof of the circumstances under which prosecutors were responsible for striking black jurors beyond the facts of his own case.

A number of lower courts following the teaching of *Swain* reasoned that proof of repeated striking of blacks over a number of cases was necessary to establish a violation of the Equal Protection Clause. Since this interpretation of *Swain* has placed on defendants a crippling burden of proof, prosecutors' peremptory challenges are now largely immune from constitutional scrutiny. * * * [W]e reject this evidentiary formulation as inconsistent with standards that have been developed since *Swain* for assessing a prima facie case under the Equal Protection Clause. * * *

[S]ince the decision in *Swain,* this Court has recognized that a defendant may make a prima facie showing of purposeful racial discrimination in selection of the venire by relying solely on the facts concerning its selection *in his case.* These decisions are in accordance with the proposition * * * that "a consistent pattern of official racial discrimination" is not "a necessary predicate to a violation of the Equal Protection Clause. A single invidiously discriminatory governmental act" is not "immunized by the absence of such discrimination in the making of other comparable decisions." For evidentiary requirements to dictate that "several must suffer discrimination" before one could object, would be inconsistent with the promise of equal protection to all.

* * * These principles support our conclusion that a defendant may establish a prima facie case of purposeful discrimination in selection of the petit jury solely on evidence concerning the prosecutor's exercise of peremptory challenges at the defendant's trial.[a] To establish such a case,

---

[a] Even though the *Batson* Court did not address whether the Equal Protection Clause imposes any limits on the exercise of peremptory challenges by criminal defense counsel, in a later case, the Court applied the *Batson* framework in a case where the prosecutor objected to a White defendant's use of the peremptory challenge to strike Black prospective jurors. *Georgia v. McCollum,* 505 U.S. 42 (1992). The Court explained that the racially discriminatory use of peremptory challenges by criminal defense counsel inflicts the same harms addressed in the *Batson* case. It also found state action, quoting from a previous Supreme Court decision where the Court explained that "the peremptory challenge system, as well as the jury system as a whole,

the defendant first must show that he is a member of a cognizable racial group, and that the prosecutor has exercised peremptory challenges to remove from the venire members of the defendant's race.[b] Second, the defendant is entitled to rely on the fact, as to which there can be no dispute, that peremptory challenges constitute a jury selection practice that permits "those to discriminate who are of a mind to discriminate." Finally, the defendant must show that these facts and any other relevant circumstances raise an inference that the prosecutor used that practice to exclude the veniremen from the petit jury on account of their race. * * *

Once the defendant makes a prima facie showing, the burden shifts to the State to come forward with a neutral explanation for challenging black jurors. Though this requirement imposes a limitation in some cases on the full peremptory character of the historic challenge, we emphasize that the prosecutor's explanation need not rise to the level justifying exercise of a challenge for cause.[c] But the prosecutor may not rebut the defendant's prima facie case of discrimination by stating merely that he challenged jurors of the defendant's race on the assumption—or his intuitive judgment—that they would be partial to the defendant because of their shared race. Just as the Equal Protection Clause forbids the States to exclude black persons from the venire on the assumption that blacks as a group are unqualified to serve as jurors, so it forbids the States to strike black veniremen on the assumption that they will be biased in a particular case simply because the defendant is black. The core guarantee of equal protection, ensuring citizens that their State will not discriminate on account of race, would be meaningless were we to approve the exclusion of jurors on the basis of such assumptions, which arise solely from the jurors' race. Nor may the prosecutor rebut the defendant's case merely by denying that he had a discriminatory motive or "affirm[ing] [his] good faith in making individual selections." If these general assertions were accepted as rebutting a defendant's prima facie case, the Equal Protection Clause "would be but a vain and illusory requirement." The prosecutor therefore must articulate a neutral explanation related to the particular case to be

---

'simply could not exist' without the 'overt, significant participation of the government,' *id.* at 51, and noting that "peremptory challenges perform a traditional function of the government: 'Their sole purpose is to permit litigants to assist the government in the selection of an impartial trier of fact.'" *Id.* at 52, *quoting Edmonson v. Leesville Concrete Co.,* 500 U.S. 614 (1991).

[b] In *Powers v. Ohio,* the Court held that the defendant and the prospective juror who is struck by the opposing party need not be members of the same race. 499 U.S. 400 (1991) (permitting a White defendant to object to the prosecution's use of its peremptory challenges to strike Black persons on the venire).

[c] In *Purkett v. Elem,* 514 U.S. 765 (1995), the Court noted that at this second stage, it is not necessary that the prosecutor's explanation be "minimally persuasive." *Id.* at 768. "At the third stage, however, when the trial court has to decide whether the defendant has established purposeful discrimination, 'implausible or fantastic justifications may (and probably will) be found to be pretexts for purposeful discrimination.'" *Id.*

tried. The trial court then will have the duty to determine if the defendant has established purposeful discrimination.[d] * * *

The State contends that our holding will eviscerate the fair trial values served by the peremptory challenge. Conceding that the Constitution does not guarantee a right to peremptory challenges and that *Swain* did state that their use ultimately is subject to the strictures of equal protection, the State argues that the privilege of unfettered exercise of the challenge is of vital importance to the criminal justice system.

While we recognize, of course, that the peremptory challenge occupies an important position in our trial procedures, we do not agree that our decision today will undermine the contribution the challenge generally makes to the administration of justice. The reality of practice, amply reflected in many state and federal court opinions, shows that the challenge may be, and unfortunately at times has been, used to discriminate against black jurors. By requiring trial courts to be sensitive to the racially discriminatory use of peremptory challenges, our decision enforces the mandate of equal protection and furthers the ends of justice. In view of the heterogeneous population of our Nation, public respect for our criminal justice system and the rule of law will be strengthened if we ensure that no citizen is disqualified from jury service because of his race. * * *

In this case, petitioner made a timely objection to the prosecutor's removal of all black persons on the venire. Because the trial court flatly rejected the objection without requiring the prosecutor to give an explanation for his action, we remand this case for further proceedings. If the trial court decides that the facts establish, prima facie, purposeful discrimination and the prosecutor does not come forward with a neutral explanation for his action, our precedents require that petitioner's conviction be reversed.

*It is so ordered.*

JUSTICE MARSHALL, concurring. * * *

I wholeheartedly concur in the Court's conclusion that use of the peremptory challenge to remove blacks from juries, on the basis of their race, violates the Equal Protection Clause. I would go further, however, in fashioning a remedy adequate to eliminate that discrimination. Merely allowing defendants the opportunity to challenge the racially discriminatory use of peremptory challenges in individual cases will not end the illegitimate use of the peremptory challenge.

---

[d]  In *Miller-El v. Dretke*, 545 U.S. 231 (2005), the Court noted that "[i]f a prosecutor's proffered reason for striking a black panelist applies just as well to an otherwise-similar nonblack who is permitted to serve, that is evidence tending to prove purposeful discrimination to be considered at *Batson*'s third step." *Id.* at 241.

* * * First, defendants cannot attack the discriminatory use of peremptory challenges at all unless the challenges are so flagrant as to establish a prima facie case. * * * Prosecutors are left free to discriminate against blacks in jury selection provided that they hold that discrimination to an "acceptable" level.

Second, when a defendant can establish a prima facie case, trial courts face the difficult burden of assessing prosecutors' motives. Any prosecutor can easily assert facially neutral reasons for striking a juror, and trial courts are ill equipped to second-guess those reasons. How is the court to treat a prosecutor's statement that he struck a juror because the juror had a son about the same age as defendant, or seemed "uncommunicative," or "never cracked a smile" and, therefore "did not possess the sensitivities necessary to realistically look at the issues and decide the facts in this case." If such easily generated explanations are sufficient to discharge the prosecutor's obligation to justify his strikes on nonracial grounds, then the protection erected by the Court today may be illusory.

Nor is outright prevarication by prosecutors the only danger here. * * * A prosecutor's own conscious or unconscious racism may lead him easily to the conclusion that a prospective black juror is "sullen," or "distant," a characterization that would not have come to his mind if a white juror had acted identically. A judge's own conscious or unconscious racism may lead him to accept such an explanation as well supported. As Justice Rehnquist concedes, prosecutors' peremptories are based on their "seat-of-the-pants instincts" as to how particular jurors will vote. Yet "seat-of-the-pants instincts" may often be just another term for racial prejudice. Even if all parties approach the Court's mandate with the best of conscious intentions, that mandate requires them to confront and overcome their own racism on all levels—a challenge I doubt all of them can meet. * * *

The inherent potential of peremptory challenges to distort the jury process by permitting the exclusion of jurors on racial grounds should ideally lead the Court to ban them entirely from the criminal justice system. * * * Some authors have suggested that the courts should ban prosecutors' peremptories entirely, but should zealously guard the defendant's peremptory as "essential to the fairness of trial by jury." I would not find that an acceptable solution. Our criminal justice system "requires not only freedom from any bias against the accused, but also from any prejudice against his prosecution. Between him and the state the scales are to be evenly held." We can maintain that balance, not by permitting both prosecutor and defendant to engage in racial discrimination in jury selection, but by banning the use of peremptory challenges by prosecutors and by allowing the States to eliminate the defendant's peremptories as well. * * *

I applaud the Court's holding that the racially discriminatory use of peremptory challenges violates the Equal Protection Clause, and I join the Court's opinion. However, only by banning peremptories entirely can such discrimination be ended.

CHIEF JUSTICE BURGER, joined by JUSTICE REHNQUIST, dissenting. * * *

Today the Court sets aside the peremptory challenge, a procedure which has been part of the common law for many centuries and part of our jury system for nearly 200 years. * * * Permitting unexplained peremptories has long been regarded as a means to strengthen our jury system in other ways as well. One commentator has recognized:

> The peremptory, made without giving any reason, avoids trafficking in the core of truth in most common stereotypes. . . . Common human experience, common sense, psychosociological studies, and public opinion polls tell us that it is likely that certain classes of people statistically have predispositions that would make them inappropriate jurors for particular kinds of cases. But to allow this knowledge to be expressed in the evaluative terms necessary for challenges for cause would undercut our desire for a society in which all people are judged as individuals and in which each is held reasonable and open to compromise. . . . [W]e have evolved in the peremptory challenge a system that allows the covert expression of what we dare not say but know is true more often than not.

For reasons such as these, this Court concluded in *Swain* that "the [peremptory] challenge is one of the most important of the rights" in our justice system. For close to a century, then, it has been settled that "[t]he denial or impairment of the right is reversible error without a showing of prejudice."

Instead of even considering the history or function of the peremptory challenge, the bulk of the Court's opinion is spent recounting the well-established principle that intentional exclusion of racial groups from jury venires is a violation of the Equal Protection Clause. * * * That the Court is not applying conventional equal protection analysis is shown by its limitation of its new rule to allegations of impermissible challenge on the basis of race; the Court's opinion clearly contains such a limitation. But if conventional equal protection principles apply, then presumably defendants could object to exclusions on the basis of not only race, but also sex. * * *

JUSTICE REHNQUIST, with whom THE CHIEF JUSTICE joins, dissenting. * * *

I cannot subscribe to the Court's unprecedented use of the Equal Protection Clause to restrict the historic scope of the peremptory challenge, which has been described as "a necessary part of trial by jury." In my view, there is simply nothing "unequal" about the State's using its peremptory challenges to strike blacks from the jury in cases involving black defendants, so long as such challenges are also used to exclude whites in cases involving white defendants, Hispanics in cases involving Hispanic defendants, Asians in cases involving Asian defendants, and so on. This case-specific use of peremptory challenges by the State does not single out blacks, or members of any other race for that matter, for discriminatory treatment. * * *

The use of group affiliations, such as age, race, or occupation, as a "proxy" for potential juror partiality, based on the assumption or belief that members of one group are more likely to favor defendants who belong to the same group, has long been accepted as a legitimate basis for the State's exercise of peremptory challenges. Indeed, given the need for reasonable limitations on the time devoted to *voir dire*, the use of such "proxies" by both the State and the defendant may be extremely useful in eliminating from the jury persons who might be biased in one way or another. The Court today holds that the State may not use its peremptory challenges to strike black prospective jurors on this basis without violating the Constitution. But I do not believe there is anything in the Equal Protection Clause, or any other constitutional provision, that justifies such a departure from [our precedents]. I would therefore affirm the judgment of the court below.

[JUSTICE WHITE's concurring opinion, JUSTICE STEVENS' concurring opinion, and JUSTICE O'CONNOR's concurring opinion have been omitted.]

## "GOOD" REVERSAL FOLLOWED "UNFAIR" TRIAL
Kay Stewart
The Courier-Journal, Nov. 6, 2005

His name is used regularly in courtrooms across America, but James Kirkland Batson would be happier if everyone forgot all about him. "It's so old, they ought to let it go," Batson said of the landmark U.S. Supreme Court ruling bearing his name. But the 49-year-old Louisville construction worker still gets emotional at the mention of his 1982 conviction for burglary and receiving stolen property by an all-white Jefferson Circuit Court jury. Batson, who is black, watched as the prosecutor dismissed all four blacks from the panel. "I don't *think* it was unfair. It was unfair," he said.

In 1986, while Batson was serving a 20-year prison sentence, the U.S. Supreme Court reversed his conviction and the ruling established new standards to prevent discrimination in jury selection. Rather than risk a retrial, Batson pleaded guilty to burglary as part of a plea bargain that resulted in a five-year sentence. He subsequently got in trouble with the law several times and racked up a string of burglary, theft, receiving stolen property and persistent-felon convictions, said Lisa Lamb, a Kentucky Corrections Department spokeswoman. He was released from prison in January 2003 and will remain on parole through 2026.

Joe Gutmann, the prosecutor in Batson's 1982 trial, said in a recent interview that the Supreme Court's decision in the case was "a good one," because it prevents lawyers from discriminating in jury selection. Gutmann, who now teaches at Central High School, said he removed the blacks not because of their race but because they were young and might sympathize with Batson.

Batson said he doesn't blame Gutmann. "He was doing what he thought was necessary," Batson said. "He was the prosecutor, and he didn't want to lose."

## *NOTE*

On Monday, April 27, 1987, less than a year following the *Batson* decision in May 1986, jury selection began in Timothy Foster's trial. Foster was tried for murder and burglary, convicted, and sentenced to death. During jury selection, Foster objected to the prosecution's use of its peremptory challenges, alleging discriminatory exclusion of all the potential black jurors, citing *Batson*. The trial court denied Foster's *Batson* challenge. After the Georgia Supreme Court affirmed Foster's conviction and sentence, the government argued that Foster had exhausted all his appellate remedies.

In 2015, based on newly discovered evidence from the prosecutor's file obtained through Georgia's Open Records Act, Foster petitioned the United States Supreme Court, which granted certiorari. The Court accepted the case to reevaluate whether there was race-based discrimination during jury selection at Foster's trial. The Supreme Court found that the State had engaged in purposeful discrimination with respect to two of its peremptory challenges. *Foster v. Chatman*, 136 S.Ct. 1737 (2016). The newly discovered evidence in the prosecutor's file contained: (1) copies of the jury venire list on which the names of each Black prospective juror were highlighted in bright green, with a legend indicating that the highlighting "represents blacks;" (2) a draft affidavit from an investigator comparing Black prospective jurors and concluding, "If it comes down to having to pick one of the black jurors, [this one] might be okay;" (3) notes identifying Black prospective jurors as "B#1," "B#2," and "B#3;" (4) notes with "N" (for "no") appearing next to the names of all Black prospective jurors; (5) a list titled "[D]efinite NO's" containing six names, including the names of all of the qualified Black prospective jurors; (6)

a document with notes on the Church of Christ that was annotated "*NO. No Black* Church;" and (7) the questionnaires filled out by five prospective Black jurors, on which each juror's response indicating his or her race had been circled. In light of the evidence in the prosecutor's file, the Court found the State's purportedly race-neutral justifications for exercising its peremptory challenges against black jurors to be pretextual, insufficient, and/or contradictory to the record considering the treatment of other nonblack jurors.

Foster's 29-year struggle to establish his *Batson* claims highlights the difficulty many criminal defendants face attempting to prove purposeful discrimination on the part of the prosecutor during jury selection.

## J.E.B. v. ALABAMA
Supreme Court of the United States
511 U.S. 127, 114 S.Ct. 1419, 128 L.Ed.2d 89 (1994)

JUSTICE BLACKMUN delivered the opinion of the Court.

* * * Today we are faced with the question whether the Equal Protection Clause forbids intentional discrimination on the basis of gender, just as it prohibits discrimination on the basis of race. We hold that gender, like race, is an unconstitutional proxy for juror competence and impartiality.

On behalf of relator T.B., the mother of a minor child, respondent State of Alabama filed a complaint for paternity and child support against petitioner J.E.B. in the District Court of Jackson County, Alabama. * * * The trial court assembled a panel of 36 potential jurors, 12 males and 24 females. After the court excused three jurors for cause, only 10 of the remaining 33 jurors were male. The State then used 9 of its 10 peremptory strikes to remove male jurors; petitioner used all but one of his strikes to remove female jurors. As a result, all the selected jurors were female.

Before the jury was empaneled, petitioner objected to the State's peremptory challenges on the ground that they were exercised against male jurors solely on the basis of gender, in violation of the Equal Protection Clause of the Fourteenth Amendment. Petitioner argued that the logic and reasoning of *Batson v. Kentucky*, which prohibits peremptory strikes solely on the basis of race, similarly forbids intentional discrimination on the basis of gender. The court rejected petitioner's claim and empaneled the all-female jury. The jury found petitioner to be the father of the child, and the court entered an order directing him to pay child support. On post judgment motion, the court reaffirmed its ruling that *Batson* does not extend to gender-based peremptory challenges. * * *

We granted certiorari to resolve a question that has created a conflict of authority—whether the Equal Protection Clause forbids peremptory challenges on the basis of gender as well as on the basis of race. Today we reaffirm what, by now, should be axiomatic: Intentional discrimination on the basis of gender by state actors violates the Equal Protection Clause, particularly where, as here, the discrimination serves to ratify and perpetuate invidious, archaic, and overbroad stereotypes about the relative abilities of men and women.

Discrimination on the basis of gender in the exercise of peremptory challenges is a relatively recent phenomenon. Gender-based peremptory strikes were hardly practicable during most of our country's existence, since, until the 20th century, women were completely excluded from jury service. * * *

Many States continued to exclude women from jury service well into the present century, despite the fact that women attained suffrage upon ratification of the Nineteenth Amendment in 1920. States that did permit women to serve on juries often erected other barriers, such as registration requirements and automatic exemptions, designed to deter women from exercising their right to jury service.

The prohibition of women on juries was derived from the English common law which, according to Blackstone, rightfully excluded women from juries under "the doctrine of propter defectum sexus, literally, the 'defect of sex.' " In this country, supporters of the exclusion of women from juries tended to couch their objections in terms of the ostensible need to protect women from the ugliness and depravity of trials. Women were thought to be too fragile and virginal to withstand the polluted courtroom atmosphere.

* * * Since *Reed v. Reed*, this Court consistently has subjected gender-based classifications to heightened scrutiny in recognition of the real danger that government policies that professedly are based on reasonable considerations in fact may be reflective of "archaic and overbroad" generalizations about gender, or based on "outdated misconceptions concerning the role of females in the home rather than in the marketplace and world of ideas."

Despite the heightened scrutiny afforded distinctions based on gender, respondent argues that gender discrimination in the selection of the petit jury should be permitted, though discrimination on the basis of race is not. Respondent suggests that "gender discrimination in this country . . . has never reached the level of discrimination" against African-Americans, and therefore gender discrimination, unlike racial discrimination, is tolerable in the courtroom.

While the prejudicial attitudes toward women in this country have not been identical to those held toward racial minorities, the similarities between the experiences of racial minorities and women, in some contexts, "overpower those differences." * * * Certainly, with respect to jury service, African-Americans and women share a history of total exclusion, a history which came to an end for women many years after the embarrassing chapter in our history came to an end for African-Americans.

We need not determine, however, whether women or racial minorities have suffered more at the hands of discriminatory state actors during the decades of our Nation's history. It is necessary only to acknowledge that "our Nation has had a long and unfortunate history of sex discrimination," a history which warrants the heightened scrutiny we afford all gender-based classifications today. Under our equal protection jurisprudence, gender-based classifications require "an exceedingly persuasive justification" in order to survive constitutional scrutiny. Thus, the only question is whether discrimination on the basis of gender in jury selection substantially furthers the State's legitimate interest in achieving a fair and impartial trial. In making this assessment, we do not weigh the value of peremptory challenges as an institution against our asserted commitment to eradicate invidious discrimination from the courtroom. Instead, we consider whether peremptory challenges based on gender stereotypes provide substantial aid to a litigant's effort to secure a fair and impartial jury.

Far from proffering an exceptionally persuasive justification for its gender-based peremptory challenges, respondent maintains that its decision to strike virtually all the males from the jury in this case "may reasonably have been based upon the perception, supported by history, that men otherwise totally qualified to serve upon a jury in any case might be more sympathetic and receptive to the arguments of a man alleged in a paternity action to be the father of an out-of-wedlock child, while women equally qualified to serve upon a jury might be more sympathetic and receptive to the arguments of the complaining witness who bore the child."

We shall not accept as a defense to gender-based peremptory challenges "the very stereotype the law condemns." Respondent's rationale, not unlike those regularly expressed for gender-based strikes, is reminiscent of the arguments advanced to justify the total exclusion of women from juries. Respondent offers virtually no support for the conclusion that gender alone is an accurate predictor of juror's attitudes; yet it urges this Court to condone the same stereotypes that justified the wholesale exclusion of women from juries and the ballot box. Respondent seems to assume that gross generalizations that would be deemed impermissible if made on the basis of race are somehow permissible when made on the basis of gender.

Discrimination in jury selection, whether based on race or on gender, causes harm to the litigants, the community, and the individual jurors who are wrongfully excluded from participation in the judicial process. The litigants are harmed by the risk that the prejudice that motivated the discriminatory selection of the jury will infect the entire proceedings. The community is harmed by the State's participation in the perpetuation of invidious group stereotypes and the inevitable loss of confidence in our judicial system that state-sanctioned discrimination in the courtroom engenders.

When state actors exercise peremptory challenges in reliance on gender stereotypes, they ratify and reinforce prejudicial views of the relative abilities of men and women. * * * Discriminatory use of peremptory challenges may create the impression that the judicial system has acquiesced in suppressing full participation by one gender or that the "deck has been stacked" in favor of one side.

In recent cases we have emphasized that individual jurors themselves have a right to nondiscriminatory jury selection procedures. Contrary to respondent's suggestion, this right extends to both men and women. * * * Striking individual jurors on the assumption that they hold particular views simply because of their gender is "practically a brand upon them, affixed by the law, an assertion of their inferiority." * * *

The experience in the many jurisdictions that have barred gender-based challenges belies the claim that litigants and trial courts are incapable of complying with a rule barring strikes based on gender. As with race-based *Batson* claims, a party alleging gender discrimination must make a prima facie showing of intentional discrimination before the party exercising the challenge is required to explain the basis for the strike. When an explanation is required, it need not rise to the level of a "for cause" challenge; rather, it merely must be based on a juror characteristic other than gender, and the proffered explanation may not be pretextual.

Failing to provide jurors the same protection against gender discrimination as race discrimination could frustrate the purpose of *Batson* itself. Because gender and race are overlapping categories, gender can be used as a pretext for racial discrimination. Allowing parties to remove racial minorities from the jury not because of their race, but because of their gender, contravenes well-established equal protection principles and could insulate effectively racial discrimination from judicial scrutiny.

Equal opportunity to participate in the fair administration of justice is fundamental to our democratic system. It not only furthers the goals of the jury system. It reaffirms the promise of equality under the law-that all citizens, regardless of race, ethnicity, or gender, have the chance to take part directly in our democracy. When persons are excluded from participation in our democratic processes solely because of race or gender, this promise of equality dims, and the integrity of our judicial system is jeopardized.

In view of these concerns, the Equal Protection Clause prohibits discrimination in jury selection on the basis of gender, or on the assumption that an individual will be biased in a particular case for no reason other than the fact that the person happens to be a woman or happens to be a man. * * *

The judgment of the Court of Civil Appeals of Alabama is reversed, and the case is remanded to that court for further proceedings not inconsistent with this opinion.

*It is so ordered.*

JUSTICE O'CONNOR, concurring.

I agree with the Court that the Equal Protection Clause prohibits the government from excluding a person from jury service on account of that person's gender. * * * I therefore join the Court's opinion in this case. But today's important blow against gender discrimination is not costless. I write separately to discuss some of these costs, and to express my belief that today's holding should be limited to the government's use of gender-based peremptory strikes. * * * [T]oday's decision further erodes the role of the peremptory challenge. * * *

In so doing we make the peremptory challenge less discretionary and more like a challenge for cause. We also increase the possibility that biased jurors will be allowed onto the jury, because sometimes a lawyer will be unable to provide an acceptable gender-neutral explanation even though the lawyer is in fact correct that the juror is unsympathetic. Similarly, in jurisdictions where lawyers exercise their strikes in open court, lawyers may be deterred from using their peremptories, out of the fear that if they are unable to justify the strike the court will seat a juror who knows that the striking party thought him unfit. Because I believe the peremptory remains an important litigator's tool and a fundamental part of the process of selecting impartial juries, our increasing limitation of it gives me pause.

Nor is the value of the peremptory challenge to the litigant diminished when the peremptory is exercised in a gender-based manner. We know that like race, gender matters. A plethora of studies make clear that in rape cases, for example, female jurors are somewhat more likely to vote to convict than male jurors. * * * Today's decision severely limits a litigant's ability to act on this intuition, for the import of our holding is that any correlation between a juror's gender and attitudes is irrelevant as a matter of constitutional law. * * * These concerns reinforce my conviction that today's decision should be limited to a prohibition on the government's use of gender-based peremptory challenges. * * *

JUSTICE SCALIA, with whom THE CHIEF JUSTICE and JUSTICE THOMAS join, dissenting.

Today's opinion is an inspiring demonstration of how thoroughly up-to-date and right-thinking we Justices are in matters pertaining to the sexes (or as the Court would have it, the genders), and how sternly we disapprove the male chauvinist attitudes of our predecessors. The price to be paid for this display—a modest price, surely—is that most of the opinion is quite irrelevant to the case at hand. The hasty reader will be surprised to learn, for example, that this lawsuit involves a complaint about the use of peremptory challenges to exclude men from a petit jury. To be sure, petitioner, a man, used all but one of his peremptory strikes to remove women from the jury (he used his last challenge to strike the sole remaining male from the pool), but the validity of his strikes is not before us. Nonetheless, the Court treats itself to an extended discussion of the historic exclusion of women not only from jury service, but also from service at the bar (which is rather like jury service, in that it involves going to the courthouse a lot). All this, as I say, is irrelevant, since the case involves state action that allegedly discriminates against men. The parties do not contest that discrimination on the basis of sex is subject to what our cases call "heightened scrutiny," and the citation of one of those cases (preferably one involving men rather than women), is all that was needed.

* * * The extension of *Batson* to sex, and almost certainly beyond, will provide the basis for extensive collateral litigation, which especially the criminal defendant (who litigates full time and cost free) can be expected to pursue. While demographic reality places some limit on the number of cases in which race-based challenges will be an issue, every case contains a potential sex-based claim. Another consequence, as I have mentioned, is a lengthening of the *voir dire* process that already burdens trial courts. * * *

For these reasons, I dissent.

[JUSTICE KENNEDY's opinion, concurring in the judgment, and CHIEF JUSTICE REHNQUIST's dissenting opinion have been omitted.]

# CHAPTER 29

# THE ROLE OF CRIMINAL
# DEFENSE COUNSEL

■ ■ ■

The Sixth Amendment to the U.S. Constitution provides, "In all criminal prosecutions, the accused shall . . . have the Assistance of Counsel for his defence." In *Gideon v. Wainwright*, the U.S. Supreme Court held that the States, along with the federal government, must provide indigent defendants with appointed counsel at trial. This right to appointed counsel applies even to an indigent defendant charged with a misdemeanor who is sentenced to a term of imprisonment. *Argersinger v. Hamlin*, 407 U.S. 25 (1972). The chapter starts with an article by Barry Winston entitled, *Why I Defend Guilty Clients*.

In order to give the right to counsel meaning, the Court has held that the right to counsel includes the right to effective assistance of counsel. *Strickland v. Washington* elaborates on the meaning of *effective* assistance of counsel and outlines what a defendant must do in order to prevail on a claim of ineffective assistance of counsel. The next three cases apply the *Strickland* test for ineffective assistance of counsel. *Padilla v. Kentucky* examines whether an attorney's failure to inform his immigrant client that pleading guilty would subject the client to removal from the United States constitutes ineffective assistance of counsel. *Buck v. Davis* considers whether a criminal defense attorney's decision to call an expert witness to the stand in a capital case involving an African American defendant, knowing that the witness had written a report in which he opined there is an increased probability of future violence with respect to Black offenders, constitutes ineffective assistance of counsel. *Nix v. Whiteside* considers whether a criminal defense attorney's threat to withdraw if the client takes the stand and testifies in a way that the attorney thinks would be providing false testimony constitutes ineffective assistance of counsel.

The remaining cases in this chapter focus on other issues related to the right to counsel. *Wheat v. United States* examines whether the right to counsel includes a right to counsel of one's choice. *Faretta v. California* examines whether the right to counsel includes a right to proceed without counsel—in other words, a right of self-representation.

## WHY I DEFEND GUILTY CLIENTS

Barry Winston
Harper's Magazine (December 1986)

Let me tell you a story. A true story. The court records are all there if anyone wants to check. It's three years ago. I'm sitting in my office, staring out the window, when I get a call from a lawyer I hardly know. Tax lawyer. Some kid is in trouble and would I be interested in helping him out? He's charged with manslaughter, a felony, and driving under the influence. I tell him sure, have the kid call me.

So the kid calls and makes an appointment to see me. He's a nice kid, fresh out of college, and he's come down here to spend some time with his older sister, who's in med school. One day she tells him they're invited to a cookout with some friends of hers. She's going directly from class and he's going to take her car and meet her there. It's way out in the country, but he gets there before she does, introduces himself around, and pops a beer. She shows up after a while and he pops another beer. Then he eats a hamburger and drinks a third beer. At some point his sister says, "Well, it's about time to go," and they head for the car.

And, the kid tells me, sitting there in my office, the next thing he remembers, he's waking up in a hospital room, hurting like hell, bandages and casts all over him, and somebody is telling him he's charged with manslaughter and DUI because he wrecked his sister's car, killed her in the process, and blew fourteen on the Breathalyzer. I ask him what the hell he means by "the next thing he remembers," and he looks me straight in the eye and says he can't remember anything from the time they leave the cookout until he wakes up in the hospital. He tells me the doctors say he has post-retrograde amnesia. I say of course I believe him, but I'm worried about finding a judge who'll believe him.

I agree to represent him and send somebody for a copy of the wreck report. It says there are four witnesses: a couple in a car going the other way who passed the kid and his sister just before their car ran off the road, the guy whose front yard they landed in, and the trooper who investigated. I call the guy whose yard they ended up in. He isn't home. I leave word. Then I call the couple. The wife agrees to come in the next day with her husband. While I'm talking to her, the first guy calls. I call him back, introduce myself, tell him I'm representing the kid and need to talk to him about the accident. He hems and haws and I figure he's one of those people who think it's against the law to talk to defense lawyers. I say the D.A. will tell him it's O.K. to talk to me, but he doesn't have to. I give him the name and number of the D.A. and he says he'll call me back.

Then I go out and hunt up the trooper. He tells me the whole story. The kid and his sister are coming into town on Smith Level Road, after it turns from fifty-five to forty-five. The Thornes—the couple—are heading out of town. They say this sports car passes them, going the other way, right after that bad turn just south of the new subdivision. They say it's going like a striped-ass ape, at least sixty-five or seventy. Mrs. Thorne turns around to look and Mr. Thorne watches in the rearview mirror. They both see the same thing: halfway into the curve, the car runs off the road on the right, whips back onto the road, spins, runs off on the left, and disappears. They turn around in the first driveway they come to and start back, both terrified of what they're going to find. By this time, Trooper Johnson says, the guy whose front yard the car has ended up in has pulled the kid and his sister out of the wreck and started CPR on the girl. Turns out he's an emergency medical technician. Holloway, that's his name. Johnson tells me that Holloway says he's sitting in his front room, watching television, when he hears a hell of a crash in his yard. He runs outside and finds the car flipped over, and so he pulls the kid out from the driver's side, the girl from the other side. She dies in his arms.

And that, says Trooper Johnson, is that. The kid's blood/alcohol content was fourteen, he was going way too fast, and the girl is dead. He had to charge him. It's a shame, he seems a nice kid, it was his own sister and all, but what the hell can he do, right?

The next day the Thornes come in, and they confirm everything Johnson said. By now things are looking not so hot for my client, and I'm thinking it's about time to have a little chat with the D.A. But Holloway still hasn't called me back, so I call him. Not home. Leave word. No call. I wait a couple of days and call again. Finally I get him on the phone. He's very agitated, and won't talk to me except to say that he doesn't have to talk to me.

I know I better look for a deal, so I go to the D.A. He's very sympathetic. But. There's only so far you can get on sympathy. A young woman is dead, promising career cut short, all because somebody has too much to drink and drives. The kid has to pay. Not, the D.A. says, with jail time. But he's got to plead guilty to two misdemeanors: death by vehicle and driving under the influence. That means probation, a big fine. Several thousand dollars. Still, it's hard for me to criticize the D.A. After all, he's probably going to have the MADD mothers all over him because of reducing the felony to a misdemeanor.

On the day of the trial, I get to court a few minutes early. There are the Thornes and Trooper Johnson, and someone I assume is Holloway. Sure enough, when this guy sees me, he comes over and introduces himself and starts right in: "I just want you to know how serious all this drinking and driving really is," he says. "If those young people hadn't been drinking and driving that night, that poor young girl would be alive today." Now, I'm trying to hold my temper when I spot the D.A. I bolt across the room, grab him by the arm, and say, "We gotta talk. Why the hell have you got all those people here? That jerk Holloway. Surely to God you're not going to call him as a witness. This is a guilty plea! My client's parents are sitting out there. You don't need to put them through a dog-and-pony show."

The D.A. looks at me and says, "Man, I'm sorry, but in a case like this, I gotta put on witnesses. Weird Wally is on the bench. If I try to go without witnesses, he might throw me out."

The D.A. calls his first witness. Trooper Johnson identifies himself, tells about being called to the scene of the accident, and describes what he found when he got there and what everybody told him. After he finishes, the judge looks at me. "No questions," I say. Then the D.A. calls Holloway. He describes the noise, running out of the house, the upside down car in his yard, pulling my client out of the window on the left side of the car and then going around to the other side for the girl. When he gets to this part, he really hits his stride. He describes, in minute detail, the injuries he saw and what he did to try and save her life. And then he tells, breath by breath, how she died in his arms.

The D.A. says, "No further questions, your Honor." The judge looks at me. I shake my head, and he says to Holloway, "You may step down." One of those awful silences hangs there, and nothing happens for a minute. Holloway doesn't move. Then he looks at me, and at the D.A., and then at the judge. He says, "Can I say something else, your Honor?"

All my bells are ringing at once, and my gut is screaming at me, Object! Object! I'm trying to decide in three-quarters of a second whether it'll be worse to listen to a lecture on the evils of drink from this jerk Holloway or piss off the judge by objecting. But all I say is, "No objections, your Honor." The judge smiles at me, then at Holloway, and says, "Very well, Mr. Holloway. What did you wish to say?"

It all comes out in a rush. "Well, you see, your Honor," Holloway says, "it was just like I told Trooper Johnson. It all happened so fast. I heard the noise, and I came running out, and it was night, and I was excited, and the next morning, when I had a chance to think about it, I figured out what had happened, but by then I'd already told Trooper Johnson and I didn't know what to do, but you see, the car, it was up-side down, and I did pull that boy out of the left-hand window, but don't you see, the car was upside down, and if you turned it over on its wheels like it's supposed to be, the left-hand side is really on the right-hand side, and your Honor, that boy wasn't driving that car at all. It was the girl that was driving, and when I had a chance to think about it the next morning, I realized that I'd told Trooper Johnson wrong, and I was scared and I didn't know what to do, and that's why"—and now he's looking right at me—"why I wouldn't talk to you."

Naturally, the defendant is allowed to withdraw his guilty plea. The charges are dismissed and the kid and his parents and I go into one of the back rooms in the courthouse and sit there looking at one another for a while. Finally, we recover enough to mumble some Oh my Gods and Thank yous and You're welcomes. And that's why I can stand to represent somebody when I know he's guilty.

## STRICKLAND V. WASHINGTON

Supreme Court of the United States
466 U.S. 668, 104 S.Ct. 2052, 80 L.Ed.2d 674 (1984)

JUSTICE O'CONNOR delivered the opinion of the Court.

This case requires us to consider the proper standards for judging a criminal defendant's contention that the Constitution requires a conviction or death sentence to be set aside because counsel's assistance at the trial or sentencing was ineffective.

During a 10-day period in September 1976, respondent planned and committed three groups of crimes, which included three brutal stabbing murders, torture, kidnaping, severe assaults, attempted murders, attempted extortion, and theft. After his two accomplices were arrested, respondent surrendered to police and voluntarily gave a lengthy statement confessing to the third of the criminal episodes. The State of Florida indicted respondent for kidnaping and murder and appointed an experienced criminal lawyer to represent him.

Counsel actively pursued pretrial motions and discovery. He cut his efforts short, however, and he experienced a sense of hopelessness about the case, when he learned that, against his specific advice, respondent had also confessed to the first two murders. By the date set for trial, respondent was subject to indictment for three counts of first-degree murder and multiple counts of robbery, kidnaping for ransom, breaking and entering and assault, attempted murder, and conspiracy to commit robbery. Respondent waived his right to a jury trial, again acting against counsel's advice, and pleaded guilty to all charges, including the three capital murder charges. * * *

Counsel advised respondent to invoke his right under Florida law to an advisory jury at his capital sentencing hearing. Respondent rejected the advice and waived the right. He chose instead to be sentenced by the trial judge without a jury recommendation.

In preparing for the sentencing hearing, counsel spoke with respondent about his background. He also spoke on the telephone with respondent's wife and mother, though he did not follow up on the one unsuccessful effort to meet with them. He did not otherwise seek out character witnesses for respondent. Nor did he request a psychiatric examination, since his conversations with his client gave no indication that respondent had psychological problems.

Counsel decided not to present and hence not to look further for evidence concerning respondent's character and emotional state. That decision reflected trial counsel's sense of hopelessness about overcoming the evidentiary effect of respondent's confessions to the gruesome crimes. * * * [B]y forgoing the opportunity to present new evidence on these subjects, counsel prevented the State from cross-examining respondent on his claim and from putting on psychiatric evidence of its own.

Counsel also excluded from the sentencing hearing other evidence he thought was potentially damaging. He successfully moved to exclude respondent's "rap sheet." Because he judged that a presentence report might prove more detrimental than helpful, as it would have included respondent's criminal history and thereby would have undermined the claim of no significant history of criminal activity, he did not request that one be prepared.

At the sentencing hearing, * * * [c]ounsel argued that respondent's remorse and acceptance of responsibility justified sparing him from the death penalty. Counsel also argued that respondent had no history of criminal activity and that respondent committed the crimes under extreme mental or emotional disturbance, thus coming within the statutory list of mitigating circumstances. He further argued that respondent should be spared death because he had surrendered, confessed, and offered to testify against a codefendant and because respondent was fundamentally a good person who had briefly gone badly wrong in extremely stressful circumstances. The State put on evidence and witnesses largely for the purpose of describing the details of the crimes. Counsel did not cross-examine the medical experts who testified about the manner of death of respondent's victims.

* * * [T]he trial judge found numerous aggravating circumstances and no * * * mitigating circumstance. * * * He therefore sentenced respondent to death on each of the three counts of murder and to prison terms for the other crimes. * * *

Respondent subsequently sought collateral relief in state court on numerous grounds, among them that counsel had rendered ineffective assistance at the sentencing proceeding. Respondent challenged counsel's assistance in six respects. He asserted that counsel was ineffective because he failed to move for a continuance to prepare for sentencing, to request a psychiatric report, to investigate and present character witnesses, to seek a presentence investigation report, to present meaningful arguments to the sentencing judge, and to investigate the medical examiner's reports or cross-examine the medical experts. In support of the claim, respondent submitted 14 affidavits from friends, neighbors, and relatives stating that they would have testified if asked to do so. He also submitted one psychiatric report and one psychological report stating that respondent, though not under the influence of extreme mental or emotional disturbance, was "chronically frustrated and depressed because of his economic dilemma" at the time of his crimes. * * *

Because of the vital importance of counsel's assistance, this Court has held that, with certain exceptions, a person accused of a federal or state crime has the right to have counsel appointed if retained counsel cannot be obtained. That a person who happens to be a lawyer is present at trial alongside the accused, however, is not enough to satisfy the constitutional command. The Sixth Amendment recognizes the right to the assistance of counsel because it envisions counsel's playing a role that is critical to the ability of the adversarial system to produce just results. An accused is entitled to be assisted by an attorney, whether retained or appointed, who plays the role necessary to ensure that the trial is fair.

For that reason, the Court has recognized that "the right to counsel is the right to the effective assistance of counsel." * * *

The Court has not elaborated on the meaning of the constitutional requirement of effective assistance in the latter class of cases—that is, those presenting claims of "actual ineffectiveness." In giving meaning to the requirement, however, we must take its purpose—to ensure a fair trial—as the guide. The benchmark for judging any claim of ineffectiveness must be whether counsel's conduct so undermined the proper functioning of the adversarial process that the trial cannot be relied on as having produced a just result. * * *

A convicted defendant's claim that counsel's assistance was so defective as to require reversal of a conviction or death sentence has two components. First, the defendant must show that counsel's performance was deficient. This requires showing that counsel made errors so serious that counsel was not functioning as the "counsel" guaranteed the defendant by the Sixth Amendment. Second, the defendant must show that the deficient performance prejudiced the defense. This requires showing that counsel's errors were so serious as to deprive the defendant of a fair trial, a trial whose result is reliable. Unless a defendant makes both showings, it cannot be said that the conviction or death sentence resulted from a breakdown in the adversary process that renders the result unreliable.

As all the Federal Courts of Appeals have now held, the proper standard for attorney performance is that of reasonably effective assistance. * * * When a convicted defendant complains of the ineffectiveness of counsel's assistance, the defendant must show that counsel's representation fell below an objective standard of reasonableness. * * * In any case presenting an ineffectiveness claim, the performance inquiry must be whether counsel's assistance was reasonable considering all the circumstances. * * *

Judicial scrutiny of counsel's performance must be highly deferential. It is all too tempting for a defendant to second-guess counsel's assistance after conviction or adverse sentence, and it is all too easy for a court, examining counsel's defense after it has proved unsuccessful, to conclude that a particular act or omission of counsel was unreasonable. A fair assessment of attorney performance requires that every effort be made to eliminate the distorting effects of hindsight, to reconstruct the circumstances of counsel's challenged conduct, and to evaluate the conduct from counsel's perspective at the time. Because of the difficulties inherent in making the evaluation, a court must indulge a strong presumption that counsel's conduct falls within the wide range of reasonable professional assistance; that is, the defendant must overcome the presumption that, under the circumstances, the challenged action "might be considered sound trial strategy." There are countless ways to provide effective assistance in any given case. Even the best criminal defense attorneys would not defend a particular client in the same way.

The availability of intrusive post-trial inquiry into attorney performance or of detailed guidelines for its evaluation would encourage the proliferation of ineffectiveness challenges. Criminal trials resolved unfavorably to the defendant would increasingly come to be followed by a second trial, this one of counsel's unsuccessful defense. Counsel's performance and even willingness to serve could be adversely affected. Intensive scrutiny of counsel and rigid requirements for acceptable assistance could dampen the ardor and impair the independence of defense counsel, discourage the acceptance of assigned cases, and undermine the trust between attorney and client.

Thus, a court * * * must judge the reasonableness of counsel's challenged conduct on the facts of the particular case, viewed as of the time of counsel's conduct. A convicted defendant making a claim of ineffective assistance must identify the acts or omissions of counsel that are alleged not to have been the result of reasonable professional judgment. The court must then determine whether, in light of all the circumstances, the identified acts or omissions were outside the wide range of professionally competent assistance. In making that determination, the court should keep in mind that counsel's function, as elaborated in prevailing professional norms, is to make the adversarial testing process work in the particular case. At the same time, the court should recognize that counsel is strongly presumed to have rendered adequate assistance and made all significant decisions in the exercise of reasonable professional judgment. * * *

An error by counsel, even if professionally unreasonable, does not warrant setting aside the judgment of a criminal proceeding if the error had no effect on the judgment. The purpose of the Sixth Amendment guarantee of counsel is to ensure that a defendant has the assistance necessary to justify reliance on the outcome of the proceeding. Accordingly, any deficiencies in counsel's performance must be prejudicial to the defense in order to constitute ineffective assistance under the Constitution.

It is not enough for the defendant to show that the errors had some conceivable effect on the outcome of the proceeding. Virtually every act or omission of counsel would meet that test, and not every error that conceivably could have influenced the outcome undermines the reliability of the result of the proceeding.

* * * [T]he appropriate test for prejudice finds its roots in the test for materiality of exculpatory information not disclosed to the defense by the prosecution * * *. The defendant must show that there is a reasonable probability that, but for counsel's unprofessional errors, the result of the proceeding would have been different. A reasonable probability is a probability sufficient to undermine confidence in the outcome.

* * * [T]he ultimate focus of inquiry must be on the fundamental fairness of the proceeding whose result is being challenged. In every case the court should be concerned with whether, despite the strong presumption of reliability, the result of the particular proceeding is unreliable because of a breakdown in the adversarial process that our system counts on to produce just results. * * *

Although we have discussed the performance component of an ineffectiveness claim prior to the prejudice component, there is no reason for a court deciding an ineffective assistance claim to approach the inquiry in the same order or even to address both components of the inquiry if the defendant makes an insufficient showing on one. In particular, a court need not determine whether counsel's performance was deficient before examining the prejudice suffered by the defendant as a result of the alleged deficiencies. The object of an ineffectiveness claim is not to grade counsel's performance. If it is easier to dispose of an ineffectiveness claim on the ground of lack of sufficient prejudice, which we expect will often be so, that course should be followed. Courts should strive to ensure that ineffectiveness claims not become so burdensome to defense counsel that the entire criminal justice system suffers as a result. * * *

Having articulated general standards for judging ineffectiveness claims, we think it useful to apply those standards to the facts of this case in order to illustrate the meaning of the general principles. * * * Application of the governing principles is not difficult in this case. The facts as described above make clear that the conduct of respondent's counsel at and before respondents sentencing proceeding cannot be found unreasonable. They also make clear that, even assuming the challenged conduct of counsel was unreasonable, respondent suffered insufficient prejudice to warrant setting aside his death sentence.

With respect to the performance component, the record shows that respondent's counsel made a strategic choice to argue for the extreme emotional distress mitigating circumstance and to rely as fully as possible on respondent's acceptance of responsibility for his crimes. Although counsel understandably felt hopeless about respondent's prospects, nothing in the record indicates * * * that counsel's sense of hopelessness distorted his professional judgment. Counsel's strategy choice was well within the range of professionally reasonable judgments, and the decision not to seek more character or psychological evidence than was already in hand was likewise reasonable.

* * * The aggravating circumstances were utterly overwhelming. Trial counsel could reasonably surmise from his conversations with respondent that character and psychological evidence would be of little help. * * * Restricting testimony on respondent's character to what had come in at the plea colloquy ensured that contrary character and psychological evidence and respondent's criminal history, which counsel had successfully moved to exclude, would not come in. On these facts, there can be little question, even without application of the presumption of adequate performance, that trial counsel's defense, though unsuccessful, was the result of reasonable professional judgment.

With respect to the prejudice component, the lack of merit of respondent's claim is even more stark. The evidence that respondent says his trial counsel should have offered at the sentencing hearing would barely have altered the sentencing profile presented to the sentencing judge. * * * [A]t most this evidence shows that numerous people who knew respondent thought he was generally a good person and that a psychiatrist and a psychologist believed he was under considerable emotional stress that did not rise to the level of extreme disturbance. Given the overwhelming aggravating factors, there is no reasonable probability that the omitted evidence would have changed the conclusion that the aggravating circumstances outweighed the mitigating circumstances and, hence, the sentence imposed. * * *

Failure to make the required showing of either deficient performance or sufficient prejudice defeats the ineffectiveness claim. Here there is a double failure. More generally, respondent has made no showing that the justice of his sentence was rendered unreliable by a breakdown in the adversary process caused by deficiencies in counsel's assistance. Respondent's sentencing proceeding was not fundamentally unfair. * * *

JUSTICE MARSHALL, dissenting. * * *

My objection to the performance standard adopted by the Court is that it is so malleable that, in practice, it will either have no grip at all or will yield excessive variation in the manner in which the Sixth Amendment is interpreted and applied by different courts. To tell lawyers and the lower courts that counsel for a criminal defendant must behave "reasonably" and must act like "a reasonably competent attorney," is to tell them almost nothing. In essence, the majority has instructed judges called upon to assess claims of ineffective assistance of counsel to advert to their own intuitions regarding what constitutes "professional" representation, and has discouraged them from trying to develop more detailed standards governing the performance of defense counsel. In my view, the Court has thereby not only abdicated its own responsibility to interpret the Constitution, but also impaired the ability of the lower courts to exercise theirs. * * *

I object to the prejudice standard adopted by the Court for two independent reasons. First, it is often very difficult to tell whether a defendant convicted after a trial in which he was ineffectively represented would have fared better if his lawyer had been competent. Seemingly impregnable cases can sometimes be dismantled by good defense counsel. On the basis of a cold record, it may be impossible for a reviewing court confidently to ascertain how the government's evidence and arguments would have stood up against rebuttal and cross-examination by a shrewd, well-prepared lawyer. The difficulties of estimating prejudice after the fact are exacerbated by the possibility that evidence of injury to the defendant may be missing from the record precisely because of the incompetence of defense counsel. In view of all these impediments to a fair evaluation of the probability that the outcome of a trial was affected by ineffectiveness of counsel, it seems to me senseless to impose on a defendant whose lawyer has been shown to have been incompetent the burden of demonstrating prejudice.

Second and more fundamentally, the assumption on which the Court's holding rests is that the only purpose of the constitutional guarantee of effective assistance of counsel is to reduce the chance that innocent persons will be convicted. In my view, the guarantee also functions to ensure that convictions are obtained only through fundamentally fair procedures. The majority contends that the Sixth Amendment is not violated when a manifestly guilty defendant is convicted after a trial in which he was represented by a manifestly ineffective attorney. I cannot agree. Every defendant is entitled to a trial in which his interests are vigorously and conscientiously advocated by an able lawyer. A proceeding in which the defendant does not receive meaningful assistance in meeting the forces of the State does not, in my opinion, constitute due process.

* * * I would thus hold that a showing that the performance of a defendant's lawyer departed from constitutionally prescribed standards requires a new trial regardless of whether the defendant suffered demonstrable prejudice thereby. * * *

[JUSTICE BRENNAN's opinion, concurring in part and dissenting in part, has been omitted.]

## NOTE

David LeRoy Washington was executed on July 13, 1984. *Killer tells daughter to 'do better,'* CHICAGO TRIBUNE, July 14, 1984, at 3, http://archives. chicagotribune.com/1984/07/14/page/3     or     https://perma.cc/C3Z2-ZXF6. Before being executed, he said "I'd like to say to the families of all my victims, I'm sorry for all the grief and heartache I brought to them," *Id. See also* Kenneth A. Soo, *David LeRoy Washington, a former choir boy who stabbed three,* UPI, (July 13, 1984), https://www.upi.com/Archives/1984/07/13/David-Leroy-Washington-a-former-choirboy-who-stabbed-three/3676458539200/ or https://perma.cc/D3T8-JYKN.

## PADILLA V. KENTUCKY

Supreme Court of the United States
559 U.S. 356, 130 S.Ct. 1473, 176 L.Ed.2d 284 (2010)

JUSTICE STEVENS delivered the opinion of the Court.

Petitioner Jose Padilla, a native of Honduras, has been a lawful permanent resident of the United States for more than 40 years. Padilla served this Nation with honor as a member of the U.S. Armed Forces during the Vietnam War. He now faces deportation after pleading guilty to the transportation of a large amount of marijuana in his tractor-trailer in the Commonwealth of Kentucky.

In this post-conviction proceeding, Padilla claims that his counsel not only failed to advise him of this consequence prior to his entering the plea, but also told him that he "did not have to worry about immigration status since he had been in the country so long." Padilla relied on his counsel's erroneous advice when he pleaded guilty to the drug charges that made his deportation virtually mandatory. He alleges that he would have insisted on going to trial if he had not received incorrect advice from his attorney. * * *

We granted certiorari to decide whether, as a matter of federal law, Padilla's counsel had an obligation to advise him that the offense to which he was pleading guilty would result in his removal from this country. * * *

Before deciding whether to plead guilty, a defendant is entitled to "the effective assistance of competent counsel." The Supreme Court of Kentucky rejected Padilla's ineffectiveness claim on the ground that the advice he sought about the risk of deportation concerned only collateral matters, i.e., those matters not within the sentencing authority of the state trial court. In its view, "collateral consequences are outside the scope of representation required by the Sixth Amendment," and, therefore, the "failure of defense counsel to advise the defendant of possible deportation consequences is not cognizable as a claim for ineffective assistance of counsel." The Kentucky high court is far from alone in this view.

We, however, have never applied a distinction between direct and collateral consequences to define the scope of constitutionally "reasonable professional assistance" required under *Strickland*. Whether that distinction is appropriate is a question we need not consider in this case because of the unique nature of deportation. * * *

Deportation as a consequence of a criminal conviction is, because of its close connection to the criminal process, uniquely difficult to classify as either a direct or a collateral consequence. The collateral versus direct distinction is thus ill suited to evaluating a *Strickland* claim concerning the specific risk of deportation. We conclude that advice regarding deportation is not categorically removed from the ambit of the Sixth Amendment right to counsel. *Strickland* applies to Padilla's claim.

Under *Strickland,* we first determine whether counsel's representation "fell below an objective standard of reasonableness." Then we ask whether "there is a reasonable probability that, but for counsel's unprofessional errors, the result of the proceeding would have been different." The first prong—constitutional deficiency—is necessarily linked to the practice and expectations of the legal community: "The proper measure of attorney performance remains simply reasonableness under prevailing professional norms." * * *

The weight of prevailing professional norms supports the view that counsel must advise her client regarding the risk of deportation. "[A]uthorities of every stripe—including the American Bar Association, criminal defense and public defender organizations, authoritative treatises, and state and city bar publications—universally require defense attorneys to advise as to the risk of deportation consequences for non-citizen clients. . . ."

We too have previously recognized that "[p]reserving the client's right to remain in the United States may be more important to the client than any potential jail sentence." * * *

In the instant case, the terms of the relevant immigration statute are succinct, clear, and explicit in defining the removal consequence for Padilla's conviction. This is not a hard case in which to find deficiency: The consequences of Padilla's plea could easily be determined from reading the removal statute, his deportation was presumptively mandatory, and his counsel's advice was incorrect.

Immigration law can be complex, and it is a legal specialty of its own. Some members of the bar who represent clients facing criminal charges, in either state or federal court or both, may not be well versed in it. There will, therefore, undoubtedly be numerous situations in which the deportation consequences of a particular plea are unclear or uncertain. The duty of the private practitioner in such cases is more limited. When the law is not succinct and straightforward (as it is in many of the scenarios posited by Justice Alito), a criminal defense attorney need do no more than advise a noncitizen client that pending criminal charges may carry a risk of adverse immigration consequences. But when the deportation consequence is truly clear, as it was in this case, the duty to give correct advice is equally clear.

Accepting his allegations as true, Padilla has sufficiently alleged constitutional deficiency to satisfy the first prong of *Strickland*. Whether Padilla is entitled to relief on his claim will depend on whether he can satisfy *Strickland's* second prong, prejudice, a matter we leave to the Kentucky courts to consider in the first instance.[a] * * *

In sum, we have long recognized that the negotiation of a plea bargain is a critical phase of litigation for purposes of the Sixth Amendment right to effective assistance of counsel. The severity of deportation—"the equivalent of banishment or exile,"—only underscores how critical it is for counsel to inform her noncitizen client that he faces a risk of deportation.

It is our responsibility under the Constitution to ensure that no criminal defendant—whether a citizen or not—is left to the "mercies of incompetent counsel." To satisfy this responsibility, we now hold that counsel must inform her client whether his plea carries a risk of deportation. Our longstanding Sixth Amendment precedents, the seriousness of deportation as a consequence of a criminal plea, and the concomitant impact of deportation on families living lawfully in this country demand no less. * * *

The judgment of the Supreme Court of Kentucky is reversed, and the case is remanded for further proceedings not inconsistent with this opinion.

JUSTICE ALITO, with whom THE CHIEF JUSTICE joins, concurring in the judgment.

* * * The Court * * * holds that a criminal defense attorney must provide advice in this specialized area [of immigration law] in those cases in which the law is "succinct and straightforward"—but not, perhaps, in other situations. This vague, halfway test will lead to much confusion and needless litigation.

Under *Strickland,* an attorney provides ineffective assistance if the attorney's representation does not meet reasonable professional standards. Until today, the longstanding and unanimous position of the federal courts was that reasonable defense counsel generally need only advise a client

---

[a]    On remand, the Court of Appeals of Kentucky found prejudice and ordered that Mr. Padilla's conviction be reversed. *See* Padilla v. Commonwealth, 381 S.W.2d 322 (Ky. App. 2012) (remanding the case to the Circuit Court for an order vacating Padilla's judgment and conviction). It is unlikely that Mr. Padilla was re-prosecuted because he had already served his full sentence. Margaret Love & Gabriel J. Chin, *The "Major Upheaval" of* Padilla v. Kentucky: *Extending the Right to Counsel to the Collateral Consequences of Conviction*, 25 CRIMINAL JUSTICE 173, 176 (2010).

about the *direct* consequences of a criminal conviction. While the line between "direct" and "collateral" consequences is not always clear, the collateral-consequences rule expresses an important truth: Criminal defense attorneys have expertise regarding the conduct of criminal proceedings. They are not expected to possess—and very often do not possess—expertise in other areas of the law, and it is unrealistic to expect them to provide expert advice on matters that lie outside their area of training and experience.

This case happens to involve removal, but criminal convictions can carry a wide variety of consequences other than conviction and sentencing, including civil commitment, civil forfeiture, the loss of the right to vote, disqualification from public benefits, ineligibility to possess firearms, dishonorable discharge from the Armed Forces, and loss of business or professional licenses. A criminal conviction may also severely damage a defendant's reputation and thus impair the defendant's ability to obtain future employment or business opportunities. All of those consequences are "seriou[s]," but this Court has never held that a criminal defense attorney's Sixth Amendment duties extend to providing advice about such matters. * * *

The Court's new approach is particularly problematic because providing advice on whether a conviction for a particular offense will make an alien removable is often quite complex. "Most crimes affecting immigration status are not specifically mentioned by the [Immigration and Nationality Act (INA)], but instead fall under a broad category of crimes, such as *crimes involving moral turpitude* or *aggravated felonies*." As has been widely acknowledged, determining whether a particular crime is an "aggravated felony" or a "crime involving moral turpitude [(CIMT)]" is not an easy task.

Defense counsel who consults a guidebook on whether a particular crime is an "aggravated felony" will often find that the answer is not "easily ascertained." For example, the ABA Guidebook answers the question "Does simple possession count as an aggravated felony?" as follows: "Yes, *at least in the Ninth Circuit*." After a dizzying paragraph that attempts to explain the evolution of the Ninth Circuit's view, the ABA Guidebook continues: "Adding to the confusion, however, is that the Ninth Circuit has conflicting opinions depending on the context on whether simple drug possession constitutes an aggravated felony under 8 U.S.C. § 1101(a)(43)." * * *

Determining whether a particular crime is one involving moral turpitude is no easier. See *id.*, at 134 ("Writing bad checks *may or may not* be a CIMT" (emphasis added)); *ibid.* ("[R]eckless assault coupled with an element of injury, but not serious injury, is *probably* not a CIMT" (emphasis added)); *id.*, at 135 (misdemeanor driving under the influence is generally not a CIMT, but may be a CIMT if the DUI results in injury or if the driver knew that his license had been suspended or revoked); *id.*, at 136 ("If there is no element of actual injury, the endangerment offense *may* not be a CIMT" (emphasis added)); *ibid.* ("Whether [a child abuse] conviction involves moral turpitude *may* depend on the subsection under which the individual is convicted. Child abuse done with criminal negligence *probably* is not a CIMT" (emphasis added)). * * *

The Court tries to downplay the severity of the burden it imposes on defense counsel by suggesting that the scope of counsel's duty to offer advice concerning deportation consequences may turn on how hard it is to determine those consequences. Where "the terms of the relevant immigration statute are succinct, clear, and explicit in defining the removal consequence[s]" of a conviction, the Court says, counsel has an affirmative duty to advise the client that he will be subject to deportation as a result of the plea. But "[w]hen the law is not succinct and straightforward . . . , a criminal defense attorney need do no more than advise a noncitizen client that pending criminal charges may carry a risk of adverse immigration consequences." This approach is problematic for at least four reasons.

First, it will not always be easy to tell whether a particular statutory provision is "succinct, clear, and explicit." How can an attorney who lacks general immigration law expertise be sure that a seemingly clear statutory provision actually means what it seems to say when read in isolation? What if the application of the provision to a particular case is not clear but a cursory examination of case law or administrative decisions would provide a definitive answer?

Second, if defense counsel must provide advice regarding only one of the many collateral consequences of a criminal conviction, many defendants are likely to be misled. To take just one example, a conviction for a particular offense may render an alien excludable but not removable. If an alien charged with such an offense is advised only that pleading guilty to such an offense will not result in removal, the alien may be induced to enter a guilty plea without realizing that a consequence of the plea is that the alien will be unable to reenter the United States if the alien returns to his or her home country for any reason, such as to visit an elderly parent or to attend a funeral. Incomplete legal advice may be worse than no advice at all because it may mislead and may dissuade the client from seeking advice from a more knowledgeable source.

Third, the Court's rigid constitutional rule could inadvertently head off more promising ways of addressing the underlying problem—such as statutory or administrative reforms requiring trial judges to inform a defendant on the record that a guilty plea may carry adverse immigration consequences. As *amici* point out, "28 states and the District of Columbia have *already* adopted rules, plea forms, or statutes requiring courts to advise criminal defendants of the possible immigration consequences of their pleas." * * *

Fourth, the Court's decision marks a major upheaval in Sixth Amendment law. This Court decided *Strickland* in 1984, but the majority does not cite a single case, from this or any other federal court, holding that criminal defense counsel's failure to provide advice concerning the removal consequences of a criminal conviction violates a defendant's Sixth Amendment right to counsel. * * * [T]he Court's view has been rejected by every Federal Court of Appeals to have considered the issue thus far. * * *

[JUSTICE SCALIA's dissent has been omitted.]

## NOTE

It is clear from *Padilla v. Kentucky* that a defendant has a right to effective assistance of counsel in the plea process. Claims of ineffective assistance in the plea context, just like ineffective assistance of counsel claims in other contexts, are governed by the two-part test set forth in *Strickland v. Washington*. The prejudice prong, however, is analyzed a bit differently in cases where the defendant accepts a guilty plea. When a defendant alleges ineffective assistance of counsel led him to accept a guilty plea rather than go to trial, "we do not ask whether, had he gone to trial, the result of that trial 'would have been different' than the result of the plea bargain." *Lee v. United States*, 582 U.S. ___, 137 S.Ct. 1958 (2017). Instead, in order to establish prejudice, the defendant must show "a reasonable probability that, but for counsel's errors, he would not have pled guilty and would have insisted on going to trial." *Id.*, citing *Hill v. Lockhart*, 474 U.S. 52, 59 (1985).

*Padilla v. Kentucky* involved defense counsel who gave incorrect advice relating to the plea. What if defense counsel fails to communicate a favorable plea offer to his client? In *Missouri v. Frye*, 566 U.S. 133 (2012), the Court examined whether a criminal defense attorney's failure to communicate a favorable plea offer from the prosecutor to the client before its expiration constituted ineffective assistance of counsel. The Court held that defense counsel has a duty to communicate favorable plea offers from the prosecutor and that by failing to communicate a plea offer to the client before it expired, defense counsel did not render the effective assistance of counsel that the Constitution requires. The Court, however, also held that in order to show prejudice from such ineffective assistance of counsel, "defendants must demonstrate a reasonable probability they would have accepted the earlier plea offer had they been afforded effective assistance of counsel" and that "the plea would have been entered without the prosecution canceling it or the trial court refusing to accept it." *Id.* at 1409.

In the next case, the Court has to decide whether a criminal defense attorney's decision in a capital case to call a psychologist to testify during the sentencing phase of the case constituted ineffective assistance of counsel. The psychologist, who had been appointed by the court to interview the attorney's African American client, had written a report in which he opined that there is an increased probability of future violence with Black offenders.

## BUCK V. DAVIS

Supreme Court of the United States
580 U.S. ___, 137 S.Ct. 759, 197 L.Ed.2d 1 (2017)

CHIEF JUSTICE ROBERTS delivered the opinion of the Court.

A Texas jury convicted petitioner Duane Buck of capital murder. Under state law, the jury could impose a death sentence only if it found that Buck was likely to commit acts of violence in the future. Buck's attorney called a psychologist to offer his opinion on that issue. The psychologist testified that Buck probably would not engage in violent conduct. But he also stated that one of the factors pertinent in assessing a person's propensity for violence was his race, and that Buck was statistically more likely to act violently because he is black. The jury sentenced Buck to death.* * *

On the morning of July 30, 1995, Duane Buck arrived at the home of his former girlfriend, Debra Gardner. He was carrying a rifle and a shotgun. Buck entered the home, shot Phyllis Taylor, his stepsister, and then shot Gardner's friend Kenneth Butler. Gardner fled the house, and Buck followed. So did Gardner's young children. While Gardner's son and daughter begged for their mother's life, Buck shot Gardner in the chest. Gardner and Butler died of their wounds. Taylor survived.

Police officers arrived soon after the shooting and placed Buck under arrest. An officer would later testify that Buck was laughing at the scene. He remained "happy" and "upbeat" as he was driven to the police station, "[s]miling and laughing" in the back of the patrol car.

Buck was tried for capital murder, and the jury convicted. During the penalty phase of the trial, the jury was charged with deciding two issues. The first was what the parties term the "future dangerousness" question. At the time of Buck's trial, a Texas jury could impose the death penalty only if it found—unanimously and beyond a reasonable doubt—"a probability that the defendant would commit criminal acts of violence that would constitute a continuing threat to society." The second issue, to be reached only if the jury found Buck likely to be a future danger, was whether mitigating circumstances nevertheless warranted a sentence of life imprisonment instead of death.

The parties focused principally on the first question. The State called witnesses who emphasized the brutality of Buck's crime and his evident lack of remorse in its aftermath. The State also called another former girl-friend, Vivian Jackson. She testified that, during their relationship, Buck had routinely hit her and had twice pointed a gun at her. Finally, the State introduced evidence of Buck's criminal history, including convictions for delivery of cocaine and unlawfully carrying a weapon.

Defense counsel answered with a series of lay witnesses, including Buck's father and stepmother, who testified that they had never known him to be violent. Counsel also called two psychologists to testify as experts. The first, Dr. Patrick Lawrence, observed that Buck had previously served time in prison and had been held in minimum custody. From this he concluded that Buck "did not present any problems in the prison setting." Dr. Lawrence further testified that murders within the Texas penal system tend to be gang related (there was no evidence Buck had ever been a member of a gang) and that Buck's offense had been a "crime of passion" occurring within the context of a romantic relationship. Based on these considerations, Dr. Lawrence determined that Buck was unlikely to be a danger if he were sentenced to life in prison.

Buck's second expert, Dr. Walter Quijano, had been appointed by the presiding judge to conduct a psychological evaluation. Dr. Quijano had met with Buck in prison prior to trial and shared a report of his findings with defense counsel.

Like Dr. Lawrence, Dr. Quijano thought it significant that Buck's prior acts of violence had arisen from romantic relationships with women; Buck, of course, would not form any such relationships while incarcerated. And Dr. Quijano likewise considered Buck's behavioral record in prison a good indicator that future violence was unlikely.

But there was more to the report. In determining whether Buck was likely to pose a danger in the future, Dr. Quijano considered seven "statistical factors." The fourth factor was "race." His report read, in relevant part: "4. Race. Black: Increased probability. There is an overrepresentation of Blacks among the violent offenders."

Despite knowing Dr. Quijano's view that Buck's race was competent evidence of an increased probability of future violence, defense counsel called Dr. Quijano to the stand and asked him to discuss the "statistical factors" he had "looked at in regard to this case." Dr. Quijano responded that certain factors were "know[n] to predict future dangerousness" and, consistent with his report, identified race as one of them. It's a sad commentary," he testified, "that minorities, Hispanics and black people, are over represented in the Criminal Justice System." Through further questioning, counsel elicited testimony concerning factors Dr. Quijano thought favorable to Buck, as well as his ultimate opinion that Buck was unlikely to pose a danger in the future. At the close of Dr. Quijano's testimony, his report was admitted into evidence.

After opening cross-examination with a series of general questions, the prosecutor likewise turned to the report. She asked first about the statistical factors of past crimes and age, then questioned Dr. Quijano about the roles of sex and race: "You have determined that the sex factor, that a male is more violent than a female because that's just the way it is, and that the race factor, black, increases the future dangerousness for various complicated reasons; is that correct?" Dr. Quijano replied, "Yes." * * *

The jury deliberated over the course of two days. During that time it sent out four notes, one of which requested the "psychology reports" that had been admitted into evidence. These reports—including Dr. Quijano's— were provided. The jury returned a sentence of death.

* * * The Sixth Amendment right to counsel "is the right to the effective assistance of counsel." A defendant who claims to have been denied effective assistance must show both that counsel performed deficiently and that counsel's deficient performance caused him prejudice.

*Strickland's* first prong sets a high bar. A defense lawyer navigating a criminal proceeding faces any number of choices about how best to make a client's case. The lawyer has discharged his constitutional responsibility so long as his decisions fall within the "wide range of professionally competent assistance." It is only when the lawyer's errors were "so serious that counsel was not functioning as the 'counsel' guaranteed . . . by the Sixth Amendment" that Strickland's first prong is satisfied.

The District Court determined that, in this case, counsel's performance fell outside the bounds of competent representation. We agree. Counsel knew that Dr. Quijano's report reflected the view that Buck's race disproportionately predisposed him to violent conduct; he also knew that the principal point of dispute during the trial's penalty phase was whether Buck was likely to act violently in the future. Counsel nevertheless (1) called Dr. Quijano to the stand; (2) specifically elicited testimony about the connection between Buck's race and the likelihood of future violence; and (3) put into evidence Dr. Quijano's expert report that stated, in reference to factors bearing on future dangerousness, "Race. Black: Increased probability."

Given that the jury had to make a finding of future dangerousness before it could impose a death sentence, Dr. Quijano's report said, in effect, that the color of Buck's skin made him more deserving of execution. It would be patently unconstitutional for a state to argue that a defendant is liable to be a future danger because of his race. No competent defense attorney would introduce such evidence about his own client.

To satisfy *Strickland*, a litigant must also demonstrate prejudice—"a reasonable probability that, but for counsel's unprofessional errors, the result of the proceeding would have been different." Accordingly, the question before the District Court was whether Buck had demonstrated a reasonable probability that, without Dr. Quijano's testimony on race, at least one juror would have harbored a reasonable doubt about whether Buck was likely to be violent in the future. The District Court concluded that Buck had not made such a showing. We disagree.

In arguing that the jury would have imposed a death sentence even if Dr. Quijano had not offered race-based testimony, the State primarily emphasizes the brutality of Buck's crime and his lack of remorse. A jury may conclude that a crime's vicious nature calls for a sentence of death. In this case, however, several considerations convince us that it is reasonably probable—notwithstanding the nature of Buck's crime and his behavior in its aftermath— that the proceeding would have ended differently had counsel rendered competent representation.

Dr. Quijano testified on the key point at issue in Buck's sentencing. True, the jury was asked to decide two issues—whether Buck was likely to be a future danger, and, if so, whether mitigating circumstances nevertheless justified a sentence of life imprisonment. But the focus of the proceeding was on the first question. Much of the penalty phase testimony was directed to future dangerousness, as were the summations for both sides. The jury, consistent with the focus of the parties, asked during deliberations to see the expert reports on dangerousness.

Deciding the key issue of Buck's dangerousness involved an unusual inquiry. The jurors were not asked to determine a historical fact concerning Buck's conduct, but to render a predictive judgment inevitably entailing a degree of speculation. Buck, all agreed, had committed acts of terrible violence. Would he do so again?

Buck's prior violent acts had occurred outside of prison, and within the context of romantic relationships with women. If the jury did not impose a death sentence, Buck would be sentenced to life in prison, and no such romantic relationship would be likely to arise. A jury could conclude that those changes would minimize the prospect of future dangerousness.

But one thing would never change: the color of Buck's skin. Buck would always be black. And according to Dr. Quijano, that immutable characteristic carried with it an "[i]ncreased probability" of future violence. Here was hard statistical evidence—from an expert—to guide an otherwise speculative inquiry.

And it was potent evidence. Dr. Quijano's testimony appealed to a powerful racial stereotype—that of black men as "violence prone." In combination with the substance of the jury's inquiry, this created something of a perfect storm. Dr. Quijano's opinion coincided precisely with a particularly noxious strain of racial prejudice, which itself coincided precisely with the central question at sentencing. The effect of this unusual confluence of factors was to provide support for making a decision on life or death on the basis of race.

This effect was heightened due to the source of the testimony. Dr. Quijano took the stand as a medical expert bearing the court's imprimatur. The jury learned at the outset of his testimony that he held a doctorate in clinical psychology, had conducted evaluations in some 70 capital murder cases, and had been appointed by the trial judge (at public expense) to evaluate Buck. Reasonable jurors might well have valued his opinion concerning the central question before them.

For these reasons, we cannot accept the District Court's conclusion that "the introduction of any mention of race" during the penalty phase was "*de minimis.*" There were only "two references to race in Dr. Quijano's testimony"—one during direct examination, the other on cross. But when a jury hears expert testimony that expressly makes a defendant's race directly pertinent on the question of life or death, the impact of that evidence cannot be measured simply by how much air time it received at trial or how many pages it occupies in the record. Some toxins can be deadly in small doses.

The State acknowledges, as it must, that introducing "race or ethnicity as evidence of criminality" can in some cases prejudice a defendant. But it insists that this is not such a case, because Buck's own counsel, not the prosecution, elicited the offending testimony. We are not convinced. In fact, the distinction could well cut the other way. A prosecutor is seeking a conviction. Jurors understand this and may reasonably be expected to evaluate the government's evidence and arguments in light of its motivations. When a defendant's own lawyer puts in the offending evidence, it is in the nature of an admission against interest, more likely to be taken at face value.

The effect of Dr. Quijano's testimony on Buck's sentencing cannot be dismissed as "*de minimis.*" Buck has demonstrated prejudice. * * *

For the foregoing reasons, we conclude that Buck has demonstrated * * * ineffective assistance of counsel under *Strickland.*

The judgment of the United States Court of Appeals for the Fifth Circuit is reversed, and the case is remanded for further proceedings consistent with this opinion.

*It is so ordered.*

JUSTICE THOMAS, with whom JUSTICE ALITO joins, dissenting.

* * *

The Court's application of the standard in *Strickland v. Washington,* is * * * misguided. In particular, the Court erroneously finds that petitioner's claim satisfies *Strickland's* second prong, which requires a defendant to show that his counsel's mistake materially prejudiced his defense. Prejudice exists only when correcting the alleged error would have produced a "substantial" likelihood of a different result. Here, the sentence of death hinged on the jury's finding that petitioner posed a threat of future dangerousness. Texas' standard for making such a finding is not difficult to satisfy: "The facts of the offense alone may be sufficient to sustain the jury's finding of future dangerousness," and "[a] jury may also infer a defendant's future dangerousness from evidence showing a lack of remorse."

The majority neglects even to mention the relevant legal standard in Texas, relying instead on rhetoric and speculation to craft a finding of prejudice. But the prosecution's evidence of both the heinousness of petitioner's crime and his complete lack of remorse was overwhelming. Accordingly, Dr. Quijano's "*de minimis*" racial testimony, did not prejudice petitioner.

First, the facts leave no doubt that this crime was premeditated and cruel. The Court recites defense testimony describing the killing spree here as a "crime of passion," but the record belies that characterization. The rampage occurred at the home of Debra Gardner, petitioner's ex-girlfriend. Prior to the shooting, petitioner called her house. His stepsister, Phyllis Taylor, answered, and petitioner asked to speak with Gardner. Gardner declined, and petitioner hung up. Petitioner then retrieved a shotgun and rifle, loaded both guns, and drove 28 miles to Gardner's house. Upon arrival, he broke down the door and opened fire without provocation. The shooting did not occur in the heat of the moment.

In addition to describing this as a crime of passion, the majority also parrots defense testimony that petitioner's violence was limited to "the context of romantic relationships." But this assertion is also quite wrong. Upon entering Gardner's house, petitioner first shot at an acquaintance, Harold Ebnezer. He next approached his stepsister, Taylor, who was seated on the couch. He said, " 'I'm going to shoot your ass too.' " She begged him, " 'Duane, please don't shoot me. I'm your sister. I don't deserve to be shot. Remember I do have children.' " Petitioner ignored her pleas, placed the gun on her chest, and shot her. Petitioner does not claim that he was in a romantic relationship with either Ebnezer or Taylor.

After shooting Taylor, petitioner cornered one of Gardner's friends, Kenneth Butler, and shot him, as well. He then exited the house and chased Gardner into the middle of the street. She turned to him and pleaded, " 'Please don't shoot me. Please don't shoot me. Why are you doing this in front of my kids?' Her son, Devon, watched from the sidewalk. Her daughter, Shennel, begged petitioner to spare her mother and even attempted to restrain him. Petitioner pointed the gun at Gardner and said, " 'I'm going to shoot you. I'm going to shoot your A[ss].' " He then did so. The flight path of the bullet suggests that Gardner was on her knees when petitioner shot her.

Second, the evidence of petitioner's lack of remorse, largely ignored by the majority, is startling. After shooting Gardner, petitioner walked back to his car and placed the firearms in the trunk. He then returned to taunt Gardner where she lay mortally wounded and bleeding in the street. He said, " 'It ain't funny now. You ain't laughing now.' " Police arrived shortly thereafter and arrested him. In the patrol car, petitioner was "laughing and joking and taunting." He continued to smile and laugh during the drive to the police station. When one of the officers informed petitioner that he did not find the situation humorous, petitioner replied that " '[t]he bitch got what she deserved.' " He remained happy and upbeat for the remainder of the drive, even commenting that he was going to heaven because God had already forgiven him. * * *

I respectfully dissent.

## *NOTE*

The next case deals with the question of whether it constitutes ineffective assistance of counsel for an attorney to tell his client that if the client takes the stand and says he saw a gun, he (the attorney) would have to tell the court that he thinks the client committed perjury. The Court is careful to note that "breach of an ethical standard does not necessarily make out a denial of the Sixth Amendment guarantee of assistance of counsel," yet relies heavily on the assumption that the attorney was acting ethically in concluding that the attorney rendered effective assistance to the client. Indeed, much of the opinion focuses on whether the attorney was acting ethically rather than on whether the *Strickland* test for effective assistance of counsel was satisfied even though the U.S. Supreme Court lacks authority to establish rules of ethics for attorneys practicing in state courts.

As you read the case, think about whether the attorney was rendering the effective assistance of counsel that the Sixth Amendment guarantees. Was counsel's assistance reasonable in light of the fact that both Model Rule 3.3 and Iowa's Rule 32:3.3(b) require that the attorney *know* (not merely believe) that the client has offered false testimony?[a] Was it reasonable in light of the role criminal defense counsel play in the criminal justice system? Did the attorney's advice to his client not to testify that he saw a gun prejudice the client? In other words, was there a reasonable probability that, if the attorney

---

[a] Model Rule 3.3(a)(3) provides, inter alia, "If a lawyer, the lawyer's client, or a witness called by the lawyer, has offered material evidence and the lawyer comes to know of its falsity, the lawyer shall take reasonable remedial measures, including, if necessary, disclosure to the tribunal." Rule 3.3(a)(3) further provides that "[a] lawyer may refuse to offer evidence, *other than the testimony of a defendant in a criminal matter*, that the lawyer reasonably believes is false." (emphasis added). Similarly, Iowa Rule 32:3.3(b) provides, "If a lawyer, the lawyer's client, or a witness called by the lawyer, has offered material evidence and the lawyer comes to know of its falsity, the lawyer shall take reasonable remedial measures, including, if necessary, disclosure to the tribunal. A lawyer may refuse to offer evidence, other than the testimony of a defendant in a criminal matter, that the lawyer reasonably believes is false."

had not given such advice, the outcome of the proceeding would have been different?

## NIX V. WHITESIDE

Supreme Court of the United States
475 U.S. 157, 106 S.Ct. 988, 89 L.Ed.2d 123 (1986)

CHIEF JUSTICE BURGER delivered the opinion of the Court.

We granted certiorari to decide whether the Sixth Amendment right of a criminal defendant to assistance of counsel is violated when an attorney refuses to cooperate with the defendant in presenting perjured testimony at his trial.

Whiteside was convicted of second-degree murder by a jury verdict * * *. The killing took place on February 8, 1977, in Cedar Rapids, Iowa. Whiteside and two others went to one Calvin Love's apartment late that night, seeking marihuana. Love was in bed when Whiteside and his companions arrived * * *. At one point, Love directed his girlfriend to get his "piece," and at another point got up, then returned to his bed. According to Whiteside's testimony, Love then started to reach under his pillow and moved toward Whiteside. Whiteside stabbed Love in the chest, inflicting a fatal wound.

Whiteside was charged with murder. * * * Gary L. Robinson was then appointed and immediately began an investigation. Whiteside gave him a statement that he had stabbed Love as the latter "was pulling a pistol from underneath the pillow on the bed." Upon questioning by Robinson, however, Whiteside indicated that he had not actually seen a gun, but that he was convinced that Love had a gun. No pistol was found on the premises; shortly after the police search following the stabbing, which had revealed no weapon, the victim's family had removed all of the victim's possessions from the apartment. Robinson interviewed Whiteside's companions who were present during the stabbing, and none had seen a gun during the incident. Robinson advised Whiteside that the existence of a gun was not necessary to establish the claim of self-defense, and that only a reasonable belief that the victim had a gun nearby was necessary even though no gun was actually present.

Until shortly before trial, Whiteside consistently stated to Robinson that he had not actually seen a gun, but that he was convinced that Love had a gun in his hand. About a week before trial, during preparation for direct examination, Whiteside for the first time told Robinson and his associate Donna Paulsen that he had seen something "metallic" in Love's hand. When asked about this, Whiteside responded: "[I]n Howard Cook's case there was a gun. If I don't say I saw a gun, I'm dead."

Robinson told Whiteside that such testimony would be perjury and repeated that it was not necessary to prove that a gun was available but only that Whiteside reasonably believed that he was in danger. On Whiteside's insisting that he would testify that he saw "something metallic" Robinson told him * * *:

> [W]e could not allow him to [testify falsely] because that would be perjury, and as officers of the court we would be suborning perjury if we allowed him to do it; . . . I advised him that if he did do that it would be my duty to advise the Court of what he was doing and that I felt he was committing perjury; also, that I probably would be allowed to attempt to impeach that particular testimony.

Robinson also indicated he would seek to withdraw from the representation if Whiteside insisted on committing perjury.

Whiteside testified in his own defense at trial and stated that he "knew" that Love had a gun and that he believed Love was reaching for a gun and he had acted swiftly in self-defense. On cross-examination, he admitted that he had not actually seen a gun in Love's hand. Robinson presented evidence that Love had been seen with a sawed-off shotgun on other occasions, that the police search of the apartment may have been careless, and that the victim's family had removed everything from the apartment shortly after the crime. Robinson presented this evidence to show a basis for Whiteside's asserted fear that Love had a gun.

The jury returned a verdict of second-degree murder, and Whiteside moved for a new trial * * *. The Supreme Court of Iowa affirmed respondent's conviction. * * * [After Whiteside filed a petition for habeas corpus, the] United States Court of Appeals for the Eighth Circuit reversed and directed that the writ of habeas corpus be granted. * * * We granted certiorari and we reverse.

The right of an accused to testify in his defense is of relatively recent origin. Until the latter part of the preceding century, criminal defendants in this country, as at common law, were considered to be disqualified from giving sworn testimony at their own trial by reason of their interest as a party to the case. * * * Although this Court has never explicitly held that a criminal defendant has a due process right to testify in his own behalf, cases in several Circuits have so held, and the right has long been assumed.[a] * * *

In *Strickland v. Washington*, we held that to obtain relief by way of federal habeas corpus on a claim of a deprivation of effective assistance of counsel under the Sixth Amendment, the movant must establish both

---

[a]    One year after deciding *Nix v. Whiteside*, the Supreme Court recognized that a defendant has a constitutional right to testify in her own behalf. *See* Rock v. Arkansas, 483 U.S. 44, 49 (1987) (noting "it cannot be doubted that a defendant in a criminal case has the right to take the witness stand and to testify in his or her own defense.").

serious attorney error and prejudice. To show such error, it must be established that the assistance rendered by counsel was constitutionally deficient in that "counsel made errors so serious that counsel was not functioning as 'counsel' guaranteed the defendant by the Sixth Amendment." To show prejudice, it must be established that the claimed lapses in counsel's performance rendered the trial unfair so as to "undermine confidence in the outcome" of the trial.

In *Strickland*, we acknowledged that the Sixth Amendment does not require any particular response by counsel to a problem that may arise. Rather, the Sixth Amendment inquiry is into whether the attorney's conduct was "reasonably effective." To counteract the natural tendency to fault an unsuccessful defense, a court reviewing a claim of ineffective assistance must "indulge a strong presumption that counsel's conduct falls within the wide range of reasonable professional assistance." In giving shape to the perimeters of this range of reasonable professional assistance, *Strickland* mandates that "[p]revailing norms of practice as reflected in American Bar Association Standards and the like . . . are guides to determining what is reasonable, but they are only guides."

Under the *Strickland* standard, breach of an ethical standard does not necessarily make out a denial of the Sixth Amendment guarantee of assistance of counsel. When examining attorney conduct, a court must be careful not to narrow the wide range of conduct acceptable under the Sixth Amendment so restrictively as to constitutionalize particular standards of professional conduct and thereby intrude into the state's proper authority to define and apply the standards of professional conduct applicable to those it admits to practice in its courts. In some future case challenging attorney conduct in the course of a state-court trial, we may need to define with greater precision the weight to be given to recognized canons of ethics, the standards established by the state in statutes or professional codes, and the Sixth Amendment, in defining the proper scope and limits on that conduct. Here we need not face that question, since virtually all of the sources speak with one voice.[b]

We turn next to the question presented: the definition of the range of "reasonable professional" responses to a criminal defendant client who informs counsel that he will perjure himself on the stand. We must determine whether, in this setting, Robinson's conduct fell within the wide range of professional responses to threatened client perjury acceptable under the Sixth Amendment.

---

[b]   Actually, states do not have uniform ethics rules governing criminal defense attorneys who believe their client plans to testify falsely. As discussed in the note following this case, some states prohibit disclosure and instead allow the attorney to put the client on the witness stand where the client may testify in narrative form. Generally speaking, in the states that favor the narrative approach, the attorney may not rely on anything the client said that the attorney believes to be false in the attorney's closing argument.

In *Strickland,* we recognized counsel's duty of loyalty and his "overarching duty to advocate the defendant's cause." Plainly, that duty is limited to legitimate, lawful conduct compatible with the very nature of a trial as a search for truth. Although counsel must take all reasonable lawful means to attain the objectives of the client, counsel is precluded from taking steps or in any way assisting the client in presenting false evidence or otherwise violating the law. This principle has consistently been recognized in most unequivocal terms by expositors of the norms of professional conduct since the first Canons of Professional Ethics were adopted by the American Bar Association in 1908. * * *

These principles have been carried through to contemporary codifications of an attorney's professional responsibility. Disciplinary Rule 7–102 of the Model Code of Professional Responsibility (1980), entitled "Representing a Client Within the Bounds of the Law," provides: "(A) In his representation of a client, a lawyer shall not: (4) Knowingly use perjured testimony or false evidence. (7) Counsel or assist his client in conduct that the lawyer knows to be illegal or fraudulent."

This provision has been adopted by Iowa, and is binding on all lawyers who appear in its courts. The more recent Model Rules of Professional Conduct (1983) similarly admonish attorneys to obey all laws in the course of representing a client: "RULE 1.2—Scope of Representation (d) A lawyer shall not counsel a client to engage, or assist a client, in conduct that the lawyer knows is criminal or fraudulent. . . ."

Both the Model Code of Professional Responsibility and the Model Rules of Professional Conduct also adopt the specific exception from the attorney-client privilege for disclosure of perjury that his client intends to commit or has committed. * * * Indeed, both the Model Code and the Model Rules do not merely *authorize* disclosure by counsel of client perjury; they *require* such disclosure.[c]

These standards confirm that the legal profession has accepted that an attorney's ethical duty to advance the interests of his client is limited by an equally solemn duty to comply with the law and standards of professional conduct; it specifically ensures that the client may not use false evidence. This special duty of an attorney to prevent and disclose frauds upon the court derives from the recognition that perjury is as much

---

[c]   Comment 10 to Rule 3.3 of the ABA Model Rules of Professional Conduct mandates disclosure to the tribunal only where an attorney has offered material evidence in the belief that it is true and "subsequently come[s] to *know* that the evidence is false," ABA MODEL RULES OF PROFESSIONAL CONDUCT (2015) (emphasis added). An attorney's mere belief, even if reasonable and supported by other evidence, is not a sufficient basis to refuse to provide assistance to the defendant client in a criminal case who wishes to testify. *United States v. Midgett,* 342 F.3d 321, 326 (4th Cir. 2003) (noting that the Model Rules of Professional Conduct, while requiring that a lawyer not knowingly offer evidence that the lawyer *knows* to be false, also states that "[a] lawyer may refuse to offer evidence, *other than the testimony of a defendant in a criminal matter,* that the lawyer *reasonably believes* is false").

a crime as tampering with witnesses or jurors by way of promises and threats, and undermines the administration of justice.

The offense of perjury was a crime recognized at common law and has been made a felony in most states by statute, including Iowa. An attorney who aids false testimony by questioning a witness when perjurious responses can be anticipated risks prosecution for subornation of perjury * * *.

It is universally agreed that at a minimum the attorney's first duty when confronted with a proposal for perjurious testimony is to attempt to dissuade the client from the unlawful course of conduct. * * * The commentary [to the Model Rules] also suggests that an attorney's revelation of his client's perjury to the court is a professionally responsible and acceptable response to the conduct of a client who has actually given perjured testimony. Similarly, the Model Rules and the commentary, as well as the Code of Professional Responsibility adopted in Iowa, expressly permit withdrawal from representation as an appropriate response of an attorney when the client threatens to commit perjury. * * *

Considering Robinson's representation of respondent in light of these accepted norms of professional conduct, we discern no failure to adhere to reasonable professional standards that would in any sense make out a deprivation of the Sixth Amendment right to counsel. Whether Robinson's conduct is seen as a successful attempt to dissuade his client from committing the crime of perjury, or whether seen as a "threat" to withdraw from representation and disclose the illegal scheme, Robinson's representation of Whiteside falls well within accepted standards of professional conduct and the range of reasonable professional conduct acceptable under *Strickland*. * * * Since there has been no breach of any recognized professional duty, it follows that there can be no deprivation of the right to assistance of counsel under the *Strickland* standard.

We hold that, as a matter of law, counsel's conduct complained of here cannot establish the prejudice required for relief under the second strand of the *Strickland* inquiry. Although a defendant need not establish that the attorney's deficient performance more likely than not altered the outcome in order to establish prejudice under *Strickland,* a defendant must show that "there is a reasonable probability that, but for counsel's unprofessional errors, the result of the proceeding would have been different." According to *Strickland,* "[a] reasonable probability is a probability sufficient to undermine confidence in the outcome." * * *

Whether he was persuaded or compelled to desist from perjury, Whiteside has no valid claim that confidence in the result of his trial has been diminished by his desisting from the contemplated perjury. Even if we were to assume that the jury might have believed his perjury, it does not follow that Whiteside was prejudiced. * * *

Whiteside's attorney treated Whiteside's proposed perjury in accord with professional standards, and since Whiteside's truthful testimony could not have prejudiced the result of his trial, the Court of Appeals was in error to direct the issuance of a writ of habeas corpus and must be reversed.

*Reversed.*

JUSTICE BRENNAN, concurring in the judgment.

This Court has no constitutional authority to establish rules of ethical conduct for lawyers practicing in the state courts. Nor does the Court enjoy any statutory grant of jurisdiction over legal ethics.

Accordingly, it is not surprising that the Court emphasizes that it "must be careful not to narrow the wide range of conduct acceptable under the Sixth Amendment so restrictively as to constitutionalize particular standards of professional conduct and thereby intrude into the state's proper authority to define and apply the standards of professional conduct applicable to those it admits to practice in its courts." I read this as saying in another way that the Court *cannot* tell the States or the lawyers in the States how to behave in their courts, unless and until federal rights are violated.

Unfortunately, the Court seems unable to resist the temptation of sharing with the legal community its vision of ethical conduct. But let there be no mistake: the Court's essay regarding what constitutes the correct response to a criminal client's suggestion that he will perjure himself is pure discourse without force of law. * * * [T]hat issue is a thorny one, but it is not an issue presented by this case. Lawyers, judges, bar associations, students, and others should understand that the problem has not now been "decided."

I [concur] because I agree that respondent has failed to prove the kind of prejudice necessary to make out a claim under *Strickland v. Washington.*

JUSTICE STEVENS, concurring in the judgment.

Justice Holmes taught us that a word is but the skin of a living thought. A "fact" may also have a life of its own. From the perspective of an appellate judge, after a case has been tried and the evidence has been sifted by another judge, a particular fact may be as clear and certain as a piece of crystal or a small diamond. A trial lawyer, however, must often deal with mixtures of sand and clay. Even a pebble that seems clear enough at first glance may take on a different hue in a handful of gravel.

As we view this case, it appears perfectly clear that respondent intended to commit perjury, that his lawyer knew it, and that the lawyer had a duty—both to the court and to his client, for perjured testimony can ruin an otherwise meritorious case—to take extreme measures to prevent the perjury from occurring. The lawyer was successful and, from our unanimous and remote perspective, it is now pellucidly clear that the client suffered no "legally cognizable prejudice."

Nevertheless, beneath the surface of this case there are areas of uncertainty that cannot be resolved today. A lawyer's certainty that a change in his client's recollection is a harbinger of intended perjury—as well as judicial review of such apparent certainty—should be tempered by the realization that, after reflection, the most honest witness may recall (or sincerely believe he recalls) details that he previously overlooked. * * * Thus, one can be convinced—as I am—that this lawyer's actions were a proper way to provide his client with effective representation without confronting the much more difficult questions of what a lawyer must, should, or may do after his client has given testimony that the lawyer does not believe. The answer to such questions may well be colored by the particular circumstances attending the actual event and its aftermath. * * *

[JUSTICE BLACKMUN's opinion, concurring in the judgment, has been omitted.]

## NOTE

The Court suggests there is no question that the attorney acted as he was required to act under the canons of legal ethics "since virtually all of the sources speak with one voice" on what an attorney must do when faced with a situation like the one the attorney in *Nix v. Whiteside* found himself in. In fact, however, there is considerable disagreement over what an attorney should do when the attorney thinks his or her client is going to commit perjury. At one extreme is the view of the late Monroe Freedman, Abbe Smith, and the National Association of Criminal Defense Lawyers (NACDL): the criminal defense attorney should proceed as normal, putting the client on the stand and examining the client as the attorney would do in any other case. Monroe H. Freedman & Abbe Smith, UNDERSTANDING LAWYER'S ETHICS 162–63 (4th ed. 2010). At the other extreme is the Model Rules approach, mandating disclosure to the tribunal if the lawyer knows that his client intends to testify falsely. In between these two extremes is another approach that recognizes the criminal defendant's right to testify as well as the obligation of defense counsel as an officer of the court not to assist in any criminal or fraudulent activity by the client. Under the narrative approach, a criminal defense attorney who believes the client intends to testify falsely may put the client on the stand and allow the client to testify in the narrative. Under this approach, the lawyer will simply ask the defendant if he or she wishes to make a statement concerning the case rather than engaging in direct examination of the client. *See e.g., People v. Johnson,* 62 Cal. App. 4th 608, 630 (Cal. Ct. App. 1998) ("We conclude the narrative approach best accommodates the competing interests of the defendant's constitutional right to testify and the attorney's ethical obligations."); *People v. Bolton,* 166 Cal. App. 4th 343, 358 (Cal. Ct. App. 2008)

("We reaffirm the conclusion of the *Johnson* court that where an attorney knows or suspects that his client intends to give false testimony, the 'narrative approach' best accommodates the interests of both the defendant and the attorney, who is obligated 'not to participate in the presentation of perjured testimony.' "); *People v. Lowery,* 52 Ill. App. 3d 44, 47 (Ill. App. Ct. 1977) (approving of the narrative approach outlined in the ABA Standards Relating to the Defense Function § 7.7); *State v. Fosnight,* 679 P.2d 180 (Kan. 1984) (finding no violation of the Code of Professional Responsibility where counsel permitted his client to tell his story on the witness stand without engaging in direct examination of the client); *Sanborn v. State,* 474 So. 2d 309 (Fla. Dist. Ct. App. 1985) (noting that the procedure used when there is a chance of perjured testimony being presented by the defendant is to allow the defendant to take the stand and deliver his statement in narrative form); D.C. Rules of Prof'l Conduct R. 3.3(b) (D.C. Bar 2015) ("If the lawyer is unable to dissuade the client or to withdraw without seriously harming the client, the lawyer may put the client on the stand to testify in a narrative fashion, but the lawyer shall not examine the client in such manner as to elicit testimony which the lawyer knows to be false, and shall not argue the probative value of the client's testimony in closing argument.").

## WHEAT V. UNITED STATES

Supreme Court of the United States
486 U.S. 153, 108 S.Ct. 1692, 100 L.Ed 2d 140 (1988)

CHIEF JUSTICE REHNQUIST delivered the opinion of the Court. * * *

Petitioner Mark Wheat, along with numerous codefendants, was charged with participating in a far-flung drug distribution conspiracy. * * * Petitioner acted primarily as an intermediary in the distribution ring; he received and stored large shipments of marijuana at his home, then distributed the marijuana to customers in the region.

Also charged in the conspiracy were Juvenal Gomez-Barajas and Javier Bravo, who were represented in their criminal proceedings by attorney Eugene Iredale.[a] Gomez-Barajas was tried first and was acquitted on drug charges overlapping with those against petitioner. To avoid a second trial on other charges, however, Gomez-Barajas offered to plead guilty to tax evasion and illegal importation of merchandise. At the commencement of petitioner's trial, the District Court had not accepted the

---

[a]    Eugene Iredale is considered to be one of the best criminal defense lawyers in San Diego, California. In 2013, Iredale's law firm was ranked in Tier 1 for Criminal Defense-Non-White Collar and Criminal Defense-White Collar cases by U.S. News and World Report. *See Best Law Firms 2013,* U.S. NEWS AND WORLD REPORT, http://bestlawfirms.usnews.com/profile/iredale-and-yoo-apc/rankings/13056. Additionally, Iredale himself has been chosen by Super Lawyers as a Super Lawyer each year from 2007 to 2015. *See Attorney Profile,* SUPERLAWYERS, http://profiles.superlawyers.com/california-san-diego/san-diego/lawyer/eugene-g-iredale/999bbee4-ba00-46e1-9a52-a13d38abc9bb.html.

plea; Gomez-Barajas was thus free to withdraw his guilty plea and proceed to trial.

Bravo, evidently a lesser player in the conspiracy, decided to forgo trial and plead guilty to one count of transporting approximately 2,400 pounds of marijuana from Los Angeles to a residence controlled by Victor Vidal. At the conclusion of Bravo's guilty plea proceedings * * *, Iredale notified the District Court that he had been contacted by petitioner and had been asked to try petitioner's case as well. In response, the Government registered substantial concern about the possibility of conflict in the representation.

* * * [T]he Government objected to petitioner's proposed substitution on the ground that Iredale's representation of Gomez-Barajas and Bravo created a serious conflict of interest. The Government's position was premised on two possible conflicts. First, the District Court had not yet accepted the plea and sentencing arrangement negotiated between Gomez-Barajas and the Government; in the event that arrangement were rejected by the court, Gomez-Barajas would be free to withdraw the plea and stand trial. He would then be faced with the prospect of representation by Iredale, who in the meantime would have acted as petitioner's attorney. Petitioner, through his participation in the drug distribution scheme, was familiar with the sources and size of Gomez-Barajas' income, and was thus likely to be called as a witness for the Government at any subsequent trial of Gomez-Barajas. This scenario would pose a conflict of interest for Iredale, who would be prevented from cross-examining petitioner and thereby from effectively representing Gomez-Barajas.

Second, and of more immediate concern, Iredale's representation of Bravo would directly affect his ability to act as counsel for petitioner. The Government believed that a portion of the marijuana delivered by Bravo to Vidal's residence eventually was transferred to petitioner. In this regard, the Government contacted Iredale and asked that Bravo be made available as a witness to testify against petitioner, and agreed in exchange to modify its position at the time of Bravo's sentencing. In the likely event that Bravo were called to testify, Iredale's position in representing both men would become untenable, for ethical proscriptions would forbid him to cross-examine Bravo in any meaningful way. By failing to do so, he would also fail to provide petitioner with effective assistance of counsel. Thus, because of Iredale's prior representation of Gomez-Barajas and Bravo and the potential for serious conflict of interest, the Government urged the District Court to reject the substitution of attorneys.

In response, petitioner emphasized his right to have counsel of his own choosing and the willingness of Gomez-Barajas, Bravo, and petitioner to waive the right to conflict-free counsel. Petitioner argued that the circumstances posited by the Government that would create a conflict for Iredale were highly speculative and bore no connection to the true relationship between the co-conspirators. If called to testify, Bravo would simply say that he did not know petitioner and had no dealings with him; no attempt by Iredale to impeach Bravo would be necessary. Further, in the unlikely event that Gomez-Barajas went to trial on the charges of tax evasion and illegal importation, petitioner's lack of involvement in those alleged crimes made his appearance as a witness highly improbable. Finally, and most importantly, all three defendants agreed to allow Iredale to represent petitioner and to waive any future claims of conflict of interest. In petitioner's view, the Government was manufacturing implausible conflicts in an attempt to disqualify Iredale, who had already proved extremely effective in representing Gomez-Barajas and Bravo.

* * * [T]he District Court * * * ruled: " * * * that an irreconcilable conflict of interest exists" [and denied] Mr. Wheat's request to substitute Mr. Iredale in as attorney of record. * * * Petitioner proceeded to trial with his original counsel and was convicted * * *.

The Sixth Amendment to the Constitution guarantees that "[i]n all criminal prosecutions, the accused shall enjoy the right . . . to have the Assistance of Counsel for his defence." In *United States v. Morrison* we observed that this right was designed to assure fairness in the adversary criminal process. Realizing that an unaided layman may have little skill in arguing the law or in coping with an intricate procedural system, we have held that the Sixth Amendment secures the right to the assistance of counsel, by appointment if necessary, in a trial for any serious crime. We have further recognized that the purpose of providing assistance of counsel "is simply to ensure that criminal defendants receive a fair trial," and that in evaluating Sixth Amendment claims, "the appropriate inquiry focuses on the adversarial process, not on the accused's relationship with his lawyer as such." Thus, while the right to select and be represented by one's preferred attorney is comprehended by the Sixth Amendment, the essential aim of the Amendment is to guarantee an effective advocate for each criminal defendant rather than to ensure that a defendant will inexorably be represented by the lawyer whom he prefers.

The Sixth Amendment right to choose one's own counsel is circumscribed in several important respects. Regardless of his persuasive powers, an advocate who is not a member of the bar may not represent clients (other than himself) in court. Similarly, a defendant may not insist on representation by an attorney he cannot afford or who for other reasons declines to represent the defendant. Nor may a defendant insist on the counsel of an attorney who has a previous or ongoing relationship with an opposing party, even when the opposing party is the Government. The question raised in this case is the extent to which a criminal defendant's right under the Sixth Amendment to his chosen attorney is qualified by the fact that the attorney has represented other defendants charged in the same criminal conspiracy.

In previous cases, we have recognized that multiple representation of criminal defendants engenders special dangers of which a court must be aware. While "permitting a single attorney to represent codefendants . . . is not *per se* violative of constitutional guarantees of effective assistance of counsel," a court confronted with and alerted to possible conflicts of interest must take adequate steps to ascertain whether the conflicts warrant separate counsel. As we said in *Holloway:*

> Joint representation of conflicting interests is suspect because of what it tends to prevent the attorney from doing. . . . [A] conflict may . . . prevent an attorney from challenging the admission of evidence prejudicial to one client but perhaps favorable to another, or from arguing at the sentencing hearing the relative involvement and culpability of his clients in order to minimize the culpability of one by emphasizing that of another.

Petitioner insists that the provision of waivers by all affected defendants cures any problems created by the multiple representation. But no such flat rule can be deduced from the Sixth Amendment presumption in favor of counsel of choice. Federal courts have an independent interest in ensuring that criminal trials are conducted within the ethical standards of the profession and that legal proceedings appear fair to all who observe them. * * * Not only the interest of a criminal defendant but the institutional interest in the rendition of just verdicts in criminal cases may be jeopardized by unregulated multiple representation.

For this reason, the Federal Rules of Criminal Procedure direct trial judges to investigate specially cases involving joint representation. In pertinent part, Rule 44(c) provides:

> [T]he court shall promptly inquire with respect to such joint representation and shall personally advise each defendant of his right to the effective assistance of counsel, including separate representation. Unless it appears that there is good cause to believe no conflict of interest is likely to arise, the court shall take such measures as may be appropriate to protect each defendant's right to counsel.

Although Rule 44(c) does not specify what particular measures may be taken by a district court, one option * * * is an order by the court that the defendants be separately represented in subsequent proceedings in the case. This suggestion comports with our instructions in *Holloway* and in *Glasser v. United States* that the trial courts, when alerted by objection from one of the parties, have an independent duty to ensure that criminal defendants receive a trial that is fair and does not contravene the Sixth Amendment. * * *

[W]here a court justifiably finds an actual conflict of interest, there can be no doubt that it may decline a proffer of waiver, and insist that defendants be separately represented. \* \* \* [W]e think the district court must be allowed substantial latitude in refusing waivers of conflicts of interest not only in those rare cases where an actual conflict may be demonstrated before trial, but in the more common cases where a potential for conflict exists which may or may not burgeon into an actual conflict as the trial progresses. In the circumstances of this case, with the motion for substitution of counsel made so close to the time of trial, the District Court relied on instinct and judgment based on experience in making its decision. We do not think it can be said that the court exceeded the broad latitude which must be accorded it in making this decision. \* \* \*

Here the District Court was confronted not simply with an attorney who wished to represent two coequal defendants in a straightforward criminal prosecution; rather, Iredale proposed to defend three conspirators of varying stature in a complex drug distribution scheme. The Government intended to call Bravo as a witness for the prosecution at petitioner's trial. The Government might readily have tied certain deliveries of marijuana by Bravo to petitioner, necessitating vigorous cross-examination of Bravo by petitioner's counsel. Iredale, because of his prior representation of Bravo, would have been unable ethically to provide that cross-examination.

Iredale had also represented Gomez-Barajas, one of the alleged kingpins of the distribution ring, and had succeeded in obtaining a verdict of acquittal for him. Gomez-Barajas had agreed with the Government to plead guilty to other charges, but the District Court had not yet accepted the plea arrangement. If the agreement were rejected, petitioner's probable testimony at the resulting trial of Gomez-Barajas would create an ethical dilemma for Iredale from which one or the other of his clients would likely suffer.

Viewing the situation as it did before trial, we hold that the District Court's refusal to permit the substitution of counsel in this case was within its discretion and did not violate petitioner's Sixth Amendment rights. \* \* \* The District Court must recognize a presumption in favor of petitioner's counsel of choice, but that presumption may be overcome not only by a demonstration of actual conflict but by a showing of a serious potential for conflict. The evaluation of the facts and circumstances of each case under this standard must be left primarily to the informed judgment of the trial court. \* \* \*

JUSTICE MARSHALL, with whom JUSTICE BRENNAN joins, dissenting.

\* \* \* As the Court states, \* \* \* the trial court must recognize a presumption in favor of a defendant's counsel of choice. This presumption means that a trial court may not reject a defendant's chosen counsel on the ground of a potential conflict of interest absent a showing that both the likelihood and the dimensions of the feared conflict are substantial. Unsupported or dubious speculation as to a conflict will not suffice. The

Government must show a substantial potential for the kind of conflict that would undermine the fairness of the trial process.

* * * In my view, a trial court that rejects a criminal defendant's chosen counsel on the ground of a potential conflict should make findings on the record to facilitate review, and an appellate court should scrutinize closely the basis for the trial court's decision. Only in this way can a criminal defendant's right to counsel of his choice be appropriately protected.

The Court's resolution of the instant case flows from its deferential approach to the District Court's denial of petitioner's motion to add or substitute counsel; absent deference, a decision upholding the District Court's ruling would be inconceivable. Indeed, I believe that even under the Court's deferential standard, reversal is in order. The mere fact of multiple representation, as the Court concedes, will not support an order preventing a criminal defendant from retaining counsel of his choice. As this Court has stated on prior occasions, such representation will not invariably pose a substantial risk of a serious conflict of interest and thus will not invariably imperil the prospect of a fair trial. The propriety of the District Court's order thus depends on whether the Government showed that the particular facts and circumstances of the multiple representation proposed in this case were such as to overcome the presumption in favor of petitioner's choice of counsel. I believe it is clear that the Government failed to make this showing. Neither Eugene Iredale's representation of Juvenal Gomez-Barajas nor Iredale's representation of Javier Bravo posed any threat of causing a conflict of interest.

At the time of petitioner's trial, Iredale's representation of Gomez-Barajas was effectively completed. As the Court notes, Iredale had obtained an acquittal for Gomez-Barajas on charges relating to a conspiracy to distribute marijuana. Iredale also had negotiated an agreement with the Government under which Gomez-Barajas would plead guilty to charges of tax evasion and illegal importation of merchandise, although the trial court had not yet accepted this plea arrangement. Gomez-Barajas was not scheduled to appear as a witness at petitioner's trial; thus, Iredale's conduct of that trial would not require him to question his former client. The only possible conflict this Court can divine from Iredale's representation of both petitioner and Gomez-Barajas rests on the premise that the trial court would reject the negotiated plea agreement and that Gomez-Barajas then would decide to go to trial. In this event, the Court tells us, "petitioner's probable testimony at the resulting trial of Gomez-Barajas would create an ethical dilemma for Iredale."

This argument rests on speculation of the most dubious kind. The Court offers no reason to think that the trial court would have rejected Gomez-Barajas' plea agreement; neither did the Government posit any such reason in its argument or brief before this Court. The most likely occurrence at the time petitioner moved to retain Iredale as his defense counsel was that the trial court would accept Gomez-Barajas' plea agreement, as the court in fact later did. Moreover, even if Gomez-Barajas had gone to trial, petitioner probably would not have testified. The record contains no indication that petitioner had any involvement in or information about crimes for which Gomez-Barajas might yet have stood trial. The only alleged connection between petitioner and Gomez-Barajas sprang from the conspiracy to distribute marijuana, and a jury already had acquitted Gomez-Barajas of that charge. It is therefore disingenuous to say that representation of both petitioner and Gomez-Barajas posed a serious potential for a conflict of interest.

Similarly, Iredale's prior representation of Bravo was not a cause for concern. The Court notes that the prosecution intended to call Bravo to the stand at petitioner's trial and asserts that Bravo's testimony could well have "necessitat[ed] vigorous cross-examination . . . by petitioner's counsel." The facts, however, belie the claim that Bravo's anticipated testimony created a serious potential for conflict. Contrary to the Court's inference, Bravo could not have testified about petitioner's involvement in the alleged marijuana distribution scheme. As all parties were aware at the time, Bravo did not know and could not identify petitioner; indeed, prior to the commencement of legal proceedings, the two men never had heard of each other. Bravo's eventual testimony at petitioner's trial related to a shipment of marijuana in which petitioner was not involved; the testimony contained not a single reference to petitioner. Petitioner's counsel did not cross-examine Bravo, and neither petitioner's counsel nor the prosecutor mentioned Bravo's testimony in closing argument. All of these developments were predictable when the District Court ruled on petitioner's request that Iredale serve as trial counsel; the contours of Bravo's testimony were clear at that time. Given the insignificance of this testimony to any matter that petitioner's counsel would dispute, the proposed joint representation of petitioner and Bravo did not threaten a conflict of interest.

Moreover, even assuming that Bravo's testimony might have "necessitat[ed] vigorous cross-examination," the District Court could have insured against the possibility of any conflict of interest without wholly depriving petitioner of his constitutional right to the counsel of his choice. Petitioner's motion requested that Iredale either be substituted for petitioner's current counsel or be added to petitioner's defense team. Had the District Court allowed the addition of Iredale and then ordered that he take no part in the cross-examination of Bravo, any possibility of a conflict would have been removed. Especially in light of the availability of this precautionary measure, the notion that Iredale's prior representation of

Bravo might well have caused a conflict of interest at petitioner's trial is nothing short of ludicrous.

The Court gives short shrift to the actual circumstances of this case in upholding the decision below. These circumstances show that the District Court erred in denying petitioner's motion to substitute or add Iredale as defense counsel. The proposed representation did not pose a substantial risk of a serious conflict of interest. The District Court therefore had no authority to deny petitioner's Sixth Amendment right to retain counsel of his choice. This constitutional error demands that petitioner's conviction be reversed. I accordingly dissent.

[JUSTICE STEVENS' dissenting opinion has been omitted.]

## FARETTA V. CALIFORNIA
Supreme Court of the United States
422 U.S. 806, 95 S.Ct. 2525, 45 L.Ed.2d 562 (1975)

JUSTICE STEWART delivered the opinion of the Court.

The Sixth and Fourteenth Amendments of our Constitution guarantee that a person brought to trial in any state or federal court must be afforded the right to the assistance of counsel before he can be validly convicted and punished by imprisonment. * * * The question before us now is whether a defendant in a state criminal trial has a constitutional right to proceed without counsel when he voluntarily and intelligently elects to do so. * * *

Anthony Faretta was charged with grand theft in an information filed in the Superior Court of Los Angeles County, Cal. At the arraignment, the Superior Court Judge assigned to preside at the trial appointed the public defender to represent Faretta. Well before the date of trial, however, Faretta requested that he be permitted to represent himself. Questioning by the judge revealed that Faretta had once represented himself in a criminal prosecution, that he had a high school education, and that he did not want to be represented by the public defender because he believed that that office was "very loaded down with . . . a heavy case load." The judge responded that he believed Faretta was "making a mistake" and emphasized that in further proceedings Faretta would receive no special favors. Nevertheless, after establishing that Faretta wanted to represent himself and did not want a lawyer, the judge, in a "preliminary ruling," accepted Faretta's waiver of the assistance of counsel. The judge indicated, however, that he might reverse this ruling if it later appeared that Faretta was unable adequately to represent himself.

Several weeks thereafter, but still prior to trial, the judge *sua sponte* held a hearing to inquire into Faretta's ability to conduct his own defense, and questioned him specifically about both the hearsay rule and the state law governing the challenge of potential jurors. After consideration of

Faretta's answers, and observation of his demeanor, the judge ruled that Faretta had not made an intelligent and knowing waiver of his right to the assistance of counsel, and also ruled that Faretta had no constitutional right to conduct his own defense. The judge, accordingly, reversed his earlier ruling permitting self-representation and again appointed the public defender to represent Faretta. Faretta's subsequent request for leave to act as co-counsel was rejected, as were his efforts to make certain motions on his own behalf. Throughout the subsequent trial, the judge required that Faretta's defense be conducted only through the appointed lawyer from the public defender's office. At the conclusion of the trial, the jury found Faretta guilty as charged, and the judge sentenced him to prison.

The California Court of Appeal, relying upon a then-recent California Supreme Court decision that had expressly decided the issue, affirmed the trial judge's ruling that Faretta had no federal or state constitutional right to represent himself. Accordingly, the appellate court affirmed Faretta's conviction. A petition for rehearing was denied without opinion, and the California Supreme Court denied review. We granted certiorari.

In the federal courts, the right of self-representation has been protected by statute since the beginning of our Nation. * * * With few exceptions, each of the several States also accords a defendant the right to represent himself in any criminal case. The constitutions of 36 States explicitly confer that right. Moreover, many state courts have expressed the view that the right is also supported by the Constitution of the United States.

This Court has more than once indicated the same view. * * * "[A]n accused, in the exercise of a free and intelligent choice, and with the considered approval of the court, may waive trial by jury, and so likewise may he competently and intelligently waive his Constitutional right to assistance of counsel."

* * * "[T]he Constitution does not force a lawyer upon a defendant." Whether the Constitution forbids a State from forcing a lawyer upon a defendant is a different question. * * *

This Court's past recognition of the right of self-representation, the federal-court authority holding the right to be of constitutional dimension, and the state constitutions pointing to the right's fundamental nature form a consensus not easily ignored. "[T]he mere fact that a path is a beaten one," Mr. Justice Jackson once observed, "is a persuasive reason for following it." We confront here a nearly universal conviction, on the part of our people as well as our courts, that forcing a lawyer upon an unwilling defendant is contrary to his basic right to defend himself if he truly wants to do so.

* * * The right of self-representation finds support in the structure of the Sixth Amendment, as well as in the English and colonial jurisprudence from which the Amendment emerged. * * *

The Sixth Amendment includes a compact statement of the rights necessary to a full defense:

> In all criminal prosecutions, the accused shall enjoy the right . . . to be informed of the nature and cause of the accusation; to be confronted with the witnesses against him; to have compulsory process for obtaining witnesses in his favor, and to have the Assistance of Counsel for his defence.

Because these rights are basic to our adversary system of criminal justice, they are part of the "due process of law" that is guaranteed by the Fourteenth Amendment to defendants in the criminal courts of the States. The rights to notice, confrontation, and compulsory process, when taken together, guarantee that a criminal charge may be answered in a manner now considered fundamental to the fair administration of American justice—through the calling and interrogation of favorable witnesses, the cross-examination of adverse witnesses, and the orderly introduction of evidence. In short, the Amendment constitutionalizes the right in an adversary criminal trial to make a defense as we know it.

The Sixth Amendment does not provide merely that a defense shall be made for the accused; it grants to the accused personally the right to make his defense. It is the accused, not counsel, who must be "informed of the nature and cause of the accusation," who must be "confronted with the witnesses against him," and who must be accorded "compulsory process for obtaining witnesses in his favor." Although not stated in the Amendment in so many words, the right to self-representation—to make one's own defense personally—is thus necessarily implied by the structure of the Amendment. The right to defend is given directly to the accused; for it is he who suffers the consequences if the defense fails.

The counsel provision supplements this design. It speaks of the "assistance" of counsel, and an assistant, however expert, is still an assistant. The language and spirit of the Sixth Amendment contemplate that counsel, like the other defense tools guaranteed by the Amendment, shall be an aid to a willing defendant—not an organ of the State interposed between an unwilling defendant and his right to defend himself personally. To thrust counsel upon the accused, against his considered wish, thus violates the logic of the Amendment. * * *

The Sixth Amendment, when naturally read, thus implies a right of self-representation. * * *

There can be no blinking of the fact that the right of an accused to conduct his own defense seems to cut against the grain of this Court's decisions holding that the Constitution requires that no accused can be convicted and imprisoned unless he has been accorded the right to the assistance of counsel. For it is surely true that the basic thesis of those decisions is that the help of a lawyer is essential to assure the defendant a fair trial. And a strong argument can surely be made that the whole thrust of those decisions must inevitably lead to the conclusion that a State may constitutionally impose a lawyer upon even an unwilling defendant.

But it is one thing to hold that every defendant, rich or poor, has the right to the assistance of counsel, and quite another to say that a State may compel a defendant to accept a lawyer he does not want. * * * It is undeniable that in most criminal prosecutions defendants could better defend with counsel's guidance than by their own unskilled efforts. But where the defendant will not voluntarily accept representation by counsel, the potential advantage of a lawyer's training and experience can be realized, if at all, only imperfectly. To force a lawyer on a defendant can only lead him to believe that the law contrives against him. Moreover, it is not inconceivable that in some rare instances, the defendant might in fact present his case more effectively by conducting his own defense. Personal liberties are not rooted in the law of averages. The right to defend is personal. The defendant, and not his lawyer or the State, will bear the personal consequences of a conviction. It is the defendant, therefore, who must be free personally to decide whether in his particular case counsel is to his advantage. And although he may conduct his own defense ultimately to his own detriment, his choice must be honored out of "that respect for the individual which is the lifeblood of the law."

When an accused manages his own defense, he relinquishes, as a purely factual matter, many of the traditional benefits associated with the right to counsel. For this reason, in order to represent himself, the accused must "knowingly and intelligently" forgo those relinquished benefits. Although a defendant need not himself have the skill and experience of a lawyer in order competently and intelligently to choose self-representation, he should be made aware of the dangers and disadvantages of self-representation, so that the record will establish that "he knows what he is doing and his choice is made with eyes open."[a]

Here, weeks before trial, Faretta clearly and unequivocally declared to the trial judge that he wanted to represent himself and did not want counsel. The record affirmatively shows that Faretta was literate, competent, and understanding, and that he was voluntarily exercising his informed free will. The trial judge had warned Faretta that he thought it

---

[a] While a defendant must be warned of the dangers of self-representation prior to being allowed to self-represent at trial, such a warning is not required for a defendant who chooses to self-represent at the entry of a plea. Iowa v. Tovar, 541 U.S. 77 (2004) (holding Sixth Amendment does not require trial court to warn defendant that waiving right to counsel at plea hearing entails risk that viable defenses may be overlooked and deprives defendant of independent opinion as to whether to plead guilty).

was a mistake not to accept the assistance of counsel, and that Faretta would be required to follow all the "ground rules" of trial procedure. We need make no assessment of how well or poorly Faretta had mastered the intricacies of the hearsay rule and the California code provisions that govern challenges of potential jurors on *voir dire*.[b] For his technical legal knowledge, as such, was not relevant to an assessment of his knowing exercise of the right to defend himself.[c]

In forcing Faretta, under these circumstances, to accept against his will a state-appointed public defender, the California courts deprived him of his constitutional right to conduct his own defense. Accordingly, the judgment before us is vacated, and the case is remanded for further proceedings not inconsistent with this opinion.

It is so ordered.

Judgment vacated and case remanded.

CHIEF JUSTICE BURGER, with whom JUSTICE BLACKMUN and JUSTICE REHNQUIST join, dissenting. * * *

The most striking feature of the Court's opinion is that it devotes so little discussion to the matter which it concedes is the core of the decision, that is, discerning an independent basis in the Constitution for the supposed right to represent oneself in a criminal trial. Its ultimate assertion that such a right is tucked between the lines of the Sixth Amendment is contradicted by the Amendment's language and its consistent judicial interpretation.

* * * [T]he conclusion that the right guaranteed by the Sixth Amendment are "personal" to an accused reflects nothing more than the obvious fact that it is he who is on trial and therefore has need of a defense. But neither that nearly trivial proposition nor the language of the Amendment, which speaks in uniformly mandatory terms, leads to the further conclusion that the right to counsel is merely supplementary and may be dispensed with at the whim of the accused. Rather, this Court's

---

[b]   The trial court may appoint standby counsel to assist the defendant who chooses to self-represent at trial, thus relieving the judge of the need to explain and enforce basic rules of courtroom protocol, even over the defendant's objection, without violating the Sixth Amendment. *McKaskle v. Wiggins*, 465 U.S. 168 (1984).

[c]   While the trial court may not deny a defendant the right to self-represent on the ground that the defendant lacks the technical knowledge of a skilled trial attorney, the trial court may consider the defendant's mental incapacity when deciding whether to grant or deny a motion to self-represent. In *Indiana v. Edwards*, 554 U.S. 164 (2008), the Court held that a defendant who wishes to self-represent and meets the standard for competence to stand trial, i.e. the defendant understands the nature of the proceedings against him and can assist in his own defense, may nonetheless be denied the right to self-represent if the defendant's mental illness would affect his ability to competently represent himself at trial. The Court did not set forth a test for measuring a defendant's mental capacity to self-represent, leaving it up to the states to fashion their own standards.

decisions have consistently included the right to counsel as an integral part of the bundle making up the larger "right to a defense as we know it." * * *

The reason for this hardly requires explanation. The fact of the matter is that in all but an extraordinarily small number of cases an accused will lose whatever defense he may have if he undertakes to conduct the trial himself.

* * * Nor is it accurate to suggest, as the Court seems to later in its opinion, that the quality of his representation at trial is a matter with which only the accused is legitimately concerned. Although we have adopted an adversary system of criminal justice, the prosecution is more than an ordinary litigant, and the trial judge is not simply an automaton who insures that technical rules are adhered to. Both are charged with the duty of insuring that justice, in the broadest sense of that term, is achieved in every criminal trial. That goal is ill-served, and the integrity of and public confidence in the system are undermined, when an easy conviction is obtained due to the defendant's ill-advised decision to waive counsel. * * * The system of criminal justice should not be available as an instrument of self-destruction. * * *

JUSTICE BLACKMUN, with whom THE CHIEF JUSTICE and JUSTICE REHNQUIST join, dissenting. * * *

If there is any truth to the old proverb that "one who is his own lawyer has a fool for a client," the Court by its opinion today now bestows a constitutional right on one to make a fool of himself.

# CHAPTER 30

# THE RIGHT OF PRESENCE

■ ■ ■

A criminal defendant's right to be present at trial is rooted in the Sixth Amendment's Confrontation Clause. This chapter evaluates whether the right of presence is absolute or can be limited or waived. *United States v. Gagnon* evaluates whether the right of presence includes a right to be present at an *in camera* session between the judge and a juror in judge's chambers. *Taylor v. United States* analyzes whether a defendant's failure to return to court after a mid-trial recess is sufficient to constitute a waiver of the right to presence. *Illinois v. Allen* considers the constitutionality of a judge's decision to remove a disruptive defendant from court and continue the trial without him.

## UNITED STATES V. GAGNON

Supreme Court of the United States
470 U.S. 522, 105 S.Ct. 1482, 84 L.Ed.2d 486 (1985)

PER CURIAM.

The four respondents were indicted on various counts and tried together in Federal District Court for participation in a large-scale cocaine distribution conspiracy. During the afternoon recess on the first day of trial the District Judge was discussing matters of law in open court with the respondents, their respective counsel, and the Assistant United States Attorney, outside the presence of the jury. The bailiff entered the courtroom and informed the judge that one of the jurors, Garold Graham, had expressed concern because he had noticed respondent Gagnon sketching portraits of the jury. Gagnon's attorney admitted that Gagnon had been sketching jury members during the trial. The District Judge ordered that the practice cease immediately. Gagnon's lawyer suggested that the judge question the juror to ascertain whether the sketching had prejudiced the juror against Gagnon. The judge then stated, still in open court in the presence of each respondent and his counsel: "I will talk to the juror in my chambers and make a determination. We'll stand at recess." No objections were made by any respondent and no respondent requested to be present at the discussion in chambers.

The District Judge then went into the chambers and called for juror Graham. The judge also requested the bailiff to bring Gagnon's counsel to chambers. There the judge, in the company of Gagnon's counsel, discussed the sketching with the juror. The juror stated: " . . . I just thought that perhaps because of the seriousness of the trial, and because of, whichever way the deliberations go, it kind of, it upset me, because of what could happen afterwards."

The judge then explained that Gagnon was an artist, meant no harm, and the sketchings had been confiscated. The juror was assured that Gagnon would sketch no more. Graham stated that another juror had seen the sketching and made a comment to him about it but no one else seemed to have noticed, and no other jurors had discussed the matter. The judge then elicited from Graham his willingness to continue as an impartial juror. Gagnon's counsel asked two questions of the juror and then stated that he was satisfied. The *in camera* meeting broke up, and the trial resumed. A transcript of the *in camera* proceeding was available to all of the parties; at no time did any respondent mention or object to the *in camera* interview of the juror. No motions were made to disqualify Graham or the other juror who witnessed the sketching, nor did any respondent request that cautionary instructions be given to the jury. After the jury returned guilty verdicts no post-trial motions concerning the incident were filed with the District Court.

On the consolidated appeal, however, each respondent claimed that the District Court's discussion with the juror in chambers violated respondents' Sixth Amendment rights to an impartial jury and their rights under Federal Rule of Criminal Procedure 43 to be present at all stages of the trial.[a] A divided panel of the Court of Appeals for the Ninth Circuit Court of Appeals reversed the convictions of all respondents, holding that the *in camera* discussion with the juror violated respondents' rights under Rule 43 and the Due Process Clause of the Fifth Amendment. * * *

We think it clear that respondents' rights under the Fifth Amendment Due Process Clause were not violated by the *in camera* discussion with the juror. "[T]he mere occurrence of an *ex parte* conversation between a trial judge and a juror does not constitute a deprivation of any constitutional right. The defense has no constitutional right to be present at every interaction between a judge and a juror, nor is there a constitutional right to have a court reporter transcribe every such communication."

The constitutional right to presence is rooted to a large extent in the Confrontation Clause of the Sixth Amendment, but we have recognized that this right is protected by the Due Process Clause in some situations where the defendant is not actually confronting witnesses or evidence against him. In *Snyder v. Massachusetts,* the Court explained that a

---

[a] Rule 43 of the Federal Rules of Criminal Procedure provides, "A defendant who was initially present at trial, or who had pleaded guilty or nolo contendere, waives the right to be present . . . when the defendant is voluntarily absent after the trial has begun, regardless of whether the court informed the defendant of an obligation to remain during trial." *See* FED. R. CRIM. P. 43.

defendant has a due process right to be present at a proceeding "whenever his presence has a relation, reasonably substantial, to the fullness of his opportunity to defend against the charge. . . . [T]he presence of a defendant is a condition of due process to the extent that a fair and just hearing would be thwarted by his absence, and to that extent only." The Court also cautioned in *Snyder* that the exclusion of a defendant from a trial proceeding should be considered in light of the whole record.

In this case the presence of the four respondents and their four trial counsel at the *in camera* discussion was not required to ensure fundamental fairness or a "reasonably substantial . . . opportunity to defend against the charge." The encounter between the judge, the juror, and Gagnon's lawyer was a short interlude in a complex trial; the conference was not the sort of event which every defendant had a right personally to attend under the Fifth Amendment. * * * The Fifth Amendment does not require that all the parties be present when the judge inquires into such a minor occurrence.

The Court of Appeals also held that the conference with the juror was a "stage of the trial" at which Gagnon's presence was guaranteed by Federal Rule of Criminal Procedure 43. We assume for the purposes of this opinion that the Court of Appeals was correct in this regard. We hold, however, that the court erred in concluding that respondents had not waived their rights under Rule 43 to be present at the conference with the juror.

The record shows * * * that the District Judge, in open court, announced her intention to speak with the juror in chambers, and then called a recess. The *in camera* discussion took place during the recess, and trial resumed shortly thereafter with no change in the jury. Respondents neither then nor later in the course of the trial asserted any Rule 43 rights they may have had to attend this conference. Respondents did not request to attend the conference at any time. No objections of any sort were lodged, either before or after the conference. Respondents did not even make any post-trial motions, although post-trial hearings may often resolve this sort of claim. * * * The district court need not get an express "on the record" waiver from the defendant for every trial conference which a defendant may have a right to attend. * * *

We hold that failure by a criminal defendant to invoke his right to be present under Federal Rule of Criminal Procedure 43 at a conference which he knows is taking place between the judge and a juror in chambers constitutes a valid waiver of that right. The petition for certiorari and respondents' motion to supplement the record are granted, and the judgment of the Court of Appeals is

*Reversed.*

JUSTICE POWELL took no part in the consideration or decision of this case.

[JUSTICE BRENNAN's dissenting opinion has been omitted.]

## TAYLOR V. UNITED STATES
### Supreme Court of the United States
### 414 U.S. 17, 94 S.Ct. 194, 38 L.Ed.2d 174 (1973)

PER CURIAM.

On the first day of his trial on four counts of selling cocaine * * *, petitioner failed to return for the afternoon session. He had been present at the expiration of the morning session when the court announced that the lunch recess would last until 2 p.m., and he had been told by his attorney to return to the courtroom at that time. The judge recessed the trial until the following morning, but petitioner still did not appear. His wife testified that she had left the courtroom the previous day with petitioner after the morning session; that they had separated after sharing a taxicab to Roxbury; that he had not appeared ill; and, finally, that she had not heard from him since. The trial judge then denied a motion for mistrial by defense counsel, who asserted that the jurors' minds would be tainted by petitioner's absence and that continuation of the trial in his absence deprived him of his Sixth Amendment right to confront witnesses against him. Relying upon Fed. Rules Crim. Proc. 43, which expressly provides that a defendant's voluntary absence "shall not prevent continuing the trial," the court found that petitioner had absented himself voluntarily from the proceedings.

Throughout the remainder of the trial, the court admonished the jury that no inference of guilt could be drawn from petitioner's absence. Petitioner was found guilty on all four counts. Following his subsequent arrest, he was sentenced to the statutory five-year minimum. The Court of Appeals affirmed the conviction, and we now grant the motion for leave to proceed in forma pauperis and the petition for certiorari and affirm the judgment of the Court of Appeals.

There is no challenge to the trial court's conclusion that petitioner's absence from the trial was voluntary, and no claim that the continuation of the trial was not authorized by Rule 43. Nor are we persuaded that Rule 43 is unconstitutional or that petitioner was deprived of any constitutional rights in the circumstances before us. Rule 43 has remained unchanged since the adoption of the Federal Rules of Criminal Procedure in 1945; and with respect to the consequences of the defendant's voluntary absence from trial, it reflects the long-standing rule recognized by this Court in *Diaz v. United States*:

[W]here * * * the accused is not in custody, the prevailing rule has been, that if, after the trial has begun in his presence, he voluntarily absents himself, this does not nullify what has been done or prevent the completion of the trial, but, on the contrary, operates as a waiver of his right to be present and leaves the court free to proceed with the trial in like manner and with like effect as if he were present.

Under this rule, the District Court and the Court of Appeals correctly rejected petitioner's claims.

Petitioner, however, insists that his mere voluntary absence from his trial cannot be construed as an effective waiver, that is, "an intentional relinquishment or abandonment of a known right or privilege," unless it is demonstrated that he knew or had been expressly warned by the trial court not only that he had a right to be present but also that the trial would continue in his absence and thereby effectively foreclose his right to testify and to confront personally the witnesses against him.

Like the Court of Appeals, we cannot accept this position. Petitioner had no right to interrupt the trial by his voluntary absence, as he implicitly concedes by urging only that he should have been warned that no such right existed and that the trial would proceed in his absence. The right at issue is the right to be present, and the question becomes whether that right was effectively waived by his voluntary absence. Consistent with Rule 43 and *Diaz*, we conclude that it was.

It is wholly incredible to suggest that petitioner, who was at liberty on bail, had attended the opening session of his trial, and had a duty to be present at the trial, entertained any doubts about his right to be present at every stage of his trial. It seems equally incredible to us, as it did to the Court of Appeals, "that a defendant who flees from a courtroom in the midst of a trial—where judge, jury, witnesses and lawyers are present and ready to continue—would not know that as a consequence the trial could continue in his absence." Here the Court of Appeals noted that when petitioner was questioned at sentencing regarding his flight, he never contended that he was unaware that a consequence of his flight would be a continuation of the trial without him. Moreover, no issue of the voluntariness of his disappearance was ever raised. As was recently noted, "there can be no doubt whatever that the governmental prerogative to proceed with a trial may not be defeated by conduct of the accused that prevents the trial from going forward." Under the circumstances present here, the Court of Appeals properly applied Rule 43 and affirmed the judgment of conviction.

Affirmed.

## ILLINOIS V. ALLEN

Supreme Court of the United States
397 U.S. 337, 90 S.Ct. 1057, 25 L.Ed.2d 353 (1970)

JUSTICE BLACK delivered the opinion of the Court.

* * * One of the most basic of the rights guaranteed by the Confrontation Clause is the accused's right to be present in the courtroom at every stage of his trial. The question presented in this case is whether an accused can claim the benefit of this constitutional right to remain in the courtroom while at the same time he engages in speech and conduct which is so noisy, disorderly, and disruptive that it is exceedingly difficult or wholly impossible to carry on the trial.

* * * Allen's expulsion from the courtroom [is] set out in the Court of Appeals' opinion * * *:

After his indictment [for armed robbery] and during the pretrial stage, the petitioner [Allen] refused court-appointed counsel and indicated to the trial court on several occasions that he wished to conduct his own defense. After considerable argument by the petitioner, the trial judge told him, "I'll let you be your own lawyer, but I'll ask Mr. Kelly (court-appointed counsel) [to] sit in and protect the record for you, insofar as possible."

The trial began on September 9, 1957. After the State's Attorney had accepted the first four jurors following their voir dire examination, the petitioner began examining the first juror and continued at great length. Finally, the trial judge interrupted the petitioner, requesting him to confine his questions solely to matters relating to the prospective juror's qualifications. At that point, the petitioner started to argue with the judge in a most abusive and disrespectful manner. At last, and seemingly in desperation, the judge asked appointed counsel to proceed with the examination of the jurors. The petitioner continued to talk, proclaiming that the appointed attorney was not going to act as his lawyer. He terminated his remarks by saying, "When I go out for lunchtime, you're [the judge] going to be a corpse here." At that point he tore the file which his attorney had and threw the papers on the floor. The trial judge thereupon stated to the petitioner, "One more outbreak of that sort and I'll remove you from the courtroom." This warning had no effect on the petitioner. He continued to talk back to the judge, saying, "There's not going to be no trial, either. I'm going to sit here and you're going to talk and you can bring your shackles out and straight jacket and put them on me and tape my mouth, but it will do no good because there's not going to be no trial." After more abusive remarks by the petitioner, the trial judge ordered the trial to proceed in the petitioner's absence. The petitioner was removed from the courtroom. The voir dire examination then continued and the jury was selected in the absence of the petitioner.

After a noon recess and before the jury was brought into the courtroom, the petitioner, appearing before the judge, complained about the fairness of the trial and his appointed attorney. He also said he wanted to be present in the court during his trial. In reply, the judge said that the petitioner would be permitted to remain in the courtroom if he "behaved [himself] and [did] not interfere with the introduction of the case." The jury was brought in and seated. Counsel for the petitioner then moved to exclude the witnesses from the courtroom. The [petitioner] protested this effort on the part of his attorney, saying: "There is going to be no proceeding. I'm going to start talking and I'm going to keep on talking all through the trial. There's not going to be no trial like this. I want my sister and my friends here in court to testify for me." The trial judge thereupon ordered the petitioner removed from the courtroom.

After this second removal, Allen remained out of the courtroom during the presentation of the State's case-in-chief, except that he was brought in on several occasions for purposes of identification. During one of these latter appearances, Allen responded to one of the judge's questions with vile and abusive language. After the prosecution's case had been presented, the trial judge reiterated his promise to Allen that he could return to the courtroom whenever he agreed to conduct himself properly. Allen gave some assurances of proper conduct and was permitted to be present through the remainder of the trial, principally his defense, which was conducted by his appointed counsel. * * *

The Court of Appeals felt that the defendant's Sixth Amendment right to be present at his own trial was so "absolute" that, no matter how unruly or disruptive the defendant's conduct might be, he could never be held to have lost that right so long as he continued to insist upon it, as Allen clearly did. Therefore the Court of Appeals concluded that a trial judge could never expel a defendant from his own trial and that the judge's ultimate remedy when faced with an obstreperous defendant like Allen who determines to make his trial impossible is to bind and gag him. We cannot agree that the Sixth Amendment, the cases upon which the Court of Appeals relied, or any other cases of this Court so handicap a trial judge in conducting a criminal trial. * * * We accept instead the statement of Mr. Justice Cardozo who, speaking for the Court in *Snyder v. Massachusetts*, said: "No doubt the privilege [of personally confronting witnesses] may be lost by consent or at times even by misconduct." Although mindful that courts must indulge every reasonable presumption against the loss of constitutional rights, we explicitly hold today that a defendant can lose his right to be present at trial if, after he has been warned by the judge that he will be removed if he continues his disruptive behavior, he nevertheless insists on conducting himself in a manner so disorderly, disruptive, and disrespectful of the court that his trial cannot be carried on with him in the courtroom. Once lost, the right to be present can, of course, be reclaimed as soon as the defendant is willing to conduct himself consistently with the decorum and respect inherent in the concept of courts and judicial proceedings.

It is essential to the proper administration of criminal justice that dignity, order, and decorum be the hallmarks of all court proceedings in our country. The flagrant disregard in the courtroom of elementary standards of proper conduct should not and cannot be tolerated. We believe trial judges confronted with disruptive, contumacious, stubbornly defiant defendants must be given sufficient discretion to meet the circumstances of each case. No one formula for maintaining the appropriate courtroom atmosphere will be best in all situations. We think there are at least three constitutionally permissible ways for a trial judge to handle an obstreperous defendant like Allen: (1) bind and gag him, thereby keeping him present; (2) cite him for contempt; (3) take him out of the courtroom until he promises to conduct himself properly.

Trying a defendant for a crime while he sits bound and gagged before the judge and jury would to an extent comply with that part of the Sixth Amendment's purposes that accords the defendant an opportunity to confront the witnesses at the trial. But even to contemplate such a technique, much less see it, arouses a feeling that no person should be tried while shackled and gagged except as a last resort. Not only is it possible that the sight of shackles and gags might have a significant effect on the jury's feelings about the defendant, but the use of this technique is itself something of an affront to the very dignity and decorum of judicial proceedings that the judge is seeking to uphold. Moreover, one of the defendant's primary advantages of being present at the trial, his ability to communicate with his counsel, is greatly reduced when the defendant is in a condition of total physical restraint. * * * However, in some situations * * *, binding and gagging might possibly be the fairest and most reasonable way to handle a defendant who acts as Allen did here.

* * * [C]iting or threatening to cite a contumacious defendant for criminal contempt might in itself be sufficient to make a defendant stop interrupting a trial. If so, the problem would be solved easily, and the defendant could remain in the courtroom. Of course, if the defendant is determined to prevent any trial, then a court in attempting to try the defendant for contempt is still confronted with the identical dilemma * * *. And criminal contempt has obvious limitations as a sanction when the defendant is charged with a crime so serious that a very severe sentence such as death or life imprisonment is likely to be imposed. In such a case the defendant might not be affected by a mere contempt sentence when he

ultimately faces a far more serious sanction. Nevertheless, the contempt remedy should be borne in mind by a judge in the circumstances of this case.

Another aspect of the contempt remedy is the judge's power, when exercised consistently with state and federal law, to imprison an unruly defendant such as Allen for civil contempt and discontinue the trial until such time as the defendant promises to behave himself. This procedure is consistent with the defendant's right to be present at trial, and yet it avoids the serious shortcomings of the use of shackles and gags. It must be recognized, however, that a defendant might conceivably, as a matter of calculated strategy, elect to spend a prolonged period in confinement for contempt in the hope that adverse witnesses might be unavailable after a lapse of time. A court must guard against allowing a defendant to profit from his own wrong in this way.

The trial court in this case decided under the circumstances to remove the defendant from the courtroom and to continue his trial in his absence until and unless he promised to conduct himself in a manner befitting an American courtroom. As we said earlier, we find nothing unconstitutional about this procedure. Allen's behavior was clearly of such an extreme and aggravated nature as to justify either his removal from the courtroom or his total physical restraint. Prior to his removal he was repeatedly warned by the trial judge that he would be removed from the courtroom if he persisted in his unruly conduct * * *. Allen was constantly informed that he could return to the trial when he would agree to conduct himself in an orderly manner. Under these circumstances we hold that Allen lost his right guaranteed by the Sixth and Fourteenth Amendments to be present throughout his trial. * * *

We do not hold that removing this defendant from his own trial was the only way the Illinois judge could have constitutionally solved the problem he had. We do hold, however, that there is nothing whatever in this record to show that the judge did not act completely within his discretion. Deplorable as it is to remove a man from his own trial, even for a short time, we hold that the judge did not commit legal error in doing what he did.

The judgment of the Court of Appeals is reversed. * * *

[JUSTICE BRENNAN's and JUSTICE DOUGLAS' concurring opinions have been omitted.]

# CHAPTER 31

# THE CONFRONTATION CLAUSE

■ ■ ■

The right of a criminal defendant to confront adversarial witnesses is rooted in the Sixth Amendment, which provides, "In all criminal prosecutions, the accused shall enjoy the right . . . to be confronted with the witnesses against him." The Confrontation Clause is vital to a defendant's ability to present an adequate defense at trial. It prevents trial by affidavit or private testimony and provides the defendant with a meaningful opportunity to challenge the evidence through the process of "face to face" cross-examination of the witnesses against him or her.

*Crawford v. Washington*, the first case in this chapter, is the principal case on the Confrontation Clause and articulates the current standard for determining whether a defendant's confrontation rights have been violated when an out-of-court statement is admitted at trial. Before *Crawford* was decided in 2004, a defendant's confrontation rights were governed by the rule against hearsay and its exceptions. If an out-of-court statement contained adequate indicia of reliability, either by falling within a firmly rooted exception to the hearsay rule or by bearing particularized guarantees of trustworthiness, its admission at trial would not violate the defendant's confrontation rights. *See Ohio v. Roberts*, 448 U.S. 56 (1980). *Crawford* abandoned the hearsay-exception-centered approach to confrontation and replaced it with a test that focuses on the availability of the witness whose statement is at issue to testify at trial and the nature of the out-of-court statement. Under *Crawford*, a defendant's confrontation rights are not implicated unless the out-of-court statement is testimonial. In *Davis v. Washington*, the Court articulates the test that is currently used to determine whether a statement is testimonial or non-testimonial for purposes of the Confrontation Clause.

This chapter also covers some of the limitations on the defendant's right of confrontation. In *Giles v. California*, the Court examines the common law doctrine of forfeiture by wrongdoing, which permitted the admission of out-of-court statements of witnesses who were kept from testifying by the defendant. The *Giles* Court considers whether the Confrontation Clause requires proof that the defendant intended to keep the witness from testifying before that witness' statement can be admitted at trial under the forfeiture by wrongdoing doctrine. *Richardson v. Marsh*, the last case in the chapter, examines whether the *Bruton* rule—the rule that forbids the admission of a non-testifying codefendant's confession naming the defendant as a participant in the crime—applies to a situation in which a non-testifying codefendant's confession has been redacted to omit any reference to the defendant.

## CRAWFORD V. WASHINGTON

Supreme Court of the United States
541 U.S. 36, 124 S.Ct. 1354, 158 L.Ed.2d 177 (2004)

JUSTICE SCALIA delivered the opinion of the Court.

Petitioner Michael Crawford stabbed a man who allegedly tried to rape his wife, Sylvia. At his trial, the State played for the jury Sylvia's tape-recorded statement to the police describing the stabbing, even though he had no opportunity for cross-examination. The Washington Supreme Court upheld petitioner's conviction after determining that Sylvia's statement was reliable. The question presented is whether this procedure complied with the Sixth Amendment's guarantee that, "[i]n all criminal prosecutions, the accused shall enjoy the right . . . to be confronted with the witnesses against him."

On August 5, 1999, Kenneth Lee was stabbed at his apartment. Police arrested petitioner later that night. After giving petitioner and his wife *Miranda* warnings, detectives interrogated each of them twice. Petitioner eventually confessed that he and Sylvia had gone in search of Lee because he was upset over an earlier incident in which Lee had tried to rape her. The two had found Lee at his apartment, and a fight ensued in which Lee was stabbed in the torso and petitioner's hand was cut.

Petitioner gave the following account of the fight:

Q.  Okay. Did you ever see anything in [Lee's] hands?

A.  I think so, but I'm not positive.

Q.  Okay, when you think so, what do you mean by that?

A.  I could a swore I seen him goin' for somethin' before, right before everything happened. He was like reachin', fiddlin' around down here and stuff . . . and I just . . . I don't know, I think, this is just a possibility, but I think, I think that he pulled somethin' out and I grabbed for it and that's how I got cut . . . but I'm not positive. I, I, my mind goes blank when things like this happen. I mean, I just, I remember things wrong, I remember things that just doesn't, don't make sense to me later.

Sylvia generally corroborated petitioner's story about the events leading up to the fight, but her account of the fight itself was arguably different—particularly with respect to whether Lee had drawn a weapon before petitioner assaulted him:

Q. Did Kenny do anything to fight back from this assault?

A. (pausing) I know he reached into his pocket . . . or somethin'
. . . I don't know what.

Q. After he was stabbed?

A. He saw Michael coming up. He lifted his hand . . . his chest
open, he might [have] went to go strike his hand out or something
and then (inaudible).

Q. Okay, you, you gotta speak up.

A. Okay, he lifted his hand over his head maybe to strike
Michael's hand down or something and then he put his hands in
his . . . put his right hand in his right pocket . . . took a step back
. . . Michael proceeded to stab him . . . then his hands were like . . .
how do you explain this . . . open arms . . . with his hands open
and he fell down . . . and we ran (describing subject holding hands
open, palms toward assailant).

Q. Okay, when he's standing there with his open hands, you're
talking about Kenny, correct?

A. Yeah, after, after the fact, yes.

Q. Did you see anything in his hands at that point?

A. (pausing) um um (no).

The State charged petitioner with assault and attempted murder. At
trial, he claimed self-defense. Sylvia did not testify because of the state
marital privilege, which generally bars a spouse from testifying without
the other spouse's consent. In Washington, this privilege does not extend
to a spouse's out-of-court statements admissible under a hearsay exception,
so the State sought to introduce Sylvia's tape-recorded statements to the
police as evidence that the stabbing was not in self-defense. Noting that
Sylvia had admitted she led petitioner to Lee's apartment and thus had
facilitated the assault, the State invoked the hearsay exception for
statements against penal interest.

Petitioner countered that * * * admitting the evidence would violate
his federal constitutional right to be "confronted with the witnesses against
him." According to our description of that right in *Ohio v. Roberts*, it does
not bar admission of an unavailable witness's statement against a criminal
defendant if the statement bears "adequate 'indicia of reliability.' " To meet
that test, evidence must either fall within a "firmly rooted hearsay
exception" or bear "particularized guarantees of trustworthiness." The trial
court here admitted the statement on the latter ground, offering several
reasons why it was trustworthy: Sylvia was not shifting blame but rather
corroborating her husband's story that he acted in self-defense or "justified
reprisal"; she had direct knowledge as an eyewitness; she was describing

recent events; and she was being questioned by a "neutral" law enforcement officer. The prosecution played the tape for the jury and relied on it in closing, arguing that it was "damning evidence" that "completely refutes [petitioner's] claim of self-defense." The jury convicted petitioner of assault.

The Washington Court of Appeals reversed [the conviction on the ground that Sylvia's statement lacked particularized guarantees of trustworthiness]. * * * The Washington Supreme Court reinstated the conviction unanimously concluding that, although Sylvia's statement did not fall under a firmly rooted hearsay exception, it bore guarantees of trustworthiness * * *. We granted certiorari to determine whether the State's use of Sylvia's statement violated the Confrontation Clause.

The Sixth Amendment's Confrontation Clause provides that, "[i]n all criminal prosecutions, the accused shall enjoy the right . . . to be confronted with the witnesses against him." We have held that this bedrock procedural guarantee applies to both federal and state prosecutions. As noted above, *Roberts* says that an unavailable witness's out-of-court statement may be admitted so long as it has adequate indicia of reliability—i.e., falls within a "firmly rooted hearsay exception" or bears "particularized guarantees of trustworthiness." Petitioner argues that this test strays from the original meaning of the Confrontation Clause and urges us to reconsider it.

The Constitution's text does not alone resolve this case. One could plausibly read "witnesses against" a defendant to mean those who actually testify at trial, those whose statements are offered at trial, or something in-between. We must therefore turn to the historical background of the Clause to understand its meaning.

* * * [H]istory supports two inferences about the meaning of the Sixth Amendment. First, the principal evil at which the Confrontation Clause was directed was the civil law mode of criminal procedure, and particularly its use of *ex parte* examinations as evidence against the accused. It was these practices * * * that English law's assertion of a right to confrontation was meant to prohibit; and that the founding-era rhetoric decried. The Sixth Amendment must be interpreted with this focus in mind. * * *

The text of the Confrontation Clause reflects this focus. It applies to "witnesses" against the accused—in other words, those who "bear testimony." "Testimony," in turn, is typically "[a] solemn declaration or affirmation made for the purpose of establishing or proving some fact." An accuser who makes a formal statement to government officers bears testimony in a sense that a person who makes a casual remark to an acquaintance does not. The constitutional text, like the history underlying the common-law right of confrontation, thus reflects an especially acute concern with a specific type of out-of-court statement.

Various formulations of this core class of "testimonial" statements exist: "*ex parte* in-court testimony or its functional equivalent—that is, material such as affidavits, custodial examinations, prior testimony that the defendant was unable to cross-examine, or similar pretrial statements that declarants would reasonably expect to be used prosecutorially"; "extrajudicial statements ... contained in formalized testimonial materials, such as affidavits, depositions, prior testimony, or confessions"; "statements that were made under circumstances which would lead an objective witness reasonably to believe that the statement would be available for use at a later trial." These formulations all share a common nucleus and then define the Clause's coverage at various levels of abstraction around it. Regardless of the precise articulation, some statements qualify under any definition—for example, *ex parte* testimony at a preliminary hearing. Statements taken by police officers in the course of interrogations are also testimonial * * *.

The historical record also supports a second proposition: that the Framers would not have allowed admission of testimonial statements of a witness who did not appear at trial unless he was unavailable to testify, and the defendant had had a prior opportunity for cross-examination. The text of the Sixth Amendment does not suggest any open-ended exceptions from the confrontation requirement to be developed by the courts. Rather, the "right ... to be confronted with the witnesses against him," is most naturally read as a reference to the right of confrontation at common law, admitting only those exceptions established at the time of the founding. * * * [T]he common law in 1791 conditioned admissibility of an absent witness's examination on unavailability and a prior opportunity to cross-examine. The Sixth Amendment therefore incorporates those limitations. The numerous early state decisions applying the same test confirm that these principles were received as part of the common law in this country.

We do not read the historical sources to say that a prior opportunity to cross-examine was merely a sufficient, rather than a necessary, condition for admissibility of testimonial statements. They suggest that this requirement was dispositive, and not merely one of several ways to establish reliability. This is not to deny, as the Chief Justice notes, that "[t]here were always exceptions to the general rule of exclusion" of hearsay evidence. Several had become well established by 1791. But there is scant evidence that exceptions were invoked to admit *testimonial* statements against the accused in a *criminal* case. Most of the hearsay exceptions covered statements that by their nature were not testimonial—for example, business records or statements in furtherance of a conspiracy. We do not infer from these that the Framers thought exceptions would apply even to prior testimony.

Our case law has been largely consistent with these two principles. * * * [P]rior trial or preliminary hearing testimony is admissible only if the defendant had an adequate opportunity to cross-examine. Even where the defendant had such an opportunity, we excluded the testimony where the government had not established unavailability of the witness.[a] We similarly excluded accomplice confessions where the defendant had no opportunity to cross-examine. In contrast, we considered reliability factors beyond prior opportunity for cross-examination when the hearsay statement at issue was not testimonial. * * *

Our cases have * * * remained faithful to the Framers' understanding: Testimonial statements of witnesses absent from trial have been admitted only where the declarant is unavailable, and only where the defendant has had a prior opportunity to cross-examine. Although the results of our decisions have generally been faithful to the original meaning of the Confrontation Clause, the same cannot be said of our rationales. *Roberts* conditions the admissibility of all hearsay evidence on whether it falls under a "firmly rooted hearsay exception" or bears "particularized guarantees of trustworthiness." This test departs from the historical principles identified above in two respects. First, it is too broad: It applies the same mode of analysis whether or not the hearsay consists of *ex parte* testimony. This often results in close constitutional scrutiny in cases that are far removed from the core concerns of the Clause. At the same time, however, the test is too narrow: It admits statements that *do* consist of *ex parte* testimony upon a mere finding of reliability. This malleable standard often fails to protect against paradigmatic confrontation violations. * * *

Where testimonial statements are involved, we do not think the Framers meant to leave the Sixth Amendment's protection to the vagaries of the rules of evidence, much less to amorphous notions of "reliability." Certainly none of the authorities discussed above acknowledges any general reliability exception to the common-law rule. Admitting statements deemed reliable by a judge is fundamentally at odds with the right of confrontation. To be sure, the Clause's ultimate goal is to ensure reliability of evidence, but it is a procedural rather than a substantive guarantee. It commands, not that evidence be reliable, but that reliability be assessed in a particular manner: by testing in the crucible of cross-examination. The Clause thus reflects a judgment, not only about the desirability of reliable evidence (a point on which there could be little dissent), but about how reliability can best be determined.

The *Roberts* test allows a jury to hear evidence, untested by the adversary process, based on a mere judicial determination of reliability. It thus replaces the constitutionally prescribed method of assessing reliability with a wholly foreign one. * * *

---

[a]  In *Barber v. Page*, the Court held that "a witness is not 'unavailable' for purposes of [the Confrontation Clause] unless the prosecutorial authorities have made a good-faith effort to obtain his presence at trial." 390 U.S. 719, 724–25 (1968).

Dispensing with confrontation because testimony is obviously reliable is akin to dispensing with jury trial because a defendant is obviously guilty. This is not what the Sixth Amendment prescribes. * * *

Reliability is an amorphous, if not entirely subjective, concept. There are countless factors bearing on whether a statement is reliable * * *. Whether a statement is deemed reliable depends heavily on which factors the judge considers and how much weight he accords each of them. * * * The unpardonable vice of the *Roberts* test, however, is not its unpredictability, but its demonstrated capacity to admit core testimonial statements that the Confrontation Clause plainly meant to exclude. * * *

*Roberts'* failings were on full display in the proceedings below. Sylvia Crawford made her statement while in police custody, herself a potential suspect in the case. Indeed, she had been told that whether she would be released "depend[ed] on how the investigation continues." In response to often leading questions from police detectives, she implicated her husband in Lee's stabbing and at least arguably undermined his self-defense claim. Despite all this, the trial court admitted her statement, listing several reasons why it was reliable. In its opinion reversing, the Court of Appeals listed several *other* reasons why the statement was *not* reliable. Finally, the State Supreme Court relied exclusively on the interlocking character of the statement and disregarded every other factor the lower courts had considered. The case is thus a self-contained demonstration of *Roberts'* unpredictable and inconsistent application. Each of the courts also made assumptions that cross-examination might well have undermined. * * *

Where nontestimonial hearsay is at issue, it is wholly consistent with the Framers' design to afford the States flexibility in their development of hearsay law—as does *Roberts,* and as would an approach that exempted such statements from Confrontation Clause scrutiny altogether. Where testimonial evidence is at issue, however, the Sixth Amendment demands what the common law required: unavailability and a prior opportunity for cross-examination. We leave for another day any effort to spell out a comprehensive definition of "testimonial." Whatever else the term covers, it applies at a minimum to prior testimony at a preliminary hearing, before a grand jury, or at a former trial; and to police interrogations. These are the modern practices with closest kinship to the abuses at which the Confrontation Clause was directed.

In this case, the State admitted Sylvia's testimonial statement against petitioner, despite the fact that he had no opportunity to cross-examine her. That alone is sufficient to make out a violation of the Sixth Amendment. *Roberts* notwithstanding, we decline to mine the record in search of indicia of reliability. Where testimonial statements are at issue, the only indicium of reliability sufficient to satisfy constitutional demands is the one the Constitution actually prescribes: confrontation.

The judgment of the Washington Supreme Court is reversed, and the case is remanded for further proceedings not inconsistent with this opinion. * * *

CHIEF JUSTICE REHNQUIST, with whom JUSTICE O'CONNOR joins, concurring in the judgment.[b]

I dissent from the Court's decision to overrule *Ohio v. Roberts*. I believe that the Court's adoption of a new interpretation of the Confrontation Clause is not backed by sufficiently persuasive reasoning to overrule long-established precedent. Its decision casts a mantle of uncertainty over future criminal trials in both federal and state courts, and is by no means necessary to decide the present case.

The Court's distinction between testimonial and nontestimonial statements, contrary to its claim, is no better rooted in history than our current doctrine. Under the common law, although the courts were far from consistent, out-of-court statements made by someone other than the accused and not taken under oath, unlike *ex parte* depositions or affidavits, were generally not considered substantive evidence upon which a conviction could be based. Testimonial statements such as accusatory statements to police officers likely would have been disapproved of in the 18th century, not necessarily because they resembled *ex parte* affidavits or depositions as the Court reasons, but more likely than not because they were not made under oath. Without an oath, one usually did not get to the second step of whether confrontation was required.

Thus, while I agree that the Framers were mainly concerned about sworn affidavits and depositions, it does not follow that they were similarly concerned about the Court's broader category of testimonial statements. As far as I can tell, unsworn testimonial statements were treated no differently at common law than were nontestimonial statements, and it seems to me any classification of statements as testimonial beyond that of sworn affidavits and depositions will be somewhat arbitrary, merely a proxy for what the Framers might have intended had such evidence been liberally admitted as substantive evidence like it is today.

I therefore see no reason why the distinction the Court draws is preferable to our precedent. * * * [W]e have never drawn a distinction between testimonial and nontestimonial statements. * * * I see little value in trading our precedent for an imprecise approximation at this late date. I am also not convinced that the Confrontation Clause categorically requires the exclusion of testimonial statements. * * *

---

[b]   Chief Justice Rehnquist agreed with the majority that Sylvia's statement was inadmissible but reached this conclusion by applying the *Ohio v. Roberts* reliability test.

## DAVIS V. WASHINGTON

Supreme Court of the United States
547 U.S. 813, 126 S.Ct. 2266, 165 L.Ed.2d 224 (2006)

JUSTICE SCALIA delivered the opinion of the Court.

These cases require us to determine when statements made to law enforcement personnel during a 911 call or at a crime scene are "testimonial" and thus subject to the requirements of the Sixth Amendment's Confrontation Clause.

The relevant statements in *Davis v. Washington,* were made to a 911 emergency operator on February 1, 2001. When the operator answered the initial call, the connection terminated before anyone spoke. She reversed the call, and Michelle McCottry answered. In the ensuing conversation, the operator ascertained that McCottry was involved in a domestic disturbance with her former boyfriend Adrian Davis, the petitioner in this case:

911 Operator: Hello.

Complainant: Hello.

911 Operator: What's going on?

Complainant: He's here jumpin' on me again.

911 Operator: Okay. Listen to me carefully. Are you in a house or an apartment?

Complainant: I'm in a house.

911 Operator: Are there any weapons?

Complainant: No. He's usin' his fists.

911 Operator: Okay. Has he been drinking?

Complainant: No.

911 Operator: Okay, sweetie. I've got help started. Stay on the line with me, okay?

Complainant: I'm on the line.

911 Operator: Listen to me carefully. Do you know his last name?

Complainant: It's Davis.

911 Operator: Davis? Okay, what's his first name?

Complainant: Adrian.

911 Operator: What is it?

Complainant: Adrian.

911 Operator: Adrian?

Complainant: Yeah.

911 Operator: Okay. What's his middle initial?

Complainant: Martell. He's runnin' now.

As the conversation continued, the operator learned that Davis had "just r[un] out the door" after hitting McCottry, and that he was leaving in a car with someone else. McCottry started talking, but the operator cut her off, saying, "Stop talking and answer my questions." She then gathered more information about Davis (including his birthday), and learned that Davis had told McCottry that his purpose in coming to the house was "to get his stuff," since McCottry was moving. McCottry described the context of the assault, after which the operator told her that the police were on their way. "They're gonna check the area for him first," the operator said, "and then they're gonna come talk to you."

The police arrived within four minutes of the 911 call and observed McCottry's shaken state, the "fresh injuries on her forearm and her face," and her "frantic efforts to gather her belongings and her children so that they could leave the residence."

The State charged Davis with felony violation of a domestic no-contact order. "The State's only witnesses were the two police officers who responded to the 911 call. Both officers testified that McCottry exhibited injuries that appeared to be recent, but neither officer could testify as to the cause of the injuries." McCottry presumably could have testified as to whether Davis was her assailant, but she did not appear. Over Davis's objection, based on the Confrontation Clause of the Sixth Amendment, the trial court admitted the recording of her exchange with the 911 operator, and the jury convicted him. The Washington Court of Appeals affirmed. The Supreme Court of Washington * * * also affirmed concluding that the portion of the 911 conversation in which McCottry identified Davis was not testimonial, and that if other portions of the conversation were testimonial, admitting them was harmless beyond a reasonable doubt. We granted certiorari.

In *Hammon v. Indiana,* police responded late on the night of February 26, 2003, to a "reported domestic disturbance" at the home of Hershel and Amy Hammon. They found Amy alone on the front porch, appearing "somewhat frightened," but she told them that "nothing was the matter." She gave them permission to enter the house, where an officer saw "a gas heating unit in the corner of the living room" that had "flames coming out of the . . . partial glass front. There were pieces of glass on the ground in front of it and there was flame emitting from the front of the heating unit."

Hershel, meanwhile, was in the kitchen. He told the police "that he and his wife had 'been in an argument' but 'everything was fine now' and the argument 'never became physical.'" By this point Amy had come back inside. One of the officers remained with Hershel; the other went to the living room to talk with Amy, and "again asked [her] what had occurred."

Hershel made several attempts to participate in Amy's conversation with the police, but was rebuffed. The officer later testified that Hershel "became angry when I insisted that [he] stay separated from Mrs. Hammon so that we can investigate what had happened." After hearing Amy's account, the officer "had her fill out and sign a battery affidavit." Amy handwrote the following: "Broke our [f]urnace & shoved me down on the floor into the broken glass. Hit me in the chest and threw me down. Broke our lamps & phone. Tore up my van where I couldn't leave the house. Attacked my daughter."

The State charged Hershel with domestic battery and with violating his probation. Amy was subpoenaed, but she did not appear at his subsequent bench trial. The State called the officer who had questioned Amy, and asked him to recount what Amy told him and to authenticate the affidavit. Hershel's counsel repeatedly objected to the admission of this evidence. At one point, after hearing the prosecutor defend the affidavit because it was made "under oath," defense counsel said, "That doesn't give us the opportunity to cross examine [the] person who allegedly drafted it. Makes me mad." Nonetheless, the trial court admitted the affidavit as a "present sense impression," and Amy's statements as "excited utterances" that "are expressly permitted in these kinds of cases even if the declarant is not available to testify." The officer thus testified that Amy

> informed me that she and Hershel had been in an argument. That he became irrate [sic] over the fact of their daughter going to a boyfriend's house. The argument became . . . physical after being verbal and she informed me that Mr. Hammon, during the verbal part of the argument was breaking things in the living room and I believe she stated he broke the phone, broke the lamp, broke the front of the heater. When it became physical he threw her down into the glass of the heater. . . . She informed me Mr. Hammon had pushed her onto the ground, had shoved her head into the broken glass of the heater and that he had punched her in the chest twice I believe.

The trial judge found Hershel guilty on both charges, and the Indiana Court of Appeals affirmed in relevant part. The Indiana Supreme Court also affirmed, concluding that Amy's statement was admissible for state-law purposes as an excited utterance, that "a 'testimonial' statement is one given or taken in significant part for purposes of preserving it for potential future use in legal proceedings," where "the motivations of the questioner and declarant are the central concerns;" and that Amy's oral statement was not "testimonial" under these standards. It also concluded that, although the affidavit was testimonial and thus wrongly admitted, it was harmless beyond a reasonable doubt, largely because the trial was to the bench. We granted certiorari.

The Confrontation Clause of the Sixth Amendment provides: "In all criminal prosecutions, the accused shall enjoy the right . . . to be confronted with the witnesses against him." In *Crawford v. Washington* we held that this provision bars "admission of testimonial statements of a witness who did not appear at trial unless he was unavailable to testify, and the defendant had had a prior opportunity for cross-examination." A critical portion of this holding, and the portion central to resolution of the two cases now before us, is the phrase "testimonial statements." Only statements of this sort cause the declarant to be a "witness" within the meaning of the Confrontation Clause. It is the testimonial character of the statement that separates it from other hearsay that, while subject to traditional limitations upon hearsay evidence, is not subject to the Confrontation Clause.

Our opinion in *Crawford* set forth "[v]arious formulations" of the core class of "testimonial" statements, but found it unnecessary to endorse any of them, because "some statements qualify under any definition." Among those, we said, were "[s]tatements taken by police officers in the course of interrogations." * * *

Without attempting to produce an exhaustive classification of all conceivable statements—or even all conceivable statements in response to police interrogation—as either testimonial or nontestimonial, it suffices to decide the present cases to hold as follows: Statements are nontestimonial when made in the course of police interrogation under circumstances objectively indicating that the primary purpose of the interrogation is to enable police assistance to meet an ongoing emergency. They are testimonial when the circumstances objectively indicate that there is no such ongoing emergency, and that the primary purpose of the interrogation is to establish or prove past events potentially relevant to later criminal prosecution. * * *

The question before us in *Davis,* then, is whether, objectively considered, the interrogation that took place in the course of the 911 call produced testimonial statements. When we said in *Crawford,* that "interrogations by law enforcement officers fall squarely within [the] class" of testimonial hearsay, we had immediately in mind (for that was the case before us) interrogations solely directed at establishing the facts of a past crime, in order to identify (or provide evidence to convict) the perpetrator. The product of such interrogation, whether reduced to a writing signed by the declarant or embedded in the memory (and perhaps notes) of the interrogating officer, is testimonial. * * * A 911 call, on the other hand, and at least the initial interrogation conducted in connection with a 911 call, is ordinarily not designed primarily to "establis[h] or prov[e]" some past fact, but to describe current circumstances requiring police assistance.

The difference between the interrogation in *Davis* and the one in *Crawford* is apparent on the face of things. In *Davis,* McCottry was speaking about events *as they were actually happening,* rather than "describ[ing] past events." Sylvia Crawford's interrogation, on the other hand, took place hours after the events she described had occurred. Moreover, any reasonable listener would recognize that McCottry (unlike Sylvia Crawford) was facing an ongoing emergency. Although one *might* call 911 to provide a narrative report of a crime absent any imminent danger, McCottry's call was plainly a call for help against bona fide physical threat. Third, the nature of what was asked and answered in *Davis,* again viewed objectively, was such that the elicited statements were necessary to be able to *resolve* the present emergency, rather than simply to learn (as in *Crawford*) what had happened in the past. That is true even of the operator's effort to establish the identity of the assailant, so that the dispatched officers might know whether they would be encountering a violent felon. And finally, the difference in the level of formality between the two interviews is striking. Crawford was responding calmly, at the station house, to a series of questions, with the officer-interrogator taping and making notes of her answers; McCottry's frantic answers were provided over the phone, in an environment that was not tranquil, or even (as far as any reasonable 911 operator could make out) safe.

We conclude from all this that the circumstances of McCottry's interrogation objectively indicate its primary purpose was to enable police assistance to meet an ongoing emergency.[a] She simply was not acting as a *witness*; she was not *testifying.* * * *

This is not to say that a conversation which begins as an interrogation to determine the need for emergency assistance cannot, as the Indiana Supreme Court put it, "evolve into testimonial statements," once that purpose has been achieved. In this case, for example, after the operator gained the information needed to address the exigency of the moment, the emergency appears to have ended (when Davis drove away from the

---

[a]   In 2015, the Court addressed the admissibility under the Confrontation Clause of out-of-court statements made by a child to a private individual to meet an ongoing emergency. In *Ohio v. Clark,* 576 U.S. ___, 135 S.Ct. 2173 (2015), the government introduced the out-of-court responses of a 3-year-old child to questions by his preschool teacher about who had injured him. The defendant challenged the child's statements on confrontation grounds since he had no prior opportunity to cross-examine the child. Applying the primary purpose test articulated in *Davis v. Washington,* the Court unanimously held that the child's statements were not testimonial since they "clearly were not made with the primary purpose of creating evidence for Clark's prosecution." *Id.* at 2181. The Court noted, "statements by very young children will rarely, if ever, implicate the Confrontation Clause," *id.* at 2177, because "it is extremely unlikely that a 3-year-old child . . . would intend his statements to be a substitute for trial testimony." *Id.* at 2182. The Court also pointed out that "statements made to someone who is not principally charged with uncovering and prosecuting criminal behavior are significantly less likely to be testimonial than statements given to law enforcement officers," *id.* at 2182, but stopped short of adopting a categorical rule exempting all statements to private individuals from the Confrontation Clause's reach. The fact that teachers were mandated to report child abuse under Ohio law did not change the Court's opinion regarding the non-testimonial nature of the statement.

premises). The operator then told McCottry to be quiet, and proceeded to pose a battery of questions. It could readily be maintained that, from that point on, McCottry's statements were testimonial, not unlike the "structured police questioning" that occurred in Crawford. This presents no great problem. Just as, for Fifth Amendment purposes, "police officers can and will distinguish almost instinctively between questions necessary to secure their own safety or the safety of the public and questions designed solely to elicit testimonial evidence from a suspect," trial courts will recognize the point at which, for Sixth Amendment purposes, statements in response to interrogations become testimonial. Through *in limine* procedure, they should redact or exclude the portions of any statement that have become testimonial, as they do, for example, with unduly prejudicial portions of otherwise admissible evidence. Davis's jury did not hear the *complete* 911 call, although it may well have heard some testimonial portions. We were asked to classify only McCottry's early statements identifying Davis as her assailant, and we agree with the Washington Supreme Court that they were not testimonial. That court also concluded that, even if later parts of the call were testimonial, their admission was harmless beyond a reasonable doubt. Davis does not challenge that holding, and we therefore assume it to be correct.

Determining the testimonial or nontestimonial character of the statements that were the product of the interrogation in *Hammon* is a much easier task, since they were not much different from the statements we found to be testimonial in *Crawford*. It is entirely clear from the circumstances that the interrogation was part of an investigation into possibly criminal past conduct—as, indeed, the testifying officer expressly acknowledged. There was no emergency in progress; the interrogating officer testified that he had heard no arguments or crashing and saw no one throw or break anything. When the officers first arrived, Amy told them that things were fine, and there was no immediate threat to her person. When the officer questioned Amy for the second time, and elicited the challenged statements, he was not seeking to determine (as in *Davis*) "what is happening," but rather "what happened." Objectively viewed, the primary, if not indeed the sole, purpose of the interrogation was to investigate a possible crime—which is, of course, precisely what the officer *should* have done.[b]

---

[b] In *Michigan v. Bryant*, 562 U.S. 344 (2011), the Court answered a question left open in *Davis*: whose purpose matters when assessing the primary purpose of the interrogation? The Court held that in deciding whether the primary purpose of an interrogation is to meet an ongoing emergency, "the relevant inquiry is not the subjective or actual purpose of the individuals involved in a particular encounter, but rather the purpose that reasonable participants would have had, as ascertained from the individuals' statements and actions and the circumstances in which the encounter occurred." *Id.* at 360. In a strongly worded dissent, Justice Scalia opined that the declarant's intent is the only intent that matters when applying the primary purpose test. Justice Scalia explained that in order for a statement to be testimonial, "the declarant must intend the statement to be a solemn declaration rather than an unconsidered or offhand remark; and he must make the statement with the understanding that it may be used to invoke the coercive machinery

It is true that the *Crawford* interrogation was more formal. It followed a *Miranda* warning, was tape-recorded, and took place at the station house. While these features certainly strengthened the statements' testimonial aspect—made it more objectively apparent, that is, that the purpose of the exercise was to nail down the truth about past criminal events—none was essential to the point. It was formal enough that Amy's interrogation was conducted in a separate room, away from her husband (who tried to intervene), with the officer receiving her replies for use in his "investigat[ion]." What we called the "striking resemblance" of the *Crawford* statement to civil-law *ex parte* examinations, is shared by Amy's statement here. Both declarants were actively separated from the defendant—officers forcibly prevented Hershel from participating in the interrogation. Both statements deliberately recounted, in response to police questioning, how potentially criminal past events began and progressed. And both took place some time after the events described were over. Such statements under official interrogation are an obvious substitute for live testimony, because they do precisely *what a witness does* on direct examination; they are inherently testimonial. * * *

Respondents in both cases, joined by a number of their *amici,* contend that the nature of the offenses charged in these two cases—domestic violence—requires greater flexibility in the use of testimonial evidence. This particular type of crime is notoriously susceptible to intimidation or coercion of the victim to ensure that she does not testify at trial. * * * But when defendants seek to undermine the judicial process by procuring or coercing silence from witnesses and victims, the Sixth Amendment does not require courts to acquiesce. While defendants have no duty to assist the State in proving their guilt, they *do* have the duty to refrain from acting in ways that destroy the integrity of the criminal-trial system. * * * [O]ne who obtains the absence of a witness by wrongdoing forfeits the constitutional right to confrontation. * * *

We have determined that, absent a finding of forfeiture by wrongdoing, the Sixth Amendment operates to exclude Amy Hammon's affidavit. The Indiana courts may (if they are asked) determine on remand whether such a claim of forfeiture is properly raised and, if so, whether it is meritorious.

We affirm the judgment of the Supreme Court of Washington in No. 05–5224. We reverse the judgment of the Supreme Court of Indiana in No. 05–5705, and remand the case to that Court for proceedings not inconsistent with this opinion.

*It is so ordered.*

---

of the State against the accused." *Id.* at 381. Justice Scalia also noted that the Court's approach created a mixed motive problem: how can a court decide what constitutes the primary purpose if the police and the declarant each have motives or purposes that conflict?

[JUSTICE THOMAS' opinion, concurring in the judgment in part and dissenting in part, has been omitted.]

## NOTE

After *Crawford* and *Davis,* the Court decided a series of cases that tested the definitional boundaries of testimonial versus non-testimonial statements. In *Melendez-Diaz v. Massachusetts,* 557 U.S. 305 (2009), the Court considered whether a forensic lab report, prepared for use by the government at trial, was testimonial. The Court found that the lab report was akin to an affidavit, and therefore was testimonial. The Court held that because the lab report was testimonial, allowing the government to present the lab report at trial without calling the forensic analyst to testify violated the defendant's confrontation rights. *Id.* at 310–11.

In 2011, the Court extended its holding in *Melendez-Diaz* to a case in which the government offered into evidence at trial a forensic lab report and, in an attempt to satisfy the Confrontation Clause, presented an analyst from the same lab as the analyst who prepared the report to validate the report. *Bullcoming v. New Mexico,* 564 U.S. 647 (2011). The analyst who testified at trial had familiarity with the lab's testing procedures but was not involved in the testing of the defendant's blood sample. The Court found the "surrogate testimony" insufficient to satisfy the Confrontation Clause, explaining that "[t]he accused's right is to be confronted with the analyst who made the certification, unless the analyst is unavailable at trial, and the accused has an opportunity, pretrial, to cross examine that particular scientist." *Id.* at 2710.

## GILES V. CALIFORNIA

Supreme Court of the United States
554 U.S. 353, 128 S.Ct. 2678, 171 L.Ed.2d 488 (2008)

JUSTICE SCALIA delivered the opinion of the Court.

We consider whether a defendant forfeits his Sixth Amendment right to confront a witness against him when a judge determines that a wrongful act by the defendant made the witness unavailable to testify at trial.

On September 29, 2002, petitioner Dwayne Giles shot his ex-girlfriend, Brenda Avie, outside the garage of his grandmother's house. No witness saw the shooting, but Giles' niece heard what transpired from inside the house. She heard Giles and Avie speaking in conversational tones. Avie then yelled "Granny" several times and a series of gunshots sounded. Giles' niece and grandmother ran outside and saw Giles standing near Avie with a gun in his hand. Avie, who had not been carrying a weapon, had been shot six times. One wound was consistent with Avie's holding her hand up at the time she was shot, another was consistent with her having turned to her side, and a third was consistent with her having been shot while lying on the ground. Giles fled the scene after the shooting. He was apprehended by police about two weeks later and charged with murder.

At trial, Giles testified that he had acted in self-defense. Giles described Avie as jealous, and said he knew that she had once shot a man, that he had seen her threaten people with a knife, and that she had vandalized his home and car on prior occasions. He said that on the day of the shooting, Avie came to his grandmother's house and threatened to kill him and his new girlfriend, who had been at the house earlier. * * * Giles testified that after Avie threatened him at the house, he went into the garage and retrieved a gun, took the safety off, and started walking toward the back door of the house. He said that Avie charged at him, and that he was afraid she had something in her hand. According to Giles, he closed his eyes and fired several shots, but did not intend to kill Avie.

Prosecutors sought to introduce statements that Avie had made to a police officer responding to a domestic-violence report about three weeks before the shooting. Avie, who was crying when she spoke, told the officer that Giles had accused her of having an affair, and that after the two began to argue, Giles grabbed her by the shirt, lifted her off the floor, and began to choke her. According to Avie, when she broke free and fell to the floor, Giles punched her in the face and head, and after she broke free again, he opened a folding knife, held it about three feet away from her, and threatened to kill her if he found her cheating on him. Over Giles' objection, the trial court admitted these statements into evidence under a provision of California law that permits admission of out-of-court statements describing the infliction or threat of physical injury on a declarant when the declarant is unavailable to testify at trial and the prior statements are deemed trustworthy.

A jury convicted Giles of first-degree murder. He appealed. While his appeal was pending, this Court decided in *Crawford v. Washington,* that the Confrontation Clause requires that a defendant have the opportunity to confront the witnesses who give testimony against him, except in cases where an exception to the confrontation right was recognized at the time of the founding. The California Court of Appeal held that the admission of Avie's unconfronted statements at Giles' trial did not violate the Confrontation Clause as construed by *Crawford* because *Crawford* recognized a doctrine of forfeiture by wrongdoing. It concluded that Giles had forfeited his right to confront Avie because he had committed the murder for which he was on trial, and because his intentional criminal act made Avie unavailable to testify. The California Supreme Court affirmed on the same ground. We granted certiorari.

* * * The State does not dispute here, and we accept without deciding, that Avie's statements accusing Giles of assault were testimonial. But it maintains (as did the California Supreme Court) that the Sixth

Amendment did not prohibit prosecutors from introducing the statements because an exception to the confrontation guarantee permits the use of a witness's unconfronted testimony if a judge finds, as the judge did in this case, that the defendant committed a wrongful act that rendered the witness unavailable to testify at trial. We held in *Crawford* that the Confrontation Clause is "most naturally read as a reference to the right of confrontation at common law, admitting only those exceptions established at the time of the founding." We therefore ask whether the theory of forfeiture by wrongdoing accepted by the California Supreme Court is a founding-era exception to the confrontation right.

We have previously acknowledged that two forms of testimonial statements were admitted at common law even though they were unconfronted. The first of these were declarations made by a speaker who was both on the brink of death and aware that he was dying. Avie did not make the unconfronted statements admitted at Giles' trial when she was dying, so her statements do not fall within this historic exception.

A second common-law doctrine, which we will refer to as forfeiture by wrongdoing, permitted the introduction of statements of a witness who was "detained" or "kept away" by the "means or procurement" of the defendant. The doctrine has roots in the 1666 decision in *Lord Morley's Case,* at which judges concluded that a witness's having been "detained by the means or procurement of the prisoner" provided a basis to read testimony previously given at a coroner's inquest. * * *

The terms used to define the scope of the forfeiture rule suggest that the exception applied only when the defendant engaged in conduct *designed* to prevent the witness from testifying. The rule required the witness to have been "kept back" or "detained" by "means or procurement" of the defendant. Although there are definitions of "procure" and "procurement" that would merely require that a defendant have caused the witness's absence, other definitions would limit the causality to one that was *designed* to bring about the result "procured." * * *

Cases and treatises of the time indicate that a purpose-based definition of these terms governed. A number of them said that prior testimony was admissible when a witness was kept away by the defendant's "means and contrivance." * * * An 1858 treatise made the purpose requirement more explicit still, stating that the forfeiture rule applied when a witness "had been kept out of the way by the prisoner, or by someone on the prisoner's behalf, *in order to prevent him from giving evidence against him.*" * * *

The manner in which the rule was applied makes plain that unconfronted testimony would *not* be admitted without a showing that the defendant intended to prevent a witness from testifying. In cases where the evidence suggested that the defendant had caused a person to be absent, but had not done so to prevent the person from testifying—as in the typical murder case involving accusatorial statements by the victim—the testimony was excluded unless it was confronted or fell within the dying-declarations exception. * * *

The dissent closes by pointing out that a forfeiture rule which ignores *Crawford* would be particularly helpful to women in abusive relationships—or at least particularly helpful in punishing their abusers. * * * [W]e are puzzled by the dissent's decision to devote its peroration to domestic abuse cases. Is the suggestion that we should have one Confrontation Clause (the one the Framers adopted and *Crawford* described) for all other crimes, but a special, improvised Confrontation Clause for those crimes that are frequently directed against women? Domestic violence is an intolerable offense that legislatures may choose to combat through many means—from increasing criminal penalties to adding resources for investigation and prosecution to funding awareness and prevention campaigns. But for that serious crime, as for others, abridging the constitutional rights of criminal defendants is not in the State's arsenal.

The domestic-violence context is, however, relevant for a separate reason. Acts of domestic violence often are intended to dissuade a victim from resorting to outside help, and include conduct designed to prevent testimony to police officers or cooperation in criminal prosecutions. Where such an abusive relationship culminates in murder, the evidence may support a finding that the crime expressed the intent to isolate the victim and to stop her from reporting abuse to the authorities or cooperating with a criminal prosecution—rendering her prior statements admissible under the forfeiture doctrine. Earlier abuse, or threats of abuse, intended to dissuade the victim from resorting to outside help would be highly relevant to this inquiry, as would evidence of ongoing criminal proceedings at which the victim would have been expected to testify. * * *

The state courts in this case did not consider the intent of the defendant because they found that irrelevant to application of the forfeiture doctrine. This view of the law was error, but the court is free to consider evidence of the defendant's intent on remand.

The judgment of the California Supreme Court is vacated, and the case is remanded for further proceedings not inconsistent with this opinion.

*It is so ordered.*

JUSTICE BREYER, with whom JUSTICE STEVENS and JUSTICE KENNEDY join, dissenting.

There are several strong reasons for concluding that the forfeiture by wrongdoing exception applies here—reasons rooted in common-law history, established principles of criminal law and evidence, and the need for a rule that can be applied without creating great practical difficulties and evidentiary anomalies.

First, the language that courts have used in setting forth the exception is broad enough to cover the wrongdoing at issue in the present case (murder) and much else besides. * * * I have found no case that uses language that would not bring a murder and a subsequent trial for murder within its scope.

Second, an examination of the forfeiture rule's basic purposes and objectives indicates that the rule applies here. At the time of the founding, a leading treatise writer described the forfeiture rule as designed to ensure that the prisoner "shall never be admitted to shelter himself by such evil Practices on the Witness, that being to give him Advantage of his own Wrong." This Court's own leading case explained the exception as finding its "foundation in the maxim that no one shall be permitted to take advantage of his own wrong." What more "evil practice," what greater "wrong," than to murder the witness? And what greater evidentiary "advantage" could one derive from that wrong than thereby to prevent the witness from testifying, e.g., preventing the witness from describing a history of physical abuse that is not consistent with the defendant's claim that he killed her in self-defense?

Third, related areas of the law motivated by similar equitable principles treat forfeiture or its equivalent similarly. The common law, for example, prohibits a life insurance beneficiary who murders an insured from recovering under the policy. And it forbids recovery when the beneficiary "feloniously kills the insured, irrespective of the purpose." Similarly, a beneficiary of a will who murders the testator cannot inherit under the will. And this is so "whether the crime was committed for that very purpose or with some other felonious design."

Fourth, under the circumstances presented by this case, there is no difficulty demonstrating the defendant's intent. This is because the defendant here knew that murdering his ex-girlfriend would keep her from testifying; and that knowledge is sufficient to show the *intent* that law ordinarily demands. As this Court put the matter more than a century ago: A "man who performs an act which it is known will produce a particular result is from our common experience presumed to have anticipated that result and to have intended it."

With a few criminal law exceptions not here relevant, the law holds an individual responsible for consequences known likely to follow just as if that individual had intended to achieve them. A defendant, in a criminal or a civil case, for example, cannot escape criminal or civil liability for murdering an airline passenger by claiming that his purpose in blowing up the airplane was to kill only a single passenger for her life insurance, not the others on the same flight.

This principle applies here. Suppose that a husband, H, knows that after he assaulted his wife, W, she gave statements to the police. Based on the fact that W gave statements to the police, H also knows that it is possible he will be tried for assault. If H then kills W, H cannot avoid responsibility for intentionally preventing W from testifying, not even if H says he killed W because he was angry with her and not to keep her away from the assault trial. Of course, the trial here is not for assault; it is for murder. But I should think that this fact, because of the nature of the crime, would count as a stronger, not a weaker, reason for applying the forfeiture rule. Nor should it matter that H, at the time of the murder, may have *believed* an assault trial *more likely* to take place than a murder trial, for W's unavailability to testify at *any* future trial was a *certain* consequence of the murder. And any reasonable person would have known it. Cf. *United States v. Falstaff Brewing Corp.* (Marshall, J., concurring in result) ("[P]erhaps the oldest rule of evidence—that a man is presumed to intend the natural and probable consequences of his acts—is based on the common law's preference for objectively measurable data over subjective statements of opinion and intent").

The majority tries to overcome this elementary legal logic by claiming that the "forfeiture rule" applies, not where the defendant *intends* to prevent the witness from testifying, but only where that is the defendant's *purpose, i.e.,* that the rule applies only where the defendant acts from a particular *motive,* a *desire* to keep the witness from trial. But the law does not often turn matters of responsibility upon *motive,* rather than *intent.* And there is no reason to believe that application of the rule of forfeiture constitutes an exception to this general legal principle.

Indeed, to turn application of the forfeiture rule upon proof of the defendant's *purpose* (rather than *intent*), as the majority does, creates serious practical evidentiary problems. Consider H who assaults W, knows she has complained to the police, and then murders her. H *knows* that W will be unable to testify against him at any future trial. But who knows whether H's knowledge played a major role, a middling role, a minor role, or no role at all, in H's decision to kill W? Who knows precisely what passed through H's mind at the critical moment?

Moreover, the majority's insistence upon a showing of *purpose* or *motive* cannot be squared with the exception's basically ethical objective. If H, by killing W, is able to keep W's testimony out of court, then he has successfully "take[n] advantage of his own wrong." And he does so whether he killed her *for the purpose of* keeping her from testifying, with *certain knowledge* that she will not be able to testify, or with *a belief* that rises to a *reasonable level of probability*. The inequity consists of his being able to *use* the killing to keep out of court her statements against him. That inequity exists whether the defendant's state of mind is purposeful, intentional (*i.e.,* with knowledge), or simply probabilistic. * * *

The rule of forfeiture is implicated primarily where domestic abuse is at issue. In such a case, a murder victim may have previously given a testimonial statement, say, to the police, about an abuser's attacks; and introduction of that statement may be at issue in a later trial for the abuser's subsequent murder of the victim. This is not an uncommon occurrence. Each year, domestic violence results in more than 1,500 deaths and more than 2 million injuries; it accounts for a substantial portion of all homicides; it typically involves a history of repeated violence; and it is difficult to prove in court because the victim is generally reluctant or unable to testify.

Regardless of a defendant's purpose, threats, further violence, and ultimately murder can stop victims from testifying. A *constitutional* evidentiary requirement that insists upon a showing of purpose (rather than simply intent or probabilistic knowledge) may permit the domestic partner who made the threats, caused the violence, or even murdered the victim to avoid conviction for earlier crimes by taking advantage of later ones.

In *Davis,* we recognized that "domestic violence" cases are "notoriously susceptible to intimidation or coercion of the victim to ensure that she does not testify at trial." We noted the concern that "[w]hen this occurs, the Confrontation Clause gives the criminal a windfall." And we replied to that concern by stating that "one who obtains the absence of a witness by wrongdoing forfeits the constitutional right to confrontation." To the extent that it insists upon an additional showing of purpose, the Court breaks the promise implicit in those words and, in doing so, grants the defendant not fair treatment, but a windfall. I can find no history, no underlying purpose, no administrative consideration, and no constitutional principle that requires this result.

[JUSTICE ALITO's concurring opinion, JUSTICE THOMAS' concurring opinion, and JUSTICE SOUTER's concurring opinion have been omitted.]

### NOTE

On remand, the Court of Appeal reversed Giles' first degree murder conviction without prejudice, finding no evidence in the record that Giles intended to make Avie unavailable to testify. *People v. Giles* (Feb. 25, 2009, B166937, unpublished opinion). On retrial, the prosecutor did not seek to introduce Avie's extrajudicial statements. Giles was again convicted of first degree murder, and his conviction was affirmed on appeal. *People v. Giles,* 2012 Cal. App. Unpub. LEXIS 366 (Jan. 18, 2012, B224629).

## RICHARDSON V. MARSH

Supreme Court of the United States
481 U.S. 200, 107 S.Ct. 1702, 95 L.Ed.2d 176 (1987)

JUSTICE SCALIA delivered the opinion of the Court.

In *Bruton v. United States*, we held that a defendant is deprived of his rights under the Confrontation Clause when his nontestifying codefendant's confession naming him as a participant in the crime is introduced at their joint trial, even if the jury is instructed to consider that confession only against the codefendant. Today we consider whether *Bruton* requires the same result when the codefendant's confession is redacted to omit any reference to the defendant, but the defendant is nonetheless linked to the confession by evidence properly admitted against him at trial.

Respondent Clarissa Marsh, Benjamin Williams, and Kareem Martin were charged with assaulting Cynthia Knighton and murdering her 4-year-old son, Koran, and her aunt, Ollie Scott. Respondent and Williams were tried jointly, over her objection. (Martin was a fugitive at the time of trial.) At the trial, Knighton testified as follows: On the evening of October 29, 1978, she and her son were at Scott's home when respondent and her boyfriend Martin visited. After a brief conversation in the living room, respondent announced that she had come to "pick up something" from Scott and rose from the couch. Martin then pulled out a gun, pointed it at Scott and the Knightons, and said that "someone had gotten killed and [Scott] knew something about it." Respondent immediately walked to the front door and peered out the peephole. The doorbell rang, respondent opened the door, and Williams walked in, carrying a gun. As Williams passed respondent, he asked, "Where's the money?" Martin forced Scott upstairs, and Williams went into the kitchen, leaving respondent alone with the Knightons. Knighton and her son attempted to flee, but respondent grabbed Knighton and held her until Williams returned. Williams ordered the Knightons to lie on the floor and then went upstairs to assist Martin. Respondent, again left alone with the Knightons, stood by the front door and occasionally peered out the peephole. A few minutes later, Martin, Williams, and Scott came down the stairs, and Martin handed a paper grocery bag to respondent. Martin and Williams then forced Scott and the Knightons into the basement, where Martin shot them. Only Cynthia Knighton survived.

In addition to Knighton's testimony, the State introduced (over respondent's objection) a confession given by Williams to the police shortly after his arrest. The confession was redacted to omit all reference to respondent—indeed, to omit all indication that *anyone* other than Martin and Williams participated in the crime. The confession largely corroborated Knighton's account of the activities of persons other than respondent in the house. In addition, the confession described a conversation Williams had with Martin as they drove to the Scott home, during which, according to Williams, Martin said that he would have to kill the victims after the robbery. At the time the confession was admitted, the jury was admonished not to use it in any way against respondent. Williams did not testify.

After the State rested, respondent took the stand. She testified that on October 29, 1978, she had lost money that Martin intended to use to buy drugs. Martin was upset, and suggested to respondent that she borrow money from Scott, with whom she had worked in the past. Martin and respondent picked up Williams and drove to Scott's house. During the drive, respondent, who was sitting in the backseat, "knew that [Martin and Williams] were talking" but could not hear the conversation because "the radio was on and the speaker was right in [her] ear." Martin and respondent were admitted into the home, and respondent had a short conversation with Scott, during which she asked for a loan. Martin then pulled a gun, and respondent walked to the door to see where the car was. When she saw Williams, she opened the door for him. Respondent testified that during the robbery she did not feel free to leave and was too scared to flee. She said that she did not know why she prevented the Knightons from escaping. She admitted taking the bag from Martin, but said that after Martin and Williams took the victims into the basement, she left the house without the bag. Respondent insisted that she had possessed no prior knowledge that Martin and Williams were armed, had heard no conversation about anyone's being harmed, and had not intended to rob or kill anyone.

During his closing argument, the prosecutor admonished the jury not to use Williams' confession against respondent. Later in his argument, however, he linked respondent to the portion of Williams' confession describing his conversation with Martin in the car. (Respondent's attorney did not object to this.) After closing arguments, the judge again instructed the jury that Williams' confession was not to be considered against respondent. The jury convicted respondent of two counts of felony murder in the perpetration of an armed robbery and one count of assault with intent to commit murder. * * *

Respondent then filed a petition for a writ of habeas corpus * * *. She alleged * * * that introduction of Williams' confession at the joint trial had violated her rights under the Confrontation Clause. * * * The Court of Appeals held that in determining whether *Bruton* bars the admission of a nontestifying codefendant's confession, a court must assess the confession's "inculpatory value" by examining not only the face of the confession, but also all of the evidence introduced at trial. Here, Williams' account of the conversation in the car was the only *direct* evidence that respondent knew before entering Scott's house that the victims would be robbed and killed. Respondent's own testimony placed her in that car. In light of the "paucity" of other evidence of malice and the prosecutor's linkage of respondent and the statement in the car during closing argument, admission of Williams' confession "was powerfully incriminating to [respondent] with respect to the critical element of intent." Thus, the Court of Appeals concluded, the Confrontation Clause was violated. We granted certiorari * * *.

The Confrontation Clause of the Sixth Amendment, extended against the States by the Fourteenth Amendment, guarantees the right of a criminal defendant "to be confronted with the witnesses against him." The right of confrontation includes the right to cross-examine witnesses. Therefore, where two defendants are tried jointly, the pretrial confession of one cannot be admitted against the other unless the confessing defendant takes the stand.

Ordinarily, a witness whose testimony is introduced at a joint trial is not considered to be a witness "against" a defendant if the jury is instructed to consider that testimony only against a codefendant. * * * In *Bruton*, however, we recognized a narrow exception to this principle: We held that a defendant is deprived of his Sixth Amendment right of confrontation when the facially incriminating confession of a nontestifying codefendant is introduced at their joint trial, even if the jury is instructed to consider the confession only against the codefendant. We said:

> [T]here are some contexts in which the risk that the jury will not, or cannot, follow instructions is so great, and the consequences of failure so vital to the defendant, that the practical and human limitations of the jury system cannot be ignored. Such a context is presented here, where the powerfully incriminating extrajudicial statements of a codefendant, who stands accused side-by-side with the defendant, are deliberately spread before the jury in a joint trial. . . .

There is an important distinction between this case and *Bruton*, which causes it to fall outside the narrow exception we have created. In *Bruton*, the codefendant's confession "expressly implicat[ed]" the defendant as his accomplice. Thus, at the time that confession was introduced there was not the slightest doubt that it would prove "powerfully incriminating." By contrast, in this case the confession was not incriminating on its face, and became so only when linked with evidence introduced later at trial (the defendant's own testimony).

Where the necessity of such linkage is involved, it is a less valid generalization that the jury will not likely obey the instruction to disregard the evidence. Specific testimony that "the defendant helped me commit the crime" is more vivid than inferential incrimination, and hence more difficult to thrust out of mind. Moreover, with regard to such an explicit statement the only issue is, plain and simply, whether the jury can possibly be expected to forget it in assessing the defendant's guilt; whereas with regard to inferential incrimination the judge's instruction may well be successful in dissuading the jury from entering onto the path of inference in the first place, so that there is no incrimination to forget. In short, while it may not always be simple for the members of a jury to obey the instruction that they disregard an incriminating inference, there does not exist the overwhelming probability of their inability to do so that is the foundation of *Bruton*'s exception to the general rule.

Even more significantly, evidence requiring linkage differs from evidence incriminating on its face in the practical effects which application of the *Bruton* exception would produce. If limited to facially incriminating confessions, *Bruton* can be complied with by redaction—a possibility suggested in that opinion itself. If extended to confessions incriminating by connection, not only is that not possible, but it is not even possible to predict the admissibility of a confession in advance of trial. * * *

One might say, of course, that a certain way of assuring compliance would be to try defendants separately whenever an incriminating statement of one of them is sought to be used. * * * It would impair both the efficiency and the fairness of the criminal justice system to require, in all these cases of joint crimes where incriminating statements exist, that prosecutors bring separate proceedings, presenting the same evidence again and again, requiring victims and witnesses to repeat the inconvenience (and sometimes trauma) of testifying, and randomly favoring the last-tried defendants who have the advantage of knowing the prosecution's case beforehand. * * * The other way of assuring compliance with an expansive *Bruton* rule would be to forgo use of codefendant confessions. That price also is too high, since confessions "are more than merely 'desirable'; they are essential to society's compelling interest in finding, convicting, and punishing those who violate the law."

The rule that juries are presumed to follow their instructions is a pragmatic one, rooted less in the absolute certitude that the presumption is true than in the belief that it represents a reasonable practical accommodation of the interests of the state and the defendant in the criminal justice process. On the precise facts of *Bruton*, involving a facially incriminating confession, we found that accommodation inadequate. As our discussion above shows, the calculus changes when confessions that do not name the defendant are at issue. While we continue to apply *Bruton* where we have found that its rationale validly applies, we decline to extend it further. We hold that the Confrontation Clause is not violated by the admission of a nontestifying codefendant's confession with a proper limiting instruction when, as here, the confession is redacted to eliminate not only the defendant's name, but any reference to his or her existence. * * *

The judgment of the Court of Appeals is reversed, and the case is remanded for further proceedings consistent with this opinion. * * *

JUSTICE STEVENS, with whom JUSTICE BRENNAN and JUSTICE MARSHALL join, dissenting. * * *

The rationale of our decision in *Bruton v. United States* applies without exception to all inadmissible confessions that are "powerfully incriminating." Today, however, the Court draws a distinction of constitutional magnitude between those confessions that directly identify the defendant and those that rely for their inculpatory effect on the factual and legal relationships of their contents to other evidence before the jury. Even if the jury's indirect inference of the defendant's guilt based on an inadmissible confession is much more devastating to the defendant's case than its inference from a direct reference in the codefendant's confession, the Court requires the exclusion of only the latter statement. This illogical result demeans the values protected by the Confrontation Clause. * * *

It is a "basic premise" of the Confrontation Clause that certain kinds of hearsay "are at once so damaging, so suspect, and yet so difficult to discount, that jurors cannot be trusted to give such evidence the minimal weight it logically deserves, *whatever* instructions the trial judge might give." This constitutionally mandated skepticism undergirds the *Bruton* holding and is equally applicable to this case. The Court framed the issue in *Bruton* as "whether the conviction of a defendant at a joint trial should be set aside although the jury was instructed that a codefendant's confession inculpating the defendant had to be disregarded in determining his guilt or innocence." We answered that question in the affirmative, noting that the Sixth Amendment is violated "where the powerfully incriminating extrajudicial statements of a codefendant, who stands accused side-by-side with the defendant, are deliberately spread before the jury in a joint trial."

Today the Court nevertheless draws a line between codefendant confessions that expressly name the defendant and those that do not. The Court relies on the presumption that in the latter category "it is a less valid generalization that the jury will not likely obey the instruction to disregard the evidence." I agree; but I do not read *Bruton* to require the exclusion of *all* codefendant confessions that do not mention the defendant. Some such confessions may not have any significant impact on the defendant's case. But others will. If we presume, as we must, that jurors give their full and vigorous attention to every witness and each item of evidence, the very acts of listening and seeing will sometimes lead them down "the path of inference." Indeed, the Court tacitly acknowledges this point; while the Court speculates that the judge's instruction may dissuade the jury from making inferences at all, it also concedes the probability of their occurrence, arguing that there is no overwhelming probability that jurors will be unable to "disregard an incriminating inference." *Bruton* has always required trial judges to answer the question whether a particular confession is or is not "powerfully incriminating" on a case-by-case basis; they should follow the same analysis whether or not the defendant is actually named by his or her codefendant.

Instructing the jury that it was to consider Benjamin Williams' confession only against him, and not against Clarissa Marsh, failed to guarantee the level of certainty required by the Confrontation Clause. * * * The facts in this case are, admittedly, different from those in *Bruton* because Williams' statement did not directly mention respondent. Thus, instead of being "incriminating on its face," it became so only when considered in connection with the other evidence presented to the jury. The difference between the facts of *Bruton* and the facts of this case does not eliminate their common, substantial, and constitutionally unacceptable risk that the jury, when resolving a critical issue against respondent, may have relied on impermissible evidence.

The facts that joint trials conserve prosecutorial resources, diminish inconvenience to witnesses, and avoid delays in the administration of criminal justice have been well known for a long time. It is equally well known that joint trials create special risks of prejudice to one of the defendants, and that such risks often make it necessary to grant severances. * * * The concern about the cost of joint trials, even if valid, does not prevail over the interests of justice. * * *

I respectfully dissent.

# CHAPTER 32

# DOUBLE JEOPARDY

■ ■ ■

The Double Jeopardy Clause contained in the Fifth Amendment provides: "nor shall any person be subject for the same offence to be twice put in jeopardy of life or limb. . . ." The Double Jeopardy Clause protects a defendant against multiple prosecutions for the same offense. It also protects a defendant against multiple punishments for the same offense.

The Double Jeopardy Clause applies only after a defendant has been placed "in jeopardy." In a jury trial, jeopardy does not attach until after the jury is empaneled and sworn. In a bench trial (a trial in which a judge rather than a jury decides whether to acquit or convict the defendant), jeopardy does not attach until the first witness is sworn. If the defendant pleads guilty and there is no trial, jeopardy attaches once the court accepts the defendant's guilty plea.

The Double Jeopardy Clause has wide application in criminal procedure. This chapter reflects the broad reach of the doctrine and covers multiple topics, including collateral estoppel, the "same offense" limitation, the dual sovereignty doctrine, criminal versus civil punishment, retrial following a mistrial, acquittals versus dismissals, retrial following the reversal of a conviction, and jury nullification.

## A. COLLATERAL ESTOPPEL

Collateral estoppel is a familiar doctrine from civil procedure. Does the doctrine also have application in criminal procedure? Is it part of the Double Jeopardy Clause? *Ashe v. Swenson* addresses these and other questions.

### ASHE V. SWENSON
Supreme Court of the United States
397 U.S. 436, 90 S.Ct. 1189, 25 L.Ed.2d 469 (1970)

JUSTICE STEWART delivered the opinion of the Court. * * *

Sometime in the early hours of the morning of January 10, 1960, six men were engaged in a poker game in the basement of the home of John Gladson at Lee's Summit, Missouri. Suddenly three or four masked men, armed with a shotgun and pistols, broke into the basement and robbed each of the poker players of money and various articles of personal property. The robbers—and it has never been clear whether there were three or four of them—then fled in a car belonging to one of the victims of the robbery. Shortly thereafter the stolen car was discovered in a field, and later that morning three men were arrested by a state trooper while they were walking on a highway not far from where the abandoned car had been found. The petitioner was arrested by another officer some distance away.

The four were subsequently charged with seven separate offenses— the armed robbery of each of the six poker players and the theft of the car. In May 1960 the petitioner went to trial on the charge of robbing Donald Knight, one of the participants in the poker game. At the trial the State called Knight and three of his fellow poker players as prosecution witnesses. Each of them described the circumstances of the holdup and itemized his own individual losses. The proof that an armed robbery had occurred and that personal property had been taken from Knight as well as from each of the others was unassailable. The testimony of the four victims in this regard was consistent both internally and with that of the others. But the State's evidence that the petitioner had been one of the robbers was weak. Two of the witnesses thought that there had been only three robbers altogether, and could not identify the petitioner as one of them. Another of the victims, who was the petitioner's uncle by marriage, said that at the "patrol station" he had positively identified each of the other three men accused of the holdup, but could say only that the petitioner's voice "sounded very much like" that of one of the robbers. The fourth participant in the poker game did identify the petitioner, but only by his "size and height, and his actions."

The cross-examination of these witnesses was brief, and it was aimed primarily at exposing the weakness of their identification testimony. Defense counsel made no attempt to question their testimony regarding the holdup itself or their claims as to their losses. Knight testified without contradiction that the robbers had stolen from him his watch, $250 in cash, and about $500 in checks. His billfold, which had been found by the police in the possession of one of the three other men accused of the robbery, was admitted in evidence. The defense offered no testimony and waived final argument.

The trial judge instructed the jury that if it found that the petitioner was one of the participants in the armed robbery, the theft of "any money" from Knight would sustain a conviction. He also instructed the jury that if the petitioner was one of the robbers, he was guilty under the law even if he had not personally robbed Knight. The jury—though not instructed to elaborate upon its verdict—found the petitioner "not guilty due to insufficient evidence."

Six weeks later the petitioner was brought to trial again, this time for the robbery of another participant in the poker game, a man named

Roberts. The petitioner filed a motion to dismiss, based on his previous acquittal. The motion was overruled, and the second trial began. The witnesses were for the most part the same, though this time their testimony was substantially stronger on the issue of the petitioner's identity. For example, two witnesses who at the first trial had been wholly unable to identify the petitioner as one of the robbers, now testified that his features, size, and mannerisms matched those of one of their assailants. Another witness who before had identified the petitioner only by his size and actions now also remembered him by the unusual sound of his voice. The State further refined its case at the second trial by declining to call one of the participants in the poker game whose identification testimony at the first trial had been conspicuously negative. The case went to the jury on instructions virtually identical to those given at the first trial. This time the jury found the petitioner guilty, and he was sentenced to a 35-year term in the state penitentiary.

* * * The question is * * * whether collateral estoppel is a part of the Fifth Amendment's guarantee against double jeopardy. And if collateral estoppel is embodied in that guarantee, then its applicability in a particular case is no longer a matter to be left for state court determination within the broad bounds of "fundamental fairness," but a matter of constitutional fact we must decide through an examination of the entire record.

"Collateral estoppel" is an awkward phrase, but it stands for an extremely important principle in our adversary system of justice. It means simply that when an issue of ultimate fact has once been determined by a valid and final judgment, that issue cannot again be litigated between the same parties in any future lawsuit. Although first developed in civil litigation, collateral estoppel has been an established rule of federal criminal law at least since this Court's decision more than 50 years ago in *United States v. Oppenheimer*. As Mr. Justice Holmes put the matter in that case, "It cannot be that the safeguards of the person, so often and so rightly mentioned with solemn reverence, are less than those that protect from a liability in debt."

The federal decisions have made clear that the rule of collateral estoppel in criminal cases is not to be applied with the hypertechnical and archaic approach of a 19th century pleading book, but with realism and rationality. Where a previous judgment of acquittal was based upon a general verdict, as is usually the case, this approach requires a court to "examine the record of a prior proceeding, taking into account the pleadings, evidence, charge, and other relevant matter, and conclude whether a rational jury could have grounded its verdict upon an issue other than that which the defendant seeks to foreclose from consideration." * * *

Straightforward application of the federal rule to the present case can lead to but one conclusion. For the record is utterly devoid of any indication that the first jury could rationally have found that an armed robbery had not occurred, or that Knight had not been a victim of that robbery. The single rationally conceivable issue in dispute before the jury was whether the petitioner had been one of the robbers. And the jury by its verdict found that he had not. The federal rule of law, therefore, would make a second prosecution for the robbery of Roberts wholly impermissible.

The ultimate question to be determined * * * is whether this established rule of federal law is embodied in the Fifth Amendment guarantee against double jeopardy. We do not hesitate to hold that it is. For whatever else that constitutional guarantee may embrace, it surely protects a man who has been acquitted from having to "run the gantlet" a second time.

The question is not whether Missouri could validly charge the petitioner with six separate offenses for the robbery of the six poker players. It is not whether he could have received a total of six punishments if he had been convicted in a single trial of robbing the six victims. It is simply whether, after a jury determined by its verdict that the petitioner was not one of the robbers, the State could constitutionally hale him before a new jury to litigate that issue again.

After the first jury had acquitted the petitioner of robbing Knight, Missouri could certainly not have brought him to trial again upon that charge. Once a jury had determined upon conflicting testimony that there was at least a reasonable doubt that the petitioner was one of the robbers, the State could not present the same or different identification evidence in a second prosecution for the robbery of Knight in the hope that a different jury might find that evidence more convincing. The situation is constitutionally no different here, even though the second trial related to another victim of the same robbery. For the name of the victim, in the circumstances of this case, had no bearing whatever upon the issue of whether the petitioner was one of the robbers.

In this case the State in its brief has frankly conceded that following the petitioner's acquittal, it treated the first trial as no more than a dry run for the second prosecution: "No doubt the prosecutor felt the state had a provable case on the first charge and, when he lost, he did what every good attorney would do—he refined his presentation in light of the turn of events at the first trial." But this is precisely what the constitutional guarantee forbids.

Reversed and remanded.

JUSTICE BRENNAN, whom JUSTICE DOUGLAS and JUSTICE MARSHALL join, concurring.

I agree that the Double Jeopardy Clause incorporates collateral estoppel as a constitutional requirement and therefore join the Court's opinion. However, even if the rule of collateral estoppel had been inapplicable to the facts of this case, it is my view that the Double Jeopardy Clause nevertheless bars the prosecution of petitioner a second time for armed robbery. The two prosecutions, the first for the robbery of Knight and the second for the robbery of Roberts, grew out of one criminal episode, and therefore I think it clear on the facts of this case that the Double Jeopardy Clause prohibited Missouri from prosecuting petitioner for each robbery at a different trial. * * *

In my view, the Double Jeopardy Clause requires the prosecution, except in most limited circumstances, to join at one trial all the charges against a defendant that grow out of a single criminal act, occurrence, episode, or transaction. This "same transaction" test of "same offence" not only enforces the ancient prohibition against vexatious multiple prosecutions embodied in the Double Jeopardy Clause, but responds as well to the increasingly widespread recognition that the consolidation in one lawsuit of all issues arising out of a single transaction or occurrence best promotes justice, economy, and convenience. * * *

CHIEF JUSTICE BURGER, dissenting. * * *

The essence of Mr. Justice Brennan's concurrence is that this was all one transaction, one episode, or, if I may so characterize it, one frolic, and, hence, only one crime. His approach, like that taken by the Court, totally overlooks the significance of there being six entirely separate charges of robbery against six individuals.

This "single frolic" concept is not a novel notion; it has been urged in various courts including this Court. One of the theses underlying the "single frolic" notion is that the criminal episode is "indivisible." The short answer to that is that to the victims, the criminal conduct is readily divisible and intensely personal; each offense is an offense against a person. For me it demeans the dignity of the human personality and individuality to talk of "a single transaction" in the context or six separate assaults on six individuals. * * *

I therefore join with the four courts that have found no double jeopardy in this case.

[JUSTICE BLACK's concurring opinion and JUSTICE HARLAN's concurring opinion have been omitted.]

## B. THE "SAME OFFENSE" REQUIREMENT

The Double Jeopardy Clause protects a defendant against multiple prosecutions for the "same offense." Determining whether a subsequent prosecution is for the "same offense," however, is not always easy. Offenses may have different titles and come from different statutory provisions, yet constitute the "same offense" for purposes of double jeopardy. In *United States v. Dixon*, we see the Justices arguing over how best to determine whether two offenses are the "same offense" for double jeopardy purposes.

### UNITED STATES V. DIXON

Supreme Court of the United States
509 U.S. 688, 113 S.Ct. 2849, 125 L.Ed.2d 556 (1993)

JUSTICE SCALIA announced the judgment of the Court and delivered the opinion of the Court with respect to Parts I, II, and IV, and an opinion with respect to Parts III and V, in which JUSTICE KENNEDY joins. * * *

### I

Respondent Alvin Dixon was arrested for second-degree murder and was released on bond. Consistent with the District of Columbia's bail law authorizing the judicial officer to impose any condition that "will reasonably assure the appearance of the person for trial or the safety of any other person or the community," Dixon's release form specified that he was not to commit "any criminal offense," and warned that any violation of the conditions of release would subject him "to revocation of release, an order of detention, and prosecution for contempt of court."

While awaiting trial, Dixon was arrested and indicted for possession of cocaine with intent to distribute, in violation of D.C. Code Ann. § 33–541(a)(1) (1988). The court issued an order requiring Dixon to show cause why he should not be held in contempt or have the terms of his pretrial release modified. At the show-cause hearing, * * * [t]he court * * * found Dixon guilty of criminal contempt under § 23–1329(c), [and sentenced him] * * * to 180 days in jail. * * * He later moved to dismiss the cocaine indictment on double jeopardy grounds; the trial court granted the motion.

Respondent Michael Foster's route to this Court is similar. Based on Foster's alleged physical attacks upon her in the past, Foster's estranged wife Ana obtained a civil protection order (CPO) in Superior Court of the District of Columbia. The order, to which Foster consented, required that he not "molest, assault, or in any manner threaten or physically abuse" Ana Foster. * * *

Over the course of eight months, Ana Foster filed three separate motions to have her husband held in contempt for numerous violations of the CPO. Of the 16 alleged episodes, the only charges relevant here are three separate instances of threats (on November 12, 1987, and March 26 and May 17, 1988) and two assaults (on November 6, 1987, and May 21, 1988) * * *.

After issuing a notice of hearing and ordering Foster to appear, the court held a 3-day bench trial. Counsel for Ana Foster and her mother prosecuted the action; the United States was not represented at trial, although the United States Attorney was apparently aware of the action, as was the court aware of a separate grand jury proceeding on some of the alleged criminal conduct. As to the assault charges, the court stated that Ana Foster would have "to prove as an element, first that there was a Civil Protection Order, and then [that] . . . the assault as defined by the criminal code, in fact occurred." * * * [T]he court granted Foster's motion for acquittal on various counts, including the alleged threats on November 12 and May 17 * * * [but] found Foster guilty beyond a reasonable doubt of four counts of criminal contempt (three violations of Ana Foster's CPO, and one violation of the CPO obtained by her mother), including the November 6, 1987, and May 21, 1988, assaults, but acquitted him on other counts, including the March 26 alleged threats. He was sentenced to an aggregate 600 days' imprisonment.

The United States Attorney's Office later obtained an indictment charging Foster with simple assault on or about November 6, 1987 (Count I, violation of § 22–504); threatening to injure another on or about November 12, 1987, and March 26 and May 17, 1988 (Counts II–IV, violation of § 22–2307); and assault with intent to kill on or about May 21, 1988 (Count V, violation of § 22–501). Ana Foster was the complainant in all counts; the first and last counts were based on the events for which Foster had been held in contempt, and the other three were based on the alleged events for which Foster was acquitted of contempt. Like Dixon, Foster filed a motion to dismiss, claiming a double jeopardy bar to all counts, and also collateral estoppel as to Counts II–IV. The trial court denied the double jeopardy claim and did not rule on the collateral-estoppel assertion.

The Government appealed the double jeopardy ruling in *Dixon,* and Foster appealed the trial court's denial of his motion. The District of Columbia Court of Appeals consolidated the two cases, reheard them en banc, and, relying on our recent decision in *Grady v. Corbin*, ruled that both subsequent prosecutions were barred by the Double Jeopardy Clause. * * *

## II

* * * In both *Dixon* and *Foster,* a court issued an order directing a particular individual not to commit criminal offenses. (In Dixon's case, the court incorporated the entire criminal code; in Foster's case, the criminal offense of simple assault.) * * * [T]he double jeopardy issue presented here [is] whether prosecution for criminal contempt based on violation of a criminal law incorporated into a court order bars a subsequent prosecution for the criminal offense.

The Double Jeopardy Clause, whose application to this new context we are called upon to consider, provides that no person shall "be subject for the same offence to be twice put in jeopardy of life or limb." This protection applies both to successive punishments and to successive prosecutions for the same criminal offense. It is well established that criminal contempt, at least the sort enforced through nonsummary proceedings, is "a crime in the ordinary sense."

We have held that constitutional protections for criminal defendants other than the double jeopardy provision apply in nonsummary criminal contempt prosecutions just as they do in other criminal prosecutions. We think it obvious, and today hold, that the protection of the Double Jeopardy Clause likewise attaches.

In both the multiple punishment and multiple prosecution contexts, this Court has concluded that where the two offenses for which the defendant is punished or tried cannot survive the "same-elements" test, the double jeopardy bar applies. The same-elements test, sometimes referred to as the *"Blockburger"* test, inquires whether each offense contains an element not contained in the other; if not, they are the "same offence" and double jeopardy bars additional punishment and successive prosecution. * * *

We recently held in *Grady* that in addition to passing the *Blockburger* test, a subsequent prosecution must satisfy a "same-conduct" test to avoid the double jeopardy bar. The *Grady* test provides that, "if, to establish an essential element of an offense charged in that prosecution, the government will prove conduct that constitutes an offense for which the defendant has already been prosecuted," a second prosecution may not be had.

### III

### A

The first question before us today is whether *Blockburger* analysis permits subsequent prosecution in this new criminal contempt context, where judicial order has prohibited criminal act. If it does, we must then proceed to consider whether *Grady* also permits it.

We begin with *Dixon*. The statute applicable in Dixon's contempt prosecution provides that "[a] person who has been conditionally released . . . and who has violated a condition of release shall be subject to . . . prosecution for contempt of court." § 23–1329(a). Obviously, Dixon could not commit an "offence" under this provision until an order setting out conditions was issued. The statute by itself imposes no legal obligation on anyone. Dixon's cocaine possession, although an offense under D.C. Code Ann. § 33–541(a), was not an offense under § 23–1329 until a judge incorporated the statutory drug offense into his release order.

In this situation, in which the contempt sanction is imposed for violating the order through commission of the incorporated drug offense, the later attempt to prosecute Dixon for the drug offense resembles the situation that produced our judgment of double jeopardy in *Harris v. Oklahoma.* There we held that a subsequent prosecution for robbery with a firearm was barred by the Double Jeopardy Clause, because the defendant had already been tried for felony murder based on the same underlying felony. We have described * * * *Harris* as standing for the proposition that, for double jeopardy purposes, "the crime generally described as felony murder" is not "a separate offense distinct from its various elements." So too here, the "crime" of violating a condition of release cannot be abstracted from the "element" of the violated condition. The *Dixon* court order incorporated the entire governing criminal code in the same manner as the *Harris* felony-murder statute incorporated the several enumerated felonies. Here, as in *Harris,* the underlying substantive criminal offense is "a species of lesser-included offense." * * *

The foregoing analysis obviously applies as well to Count I of the indictment against Foster, charging assault in violation of § 22–504, based on the same event that was the subject of his prior contempt conviction for violating the provision of the CPO forbidding him to commit simple assault under § 22–504. The subsequent prosecution for assault fails the *Blockburger* test, and is barred.

### B

The remaining four counts in *Foster,* assault with intent to kill (Count V; § 22–501) and threats to injure or kidnap (Counts II–IV; § 22–2307), are not barred under *Blockburger.* As to Count V: Foster's conduct on May 21, 1988, was found to violate the Family Division's order that he not "molest, assault, or in any manner threaten or physically abuse" his wife. At the contempt hearing, the court stated that Ana Foster's attorney, who prosecuted the contempt, would have to prove, first, knowledge of a CPO, and, second, a willful violation of one of its conditions, here simple assault as defined by the criminal code. On the basis of the same episode, Foster was then indicted for violation of § 22–501, which proscribes assault with intent to kill. Under governing law, that offense requires proof of specific intent to kill; simple assault does not. Similarly, the contempt offense required proof of knowledge of the CPO, which assault with intent to kill does not. Applying the *Blockburger* elements test, the result is clear: These crimes were different offenses, and the subsequent prosecution did not violate the Double Jeopardy Clause.

Counts II, III, and IV of Foster's indictment are likewise not barred. These charged Foster under § 22–2307 (forbidding anyone to "threate[n] . . . to kidnap any person or to injure the person of another or physically damage the property of any person") for his alleged threats on three separate dates. Foster's contempt prosecution included charges that, on the same dates, he violated the CPO provision ordering that he not "in any manner threaten" Ana Foster. Conviction of the contempt required willful violation of the CPO—which conviction under § 22–2307 did not; and conviction under § 22–2307 required that the threat be a threat to kidnap, to inflict bodily injury, or to damage property—which conviction of the contempt (for violating the CPO provision that Foster not "in any manner threaten") did not. Each offense therefore contained a separate element, and the *Blockburger* test for double jeopardy was not met.

IV

Having found that at least some of the counts at issue here are not barred by the *Blockburger* test, we must consider whether they are barred by the new, additional double jeopardy test we announced three Terms ago in *Grady v. Corbin*.[a] They undoubtedly are, since *Grady* prohibits "a subsequent prosecution if, to establish an essential element of an offense charged in that prosecution [here, assault as an element of assault with intent to kill, or threatening as an element of threatening bodily injury], the government will prove conduct that constitutes an offense for which the defendant has already been prosecuted [here, the assault and the threatening, which conduct constituted the offense of violating the CPO]."

We have concluded, however, that *Grady* must be overruled. Unlike *Blockburger* analysis, whose definition of what prevents two crimes from being the "same offence," has deep historical roots and has been accepted in numerous precedents of this Court, *Grady* lacks constitutional roots. The "same-conduct" rule it announced is wholly inconsistent with earlier Supreme Court precedent and with the clear common-law understanding of double jeopardy. We need not discuss the many proofs of these statements, which were set forth at length in the *Grady* dissent.

---

[a]   *In Grady v. Corbin*, 495 U.S. 508 (1990), the Court noted that the *Blockburger* test was not the exclusive test for determining whether or not double jeopardy bars a subsequent prosecution, explaining:

> To determine whether a subsequent prosecution is barred by the Double Jeopardy Clause, a court must first apply the traditional Blockburger test. If application of that test reveals that the offenses have identical statutory elements or that one is a lesser included offense of the other, then the inquiry must cease, and the subsequent prosecution is barred.

*Id.* at 516. Under the *Grady v. Corbin* conduct test, if application of the *Blockburger* test suggests that the offenses in question are not the same offense, the subsequent prosecution will be barred if "the government, to establish an essential element of an offense charged in that prosecution, will prove conduct that constitutes an offense for which the defendant has already been prosecuted." *Id.* at 521.

The defendant in *Grady* pled guilty to two misdemeanor traffic offenses: driving while intoxicated and failing to keep to the right of the median. He was subsequently indicted on charges of reckless manslaughter, second-degree vehicular manslaughter, and criminally negligent homicide, and moved to dismiss the indictment on double jeopardy grounds. The bill of particulars in the subsequent prosecution stated that the prosecution would demonstrate recklessness and criminal negligence by proving that the defendant had operated a motor vehicle on a public highway in an intoxicated condition and failed to keep to the right of the median. Since the government, in order to establish the *mens rea* element of the homicide charges in the subsequent prosecution, would be proving *conduct* that constituted offenses for which Grady had already been prosecuted, the Court held that the subsequent prosecution was barred by double jeopardy.

\* \* \* *Grady* was not only wrong in principle; it has already proved unstable in application. Less than two years after it came down, in *United States v. Felix,* we were forced to recognize a large exception to it. \* \* \* A hypothetical based on the facts in *Harris* reinforces the conclusion that *Grady* is a continuing source of confusion and must be overruled. Suppose the State first tries the defendant for felony murder, based on robbery, and then indicts the defendant for robbery with a firearm in the same incident.[b] Absent *Grady,* our cases provide a clear answer to the double jeopardy claim in this situation. Under *Blockburger,* the second prosecution is not barred—as it clearly was not barred at common law, as a famous case establishes. In *King v. Vandercomb,* the government abandoned, midtrial, prosecution of defendant for burglary by breaking and entering and stealing goods, because it turned out that no property had been removed on the date of the alleged burglary. The defendant was then prosecuted for burglary by breaking and entering with intent to steal. That second prosecution was allowed, because "these two offences are so distinct in their nature, that evidence of one of them will not support an indictment for the other."

Having encountered today yet another situation in which the pre-*Grady* understanding of the Double Jeopardy Clause allows a second trial, though the "same-conduct" test would not, we think it time to acknowledge what is now, three years after *Grady,* compellingly clear: the case was a mistake. We do not lightly reconsider a precedent, but, because *Grady* contradicted an "unbroken line of decisions," contained "less than accurate" historical analysis, and has produced "confusion," we do so here. Although *stare decisis* is the "preferred course" in constitutional adjudication, "when governing decisions are unworkable or are badly reasoned, 'this Court has never felt constrained to follow precedent.'" We would mock *stare decisis* and only add chaos to our double jeopardy jurisprudence by pretending that *Grady* survives when it does not. We therefore accept the Government's invitation to overrule *Grady.* \* \* \*

CHIEF JUSTICE REHNQUIST, with whom JUSTICE O'CONNOR and JUSTICE THOMAS join, concurring in part and dissenting in part.

\* \* \* I do not join Part III of Justice Scalia's opinion because I think that none of the criminal prosecutions in this case were barred under *Blockburger.* \* \* \* For the reasons set forth in the dissent in *Grady* (opinion of Scalia, J.), and in Part IV of the Court's opinion, I, too, think that *Grady*

---

[b] In *Harris v. Oklahoma,* 433 U.S. 682 (1977), the defendant was convicted of felony murder where the underlying felony was robbery with firearms. He was then prosecuted for robbery with firearms. In a per curiam opinion, the Supreme Court held that the Double Jeopardy Clause barred the subsequent prosecution, explaining that "[w]hen, as here, conviction of a greater crime, murder, cannot be had without conviction of the lesser crime, robbery with firearms, the Double Jeopardy Clause bars prosecution for the lesser crime after conviction of the greater one." *Id.* at 682.

must be overruled. I therefore join Parts I, II, and IV of the Court's opinion
* * *.

In my view, *Blockburger*'s same-elements test requires us to focus, not
on the terms of the particular court orders involved, but on the elements of
contempt of court in the ordinary sense. Relying on *Harris v. Oklahoma,*
* * * Justice Scalia concludes otherwise today, and thus incorrectly finds in
Part III-A of his opinion that the subsequent prosecutions of Dixon for drug
distribution and of Foster for assault violated the Double Jeopardy Clause.
In so doing, Justice Scalia rejects the traditional view—shared by every
federal court of appeals and state supreme court that addressed the issue
prior to *Grady*—that, as a general matter, double jeopardy does not bar a
subsequent prosecution based on conduct for which a defendant has been
held in criminal contempt. * * *

At the heart of this pre-*Grady* consensus lay the common belief that
there was no double jeopardy bar under *Blockburger*. There, we stated that
two offenses are different for purposes of double jeopardy if "each *provision*
requires proof of a fact which the other does not." Applying this test to the
offenses at bar, it is clear that the elements of the governing contempt
*provision* are entirely different from the elements of the substantive
crimes. Contempt of court comprises two elements: (i) a court order made
known to the defendant, followed by (ii) willful violation of that order.
Neither of those elements is necessarily satisfied by proof that a defendant
has committed the substantive offenses of assault or drug distribution.
Likewise, no element of either of those substantive offenses is necessarily
satisfied by proof that a defendant has been found guilty of contempt of
court. * * *

Our double jeopardy cases applying *Blockburger* have focused on the
statutory elements of the offenses charged, not on the facts that must be
proved under the particular indictment at issue—an indictment being the
closest analogue to the court orders in this case. * * * By focusing on the
facts needed to show a violation of the specific court orders involved in this
case, and not on the generic elements of the crime of contempt of court,
Justice Scalia's double jeopardy analysis bears a striking resemblance to
that found in *Grady*—not what one would expect in an opinion that
overrules *Grady*.

Close inspection of the crimes at issue in *Harris* reveals, moreover,
that our decision in that case was not a departure from *Blockburger*'s focus
on the *statutory* elements of the offenses charged. * * * [T]he *ratio
decidendi* of our *Harris* decision was that the two crimes there were akin
to greater and lesser included offenses. The crimes at issue here, however,
cannot be viewed as greater and lesser included offenses, either intuitively
or logically. A crime such as possession with intent to distribute cocaine is
a serious felony that cannot easily be conceived of as a lesser included

offense of criminal contempt, a relatively petty offense as applied to the conduct in this case. Indeed, to say that criminal contempt is an aggravated form of that offense defies common sense. * * *

JUSTICE SOUTER, with whom JUSTICE STEVENS joins, concurring in the judgment in part and dissenting in part.

* * * I cannot join the Court in restricting the Clause's reach and dismembering the protection against successive prosecution that the Constitution was meant to provide. The Court has read our precedents so narrowly as to leave them bereft of the principles animating that protection, and has chosen to overrule the most recent of the relevant cases, *Grady v. Corbin,* decided three years ago. Because I think that *Grady* was correctly decided, amounting merely to an expression of just those animating principles, and because, even if the decision had been wrong in the first instance, there is no warrant for overruling it now, I respectfully dissent. * * *

The Double Jeopardy Clause prevents the government from "mak[ing] repeated attempts to convict an individual for an alleged offense, thereby subjecting him to embarrassment, expense and ordeal and compelling him to live in a continuing state of anxiety and insecurity." The Clause addresses a further concern as well, that the government not be given the opportunity to rehearse its prosecution, "honing its trial strategies and perfecting its evidence through successive attempts at conviction," because this "enhanc[es] the possibility that even though innocent [the defendant] may be found guilty."

Consequently, while the government may punish a person separately for each conviction of at least as many different offenses as meet the *Blockburger* test, we have long held that it must sometimes bring its prosecutions for these offenses together. If a separate prosecution were permitted for every offense arising out of the same conduct, the government could manipulate the definitions of offenses, creating fine distinctions among them and permitting a zealous prosecutor to try a person again and again for essentially the same criminal conduct. While punishing different combinations of elements is consistent with the Double Jeopardy Clause in its limitation on the imposition of multiple punishments (a limitation rooted in concerns with legislative intent), permitting such repeated prosecutions would not be consistent with the principles underlying the Clause in its limitation on successive prosecutions. The limitation on successive prosecutions is thus a restriction on the government different in kind from that contained in the limitation on multiple punishments, and the government cannot get around the restriction on repeated prosecution of a single individual merely by precision in the way it defines its statutory offenses. Thus, "[t]he *Blockburger* test is not the only standard for determining whether successive prosecutions impermissibly involve the same offense. Even if two offenses are sufficiently different to permit the imposition of consecutive sentences, successive prosecutions will be barred in some circumstances where the second prosecution requires the relitigation of factual issues already resolved by the first."

An example will show why this should be so. Assume three crimes: robbery with a firearm, robbery in a dwelling, and simple robbery. The elements of the three crimes are the same, except that robbery with a firearm has the element that a firearm be used in the commission of the robbery while the other two crimes do not, and robbery in a dwelling has the element that the robbery occur in a dwelling while the other two crimes do not.

If a person committed a robbery in a dwelling with a firearm and was prosecuted for simple robbery, all agree he could not be prosecuted subsequently for either of the greater offenses of robbery with a firearm or robbery in a dwelling. Under the lens of *Blockburger*, however, if that same person were prosecuted first for robbery with a firearm, he could be prosecuted subsequently for robbery in a dwelling, even though he could not subsequently be prosecuted on the basis of that same robbery for simple robbery.[3] This is true simply because neither of the crimes, robbery with a firearm and robbery in a dwelling, is either identical to or a lesser included offense of the other. But since the purpose of the Double Jeopardy Clause's protection against successive prosecutions is to prevent repeated trials in which a defendant will be forced to defend against the same charge again and again, and in which the government may perfect its presentation with dress rehearsal after dress rehearsal, it should be irrelevant that the second prosecution would require the defendant to defend himself not only from the charge that he committed the robbery, but also from the charge of some additional fact, in this case, that the scene of the crime was a dwelling. If, instead, protection against successive prosecutions were as limited as it would be by *Blockburger* alone, the doctrine would be as striking for its anomalies as for the limited protection it would provide. Thus, in the relatively few successive prosecution cases we have had over the years, we have not held that the *Blockburger* test is the only hurdle the government must clear. * * *

In the past 20 years the Court has addressed just this problem of successive prosecution on three occasions. In *Harris v. Oklahoma* we held that prosecution for a robbery with firearms was barred by the Double Jeopardy Clause when the defendant had already been convicted of felony murder comprising the same robbery with firearms as the underlying felony. Of course the elements of the two offenses were different enough to permit more than one punishment under the *Blockburger* test: felony

---

[3]    Our cases have long made clear that the order in which one is prosecuted for two crimes alleged to be the same matters not in demonstrating a violation of double jeopardy. See *Brown* v. *Ohio*, 432 U.S. 161, 168, 97 S.Ct. 2221, 53 L.Ed.2d 187 (1977) ("The sequence is immaterial").

murder required the killing of a person by one engaged in the commission of a felony; robbery with firearms required the use of a firearm in the commission of a robbery.

In *Harris*, however, we held that "[w]hen, as here, conviction of a greater crime, murder, cannot be had without conviction of the lesser crime, robbery with firearms, the Double Jeopardy Clause bars prosecution for the lesser crime after conviction of the greater one."

* * * [T]he analysis in *Harris* turned on considering the prior conviction in terms of the conduct actually charged. While that process might be viewed as a misapplication of a *Blockburger* lesser included offense analysis, the crucial point is that the *Blockburger* elements test would have produced a different result. The case thus [shows] that the *Blockburger* test is not the exclusive standard for determining whether the rule against successive prosecutions applies in a given case.

Subsequently, in *Illinois v. Vitale*, the Court again indicated that a valid claim of double jeopardy would not necessarily be defeated by the fact that the two offenses are not the "same" under the *Blockburger* test. In that case, we were confronted with a prosecution for failure to reduce speed and a subsequent prosecution for involuntary manslaughter. * * * We held that "[i]f, as a matter of Illinois law, a careless failure to slow is always a necessary element of manslaughter by automobile, then the two offenses are the 'same' under *Blockburger* and Vitale's trial on the latter charge would constitute double jeopardy. . . ." But that was not all. Writing for the Court, Justice White went on to say that, "[i]n any event, it may be that to sustain its manslaughter case the State may find it necessary to prove a failure to slow or to rely on conduct necessarily involving such failure. . . . In that case, because Vitale has already been convicted for conduct that is a necessary element of the more serious crime for which he has been charged, his claim of double jeopardy would be substantial under * * * *Harris v. Oklahoma*."

Over a decade ago, then, we clearly understood *Harris* to stand for the proposition that when one has already been tried for a crime comprising certain conduct, a subsequent prosecution seeking to prove the same conduct is barred by the Double Jeopardy Clause. Even if this had not been clear * * *, any debate should have been settled by our decision three Terms ago in *Grady v. Corbin*, that "the Double Jeopardy Clause bars a subsequent prosecution if, to establish an essential element of an offense charged in that prosecution, the government will prove conduct that constitutes an offense for which the defendant has already been prosecuted."

* * * Whatever may have been the merits of the debate in *Grady,* the decision deserves more respect than it receives from the Court today. "Although adherence to precedent is not rigidly required in constitutional

cases, any departure from the doctrine of *stare decisis* demands special justification." * * *

[JUSTICE WHITE's opinion, concurring in the judgment in part and dissenting in part, and JUSTICE BLACKMUN's opinion, concurring in the judgment in part and dissenting in part, have been omitted. Justice White believed the subsequent prosecutions in both *Dixon* and *Foster* were barred by double jeopardy. Justice Blackmun wrote separately because he did not see how contempt of court could be considered the "same offense" as either assault with intent to kill or possession of cocaine with intent to distribute it. Justice Blackmun also disagreed with the decision to overrule *Grady v. Corbin.*]

### *NOTE*

In *Brown v. Ohio*, the Court recognized an exception to the usual double jeopardy rule prohibiting the government from retrying a defendant for the same offense. The Court explained that where application of its traditional double jeopardy analysis would bar a subsequent prosecution, "[a]n exception may exist where the State is unable to proceed on the more serious charge at the outset because the additional facts necessary to sustain that charge have not occurred or have not been discovered despite the exercise of due diligence." 432 U.S. 161, 169 n.7 (1977), *citing Diaz v. United States*, 223 U.S. 442, 448–49 (1912). This exception has been called the *Brown-Diaz* exception.

## C. THE DUAL SOVEREIGNTY DOCTRINE

Notwithstanding the "same offense" limitation discussed in the previous section, a subsequent prosecution for the same offense will not be barred if brought by a different sovereign. Under the dual sovereignty doctrine, a sovereign has the right to prosecute criminal violations in its jurisdiction even if a separate sovereign has chosen to prosecute the defendant for the same criminal offense. *Heath v. Alabama* explains the rationale behind the dual sovereignty doctrine and considers whether the doctrine allows one state to prosecute a defendant who has been convicted of the same offense in another state. The note following *Heath v. Alabama* discusses the U.S. Department of Justice's Petite Policy, a policy that federal prosecutors use as a guide when deciding whether to pursue a federal prosecution following a state prosecution for the same offense.

### HEATH V. ALABAMA
Supreme Court of the United States
474 U.S. 82, 106 S.Ct. 433, 88 L.Ed.2d 387 (1985)

JUSTICE O'CONNOR delivered the opinion of the Court.

In August 1981, petitioner, Larry Gene Heath, hired Charles Owens and Gregory Lumpkin to kill his wife, Rebecca Heath, who was then nine months pregnant, for a sum of $2,000. On the morning of August 31, 1981, petitioner left the Heath residence in Russell County, Alabama, to meet with Owens and Lumpkin in Georgia, just over the Alabama border from the Heath home. Petitioner led them back to the Heath residence, gave them the keys to the Heaths' car and house, and left the premises in his girlfriend's truck. Owens and Lumpkin then kidnaped Rebecca Heath from her home. The Heath car, with Rebecca Heath's body inside, was later found on the side of a road in Troup County, Georgia. The cause of death was a gunshot wound in the head.

Georgia and Alabama authorities pursued dual investigations in which they cooperated to some extent. On September 4, 1981, petitioner was arrested by Georgia authorities. Petitioner waived his Miranda rights and gave a full confession admitting that he had arranged his wife's kidnaping and murder. In November 1981, the grand jury of Troup County, Georgia, indicted petitioner for the offense of "malice" murder. Georgia then served petitioner with notice of its intention to seek the death penalty, citing as the aggravating circumstance the fact that the murder was "caused and directed" by petitioner. On February 10, 1982, petitioner pleaded guilty to the Georgia murder charge in exchange for a sentence of life imprisonment, which he understood could involve his serving as few as seven years in prison.

On May 5, 1982, the grand jury of Russell County, Alabama, returned an indictment against petitioner for the capital offense of murder during a kidnaping. Before trial on this indictment, petitioner entered pleas of *autrefois convict* and former jeopardy under the Alabama and United States Constitutions, arguing that his conviction and sentence in Georgia barred his prosecution in Alabama for the same conduct. * * *

After a hearing, the trial court rejected petitioner's double jeopardy claims. It assumed, *arguendo*, that the two prosecutions could not have been brought in succession by one State but held that double jeopardy did not bar successive prosecutions by two different States for the same act. * * * On January 12, 1983, the Alabama jury convicted petitioner of murder during a kidnaping in the first degree. After a sentencing hearing, the jury recommended the death penalty. * * *

[On appeal of the conviction] the Alabama Supreme Court noted that "[p]rosecutions under the laws of separate sovereigns do not improperly subject an accused twice to prosecutions for the same offense," citing this Court's cases applying the dual sovereignty doctrine. The court acknowledged that this Court has not considered the applicability of the dual sovereignty doctrine to successive prosecutions by different States. It reasoned, however, that "[i]f, for double jeopardy purposes, Alabama is considered to be a sovereign entity vis-à-vis the federal government then surely it is a sovereign entity vis-à-vis the State of Georgia." * * *

Successive prosecutions are barred by the Fifth Amendment only if the two offenses for which the defendant is prosecuted are the "same" for double jeopardy purposes. Respondent does not contravene petitioner's contention that the offenses of "murder during a kidnaping" and "malice murder," as construed by the courts of Alabama and Georgia respectively, may be considered greater and lesser offenses and, thus, the "same" offense, absent operation of the dual sovereignty principle. We therefore assume, *arguendo,* that, had these offenses arisen under the laws of one State and had petitioner been separately prosecuted for both offenses in that State, the second conviction would have been barred by the Double Jeopardy Clause.

The * * * question upon which we granted certiorari is whether the dual sovereignty doctrine permits successive prosecutions under the laws of different States which otherwise would be held to "subject [the defendant] for the same offence to be twice put in jeopardy." Although we have not previously so held, we believe the answer to this query is inescapable. The dual sovereignty doctrine, as originally articulated and consistently applied by this Court, compels the conclusion that successive prosecutions by two States for the same conduct are not barred by the Double Jeopardy Clause.

The dual sovereignty doctrine is founded on the common-law conception of crime as an offense against the sovereignty of the government. When a defendant in a single act violates the "peace and dignity" of two sovereigns by breaking the laws of each, he has committed two distinct "offences." * * * Consequently, when the same act transgresses the laws of two sovereigns, "it cannot be truly averred that the offender has been twice punished for the same offence; but only that by one act he has committed two offences, for each of which he is justly punishable."

In applying the dual sovereignty doctrine, then, the crucial determination is whether the two entities that seek successively to prosecute a defendant for the same course of conduct can be termed separate sovereigns. This determination turns on whether the two entities draw their authority to punish the offender from distinct sources of power. Thus, the Court has uniformly held that the States are separate sovereigns with respect to the Federal Government because each State's power to prosecute is derived from its own "inherent sovereignty," not from the Federal Government. * * *

The States are no less sovereign with respect to each other than they are with respect to the Federal Government. Their powers to undertake criminal prosecutions derive from separate and independent sources of power and authority originally belonging to them before admission to the Union and preserved to them by the Tenth Amendment. The States are equal to each other "in power, dignity and authority, each competent to exert that residuum of sovereignty not delegated to the United States by the Constitution itself." Thus, "[e]ach has the power, inherent in any sovereign, independently to determine what shall be an offense against its authority and to punish such offenses, and in doing so each 'is exercising its own sovereignty, not that of the other.' " * * *

In those instances where the Court has found the dual sovereignty doctrine inapplicable, it has done so because the two prosecuting entities did not derive their powers to prosecute from independent sources of authority. Thus, the Court has held that successive prosecutions by federal and territorial courts are barred because such courts are "creations emanating from the same sovereignty."[a] Similarly, municipalities that derive their power to try a defendant from the same organic law that empowers the State to prosecute are not separate sovereigns with respect to the State. These cases confirm that it is the presence of independent sovereign authority to prosecute, not the relation between States and the Federal Government in our federalist system that constitutes the basis for the dual sovereignty doctrine.

* * * The Court's express rationale for the dual sovereignty doctrine is not simply a fiction that can be disregarded in difficult cases. It finds weighty support in the historical understanding and political realities of the States' role in the federal system and in the words of the Double Jeopardy Clause itself, "nor shall any person be subject for the same *offence* to be twice put in jeopardy of life or limb."

---

[a]  In *Puerto Rico v. Sanchez Valle*, 579 U.S. ___, 135 S.Ct. 1863 (2016), the Supreme Court found that Puerto Rico, a territory of the United States, is not a separate sovereign from the U.S. government for purposes of the dual sovereignty doctrine despite the fact that Puerto Rico has its own Constitution, its own criminal code, and local prosecutors who prosecute crimes under Puerto Rico's criminal law. Justice Kagan, writing for the Court, explained:

[T]he test we have devised to decide whether two governments are distinct for double jeopardy purposes overtly disregards common indicia of sovereignty. * * * The degree to which an entity exercises self-governance—whether autonomously managing its own affairs or continually submitting to outside direction—plays no role in the analysis. Nor do we care about a government's more particular ability to enact and enforce its own criminal laws. Rather, as Puerto Rico itself acknowledges, our test hinges on a single criterion: the "ultimate source" of the power undergirding the respective prosecutions. The inquiry is thus historical, not functional—looking at the deepest wellsprings, not the current exercise, of prosecutorial authority. If two entities derive their power to punish from wholly independent sources (imagine here a pair of parallel lines), then they may bring successive prosecutions. Conversely, if those entities draw their power from the same ultimate source (imagine now two lines merging from a common point, even if later diverging), then they may not.

Because the ultimate source of Puerto Rico's power to prosecute was the U.S. Congress, the Court found that Puerto Rico was not a separate sovereign for purposes of the dual sovereignty doctrine. Accordingly, the Double Jeopardy Clause bars Puerto Rico from prosecuting an individual after that individual has been prosecuted by the U.S. government for the same offense. On June 11, 2017, Puerto Ricans voted in favor of statehood in a non-binding referendum. Colin Dwyer, *Puerto Ricans Overwhelmingly Vote on U.S. Statehood in Nonbinding Referendum*, NPR News, June 11, 2017, http://www.npr.org/sections/thetwo-way/2017/06/11/532482957/puerto-rico-votes-on-state hood-though-congress-will-make-final-call. Congress, however, must take action before Puerto Rico can become a state. *Id.*

It is axiomatic that "[i]n America, the powers of sovereignty are divided between the government of the Union, and those of the States. They are each sovereign, with respect to the objects committed to it, and neither sovereign with respect to the objects committed to the other." It is as well established that the States, "as political communities, [are] distinct and sovereign, and consequently foreign to each other." The Constitution leaves in the possession of each State "certain exclusive and very important portions of sovereign power." Foremost among the prerogatives of sovereignty is the power to create and enforce a criminal code. To deny a State its power to enforce its criminal laws because another State has won the race to the courthouse "would be a shocking and untoward deprivation of the historic right and obligation of the States to maintain peace and order within their confines." * * *

The judgment of the Supreme Court of Alabama is affirmed.

*It is so ordered.*

JUSTICE MARSHALL, with whom JUSTICE BRENNAN joins, dissenting.

Seizing upon the suggestion in past cases that every "independent" sovereign government may prosecute violations of its laws even when the defendant has already been tried for the same crime in another jurisdiction, the Court today gives short shrift to the policies underlying those precedents. The "dual sovereignty" doctrine, heretofore used to permit federal and state prosecutions for the same offense, was born of the need to accommodate complementary state and federal concerns within our system of concurrent territorial jurisdictions. It cannot justify successive prosecutions by different States. Moreover, even were the dual sovereignty doctrine to support successive state prosecutions as a general matter, it simply could not legitimate the collusion between Georgia and Alabama in this case to ensure that petitioner is executed for his crime.

On August 31, 1981, the body of Rebecca Heath was discovered in an abandoned car in Troup County, Georgia. Because the deceased was a resident of Russell County, Alabama, members of the Russell County Sheriff's Department immediately joined Troup County authorities in investigating the causes and agents of her death. This cooperative effort proved fruitful. On September 4, petitioner Larry Heath, the deceased's husband, was arrested and brought to the Georgia State Patrol barracks in Troup County, where he confessed to having hired other men to murder his wife. Shortly thereafter, petitioner was indicted by the grand jury of Troup County for malice murder. The prosecution's notice to petitioner that it was seeking the death penalty triggered the beginning of the Unified Appeals Procedure that Georgia requires in capital cases. But while these pretrial proceedings were still in progress, petitioner seized the prosecution's offer of a life sentence in exchange for a guilty plea. Upon entry of his plea in February 1982, petitioner was sentenced in Troup County Superior Court to life imprisonment. His stay in the custody of Georgia authorities proved short, however. Three months later, a Russell County, Alabama, grand jury indicted him for the capital offense of murdering Rebecca Heath during the course of a kidnaping in the first degree.

The murder of Rebecca Heath must have been quite noteworthy in Russell County, Alabama. By petitioner's count, of the 82 prospective jurors questioned before trial during *voir dire,* all but 7 stated that they were aware that petitioner had pleaded guilty to the same crime in Georgia. The *voir dire* responses of almost all of the remaining 75 veniremen can only be characterized as remarkable. When asked whether they could put aside their knowledge of the prior guilty plea in order to give petitioner a fair trial in Alabama, the vast majority answered in the affirmative. These answers satisfied the trial judge, who denied petitioner's challenges for cause except as to those jurors who explicitly admitted that the Georgia proceedings would probably affect their assessment of petitioner's guilt.

With such a well-informed jury, the outcome of the trial was surely a foregone conclusion. Defense counsel could do little but attempt to elicit information from prosecution witnesses tending to show that the crime was committed exclusively in Georgia. The court having rejected petitioner's constitutional and jurisdictional claims, the defense was left to spend most of its summation arguing that Rebecca Heath may not actually have been kidnaped from Alabama before she was murdered and that petitioner was already being punished for ordering that murder. Petitioner was convicted and, after sentencing hearings, was condemned to die. The conviction and sentence were upheld by the Alabama Court of Criminal Appeals and the Alabama Supreme Court.

Had the Georgia authorities suddenly become dissatisfied with the life sentence petitioner received in their courts and reindicted petitioner in order to seek the death penalty once again, that indictment would without question be barred by the Double Jeopardy Clause of the Fifth Amendment, as applied to the States by the Fourteenth Amendment. Whether the second indictment repeated the charge of malice murder or instead charged murder in the course of a kidnaping, it would surely, under any reasonable constitutional standard, offend the bar to successive prosecutions for the same offense.

The only difference between this case and such a hypothetical *volte-face* by Georgia is that here Alabama, not Georgia, was offended by the notion that petitioner might not forfeit his life in punishment for his crime. The only reason the Court gives for permitting Alabama to go forward is that Georgia and Alabama are separate sovereigns.

The dual sovereignty theory posits that where the same act offends the laws of two sovereigns, "it cannot be truly averred that the offender has been twice punished for the same offence; but only that by one act he has committed two offences, for each of which he is justly punishable." Therefore, "prosecutions under the laws of separate sovereigns do not, in the language of the Fifth Amendment, 'subject [the defendant] for the same offence to be twice put in jeopardy.' " * * *

This strained reading of the Double Jeopardy Clause has survived and indeed flourished in this Court's cases not because of any inherent plausibility, but because it provides reassuring interpretivist support for a rule that accommodates the unique nature of our federal system. Before this rule is extended to cover a new class of cases, the reasons for its creation should therefore be made clear.

Under the constitutional scheme, the Federal Government has been given the exclusive power to vindicate certain of our Nation's sovereign interests, leaving the States to exercise complementary authority over matters of more local concern. The respective spheres of the Federal Government and the States may overlap at times, and even where they do not, different interests may be implicated by a single act. Yet were a prosecution by a State, however zealously pursued, allowed to preclude further prosecution by the Federal Government for the same crime, an entire range of national interests could be frustrated. The importance of those federal interests has thus quite properly been permitted to trump a defendant's interest in avoiding successive prosecutions or multiple punishments for the same crime. Conversely, because "the States under our federal system have the principal responsibility for defining and prosecuting crimes," it would be inappropriate—in the absence of a specific congressional intent to pre-empt state action pursuant to the Supremacy Clause—to allow a federal prosecution to preclude state authorities from vindicating "the historic right and obligation of the States to maintain peace and order within their confines." * * *

Where two States seek to prosecute the same defendant for the same crime in two separate proceedings, the justifications found in the federal-state context for an exemption from double jeopardy constraints simply do not hold. Although the two States may have opted for different policies within their assigned territorial jurisdictions, the sovereign concerns with whose vindication each State has been charged are identical. Thus, in contrast to the federal-state context, barring the second prosecution would still permit one government to act upon the broad range of sovereign concerns that have been reserved to the States by the Constitution. The compelling need in the federal-state context to subordinate double jeopardy concerns is thus considerably diminished in cases involving successive prosecutions by different States. * * *

To be sure, a refusal to extend the dual sovereignty rule to state-state prosecutions would preclude the State that has lost the "race to the courthouse" from vindicating legitimate policies distinct from those underlying its sister State's prosecution. But as yet, I am not persuaded that a State's desire to further a particular policy should be permitted to deprive a defendant of his constitutionally protected right not to be brought to bar more than once to answer essentially the same charges. * * *

[JUSTICE BRENNAN's dissenting opinion has been omitted.]

## NOTE

Although the dual sovereignty doctrine permits the federal government to prosecute a defendant after a state prosecution for the same offense, the federal government disfavors such prosecutions. The U.S. Department of Justice's "Dual and Successive Prosecution Policy," also known as the "Petite Policy," establishes the following guidelines for the exercise of prosecutorial charging discretion in cases in which there has already been a previous state or federal prosecution of the defendant:

> This policy precludes the initiation or continuation of a federal prosecution, following a prior state or federal prosecution based on substantially the same act(s) or transaction(s) unless three substantive prerequisites are satisfied: first, the matter must involve a substantial federal interest; second, the prior prosecution must have left that interest demonstrably unvindicated; and third, applying the same test that is applicable to all federal prosecutions, the government must believe that the defendant's conduct constitutes a federal offense, and that the admissible evidence probably will be sufficient to obtain and sustain a conviction by an unbiased trier of fact. In addition, there is a procedural prerequisite to be satisfied, that is, the prosecution must be approved by the appropriate Assistant Attorney General.

> Satisfaction of the three substantive prerequisites does not mean that a proposed prosecution must be approved or brought. The traditional elements of federal prosecutorial discretion continue to apply.

U.S. DEP'T OF JUSTICE, UNITED STATES ATTORNEYS' MANUAL (1997), *available at* http://www.justice.gov/usam/usam-9-2000-authority-us-attorney-criminal-division-mattersprior-approvals#9-2.031. Since the Petite Policy is just an internal guideline, a defendant cannot use the Petite Policy to challenge a federal prosecution that follows a state or federal prosecution for the same offense. Ellen S. Podgor, *Department of Justice Guidelines: Balancing "Discretionary Justice,"* 13 CORNELL J.L. & PUB. POL'Y 167 (2004).

## D. CRIMINAL VERSUS CIVIL PUNISHMENT

In addition to its prohibition against multiple prosecutions for the same offense, the Double Jeopardy Clause also bars multiple punishments—that is, *criminal* punishments—for the same offense. A penalty imposed after a civil proceeding may constitute criminal punishment under certain circumstances. In order to determine whether a penalty imposed after a civil proceeding should be considered a criminal punishment or merely a civil penalty, the infringed statute, as well as the legislative intent behind the statute, must be examined. *Hudson v. United States* examines when a penalty imposed after a civil proceeding constitutes criminal punishment for double jeopardy purposes.

## HUDSON V. UNITED STATES

Supreme Court of the United States
522 U.S. 93, 118 S.Ct. 488, 139 L.Ed.2d 450 (1997)

CHIEF JUSTICE REHNQUIST delivered the opinion of the Court.

The Government administratively imposed monetary penalties and occupational debarment on petitioners for violation of federal banking statutes, and later criminally indicted them for essentially the same conduct. * * *

During the early and mid-1980's, petitioner John Hudson was the chairman and controlling shareholder of the First National Bank of Tipton (Tipton) and the First National Bank of Hammon (Hammon). During the same period, petitioner Jack Rackley was president of Tipton and a member of the board of directors of Hammon, and petitioner Larry Baresel was a member of the board of directors of both Tipton and Hammon.

An examination of Tipton and Hammon led the Office of the Comptroller of the Currency (OCC) to conclude that petitioners had used their bank positions to arrange a series of loans to third parties in violation of various federal banking statutes and regulations. According to the OCC, those loans, while nominally made to third parties, were in reality made to Hudson in order to enable him to redeem bank stock that he had pledged as collateral on defaulted loans. * * *

In October 1989, petitioners resolved the OCC proceedings against them by each entering into a "Stipulation and Consent Order." These consent orders provided that Hudson, Baresel, and Rackley would pay assessments of $16,500, $15,000, and $12,500 respectively. In addition, each petitioner agreed not to "participate in any manner" in the affairs of any banking institution without the written authorization of the OCC and all other relevant regulatory agencies.

In August 1992, petitioners were indicted * * * [for conspiracy, misapplication of bank funds, and making false bank entries]. The violations charged in the indictment rested on the same lending transactions that formed the basis for the prior administrative actions brought by OCC. Petitioners moved to dismiss the indictment on double jeopardy grounds, but the District Court denied the motions. * * *

The Double Jeopardy Clause provides that no "person [shall] be subject for the same offence to be twice put in jeopardy of life or limb." We have long recognized that the Double Jeopardy Clause does not prohibit the imposition of all additional sanctions that could, "in common parlance," be described as punishment. The Clause protects only against the imposition of multiple *criminal* punishments for the same offense.

Whether a particular punishment is criminal or civil is, at least initially, a matter of statutory construction. A court must first ask whether the legislature, "in establishing the penalizing mechanism, indicated either expressly or impliedly a preference for one label or the other." Even in those cases where the legislature "has indicated an intention to establish a civil penalty, we have inquired further whether the statutory scheme was so punitive either in purpose or effect," as to "transfor[m] what was clearly intended as a civil remedy into a criminal penalty."

In making this latter determination, the factors listed in *Kennedy v. Mendoza-Martinez* provide useful guideposts, including: (1) "[w]hether the sanction involves an affirmative disability or restraint"; (2) "whether it has historically been regarded as a punishment"; (3) "whether it comes into play only on a finding of *scienter*"; (4) "whether its operation will promote the traditional aims of punishment-retribution and deterrence"; (5) "whether the behavior to which it applies is already a crime"; (6) "whether an alternative purpose to which it may rationally be connected is assignable for it"; and (7) "whether it appears excessive in relation to the alternative purpose assigned." It is important to note, however, that "these factors must be considered in relation to the statute on its face," and "only the clearest proof" will suffice to override legislative intent and transform what has been denominated a civil remedy into a criminal penalty. * * *

Applying traditional double jeopardy principles to the facts of this case, it is clear that the criminal prosecution of these petitioners would not violate the Double Jeopardy Clause. It is evident that Congress intended the OCC money penalties and debarment sanctions * * * to be civil in nature. As for the money penalties, * * * [the statutes] expressly provide that such penalties are "civil." While the provision authorizing debarment contains no language explicitly denominating the sanction as civil, we think it significant that the authority to issue debarment orders is conferred upon the "appropriate Federal banking agenc[ies]." That such authority was conferred upon administrative agencies is prima facie evidence that Congress intended to provide for a civil sanction.

Turning to the second stage of the * * * test, we find that there is little evidence, much less the clearest proof that we require, suggesting that either OCC money penalties or debarment sanctions are "so punitive in form and effect as to render them criminal despite Congress' intent to the contrary." First, neither money penalties nor debarment has historically been viewed as punishment. We have long recognized that "revocation of a privilege voluntarily granted," such as a debarment, "is characteristically free of the punitive criminal element." Similarly, "the payment of fixed or variable sums of money [is a] sanction which ha[s] been recognized as enforcible by civil proceedings since the original revenue law of 1789."

Second, the sanctions imposed do not involve an "affirmative disability or restraint," as that term is normally understood. While petitioners have been prohibited from further participating in the banking industry, this is "certainly nothing approaching the 'infamous punishment' of imprisonment." Third, neither sanction comes into play "only" on a finding of scienter. The provisions under which the money penalties were imposed, allow for the assessment of a penalty against any person "who violates" any of the underlying banking statutes, without regard to the violator's state of mind. * * *

Fourth, the conduct for which OCC sanctions are imposed may also be criminal (and in this case formed the basis for petitioners' indictments). This fact is insufficient to render the money penalties and debarment sanctions criminally punitive, particularly in the double jeopardy context.

Finally, we recognize that the imposition of both money penalties and debarment sanctions will deter others from emulating petitioners' conduct, a traditional goal of criminal punishment. But the mere presence of this purpose is insufficient to render a sanction criminal, as deterrence "may serve civil as well as criminal goals." For example, the sanctions at issue here, while intended to deter future wrongdoing, also serve to promote the stability of the banking industry. To hold that the mere presence of a deterrent purpose renders such sanctions "criminal" for double jeopardy purposes would severely undermine the Government's ability to engage in effective regulation of institutions such as banks.

In sum, there simply is very little showing, * * * that OCC money penalties and debarment sanctions are criminal. The Double Jeopardy Clause is therefore no obstacle to their trial on the pending indictments, and it may proceed.

The judgment of the Court of Appeals for the Tenth Circuit is accordingly

*Affirmed.*

JUSTICE STEVENS, concurring in the judgment.

* * * [In prior cases, we have] held that sanctions imposed in civil proceedings [may constitute] "punishment" barred by the Double Jeopardy Clause. * * * [T]he Government cannot use the "civil" label to escape entirely the Double Jeopardy Clause's command, as we have recognized for at least six decades. That proposition is extremely important because the States and the Federal Government have an enormous array of civil

administrative sanctions at their disposal that are capable of being used to punish persons repeatedly for the same offense, violating the bedrock double jeopardy principle of finality. "The underlying idea, one that is deeply ingrained in at least the Anglo-American system of jurisprudence, is that the State with all its resources and power should not be allowed to make repeated attempts to convict an individual for an alleged offense, thereby subjecting him to embarrassment, expense and ordeal and compelling him to live in a continuing state of anxiety and insecurity. . . ." * * *

JUSTICE BREYER, with whom JUSTICE GINSBURG joins, concurring in the judgment.

* * * I disagree with [the Court's] reasoning in two respects. First, unlike the Court I would not say that "only the clearest proof" will "transform" into a criminal punishment what a legislature calls a "civil remedy." I understand that the Court has taken this language from earlier cases. But the limitation that the language suggests is not consistent with what the Court has actually done. Rather, in fact if not in theory, the Court has simply applied factors of the *Kennedy* variety to the matter at hand. * * * The "clearest proof" language is consequently misleading. * * *

Second, I would not decide now that a court should evaluate a statute only "on its face," rather than "assessing the character of the actual sanctions imposed." * * * That said, an analysis of the *Kennedy* factors still leads me to the conclusion that the statutory penalty in this case is not on its face a criminal penalty. Nor, in my view, does the application of the statute to the petitioners in this case amount to criminal punishment. I therefore concur in the judgment.

[JUSTICE SCALIA's concurring opinion and JUSTICE SOUTER's concurring opinion have been omitted.]

### NOTE

In *United States v. Ursery*, 518 U.S. 267 (1996), the Supreme Court considered whether a civil forfeiture action following a prosecution for manufacturing marijuana constituted punishment for purposes of the Double Jeopardy Clause. The Court answered this question in the negative, concluding that *in rem* civil forfeitures are neither criminal nor "punishment" for double jeopardy purposes, and therefore the subsequent civil forfeiture action was not barred. *Id.* at 292.

## E. MISTRIALS

A mistrial is a trial that is terminated before its normal conclusion. Whether the defendant can be retried following a mistrial depends upon various factors, including which party requested the mistrial. *Arizona v. Washington* and *Oregon v. Kennedy* outline the tests the Court has established for determining whether and when a defendant may be retried following a mistrial.

## ARIZONA V. WASHINGTON
### Supreme Court of the United States
### 434 U.S. 497, 98 S.Ct. 824, 54 L.Ed.2d (1978)

JUSTICE STEVENS delivered the opinion of the Court. * * *

In 1971 respondent was found guilty of murdering a hotel night clerk. In 1973, the Superior Court of Pima County, Ariz., ordered a new trial because the prosecutor had withheld exculpatory evidence from the defense. The Arizona Supreme Court affirmed the new trial order in an unpublished opinion.

Respondent's second trial began in January 1975. During the *voir dire* examination of prospective jurors, the prosecutor made reference to the fact that some of the witnesses whose testimony the jurors would hear had testified in proceedings four years earlier. Defense counsel told the prospective jurors "that there was evidence hidden from [respondent] at the last trial."

In his opening statement, he made this point more forcefully:

> You will hear testimony that notwithstanding the fact that we had a trial in May of 1971 in this matter, that the prosecutor hid those statements and didn't give those to the lawyer for George saying the man was Spanish speaking, didn't give those statements at all, hid them.

> You will hear that that evidence was suppressed and hidden by the prosecutor in that case. You will hear that that evidence was purposely withheld. You will hear that because of the misconduct of the County Attorney at that time and because he withheld evidence, that the Supreme Court of Arizona granted a new trial in this case.

After opening statements were completed, the prosecutor moved for a mistrial. In colloquy during argument of the motion, the trial judge expressed the opinion that evidence concerning the reasons for the new trial, and specifically the ruling of the Arizona Supreme Court, was irrelevant to the issue of guilt or innocence and therefore inadmissible. Defense counsel asked for an opportunity "to find some law" that would support his belief that the Supreme Court opinion would be admissible. After further argument, the judge stated that he would withhold ruling on the admissibility of the evidence and denied the motion for mistrial. Two witnesses then testified.

The following morning the prosecutor renewed his mistrial motion. * * * [H]e argued that there was no theory on which the basis for the new trial ruling could be brought to the attention of the jury, that the prejudice to the jury could not be repaired by any cautionary instructions, and that a mistrial was a "manifest necessity." Defense counsel * * * argued that his comment was invited by the prosecutor's reference to the witnesses' earlier testimony and that any prejudice could be avoided by curative instructions. * * *

Ultimately the trial judge granted the motion, stating that his ruling was based upon defense counsel's remarks in his opening statement concerning the Arizona Supreme Court opinion. The trial judge did not expressly find that there was "manifest necessity" for a mistrial; nor did he expressly state that he had considered alternative solutions and concluded that none would be adequate. The Arizona Supreme Court refused to review the mistrial ruling. * * * [In federal court, Respondent filed a petition for habeas corpus, alleging that a retrial would violate Double Jeopardy. His petition was granted based upon the lack of express findings by the trial judge for the mistrial. The Ninth Circuit Court of Appeals affirmed.] * * *

We are persuaded that the Court of Appeals applied an inappropriate standard of review to mistrial rulings of this kind, and attached undue significance to the form of the ruling. We therefore reverse.

A State may not put a defendant in jeopardy twice for the same offense. The constitutional protection against double jeopardy unequivocally prohibits a second trial following an acquittal. The public interest in the finality of criminal judgments is so strong that an acquitted defendant may not be retried even though "the acquittal was based upon an egregiously erroneous foundation." If the innocence of the accused has been confirmed by a final judgment, the Constitution conclusively presumes that a second trial would be unfair.

Because jeopardy attaches before the judgment becomes final, the constitutional protection also embraces the defendant's "valued right to have his trial completed by a particular tribunal." The reasons why this "valued right" merits constitutional protection are worthy of repetition. Even if the first trial is not completed, a second prosecution may be grossly unfair. It increases the financial and emotional burden on the accused, prolongs the period in which he is stigmatized by an unresolved accusation of wrongdoing, and may even enhance the risk that an innocent defendant may be convicted. The danger of such unfairness to the defendant exists whenever a trial is aborted before it is completed. Consequently, as a general rule, the prosecutor is entitled to one, and only one, opportunity to require an accused to stand trial.

Unlike the situation in which the trial has ended in an acquittal or conviction, retrial is not automatically barred when a criminal proceeding is terminated without finally resolving the merits of the charges against the accused. Because of the variety of circumstances that may make it necessary to discharge a jury before a trial is concluded, and because those circumstances do not invariably create unfairness to the accused, his valued right to have the trial concluded by a particular tribunal is sometimes subordinate to the public interest in affording the prosecutor one full and fair opportunity to present his evidence to an impartial jury. Yet in view of the importance of the right, and the fact that it is frustrated by any mistrial, the prosecutor must shoulder the burden of justifying the mistrial if he is to avoid the double jeopardy bar. His burden is a heavy one. The prosecutor must demonstrate "manifest necessity" for any mistrial declared over the objection of the defendant.

The words "manifest necessity" appropriately characterize the magnitude of the prosecutor's burden. * * * Nevertheless, those words do not describe a standard that can be applied mechanically or without attention to the particular problem confronting the trial judge. Indeed, it is manifest that the key word "necessity" cannot be interpreted literally. * * * [W]e assume that there are degrees of necessity and we require a "high degree" before concluding that a mistrial is appropriate.

The question whether that "high degree" has been reached is answered more easily in some kinds of cases than in others. At one extreme are cases in which a prosecutor requests a mistrial in order to buttress weaknesses in his evidence. * * * [T]he prohibition against double jeopardy as it evolved in this country was plainly intended to condemn this "abhorrent" practice. * * *

Thus, the strictest scrutiny is appropriate when the basis for the mistrial is the unavailability of critical prosecution evidence, or when there is reason to believe that the prosecutor is using the superior resources of the State to harass or to achieve a tactical advantage over the accused.

At the other extreme is the mistrial premised upon the trial judge's belief that the jury is unable to reach a verdict, long considered the classic basis for a proper mistrial. * * * [W]ithout exception, the courts have held that the trial judge may discharge a genuinely deadlocked jury and require the defendant to submit to a second trial. This rule accords recognition to society's interest in giving the prosecution one complete opportunity to convict those who have violated its laws.

In this case the trial judge ordered a mistrial because the defendant's lawyer made improper and prejudicial remarks during his opening statement to the jury. * * * An improper opening statement unquestionably tends to frustrate the public interest in having a just judgment reached by an impartial tribunal. * * * The trial judge, of course, may instruct the jury to disregard the improper comment. In extreme cases, he may discipline counsel, or even remove him from the trial * * *. Those actions, however, will not necessarily remove the risk of bias that may be created by improper argument. Unless unscrupulous defense counsel are to be allowed an unfair advantage, the trial judge must have the power to declare a mistrial in appropriate cases. The interest in orderly, impartial procedure would be impaired if he were deterred from exercising that power by a concern that any time a reviewing court disagreed with his assessment of the trial situation a retrial would automatically be barred. The adoption of a stringent standard of appellate review in this area, therefore, would seriously impede the trial judge in the proper performance of his "duty, in order to protect the integrity of the trial, to take prompt and affirmative action to stop . . . professional misconduct." * * *

There are compelling institutional considerations militating in favor of appellate deference to the trial judge's evaluation of the significance of possible juror bias. He has seen and heard the jurors during their *voir dire* examination. He is the judge most familiar with the evidence and the background of the case on trial. He has listened to the tone of the argument as it was delivered and has observed the apparent reaction of the jurors. In short, he is far more "conversant with the factors relevant to the determination" than any reviewing court can possibly be.

Our conclusion that a trial judge's decision to declare a mistrial based on his assessment of the prejudicial impact of improper argument is entitled to great deference does not, of course, end the inquiry. * * * [R]eviewing courts have an obligation to satisfy themselves that, * * * the trial judge exercised "sound discretion" in declaring a mistrial.

Thus, if a trial judge acts irrationally or irresponsibly, his action cannot be condoned. But our review of this record indicates that this was not such a case. Defense counsel aired improper and highly prejudicial evidence before the jury, the possible impact of which the trial judge was in the best position to assess. The trial judge did not act precipitately in response to the prosecutor's request for a mistrial. On the contrary, * * * he gave both defense counsel and the prosecutor full opportunity to explain their positions on the propriety of a mistrial. We are therefore persuaded by the record that the trial judge acted responsibly and deliberately, and accorded careful consideration to respondent's interest in having the trial concluded in a single proceeding. Since he exercised "sound discretion" in handling the sensitive problem of possible juror bias created by the improper comment of defense counsel, the mistrial order is supported by the "high degree" of necessity which is required in a case of this kind. Neither party has a right to have his case decided by a jury which may be tainted by bias; in these circumstances, "the public's interest in fair trials designed to end in just judgements" must prevail over the defendant's "valued right" to have his trial concluded before the first jury impaneled.

One final matter requires consideration. The absence of an explicit finding of "manifest necessity" appears to have been determinative for the

District Court and may have been so for the Court of Appeals. If those courts regarded that omission as critical, they required too much. Since the record provides sufficient justification for the state-court ruling, the failure to explain that ruling more completely does not render it constitutionally defective.

Review of any trial court decision, is of course, facilitated by findings and by an explanation of the reasons supporting the decision. No matter how desirable such procedural assistance may be, it is not constitutionally mandated in a case such as this. The basis for the trial judge's mistrial order is adequately disclosed by the record, which includes the extensive argument of counsel prior to the judge's ruling. The state trial judge's mistrial declaration is not subject to collateral attack in a federal court simply because he failed to find "manifest necessity" in those words or to articulate on the record all the factors which informed the deliberate exercise of his discretion. * * *

JUSTICE BLACKMUN concurs in the result.

JUSTICE MARSHALL, with whom JUSTICE BRENNAN joins, dissenting. * * *

My disagreement with the majority is a narrow one. * * * Where I part ways from the Court is in its assumption that an "assessment of the prejudicial impact of improper argument," sufficient to support the need for a mistrial may be implied from this record. * * *

I do not propose that the Constitution invariably requires a trial judge to make findings of necessity on the record to justify the declaration of a mistrial over a defendant's objections. * * * What the "manifest necessity" doctrine does require, in my view, is that the record make clear either that there were no meaningful and practical alternatives to a mistrial, or that the trial court scrupulously considered available alternatives and found all wanting but a termination of the proceedings. The record here * * * does neither. * * *

Had the court here explored alternatives on the record, or made a finding of substantial and incurable prejudice or other "manifest necessity," this would be a different case and one in which I would agree with both the majority's reasoning and its result. On this ambiguous record, however, the absence of any such finding—and indeed of any express indication that the trial court applied the manifest-necessity doctrine—leaves open the substantial possibility that there was in fact no need to terminate the proceedings. While the Court states that a "high degree" of necessity is required before a mistrial may properly be granted, its reading of the record here is inconsistent with this principle. * * *

[JUSTICE WHITE's dissenting opinion has been omitted.]

## OREGON V. KENNEDY

Supreme Court of the United States
456 U.S. 667, 102 S.Ct. 2083, 72 L.Ed.2d 416 (1982)

JUSTICE REHNQUIST delivered the opinion of the Court. * * *

Respondent was charged with the theft of an oriental rug. During his first trial, the State called an expert witness on the subject of Middle Eastern rugs to testify as to the value and the identity of the rug in question. On cross-examination, respondent's attorney apparently attempted to establish bias on the part of the expert witness by asking him whether he had filed a criminal complaint against respondent. The witness eventually acknowledged this fact, but explained that no action had been taken on his complaint. On redirect examination, the prosecutor sought to elicit the reasons why the witness had filed a complaint against respondent, but the trial court sustained a series of objections to this line of inquiry. The following colloquy then ensued:

Prosecutor: Have you ever done business with the Kennedys?

Witness: No, I have not.

Prosecutor: Is that because he is a crook?

The trial court then granted respondent's motion for a mistrial.

When the State later sought to retry respondent, he moved to dismiss the charges because of double jeopardy. After a hearing at which the prosecutor testified, the trial court found as a fact that "it was not the intention of the prosecutor in this case to cause a mistrial." On the basis of this finding, the trial court held that double jeopardy principles did not bar retrial, and respondent was then tried and convicted.

Respondent then successfully appealed to the Oregon Court of Appeals, which sustained his double jeopardy claim. * * * The Court of Appeals accepted the trial court's finding that it was not the intent of the prosecutor to cause a mistrial. Nevertheless, the court held that retrial was barred because the prosecutor's conduct in this case constituted what it viewed as "overreaching." * * *

Where the trial is terminated over the objection of the defendant, the classical test for lifting the double jeopardy bar to a second trial is the "manifest necessity" standard first enunciated in Justice Story's opinion for the Court in *United States v. Perez. Perez* dealt with the most common form of "manifest necessity": a mistrial declared by the judge following the jury's declaration that it was unable to reach a verdict. While other situations have been recognized by our cases as meeting the "manifest necessity" standard, the hung jury remains the prototypical example. The "manifest necessity" standard provides sufficient protection to the defendant's interests in having his case finally decided by the jury first selected while at the same time maintaining "the public's interest in fair trials designed to end in just judgments."

But in the case of a mistrial declared at the behest of the defendant, quite different principles come into play. Here the defendant himself has elected to terminate the proceedings against him, and the "manifest necessity" standard has no place in the application of the Double Jeopardy Clause. * * *

Our cases, however, have indicated that even where the defendant moves for a mistrial, there is a narrow exception to the rule that the Double Jeopardy Clause is no bar to retrial. The circumstances under which respondent's first trial was terminated require us to delineate the bounds of that exception more fully than we have in previous cases.

Since one of the principal threads making up the protection embodied in the Double Jeopardy Clause is the right of the defendant to have his trial completed before the first jury empaneled to try him, it may be wondered as a matter of original inquiry why the defendant's election to terminate the first trial by his own motion should not be deemed a renunciation of that right for all purposes. We have recognized, however, that there would be great difficulty in applying such a rule where the prosecutor's actions giving rise to the motion for mistrial were done "in order to goad the [defendant] into requesting a mistrial." In such a case, the defendant's valued right to complete his trial before the first jury would be a hollow shell if the inevitable motion for mistrial were held to prevent a later invocation of the bar of double jeopardy in all circumstances. But the precise phrasing of the circumstances which *will* allow a defendant to interpose the defense of double jeopardy to a second prosecution where the first has terminated on his own motion for a mistrial have been stated with less than crystal clarity in our cases which deal with this area of the law.

In *United States v. Dinitz* we said:

The Double Jeopardy Clause does protect a defendant against governmental actions intended to provoke mistrial requests and thereby to subject defendants to the substantial burdens imposed by multiple prosecutions.

* * * [I]mmediately following the quoted language we went on to say:

[The Double Jeopardy Clause] bars retrials where 'bad-faith conduct by judge or prosecutor,' threatens the '[h]arassment of an accused by successive prosecutions or declaration of a mistrial so as to afford the prosecution a more favorable opportunity to convict' the defendant.

The language just quoted would seem to broaden the test from one of *intent* to provoke a motion for a mistrial to a more generalized standard of "bad faith conduct" or "harassment" on the part of the judge or prosecutor.

It was upon this language that the Oregon Court of Appeals apparently relied in concluding that the prosecutor's colloquy with the expert witness in this case amount to "overreaching."

The difficulty with the more general standards which would permit a broader exception than one merely based on intent is that they offer virtually no standards for their application. Every act on the part of a rational prosecutor during a trial is designed to "prejudice" the defendant by placing before the judge or jury evidence leading to a finding of his guilt. Given the complexity of the rules of evidence, it will be a rare trial of any complexity in which some proffered evidence by the prosecutor or by the defendant's attorney will not be found objectionable by the trial court. Most such objections are undoubtedly curable by simply refusing to allow the proffered evidence to be admitted, or in the case of a particular line of inquiry taken by counsel with a witness, by an admonition to desist from a particular line of inquiry.

More serious infractions on the part of the prosecutor may provoke a motion for mistrial on the part of the defendant, and may in the view of the trial court warrant the granting of such a motion. The "overreaching" standard applied by the court below and urged today by Justice STEVENS, however, would add another classification of prosecutorial error, one requiring dismissal of the indictment, but without supplying any standard by which to assess that error.

By contrast, a standard that examines the intent of the prosecutor, though certainly not entirely free from practical difficulties, is a manageable standard to apply. It merely calls for the court to make a finding of fact. Inferring the existence or nonexistence of intent from objective facts and circumstances is a familiar process in our criminal justice system. When it is remembered that resolution of double jeopardy questions by state trial courts are reviewable not only within the state court system, but in the federal court system on habeas corpus as well, the desirability of an easily applied principle is apparent.

Prosecutorial conduct that might be viewed as harassment or overreaching, even if sufficient to justify a mistrial on defendant's motion, therefore, does not bar retrial absent intent on the part of the prosecutor to subvert the protections afforded by the Double Jeopardy Clause. A defendant's motion for a mistrial constitutes "a deliberate election on his part to forgo his valued right to have his guilt or innocence determined before the first trier of fact." Where prosecutorial error even of a degree sufficient to warrant a mistrial has occurred, "[t]he important consideration, for purposes of the Double Jeopardy Clause, is that the defendant retain primary control over the course to be followed in the event of such error." Only where the governmental conduct in question is intended to "goad" the defendant into moving for a mistrial may a defendant raise the bar of double jeopardy to a second trial after having succeeded in aborting the first on his own motion.

Were we to embrace the broad and somewhat amorphous standard adopted by the Oregon Court of Appeals, we are not sure that criminal defendants as a class would be aided. Knowing that the granting of the defendant's motion for mistrial would all but inevitably bring with it an attempt to bar a second trial on grounds of double jeopardy, the judge presiding over the first trial might well be more loath to grant a defendant's motion for mistrial. If a mistrial were in fact warranted under the applicable law, of course, the defendant could in many instances successfully appeal a judgment of conviction on the same grounds that he urged a mistrial, and the Double Jeopardy Clause would present no bar to retrial. But some of the advantages secured to him by the Double Jeopardy Clause—the freedom from extended anxiety, and the necessity to confront the government's case only once—would be to a large extent lost in the process of trial to verdict, reversal on appeal, and subsequent retrial.

* * * We do not by this opinion lay down a flat rule that where a defendant in a criminal trial successfully moves for a mistrial, he may not thereafter invoke the bar of double jeopardy against a second trial. But we do hold that the circumstances under which such a defendant may invoke the bar of double jeopardy in a second effort to try him are limited to those cases in which the conduct giving rise to the successful motion for a mistrial was intended to provoke the defendant into moving for a mistrial.

Since the Oregon trial court found, and the Oregon Court of Appeals accepted, that the prosecutorial conduct culminating in the termination of the first trial in this case was not so intended by the prosecutor, that is the end of the matter for purposes of the Double Jeopardy Clause of the Fifth Amendment to the United States Constitution. The judgment of the Oregon Court of Appeals is reversed, and the cause is remanded for further proceedings not inconsistent with this opinion. * * *

JUSTICE POWELL, concurring.

I join the Court's opinion holding that the *intention* of a prosecutor determines whether his conduct, viewed by the defendant and the court as justifying a mistrial, bars a retrial of the defendant under the Double Jeopardy Clause. Because "subjective" intent often may be unknowable, I emphasize that a court—in considering a double jeopardy motion—should rely primarily upon the objective facts and circumstances of the particular case.

In the present case the mistrial arose from the prosecutor's conduct in pursuing a line of redirect examination of a key witness. The Oregon Court of Appeals identified a single question as constituting "overreaching" so serious as to bar a retrial. Yet, there are few vigorously contested lawsuits—whether criminal or civil—in which improper questions are not asked. Our system *is* adversarial and vigorous advocacy is encouraged.

Nevertheless, this would have been a close case for me if there had been substantial factual evidence of intent beyond the question itself. Here, however, other relevant facts and circumstances strongly support the view that prosecutorial intent to cause a mistrial was absent. First, there was no sequence of overreaching prior to the single prejudicial question. Moreover, it is evident from a colloquy between counsel and the court, out of the presence of the jury, that the prosecutor not only resisted, but also was surprised by, the defendant's motion for a mistrial. Finally, at the hearing on respondent's double jeopardy motion, the prosecutor testified— and the trial found as a fact and the appellate court agreed—that there was no " 'intention . . . to cause a mistrial.' "

In view of these circumstances, the Double Jeopardy Clause provides no bar to retrial.

JUSTICE STEVENS, with whom JUSTICE BRENNAN, JUSTICE MARSHALL, and JUSTICE BLACKMUN join, concurring in the judgment. * * *

The Double Jeopardy Clause represents a constitutional policy of finality for the defendant's benefit in criminal proceedings. If the defendant is acquitted by the jury, or if he is convicted and the conviction is upheld on appeal, he may not be prosecuted again for the same offense. The defendant's interest in finality is not confined to final judgments; he also has a protected interest in having his guilt or innocence decided in one proceeding. That interest must be balanced against society's interest in affording the prosecutor one full and fair opportunity to present his evidence to the jury. Our decisions in the mistrial setting accordingly have accommodated the defendant's double jeopardy interests with legitimate prosecutorial interests.

The accommodation is reflected in two general rules that govern the permissibility of reprosecution after a mistrial. Which general rule applies turns on whether the defendant has retained control over the course to be followed once error has substantially tainted the initial proceeding. When a mistrial is declared over the defendant's objection, the general rule is that retrial is barred. An exception to this general rule exists for cases in which the mistrial was justified by "manifest necessity." The other general rule is that the defendant's motion for, or consent to, a mistrial removes any double jeopardy bar to reprosecution. There is an exception to this rule for cases in which the prosecutor intended to provoke a mistrial or otherwise engaged in "overreaching" or "harassment." The prosecutor has the burden of proving the former exception for manifest necessity, and the defendant has the burden of proving the latter exception for overreaching. * * *

Today the Court once again recognizes that the exception properly encompasses the situation in which the prosecutor commits prejudicial error with the intent to provoke a mistrial. But the Court reaches out to limit the exception to that one situation, rejecting the previous recognition that prosecutorial overreaching or harassment is also within the exception.

Even if I agreed that the balance of competing interests tipped in favor of a bar to reprosecution only in the situation in which the prosecutor intended to provoke a mistrial, I would not subscribe to a standard that conditioned such a bar on the determination that the prosecutor harbored such intent when he committed prejudicial error. It is almost inconceivable that a defendant could prove that the prosecutor's deliberate misconduct was motivated by an intent to provoke a mistrial instead of an intent simply to prejudice the defendant. The defendant must shoulder a strong burden to establish a bar to reprosecution when he has consented to the mistrial, but the Court's subjective intent standard would eviscerate the exception. * * *

To invoke the exception for overreaching, a court need not divine the exact motivation for the prosecutorial error. It is sufficient that the court is persuaded that egregious prosecutorial misconduct has rendered unmeaningful the defendant's choice to continue or to abort the proceeding. * * *

[JUSTICE BRENNAN's opinion, concurring in the judgment, has been omitted.]

## F.  RETRIAL FOLLOWING ACQUITTALS, DISMISSALS, AND CONVICTIONS

Generally speaking, a defendant may not be subjected to retrial following an acquittal. In *United States v. Scott*, the Court explains whether and when a dismissal of the indictment can count as an acquittal for double jeopardy purposes.

Conversely, a defendant who has been convicted can usually be retried after successfully appealing a conviction. In *Burks v. United States*, the Court considers whether this rule permitting retrial following a successful appeal applies when a defendant's conviction is reversed due to insufficiency of the evidence as opposed to trial error.

### UNITED STATES V. SCOTT
Supreme Court of the United States
437 U.S. 82, 98 S.Ct. 2187, 57 L.Ed.2d 65 (1978)

JUSTICE REHNQUIST delivered the opinion of the Court.

On March 5, 1975, respondent, a member of the police force in Muskegon, Mich., was charged * * * with distribution of various narcotics. Both before his trial, and twice during the trial, respondent moved to dismiss the two counts of the indictment which concerned transactions that took place during the preceding September, on the ground that his defense had been prejudiced by preindictment delay. At the close of all the evidence, the court granted respondent's motion. * * *

The Government sought to appeal the dismissals. [The Court of Appeals], relying on our opinion in *United States v. Jenkins*, concluded that any further prosecution of respondent was barred by the Double Jeopardy Clause of the Fifth Amendment, and therefore dismissed the appeal. We granted certiorari to give further consideration to the applicability of the Double Jeopardy Clause to Government appeals from orders granting defense motions to terminate a trial before verdict. * * *

The origin and history of the Double Jeopardy Clause are hardly a matter of dispute. The constitutional provision had its origin in the three common-law pleas of *autrefois acquit, autrefois convict*, and pardon. These three pleas prevented the retrial of a person who had previously been acquitted, convicted, or pardoned for the same offense. As this Court has described the purpose underlying the prohibition against double jeopardy:

> The underlying idea, one that is deeply ingrained in at least the Anglo-American system of jurisprudence, is that the State with all its resources and power should not be allowed to make repeated attempts to convict an individual for an alleged offense, thereby subjecting him to embarrassment, expense and ordeal and compelling him to live in a continuing state of anxiety and insecurity, as well as enhancing the possibility that even though innocent he may be found guilty.

* * * At the time the Fifth Amendment was adopted, its principles were easily applied, since most criminal prosecutions proceeded to final judgment, and neither the United States nor the defendant had any right to appeal an adverse verdict. The verdict in such a case was unquestionably final, and could be raised in bar against any further prosecution for the same offense.

* * * It was not until 1889 that Congress permitted criminal defendants to seek a writ of error in this Court, and then only in capital cases. Only then did it become necessary for this Court to deal with the issues presented by the challenge of verdicts on appeal.

And, in the very first case presenting the issues, *United States v. Ball*, the Court established principles that have been adhered to ever since. Three persons had been tried together for murder; two were convicted, the other acquitted. This Court reversed the convictions, finding the indictment fatally defective whereupon all three defendants were tried again. This time all three were convicted and they again sought review here. This Court held that the Double Jeopardy Clause precluded further prosecution of the defendant who had been *acquitted* at the original trial but that it posed no such bar to the prosecution of those defendants who had been *convicted* in the earlier proceeding. * * *

Although *Ball* firmly established that a successful appeal of a conviction precludes a subsequent plea of double jeopardy, the opinion shed no light on whether a judgment of acquittal could be reversed on appeal consistently with the Double Jeopardy Clause. * * * [I]n *United States v. Martin Linen Supply Co.,* [we] held that the Government could not appeal the granting of a motion to acquit * * * where a second trial would be required upon remand. The Court, quoting language in *Ball*, stated: "Perhaps the most fundamental rule in the history of double jeopardy jurisprudence has been that '[a] verdict of acquittal . . . could not be reviewed, on error or otherwise, without putting [a defendant] twice in jeopardy, and thereby violating the Constitution.'"

These, then, at least, are two venerable principles of double jeopardy jurisprudence. The successful appeal of a judgment of conviction, on any ground other than the insufficiency of the evidence to support the verdict, poses no bar to further prosecution on the same charge. A judgment of acquittal, whether based on a jury verdict of not guilty or on a ruling by the court that the evidence is insufficient to convict, may not be appealed and terminates the prosecution when a second trial would be necessitated by a reversal. * * * To permit a second trial after an acquittal, however mistaken the acquittal may have been, would present an unacceptably high risk that the Government, with its vastly superior resources, might wear down the defendant so that "even though innocent, he may be found guilty." On the other hand, to require a criminal defendant to stand trial again after he has successfully invoked a statutory right of appeal to upset his first conviction is not an act of governmental oppression of the sort against which the Double Jeopardy Clause was intended to protect. * * *

Although the primary purpose of the Double Jeopardy Clause was to protect the integrity of a final judgment, this Court has also developed a body of law guarding the separate but related interest of a defendant in avoiding multiple prosecutions even where no final determination of guilt or innocence has been made. Such interests may be involved in two different situations: the first, in which the trial judge declares a mistrial; the second, in which the trial judge terminates the proceedings favorably to the defendant on a basis not related to factual guilt or innocence. * * *

We turn now to the relationship between the Double Jeopardy Clause and reprosecution of a defendant who has successfully obtained not a mistrial but a termination of the trial in his favor before any determination of factual guilt or innocence. Unlike the typical mistrial, the granting of a motion such as this obviously contemplates that the proceedings will terminate then and there in favor of the defendant. The prosecution, if it wishes to reinstate the proceedings in the face of such a ruling, ordinarily must seek reversal of the decision of the trial court. * * *

In the present case, the District Court's dismissal of the first count of the indictment was based upon a claim of preindictment delay and not on the court's conclusion that the Government had not produced sufficient evidence to establish the guilt of the defendant. Respondent Scott points out quite correctly that he had moved to dismiss the indictment on this ground prior to trial, and that had the District Court chosen to grant it at that time the Government could have appealed the ruling * * *.

* * * It is quite true that the Government with all its resources and power should not be allowed to make repeated attempts to convict an individual for an alleged offense. * * * [A] defendant once acquitted may not be again subjected to trial without violating the Double Jeopardy Clause.

But that situation is obviously a far cry from the present case, where the Government was quite willing to continue with its production of evidence to show the defendant guilty before the jury first empaneled to try him, but the defendant elected to seek termination of the trial on grounds unrelated to guilt or innocence. This is scarcely a picture of an all-powerful state relentlessly pursuing a defendant who had either been found not guilty or who had at least insisted on having the issue of guilt submitted to the first trier of fact. It is instead a picture of a defendant who chooses to avoid conviction and imprisonment, not because of his assertion that the Government has failed to make out a case against him, but because of a legal claim that the Government's case against him must fail even though it might satisfy the trier of fact that he was guilty beyond a reasonable doubt. * * *

We have previously noted that "the trial judge's characterization of his own action cannot control the classification of the action." * * * Rather, a defendant is acquitted only when "the ruling of the judge, whatever its label, actually represents a resolution [in the defendant's favor], correct or not, of some or all of the factual elements of the offense charged." Where the court, before the jury returns a verdict, enters a judgment of acquittal * * *, appeal will be barred only when "it is plain that the District Court ... evaluated the Government's evidence and determined that it was legally insufficient to sustain a conviction." * * *

We think that in a case such as this the defendant, by deliberately choosing to seek termination of the proceedings against him on a basis unrelated to factual guilt or innocence of the offense of which he is accused, suffers no injury cognizable under the Double Jeopardy Clause if the Government is permitted to appeal from such a ruling of the trial court in favor of the defendant. * * * [W]e conclude that the Double Jeopardy

Clause, which guards against Government oppression, does not relieve a defendant from the consequences of his voluntary choice.

\* \* \* [W]here the defendant \* \* \* obtains the termination of the proceedings against him in the trial court without any finding by a court or jury as to his guilt or innocence[,] [h]e has not been "deprived" of his valued right to go to the first jury; only the public has been deprived of its valued right to "one complete opportunity to convict those who have violated its laws." No interest protected by the Double Jeopardy Clause is invaded when the Government is allowed to appeal and seek reversal of such a midtrial termination of the proceedings in a manner favorable to the defendant. \* \* \*

Here, "the lessons of experience" indicate that Government appeals from midtrial dismissals requested by the defendant would significantly advance the public interest in assuring that each defendant shall be subject to a just judgment on the merits of his case, without "enhancing the possibility that even though innocent he may be found guilty." \* \* \*

Justice Brennan, with whom Justice White, Justice Marshall, and Justice Stevens join, dissenting. \* \* \*

I dissent. \* \* \* The Court's attempt to draw a distinction between "true acquittals" and other final judgments favorable to the accused, quite simply, is unsupportable in either logic or policy. \* \* \*

While the Double Jeopardy Clause often has the effect of protecting the accused's interest in the finality of particular favorable determinations, this is not its objective. For the Clause often permits Government appeals from final judgments favorable to the accused. *See United States v. Wilson* (whether or not final judgment was an acquittal, Government may appeal if reversal would not necessitate a retrial). The purpose of the Clause, which the Court today fails sufficiently to appreciate, is to protect the accused against the agony and risks attendant upon undergoing more than one criminal trial for any single offense. \* \* \* Society's "willingness to limit the Government to a single criminal proceeding to vindicate its very vital interest in enforcement of criminal laws" bespeaks society's recognition of the gross unfairness of requiring the accused to undergo the strain and agony of more than one trial for any single offense. Accordingly, the policies of the Double Jeopardy Clause mandate that the Government be afforded but one complete opportunity to convict an accused and that when the first proceeding terminates in a final judgment favorable to the defendant any retrial be barred. The rule as to acquittals can only be understood as simply an application of this larger principle.

Judgments of acquittal normally result from jury or bench verdicts of not guilty. In such cases, the acquittal represents the factfinder's conclusion that, under the controlling legal principles, the evidence does not establish that the defendant can be convicted of the offense charged in the indictment. But the judgment does not necessarily establish the criminal defendant's lack of criminal culpability; the acquittal may result from erroneous evidentiary rulings or erroneous interpretations of governing legal principles induced by the defense. Yet the Double Jeopardy Clause bars a second trial.

* * * [T]he Court's new theory [is] that a criminal defendant who seeks to avoid conviction on a "ground unrelated to factual innocence" somehow stands on a different constitutional footing from a defendant whose participation in his criminal trial creates a situation in which a judgment of acquittal has to be entered. This premise is simply untenable. * * * The rule prohibiting retrials following acquittals does not and could not rest on a conclusion that the accused was factually innocent in any meaningful sense.

* * * [T]he reasons that bar a retrial following an acquittal are equally applicable to a final judgment entered on a ground "unrelated to factual innocence." The heavy personal strain of the second trial is the same in either case. So too is the risk that, though innocent, the defendant may be found guilty at a second trial. If the appeal is allowed in either situation, the Government will, following any reversal, not only obtain the benefit of the favorable appellate ruling but also be permitted to shore up any other weak points of its case and obtain all the other advantages at the second trial that the Double Jeopardy Clause was designed to forbid.

It is regrettable that the Court should introduce such confusion in an area of the law that, until today, had been crystal clear. * * * [T]oday's decision fashions an entirely arbitrary distinction that creates precisely the evils that the Double Jeopardy Clause was designed to prevent. I would affirm the judgment of the Court of Appeals.

## BURKS V. UNITED STATES

Supreme Court of the United States
437 U.S. 1, 98 S.Ct. 2141, 57 L.Ed.2d 1 (1978)

CHIEF JUSTICE BURGER delivered the opinion of the Court.

We granted certiorari to resolve the question of whether an accused may be subjected to a second trial when conviction in a prior trial was reversed by an appellate court solely for lack of sufficient evidence to sustain the jury's verdict.

Petitioner Burks was tried in the United States District Court for the crime of robbing a federally insured bank by use of a dangerous weapon * * *. Burks' principal defense was insanity. To prove this claim petitioner produced three expert witnesses who testified, albeit with differing diagnoses of his mental condition, that he suffered from a mental illness at the time of the robbery, which rendered him substantially incapable of conforming his conduct to the requirements of the law. In rebuttal the Government offered the testimony of two experts, one of whom testified that although petitioner possessed a character disorder, he was not mentally ill. The other prosecution witness acknowledged a character disorder in petitioner, but gave a rather ambiguous answer to the question of whether Burks had been capable of conforming his conduct to the law. Lay witnesses also testified for the Government, expressing their opinion that petitioner appeared to be capable of normal functioning and was sane at the time of the alleged offense.

Before the case was submitted to the jury, the court denied a motion for a judgment of acquittal. The jury found Burks guilty as charged. * * * On appeal petitioner narrowed the issues by admitting the affirmative factual elements of the charge against him, leaving only his claim concerning criminal responsibility to be resolved. With respect to this point, the Court of Appeals agreed with petitioner's claim that the evidence was insufficient to support the verdict and reversed his conviction, [explaining that] the prosecution's evidence with respect to Burks' mental condition, even when viewed in the light most favorable to the Government, did not "effectively rebu[t]" petitioner's proof with respect to insanity and criminal responsibility. * * *

Petitioner's argument is straightforward. He contends that the Court of Appeals' holding was nothing more or less than a decision that the District Court had erred by not granting his motion for a judgment of acquittal. By implication, he argues, the appellate reversal was the operative equivalent of a district court's judgment of acquittal, entered either before or after verdict. Petitioner points out, however, that had the District Court found the evidence at the first trial inadequate, as the Court of Appeals said it should have done, a second trial would violate the Double Jeopardy Clause of the Fifth Amendment. Therefore, he maintains, it makes no difference that the determination of evidentiary insufficiency was made by a *reviewing* court since the double jeopardy considerations are the same, regardless of which court decides that a judgment of acquittal is in order.

The position advanced by petitioner has not been embraced by our prior holdings. * * * It is unquestionably true that the Court of Appeals' decision "represente[d] a resolution, correct or not, of some or all of the factual elements of the offense charged." By deciding that the Government had failed to come forward with sufficient proof of petitioner's capacity to be responsible for criminal acts, that court was clearly saying that Burks' criminal culpability had not been established. If the District Court had so held in the first instance, as the reviewing court said it should have done, a judgment of acquittal would have been entered and, of course, petitioner could not be retried for the same offense. * * * [I]t should make no difference that the *reviewing* court, rather than the trial court, determined the evidence to be insufficient. The appellate decision unmistakably meant that the District Court had erred in failing to grant a judgment of acquittal. To hold otherwise would create a purely arbitrary distinction between those in petitioner's position and others who would enjoy the benefit of a correct decision by the District Court.

The Double Jeopardy Clause forbids a second trial for the purpose of affording the prosecution another opportunity to supply evidence which it failed to muster in the first proceeding. This is central to the objective of the prohibition against successive trials. The Clause does not allow "the State . . . to make repeated attempts to convict an individual for an alleged offense," since "[t]he constitutional prohibition against 'double jeopardy' was designed to protect an individual from being subjected to the hazards of trial and possible conviction more than once for an alleged offense." * * *

*United States v. Ball* * * * provides a logical starting point for unraveling the conceptual confusion arising from [several] cases * * *. This is especially true since *Ball* appears to represent the first instance in which this Court considered in any detail the double jeopardy implications of an appellate reversal.

*Ball* came before the Court twice, the first occasion being on writ of error from federal convictions for murder. On this initial review, those defendants who had been found guilty obtained a reversal of their convictions due to a fatally defective indictment. On remand after appeal, the trial court dismissed the flawed indictment and proceeded to retry the defendants on a new indictment. They were again convicted and the defendants came once more to this Court, arguing that their second trial was barred because of former jeopardy. The Court rejected this plea in a brief statement:

> [A] defendant, who procures a judgment against him upon an indictment to be set aside, may be tried anew upon the same indictment, or upon another indictment, for the same offence of which he had been convicted.

The reversal in *Ball* was therefore based not on insufficiency of evidence but rather on trial error, *i.e.*, failure to dismiss a faulty indictment. Moreover, the cases cited as authority by *Ball* were ones involving trial errors. We have no doubt that *Ball* was correct in allowing a new trial to rectify *trial error*:

> The principle that [the Double Jeopardy Clause] does not preclude the Government's retrying a defendant whose conviction is set aside because of an *error in the proceedings* leading to conviction is a well-established part of our constitutional jurisprudence. * * *

As we have seen * * *, the cases which have arisen since *Ball* generally do not distinguish between reversals due to trial error and those resulting from evidentiary insufficiency. We believe, however, that the failure to make this distinction has contributed substantially to the present state of conceptual confusion existing in this area of the law. Consequently, it is important to consider carefully the respective roles of these two types of reversals in double jeopardy analysis. Various rationales have been advanced to support the policy of allowing retrial to correct trial error, but in our view the most reasonable justification is * * *:

> It would be a high price indeed for society to pay were every accused granted immunity from punishment because of any defect sufficient to constitute reversible error in the proceedings leading to conviction.

In short, reversal for trial error, as distinguished from evidentiary insufficiency, does not constitute a decision to the effect that the government has failed to prove its case. As such, it implies nothing with respect to the guilt or innocence of the defendant. Rather, it is a determination that a defendant has been convicted through a judicial process which is defective in some fundamental respect, *e. g.*, incorrect receipt or rejection of evidence, incorrect instructions, or prosecutorial misconduct. When this occurs, the accused has a strong interest in obtaining a fair readjudication of his guilt free from error, just as society maintains a valid concern for insuring that the guilty are punished.

The same cannot be said when a defendant's conviction has been overturned due to a failure of proof at trial, in which case the prosecution cannot complain of prejudice, for it has been given one fair opportunity to offer whatever proof it could assemble. Moreover, such an appellate reversal means that the government's case was so lacking that it should not have even been *submitted* to the jury. Since we necessarily afford absolute finality to a jury's *verdict* of acquittal—no matter how erroneous its decision—it is difficult to conceive how society has any greater interest in retrying a defendant when, on review, it is decided as a matter of law that the jury could not properly have returned a verdict of guilty.

The importance of a reversal on grounds of evidentiary insufficiency for purposes of inquiry under the Double Jeopardy Clause is underscored by the fact that a federal court's role in deciding whether a case should be considered by the jury is quite limited. Even the trial court, which has heard the testimony of witnesses first hand, is not to weigh the evidence or assess the credibility of witnesses when it judges the merits of a motion for acquittal. The prevailing rule has long been that a district judge is to submit a case to the jury if the evidence and inferences therefrom most favorable to the prosecution would warrant the jury's finding the defendant guilty beyond a reasonable doubt. Obviously a federal appellate court applies no higher a standard; rather, it must sustain the verdict if there is substantial evidence, viewed in the light most favorable to the

Government, to uphold the jury's decision. While this is not the appropriate occasion to re-examine in detail the standards for appellate reversal on grounds of insufficient evidence, it is apparent that such a decision will be confined to cases where the prosecution's failure is clear. Given the requirements for entry of a judgment of acquittal, the purposes of the Clause would be negated were we to afford the government an opportunity for the proverbial "second bite at the apple."

In our view it makes no difference that a defendant has sought a new trial as one of his remedies, or even as the sole remedy. It cannot be meaningfully said that a person "waives" his right to a judgment of acquittal by moving for a new trial. * * * Since we hold today that the Double Jeopardy Clause precludes a second trial once the reviewing court has found the evidence legally insufficient, the only "just" remedy available for that court is the direction of a judgment of acquittal. To the extent that our prior decisions suggest that by moving for a new trial, a defendant waives his right to a judgment of acquittal on the basis of evidentiary insufficiency, those cases are overruled. * * *

JUSTICE BLACKMUN took no part in the consideration or decision of this case.

# G. JURY NULLIFICATION

Jury nullification occurs when a jury votes to acquit the defendant despite evidence that the defendant is guilty of the charged offense. The Double Jeopardy Clause of the Fifth Amendment prohibits reversal of a jury's decision to acquit, even if there is overwhelming evidence of guilt and it appears that the jury has engaged in jury nullification. In the first excerpt below, *Racially Based Jury Nullification: Black Power in the Criminal Justice System*, Paul Butler outlines the history of jury nullification and then proposes that African-American jurors engage in racially based jury nullification. In *The Dangers of Race-Based Jury Nullification: A Response to Professor Butler*, Andrew Leipold provides a strong counter to Butler's proposal.

## RACIALLY BASED JURY NULLIFICATION: BLACK POWER IN THE CRIMINAL JUSTICE SYSTEM
### Paul Butler
### 105 Yale L.J. 677 (1995)

\* \* \*

### II. B. *Jury Nullification*

When a jury disregards evidence presented at trial and acquits an otherwise guilty defendant because the jury objects to the law that the defendant violated or to the application of the law to that defendant, it has practiced jury nullification. * * * I argue that it is both lawful and morally right that black jurors consider race in reaching verdicts in criminal cases.

### 1. *What Is Jury Nullification?* * * *

In the United States, the doctrine of jury nullification originally was based on the common law idea that the function of a jury was, broadly, to decide justice, which included judging the law as well as the facts. If jurors believed that applying a law would lead to an unjust conviction, they were not compelled to convict someone who had broken that law. Although most American courts now disapprove of a jury's deciding anything other than the "facts," the Double Jeopardy Clause of the Fifth Amendment prohibits appellate reversal of a jury's decision to acquit, regardless of the reason for the acquittal. Thus, even when a trial judge thinks that a jury's acquittal directly contradicts the evidence, the jury's verdict must be accepted as final. The jurors, in judging the law, function as an important and necessary check on government power.

### 2. *A Brief History*

The prerogative of juries to nullify has been part of English and American law for centuries. In 1670, the landmark decision in *Bushell's Case* established the right of juries under English common law to nullify on the basis of an objection to the law the defendant had violated. Two members of an unpopular minority group—the Quakers—were prosecuted for unlawful assembly and disturbance of the peace. At trial, the defendants, William Penn and William Mead, admitted that they had assembled a large crowd on the streets of London. Upon that admission, the judge asked the men if they wished to plead guilty. Penn replied that the issue was not "whether I am guilty of this Indictment but whether this Indictment be legal," and argued that the jurors should go "behind" the law and use their consciences to decide whether he was guilty. The judge disagreed, and he instructed the jurors that the defendants' admissions compelled a guilty verdict. After extended deliberation, however, the jurors found both defendants not guilty. The judge then fined the jurors for rendering a decision contrary to the evidence and to his instructions. When one juror, Bushell, refused to pay his fine, the issue reached the Court of Common Pleas, which held that jurors in criminal cases could not be punished for voting to acquit, even when the trial judge believed that the verdict contradicted the evidence. The reason was stated by the Chief Justice of the Court of Common Pleas:

> A man cannot see by anothers eye, nor hear by anothers ear, no more can a man conclude or inferr the thing to be resolv'd by anothers understanding or reasoning; and though the verdict be right the jury give, yet they being not assur'd it is so from their own understanding, are forsworn, at least in foro conscientiae.

This decision "changed the course of jury history." It is unclear why the jurors acquitted Penn and Mead, but their act has been viewed in near mythological terms. Bushell and his fellow jurors have come to be seen as representing the best ideals of democracy because they "rebuffed the tyranny of the judiciary and vindicated their own true historical and moral purpose."

American colonial law incorporated the common law prerogative of jurors to vote according to their consciences after the British government began prosecuting American revolutionaries for political crimes. The best known of these cases involved John Peter Zenger, who was accused of seditious libel for publishing statements critical of British colonial rule in North America. In seditious libel cases, English law required that the judge determine whether the statements made by the defendant were libelous; the jury was not supposed to question the judge's finding on this issue. At trial, Zenger's attorney told the jury that it should ignore the judge's instructions that Zenger's remarks were libelous because the jury "ha[d] the right beyond all dispute to determine both the law and the facts." The lawyer then echoed the language of *Bushell's Case,* arguing that the jurors had "to see with their eyes, to hear with their own ears, and to make use of their own consciences and understandings, in judging of the lives, liberties or estates of their fellow subjects." Famously, the jury acquitted Zenger, and another case entered the canon as a shining example of the benefits of the jury system.

After Zenger's trial, the notion that juries should decide "justice," as opposed to simply applying the law to the facts, became relatively settled in American jurisprudence. In addition to pointing to political prosecutions of white American revolutionaries like Zenger, modern courts and legal historians often cite with approval nullification in trials of defendants "guilty" of helping to free black slaves. In these cases, Northern jurors with abolitionist sentiments used their power as jurors to subvert federal law that supported slavery. In *United States v. Morris,* for example, three defendants were accused of aiding and abetting a runaway slave's escape to Canada. The defense attorney told the jury that, because it was hearing a criminal case, it had the right to judge the law, and if it believed that the Fugitive Slave Act was unconstitutional, it was bound to disregard any contrary instructions given by the judge. The defendants were acquitted, and the government dropped the charges against five other people accused of the same crime. Another success story entered the canon.

### 3. Sparf *and Other Critiques*

In the mid-nineteenth century, as memories of the tyranny of British rule faded, some American courts began to criticize the idea of jurors deciding justice. A number of the state decisions that allowed this practice were overruled, and in the 1895 case of *Sparf v. United States,* the Supreme Court spoke regarding jury nullification in federal courts.

In *Sparf,* two men on trial for murder requested that the judge instruct the jury that it had the option of convicting them of manslaughter, a lesser-included offense. The trial court refused this request and instead instructed the jurors that if they convicted the defendants of any crime less than murder, or if they acquitted them, the jurors would be in violation of their legal oath and duties. The Supreme Court held that this instruction was not contrary to law and affirmed the defendants' murder convictions. The Court acknowledged that juries have the "physical power" to disregard the law, but stated that they have no "moral right" to do so. Indeed, the Court observed, "If the jury were at liberty to settle the law for themselves, the effect would be . . . that the law itself would be most uncertain, from the different views, which different juries might take of it." Despite this criticism, *Sparf* conceded that, as a matter of law, a judge could not prevent jury nullification, because in criminal cases "[a] verdict of acquittal cannot be set aside." An anomaly was thus created, and has been a feature of American criminal law ever since: Jurors have the power to nullify, but, in most jurisdictions, they have no right to be informed of this power.

Since *Sparf,* most of the appellate courts that have considered jury nullification have addressed that anomaly and have endorsed it. Some of these courts, however, have not been as critical of the concept of jury nullification as the *Sparf* Court. The D.C. Circuit's opinion in *United States v. Dougherty* is illustrative. In *Dougherty,* the court noted that the ability of juries to nullify was widely recognized and even approved "as a 'necessary counter to case-hardened judges and arbitrary prosecutors.' " This necessity, however, did not establish "as an imperative" that a jury be informed by the judge of its power to nullify. The D.C. Circuit was concerned that "[w]hat makes for health as an occasional medicine would be disastrous as a daily diet." Specifically:

> Rules of law or justice involve choice of values and ordering of objectives for which unanimity is unlikely in any society, or group representing the society, especially a society as diverse in cultures and interests as ours. To seek unity out of diversity, under the national motto, there must be a procedure for decision by vote of a majority or prescribed plurality—in accordance with democratic philosophy. To assign the role of mini-legislature to the various petit juries, who must hang if not unanimous, exposes criminal law and administration to paralysis, and to a deadlock that betrays rather than furthers the assumptions of viable democracy.
> * * *

## C.  *The Moral Case for Jury Nullification by African-Americans*

Any juror legally may vote for nullification in any case, but, certainly, jurors should not do so without some principled basis. The reason that some historical examples of nullification are viewed approvingly is that most of us now believe that the jurors in those cases did the morally right thing; it would have been unconscionable, for example, to punish those slaves who committed the crime of escaping to the North for their freedom. It is true that nullification later would be used as a means of racial subordination by some Southern jurors, but that does not mean that nullification in the approved cases was wrong. It only means that those Southern jurors erred in their calculus of justice. * * *

### 1.  *African-Americans and the "Betrayal" of Democracy*

There is no question that jury nullification is subversive of the rule of law. It appears to be the antithesis of the view that courts apply settled, standing laws and do not "dispense justice in some ad hoc, case-by-case basis." * * * [J]ury nullification "betrays rather than furthers the assumptions of viable democracy." Because the Double Jeopardy Clause makes this power part-and-parcel of the jury system, the issue becomes whether black jurors have any moral right to "betray democracy" in this sense. I believe that they do for two reasons that I borrow from the jurisprudence of legal realism and critical race theory: First, the idea of "the rule of law" is more mythological than real, and second, "democracy," as practiced in the United States, has betrayed African-Americans far more than they could ever betray it. * * *

### 2.  *The Rule of Law as Myth*

* * * The argument, in brief, is that law is indeterminate and incapable of neutral interpretation. * * * Think, for example, of the existence of slavery in a republic purportedly dedicated to the proposition that all men are created equal, or the law's support of state-sponsored segregation even after the Fourteenth Amendment guaranteed blacks equal protection. That the rule of law ultimately corrected some of the large holes in the American fabric is evidence more of its malleability than of its virtue; the rule of law had, in the first instance, justified the holes. * * *

If the rule of law is a myth, or at least is not applicable to African-Americans, the criticism that jury nullification undermines it loses force. The black juror is simply another actor in the system, using her power to fashion a particular outcome; the juror's act of nullification * * * exposes the indeterminacy of law, but does not create it.

### 3.  *The Moral Obligation to Disobey Unjust Laws*

* * * [T]here * * * is no moral obligation to follow an unjust law. This principle is familiar to many African-Americans who practiced civil disobedience during the civil rights protests of the 1950s and 1960s.

Indeed, Martin Luther King suggested that morality requires that unjust laws not be obeyed. As I state above, the difficulty of determining which laws are unjust should not obscure the need to make that determination. * * *

### 4. *Democratic Domination*

* * * Lani Guinier suggests that the moral legitimacy of majority rule hinges on two assumptions: 1) that majorities are not fixed; and 2) that minorities will be able to become members of some majorities. Racial prejudice "to such a degree that the majority consistently excludes the minority, or refuses to inform itself about the relative merit of the minority's preferences," defeats both assumptions.

* * * [African Americans] are not even proportionally represented in the U.S. House of Representatives or in the Senate. As a result, African-Americans wield little influence over criminal law, state or federal. African-Americans should embrace the antidemocratic nature of jury nullification because it provides them with the power to determine justice in a way that majority rule does not.

### D. *"[J]ustice must satisfy the appearance of justice": The Symbolic Function of Black Jurors*

* * * [O]n several occasions, the Supreme Court has referred to the usefulness of black jurors to the rule of law in the United States. In essence, black jurors symbolize the fairness and impartiality of the law. * * * [T]he Court has suggested that these jurors perform a symbolic function, especially when they sit on cases involving African-American defendants, and the Court has typically made these suggestions in the form of rhetoric about the social harm caused by the exclusion of blacks from jury service. I will refer to this role of black jurors as the "legitimization function." * * *

When blacks are excluded from juries, beyond any harm done to the juror who suffers the discrimination or to the defendant, the social injury of the exclusion is that it "undermine[s] . . . public confidence—as well [it] should." Because the United States is both a democracy and a pluralist society, it is important that diverse groups appear to have a voice in the laws that govern them. Allowing black people to serve on juries strengthens "public respect for our criminal justice system and the rule of law."

* * * In choosing [to nullify], the juror makes a decision not to be a passive symbol of support for a system for which she has no respect. Rather than signaling her displeasure with the system by breaching "community peace," the black juror invokes the political nature of her role in the criminal justice system and votes "no." In a sense, the black juror engages in an act of civil disobedience, except that her choice is better than civil disobedience because it is lawful. Is the black juror's race-conscious act moral? Absolutely. * * * [T]he doctrine of jury nullification affords African-

American jurors the opportunity to control the authority of the law over some African-American criminal defendants. * * *

### III.  C. *Some Political and Procedural Concerns*

### 1.  *What if White People Start Nullifying Too?*

One concern is that whites will nullify in cases of white-on-black crime. The best response to this concern is that often white people do nullify in those cases. The white jurors who acquitted the police officers who beat up Rodney King are a good example. There is no reason why my proposal should cause white jurors to acquit white defendants who are guilty of violence against blacks any more frequently. My model assumes that black violence against whites would be punished by black jurors; I hope that white jurors would do the same in cases involving white defendants.

If white jurors were to begin applying my proposal to cases with white defendants, then they, like the black jurors, would be choosing to opt out of the criminal justice system. For pragmatic political purposes, that would be excellent. Attention would then be focused on alternative methods of correcting antisocial conduct much sooner than it would if only African-Americans raised the issue. * * *

### THE DANGERS OF RACE-BASED JURY NULLIFICATION: A RESPONSE TO PROFESSOR BUTLER

Andrew D. Leipold
44 UCLA L. Rev. 109 (1996)

In his provocative essay, *Racially Based Jury Nullification: Black Power in the Criminal Justice System*, Professor Paul Butler argues that African-American jurors should sometimes vote to acquit in criminal cases because the defendant is black. As every lawyer knows, juries have the unreviewable power to acquit for any reason, and Professor Butler urges black jurors to exercise this power on behalf of factually guilty African-American defendants whenever the benefits of returning the defendant to the community outweigh the harms that will be caused by incarceration. Butler claims that this use of "jury nullification"—when a jury acquits for reasons unrelated to the evidence—will diminish the racially disparate impact of the criminal law, help bring about beneficial legal reform, and improve the African-American communities that are now crippled by the excessive imprisonment of their members. * * *

Curiously, Professor Butler spends little time exploring the incentives his proposal will create for those at the source of the perceived problem: the police and prosecutors who enforce the criminal law, and the legislators who hold the keys to change. Butler's vision is that, faced with widespread nullification, convictions for drug crimes will be sharply reduced, which will, in turn, force a rethinking of the war on drugs. Perhaps, Butler believes, this will lead legislators to divert money that is now being used to warehouse "criminals" into treatment and social programs, which will attack the sickness of addiction and the poverty that breeds it.

Perhaps—but don't bet on it. A more likely, and more sinister, outcome would be that police and prosecutors would simply abandon their efforts to enforce the drug laws in black neighborhoods. In most cities, there is no shortage of criminals to pursue or charges to file, so rational police and prosecutors will spend little time on drug crimes if the probable outcome is an acquittal against the evidence. To the honest citizens of drug-ravaged neighborhoods, the notion of being abandoned by the police until a drug war erupts or until an addict actually accosts them (i.e., until there is a "victim") should be a frightening one.

A second tangible harm is that prosecutors would change the way they pick juries. Prosecutors may not excuse jurors because of their race, but may remove jurors for cause if it appears they will not apply the law as given by the judge, and may challenge jurors peremptorily if they can articulate a race-neutral reason for the strike. Black jurors who become aware of Butler's proposal could surely be questioned about it during voir dire, and those who admit that they subscribe to the plan could almost certainly be removed for cause. Even if prospective jurors lied or were undecided about the wisdom of the proposal, their hesitancy to affirm that they would follow the law might be enough to permit a peremptory strike, despite the disparate impact the strikes would have on prospective black jurors. The results could only be that fewer black jurors would be seated, and many of the benefits of culturally diverse juries would be lost. * * *

By its terms, the plan is limited to nullification by African-American jurors in cases involving nonviolent, victimless crimes. These limits are by fiat; there is no logic to them. It takes little imagination to think of other groups who might also stake a claim to the use of nullification: Hispanic defendants could tell a tale of oppression by the criminal justice system, as could those of Chinese and Japanese background. Italian Americans and, more recently, Colombians, have claimed that they are disproportionately targeted for investigation when organized crime is involved; Arabic defendants believe that they are unfairly stereotyped as terrorists. Perhaps, most significantly, women have been poorly treated by the legal system throughout much of our history. Each of these groups could claim that they too have suffered systemic discrimination, and make cogent arguments about their perceived inability to bring about legal change through the legislative process.

It is hard to believe that supporters of the Butler plan could oppose strategic nullification by these groups. It is also hard to imagine, however, that reasonable people would favor a world in which each juror would begin deliberations with a presumption that defendants who are members of his or her own group should be acquitted, regardless of the evidence. The upheaval that would follow would surely prevent unjust convictions, but would do so at the cost of preventing a huge number of justified convictions. The impact would fall most heavily on future crime victims, whose perpetrators failed to learn the lesson that a prior nullification was supposed to teach. The proposal would also leave unprotected those who belong to no identifiable group (the homeless, non-citizens, the mentally impaired) who are in great need of the law's protection, but who are unlikely to be represented on juries. Jurors who come to the box with a mandate to protect their own may have no mercy to spare for those who do not fit in anywhere. * * *

Finally, even if strictly followed, the proposal still sends the wrong message to those with an interest in the criminal justice system—in other words, to all of us. It is a sad commentary on the state of race relations and legal thinking that the most obvious problem with Butler's plan needs to be made at all: deciding whether a defendant should go to prison or be set free should not depend on the color of his skin. Urging prospective jurors to return a verdict in a criminal case based on the race of the defendant is wrong, and neither good intentions nor strategic political considerations can change that.

Race-based decisionmaking by juries is wrong on so many levels it is hard to know where to begin. It is wrong because verdicts will inevitably be based on stereotypes that are harmful to all members of the group; wrong because those who are not part of the favored group are treated more harshly for reasons unrelated to their blameworthiness; wrong because it helps polarize a society that is already struggling with racial division; and most tragically, wrong because it raises the flag of surrender in the fight for equality. Butler's inescapable message is that equal treatment will never be possible, at least in court, so African Americans should take whatever small benefits they can grab on their own and be content with that. But those who have struggled for equal justice deserve better: The tangible gains that have been made over the last few decades in reducing racial bias in the criminal system should not be so casually dismissed by those who are too impatient to continue on the current course. * * *

# CHAPTER 33

# SENTENCING

■ ■ ■

The Eighth Amendment to the U.S. Constitution prohibits "cruel and unusual punishments." In *Coker v. Georgia*, the Supreme Court considers whether allowing the death penalty for rape constitutes cruel and unusual punishment. In *Ewing v. California*, the Court reviews the constitutionality of California's "Three Strikes and You're Out Law" which was meant to ensure that certain repeat felony offenders would receive harsher penalties than others. Finally, in *McCleskey v. Kemp*, the Court considers whether a sophisticated statistical study, which demonstrates a risk that race discrimination may have influenced Georgia's capital sentencing scheme, should render a death sentence unconstitutional under the Eighth and Fourteenth Amendments.

## COKER V. GEORGIA
Supreme Court of the United States
433 U.S. 584, 97 S.Ct. 2861, 53 L.Ed.2d 982 (1977)

JUSTICE WHITE announced the judgment of the Court. * * *

Georgia Code Ann. § 26–2001 (1972) provides that "[a] person convicted of rape shall be punished by death or by imprisonment for life, or by imprisonment for not less than one nor more than 20 years." * * * Petitioner Coker was convicted of rape and sentenced to death. Both the conviction and the sentence were affirmed by the Georgia Supreme Court. Coker was granted a writ of certiorari * * * limited to the single claim * * * that the punishment of death for rape violates the Eighth Amendment, which proscribes "cruel and unusual punishments" * * *.

While serving various sentences for murder, rape kidnaping, and aggravated assault, petitioner escaped from the Ware Correctional Institution near Waycross, Ga., on September 2, 1974. At approximately 11 o'clock that night, petitioner entered the house of Allen and Elnita Carver through an unlocked kitchen door. Threatening the couple with a "board," he tied up Mr. Carver in the bathroom, obtained a knife from the kitchen, and took Mr. Carver's money and the keys to the family car. Brandishing the knife and saying "you know what's going to happen to you if you try anything, don't you," Coker then raped Mrs. Carver. Soon thereafter, petitioner drove away in the Carver car, taking Mrs. Carver with him. Mr. Carver, freeing himself, notified the police; and not long thereafter petitioner was apprehended. Mrs. Carver was unharmed.

Petitioner was charged with escape, armed robbery, motor vehicle theft, kidnaping, and rape. * * * The jury returned a verdict of guilty, rejecting his general plea of insanity. A sentencing hearing was then conducted * * *. The jury's verdict on the rape count was death by electrocution.

* * * It is now settled that the death penalty is not invariably cruel and unusual punishment within the meaning of the Eighth Amendment; it is not inherently barbaric or an unacceptable mode of punishment for crime; neither is it always disproportionate to the crime for which it is imposed.

* * * [T]he Eighth Amendment bars not only those punishments that are "barbaric" but also those that are "excessive" in relation to the crime committed. Under *Gregg*, a punishment is "excessive" and unconstitutional if it (1) makes no measurable contribution to acceptable goals of punishment and hence is nothing more than the purposeless and needless imposition of pain and suffering; or (2) is grossly out of proportion to the severity of the crime. A punishment might fail the test on either ground. Furthermore, these Eighth Amendment judgments should not be, or appear to be, merely the subjective views of individual Justices; judgment should be informed by objective factors to the maximum possible extent. To this end, attention must be given to the public attitudes concerning a particular sentence—history and precedent, legislative attitudes, and the response of juries reflected in their sentencing decisions are to be consulted. In *Gregg*, after giving due regard to such sources, the Court's judgment was that the death penalty for deliberate murder was neither the purposeless imposition of severe punishment nor a punishment grossly disproportionate to the crime. But the Court reserved the question of the constitutionality of the death penalty when imposed for other crimes.

That question, with respect to rape of an adult woman, is now before us. We have concluded that a sentence of death is grossly disproportionate and excessive punishment for the crime of rape and is therefore forbidden by the Eighth Amendment as cruel and unusual punishment.

As advised by recent cases, we seek guidance in history and from the objective evidence of the country's present judgment concerning the acceptability of death as a penalty for rape of an adult woman. At no time in the last 50 years have a majority of the States authorized death as a punishment for rape. In 1925, 18 States, the District of Columbia, and the Federal Government authorized capital punishment for the rape of an adult female. By 1971 * * *, that number had declined, but not substantially, to 16 States plus the Federal Government. *Furman* then invalidated most of the capital punishment statutes in this country, including the rape statutes, because, among other reasons, of the manner in which the death penalty was imposed and utilized under those laws.

With their death penalty statutes for the most part invalidated, the States were faced with the choice of enacting modified capital punishment laws in an attempt to satisfy the requirements of *Furman* or of being satisfied with life imprisonment as the ultimate punishment for *any* offense. Thirty-five States immediately reinstituted the death penalty. * * *

In reviving death penalty laws to satisfy *Furman*'s mandate, none of the States that had not previously authorized death for rape chose to include rape among capital felonies. Of the 16 States in which rape had been a capital offense, only three provided the death penalty for rape of an adult woman in their revised statutes. * * *

The current judgment with respect to the death penalty for rape is not wholly unanimous among state legislatures, but it obviously weighs very heavily on the side of rejecting capital punishment as a suitable penalty for raping an adult woman.

It was also observed in *Gregg* that "[t]he jury . . . is a significant and reliable objective index of contemporary values because it is so directly involved" and that it is thus important to look to the sentencing decisions that juries have made in the course of assessing whether capital punishment is an appropriate penalty for the crime being tried. * * *

According to the factual submissions in this Court, out of all rape convictions in Georgia since 1973, * * * 63 cases had been reviewed by the Georgia Supreme Court as of the time of oral argument; and of these, 6 involved a death sentence, 1 of which was set aside, leaving 5 convicted rapists now under sentence of death in the State of Georgia. Georgia juries have thus sentenced rapists to death six times since 1973. This obviously is not a negligible number; and the State argues that as a practical matter juries simply reserve the extreme sanction for extreme cases of rape and that recent experience surely does not prove that jurors consider the death penalty to be a disproportionate punishment for every conceivable instance of rape, no matter how aggravated. Nevertheless, it is true that in the vast majority of cases, at least 9 out of 10, juries have not imposed the death sentence.

These recent events evidencing the attitude of state legislatures and sentencing juries do not wholly determine this controversy, for the Constitution contemplates that in the end our own judgment will be brought to bear on the question of the acceptability of the death penalty under the Eighth Amendment. Nevertheless, the legislative rejection of capital punishment for rape strongly confirms our own judgment, which is that death is indeed a disproportionate penalty for the crime of raping an adult woman. * * *

Rape is without doubt deserving of serious punishment; but in terms of moral depravity and of the injury to the person and to the public, it does not compare with murder, which does involve the unjustified taking of human life. Although it may be accompanied by another crime, rape by definition does not include the death of or even the serious injury to another person. The murderer kills; the rapist, if no more than that, does not. Life is over for the victim of the murderer; for the rape victim, life may not be nearly so happy as it was, but it is not over and normally is not beyond repair. We have the abiding conviction that the death penalty, which "is unique in its severity and irrevocability," is an excessive penalty for the rapist who, as such, does not take human life. * * *

The judgment of the Georgia Supreme Court upholding the death sentence is reversed, and the case is remanded to that court for further proceedings not inconsistent with this opinion.

*So ordered.*

CHIEF JUSTICE BURGER, with whom JUSTICE REHNQUIST joins, dissenting. * * *

Unlike the plurality, I would narrow the inquiry in this case to the question actually presented: Does the Eighth Amendment's ban against cruel and unusual punishment prohibit the State of Georgia from executing a person who has, within the space of three years, raped three separate women, killing one and attempting to kill another, who is serving prison terms exceeding his probable lifetime and who has not hesitated to escape confinement at the first available opportunity? Whatever one's view may be as to the State's constitutional power to impose the death penalty upon a rapist who stands before a court convicted for the first time, this case reveals a chronic rapist whose continuing danger to the community is abundantly clear.

* * * [O]nce the Court has held that "the punishment of death does not invariably violate the Constitution," it seriously impinges upon the State's legislative judgment to hold that it may not impose such sentence upon an individual who has shown total and repeated disregard for the welfare, safety, personal integrity, and human worth of others, and who seemingly cannot be deterred from continuing such conduct. I therefore would hold that the death sentence here imposed is within the power reserved to the State and leave for another day the question of whether such sanction would be proper under other circumstances. * * *

[JUSTICE BRENNAN's concurring opinion, JUSTICE MARSHALL's concurring opinion, and JUSTICE POWELL's concurring opinion have been omitted.]

## NOTE

Prior to the Court's decision in *Coker*, Black men were substantially more likely than other men to receive the death penalty for raping White women. Between 1930 and 1972, 455 people were executed for rape. U.S. DEP'T OF JUSTICE BUREAU OF PRISONS, NATIONAL PRISONER STATISTICS, BULLETIN No. 45, CAPITAL PUNISHMENT 1930–1968 (1969). Of those, 405 or 89.1 percent were Black. *Id.* Black men were sentenced to death for raping White women approximately 18 times more often than any other combination of defendant and victim in rape cases. Marvin E. Wolfgang & Marc Riedel, *Race, Judicial Discretion, and the Death Penalty*, 407 ANNALS OF THE AM. ACAD. OF POL. AND SOC. SCI. 119, 126–33 (1973), cited in a brief located at http://www.death penaltyinfo.org/ACLULDF.pdf at 12.

In *Kennedy v. Louisiana*, 554 U.S. 407 (2008), the Supreme Court revisited the question of whether the death penalty for the crime of rape violates the Eighth Amendment's prohibition against cruel and unusual punishment. This case involved the violent rape and sodomy of an eight year old girl. In a 5 to 4 decision, Justice Kennedy explained that since there was no national consensus that the death penalty was an appropriate punishment for child rape, the death penalty was disproportionate punishment. The Court concluded that when crimes against individual people are at issue, "the death penalty should not be expanded to instances where the victim's life was not taken." *Id.* at 437.

## EWING V. CALIFORNIA

Supreme Court of the United States
538 U.S. 11, 123 S.Ct. 1179, 155 L.Ed.2d 108 (2003)

JUSTICE O'CONNOR announced the judgment of the Court and delivered an opinion in which the Chief Justice and JUSTICE KENNEDY join.

In this case, we decide whether the Eighth Amendment prohibits the State of California from sentencing a repeat felon to a prison term of 25 years to life under the State's "Three Strikes and You're Out" law. California's three strikes law reflects a shift in the State's sentencing policies toward incapacitating and deterring repeat offenders who threaten the public safety. The law was designed "to ensure longer prison sentences and greater punishment for those who commit a felony and have been previously convicted of serious and/or violent felony offenses." * * *

> [Under California's three strikes law as initially enacted, a defendant with two or more prior "serious" or "violent" felony convictions, who was convicted of a third felony (not necessarily a serious or violent felony), faced a mandatory sentence of twenty-five years to life.]

On parole from a 9-year prison term, petitioner Gary Ewing walked into the pro shop of the El Segundo Golf Course in Los Angeles County on

March 12, 2000. He walked out with three golf clubs, priced at $399 apiece, concealed in his pants leg. A shop employee, whose suspicions were aroused when he observed Ewing limp out of the pro shop, telephoned the police. The police apprehended Ewing in the parking lot.

Ewing is no stranger to the criminal justice system. In 1984, at the age of 22, he pleaded guilty to theft. The court sentenced him to six months in jail (suspended), three years' probation, and a $300 fine. In 1988, he was convicted of felony grand theft auto and sentenced to one year in jail and three years' probation. After Ewing completed probation, however, the sentencing court reduced the crime to a misdemeanor, permitted Ewing to withdraw his guilty plea, and dismissed the case. In 1990, he was convicted of petty theft with a prior and sentenced to 60 days in the county jail and three years' probation. In 1992, Ewing was convicted of battery and sentenced to 30 days in the county jail and two years' summary probation. One month later, he was convicted of theft and sentenced to 10 days in the county jail and 12 months' probation. In January 1993, Ewing was convicted of burglary and sentenced to 60 days in the county jail and one year's summary probation. In February 1993, he was convicted of possessing drug paraphernalia and sentenced to six months in the county jail and three years' probation. In July 1993, he was convicted of appropriating lost property and sentenced to 10 days in the county jail and two years' summary probation. In September 1993, he was convicted of unlawfully possessing a firearm and trespassing and sentenced to 30 days in the county jail and one year's probation.

In October and November 1993, Ewing committed three burglaries and one robbery at a Long Beach, California, apartment complex over a 5-week period. He awakened one of his victims, asleep on her living room sofa, as he tried to disconnect her video cassette recorder from the television in that room. When she screamed, Ewing ran out the front door. On another occasion, Ewing accosted a victim in the mailroom of the apartment complex. Ewing claimed to have a gun and ordered the victim to hand over his wallet. When the victim resisted, Ewing produced a knife and forced the victim back to the apartment itself. While Ewing rifled through the bedroom, the victim fled the apartment screaming for help. Ewing absconded with the victim's money and credit cards.

On December 9, 1993, Ewing was arrested on the premises of the apartment complex for trespassing and lying to a police officer. The knife used in the robbery and a glass cocaine pipe were later found in the back seat of the patrol car used to transport Ewing to the police station. A jury convicted Ewing of first-degree robbery and three counts of residential burglary. Sentenced to nine years and eight months in prison, Ewing was paroled in 1999.

Only 10 months later, Ewing stole the golf clubs at issue in this case. He was charged with, and ultimately convicted of, one count of felony grand theft of personal property in excess of $400. As required by the three strikes law, the prosecutor formally alleged, and the trial court later found, that Ewing had been convicted previously of four serious or violent felonies for the three burglaries and the robbery in the Long Beach apartment complex.

At the sentencing hearing, Ewing asked the court to reduce the conviction for grand theft, a "wobbler" under California law, to a misdemeanor so as to avoid a three strikes sentence.[a] Ewing also asked the trial court to exercise its discretion to dismiss the allegations of some or all of his prior serious or violent felony convictions, again for purposes of avoiding a three strikes sentence. Before sentencing Ewing, the trial court took note of his entire criminal history, including the fact that he was on parole when he committed his latest offense. The court also heard arguments from defense counsel and a plea from Ewing himself.

In the end, the trial judge determined that the grand theft should remain a felony. The court also ruled that the four prior strikes for the three burglaries and the robbery in Long Beach should stand. As a newly convicted felon with two or more "serious" or "violent" felony convictions in his past, Ewing was sentenced under the three strikes law to 25 years to life.

The California Court of Appeal affirmed in an unpublished opinion. * * * The Supreme Court of California denied Ewing's petition for review, and we granted certiorari. We now affirm.

The Eighth Amendment, which forbids cruel and unusual punishments, contains a "narrow proportionality principle" that "applies to noncapital sentences." We have most recently addressed the proportionality principle as applied to terms of years in a series of cases beginning with *Rummel v. Estelle.*

In *Rummel,* we held that it did not violate the Eighth Amendment for a State to sentence a three-time offender to life in prison with the possibility of parole. Like Ewing, Rummel was sentenced to a lengthy prison term under a recidivism statute. Rummel's two prior offenses were a 1964 felony for "fraudulent use of a credit card to obtain $80 worth of goods or services," and a 1969 felony conviction for "passing a forged check in the amount of $28.36." His triggering offense was a conviction for felony theft—"obtaining $120.75 by false pretenses."

This Court ruled that "having twice imprisoned him for felonies, Texas was entitled to place upon Rummel the onus of one who is simply unable to bring his conduct within the social norms prescribed by the criminal law

---

[a]     Under California law, certain offenses can be classified as either felonies or misdemeanors. These offenses are known as "wobblers." A wobbler is presumptively a felony unless the prosecution or the trial court exercises its discretion to reduce the wobbler to a misdemeanor.

of the State." The recidivism statute "is nothing more than a societal decision that when such a person commits yet another felony, he should be subjected to the admittedly serious penalty of incarceration for life, subject only to the State's judgment as to whether to grant him parole." We noted that this Court "has on occasion stated that the Eighth Amendment prohibits imposition of a sentence that is grossly disproportionate to the severity of the crime." But "outside the context of capital punishment, successful challenges to the proportionality of particular sentences have been exceedingly rare."

Although we stated that the proportionality principle "would . . . come into play in the extreme example . . . if a legislature made overtime parking a felony punishable by life imprisonment," we held that "the mandatory life sentence imposed upon this petitioner does not constitute cruel and unusual punishment under the Eighth and Fourteenth Amendments." * * *

Three years after *Rummel*, in *Solem v. Helm*, we held that the Eighth Amendment prohibited "a life sentence without possibility of parole for a seventh nonviolent felony." The triggering offense in *Solem* was "uttering a 'no account' check for $100." We specifically stated that the Eighth Amendment's ban on cruel and unusual punishments "prohibits . . . sentences that are disproportionate to the crime committed," and that the "constitutional principle of proportionality has been recognized explicitly in this Court for almost a century." The *Solem* Court then explained that three factors may be relevant to a determination of whether a sentence is so disproportionate that it violates the Eighth Amendment: "(i) the gravity of the offense and the harshness of the penalty; (ii) the sentences imposed on other criminals in the same jurisdiction; and (iii) the sentences imposed for commission of the same crime in other jurisdictions."

Applying these factors in *Solem*, we struck down the defendant's sentence of life without parole. We specifically noted the contrast between that sentence and the sentence in *Rummel*, pursuant to which the defendant was eligible for parole. Indeed, we explicitly declined to overrule *Rummel*: "Our conclusion today is not inconsistent with *Rummel v. Estelle*."

Eight years after *Solem*, we grappled with the proportionality issue again in *Harmelin v. Michigan*. *Harmelin* was not a recidivism case, but rather involved a first-time offender convicted of possessing 672 grams of cocaine. He was sentenced to life in prison without possibility of parole. A majority of the Court rejected Harmelin's claim that his sentence was so grossly disproportionate that it violated the Eighth Amendment. The Court, however, could not agree on why his proportionality argument failed. * * *

Justice Kennedy, joined by two other Members of the Court, concurred in part and concurred in the judgment. Justice Kennedy specifically recognized that "the Eighth Amendment proportionality principle also applies to noncapital sentences." He then identified four principles of proportionality review—"the primacy of the legislature, the variety of legitimate penological schemes, the nature of our federal system, and the requirement that proportionality review be guided by objective factors"— that "inform the final one: The Eighth Amendment does not require strict proportionality between crime and sentence. Rather, it forbids only extreme sentences that are grossly disproportionate to the crime." Justice Kennedy's concurrence also stated that *Solem* "did not mandate" comparative analysis "within and between jurisdictions."

The proportionality principles in our cases distilled in Justice Kennedy's concurrence guide our application of the Eighth Amendment in the new context that we are called upon to consider.

For many years, most States have had laws providing for enhanced sentencing of repeat offenders. Yet between 1993 and 1995, three strikes laws effected a sea change in criminal sentencing throughout the Nation. These laws responded to widespread public concerns about crime by targeting the class of offenders who pose the greatest threat to public safety: career criminals. * * *

Throughout the States, legislatures enacting three strikes laws made a deliberate policy choice that individuals who have repeatedly engaged in serious or violent criminal behavior, and whose conduct has not been deterred by more conventional approaches to punishment, must be isolated from society in order to protect the public safety. Though three strikes laws may be relatively new, our tradition of deferring to state legislatures in making and implementing such important policy decisions is longstanding.

Our traditional deference to legislative policy choices finds a corollary in the principle that the Constitution "does not mandate adoption of any one penological theory." A sentence can have a variety of justifications, such as incapacitation, deterrence, retribution, or rehabilitation. Some or all of these justifications may play a role in a State's sentencing scheme. Selecting the sentencing rationales is generally a policy choice to be made by state legislatures, not federal courts.

When the California Legislature enacted the three strikes law, it made a judgment that protecting the public safety requires incapacitating criminals who have already been convicted of at least one serious or violent crime. Nothing in the Eighth Amendment prohibits California from making that choice. To the contrary, our cases establish that "States have a valid interest in deterring and segregating habitual criminals." Recidivism has long been recognized as a legitimate basis for increased punishment.

California's justification is no pretext. Recidivism is a serious public safety concern in California and throughout the Nation. According to a recent report, approximately 67 percent of former inmates released from state prisons were charged with at least one "serious" new crime within three years of their release. In particular, released property offenders like Ewing had higher recidivism rates than those released after committing violent, drug, or public-order offenses. * * *

The State's interest in deterring crime also lends some support to the three strikes law. We have long viewed both incapacitation and deterrence as rationales for recidivism statutes * * *. Four years after the passage of California's three strikes law, the recidivism rate of parolees returned to prison for the commission of a new crime dropped by nearly 25 percent. Even more dramatically:

> [A]n unintended but positive consequence of "Three Strikes" has been the impact on parolees leaving the state. More California parolees are now leaving the state than parolees from other jurisdictions entering California. This striking turnaround started in 1994. It was the first time more parolees left the state than entered since 1976. This trend has continued and in 1997 more than 1,000 net parolees left California.

To be sure, California's three strikes law has sparked controversy. Critics have doubted the law's wisdom, cost-efficiency, and effectiveness in reaching its goals. This criticism is appropriately directed at the legislature, which has primary responsibility for making the difficult policy choices that underlie any criminal sentencing scheme. We do not sit as a "superlegislature" to second-guess these policy choices. It is enough that the State of California has a reasonable basis for believing that dramatically enhanced sentences for habitual felons "advances the goals of [its] criminal justice system in any substantial way."

Against this backdrop, we consider Ewing's claim that his three strikes sentence of 25 years to life is unconstitutionally disproportionate to his offense of "shoplifting three golf clubs." We first address the gravity of the offense compared to the harshness of the penalty. At the threshold, we note that Ewing incorrectly frames the issue. The gravity of his offense was not merely "shoplifting three golf clubs." Rather, Ewing was convicted of felony grand theft for stealing nearly $1,200 worth of merchandise after previously having been convicted of at least two "violent" or "serious" felonies. * * *

In weighing the gravity of Ewing's offense, we must place on the scales not only his current felony, but also his long history of felony recidivism. Any other approach would fail to accord proper deference to the policy judgments that find expression in the legislature's choice of sanctions. In imposing a three strikes sentence, the State's interest is not merely punishing the offense of conviction, or the "triggering" offense: "It is in addition the interest . . . in dealing in a harsher manner with those who by repeated criminal acts have shown that they are simply incapable of conforming to the norms of society as established by its criminal law." To give full effect to the State's choice of this legitimate penological goal, our proportionality review of Ewing's sentence must take that goal into account.

Ewing's sentence is justified by the State's public-safety interest in incapacitating and deterring recidivist felons, and amply supported by his own long, serious criminal record. * * * To be sure, Ewing's sentence is a long one. But it reflects a rational legislative judgment, entitled to deference, that offenders who have committed serious or violent felonies and who continue to commit felonies must be incapacitated. * * *

We hold that Ewing's sentence of 25 years to life in prison, imposed for the offense of felony grand theft under the three strikes law, is not grossly disproportionate and therefore does not violate the Eighth Amendment's prohibition on cruel and unusual punishments. The judgment of the California Court of Appeal is affirmed.

*It is so ordered.*

[JUSTICE SCALIA's concurring opinion, JUSTICE THOMAS' concurring opinion, JUSTICE STEVENS' dissenting opinion, and JUSTICE BREYER's dissenting opinion have been omitted.]

## NOTE

In 2012, California voters passed Proposition 36, which amended the Three Strikes law to require the third felony, as well as the first and second, to be a "serious" or "violent" felony. Tracey Kaplan, *Proposition 36: Voters overwhelmingly ease Three Strikes law*, SAN JOSE MERCURY NEWS, Nov. 6, 2012, http://www.mercurynews.com/ci_21943951/prop-36-huge-lead-early-returns?source=infinite or https://perma.cc/X6CT-UH89; *see also* CAL. PENAL CODE §§ 667, 1170.12, 1170.125, 1170.126 (West 2014).

## MCCLESKEY V. KEMP

Supreme Court of the United States
481 U.S. 279, 107 S.Ct. 1756, 95 L.Ed.2d 262 (1987)

JUSTICE POWELL delivered the opinion of the Court.

This case presents the question whether a complex statistical study that indicates a risk that racial considerations enter into capital sentencing determinations proves that petitioner McCleskey's capital sentence is unconstitutional under the Eighth or Fourteenth Amendment.

McCleskey, a black man, was convicted of two counts of armed robbery and one count of murder in the Superior Court of Fulton County, Georgia, on October 12, 1978. McCleskey's convictions arose out of the robbery of a furniture store and the killing of a white police officer during the course of the robbery. The evidence at trial indicated that McCleskey and three accomplices planned and carried out the robbery. All four were armed. * * * During the course of the robbery, a police officer, answering a silent alarm, entered the store through the front door. As he was walking down the center aisle of the store, two shots were fired. Both struck the officer. One hit him in the face and killed him.

Several weeks later, McCleskey was arrested in connection with an unrelated offense. He confessed that he had participated in the furniture store robbery, but denied that he had shot the police officer. At trial, the State introduced evidence that at least one of the bullets that struck the officer was fired from a .38 caliber Rossi revolver. This description matched the description of the gun that McCleskey had carried during the robbery. The State also introduced the testimony of two witnesses who had heard McCleskey admit to the shooting.

The jury convicted McCleskey of murder. * * * The jury in this case found two aggravating circumstances to exist beyond a reasonable doubt: the murder was committed during the course of an armed robbery; and the murder was committed upon a peace officer engaged in the performance of his duties. * * * McCleskey offered no mitigating evidence. The jury recommended that he be sentenced to death on the murder charge and to consecutive life sentences on the armed robbery charges. The court followed the jury's recommendation and sentenced McCleskey to death.

On appeal, the Supreme Court of Georgia affirmed the convictions and the sentences. * * * McCleskey next filed a petition for a writ of habeas corpus in the Federal District Court for the Northern District of Georgia. His petition raised 18 claims, one of which was that the Georgia capital sentencing process is administered in a racially discriminatory manner in violation of the Eighth and Fourteenth Amendments to the United States Constitution. In support of his claim, McCleskey proffered a statistical study performed by Professors David C. Baldus, Charles Pulaski, and George Woodworth (the Baldus study) that purports to show a disparity in the imposition of the death sentence in Georgia based on the race of the murder victim and, to a lesser extent, the race of the defendant. The Baldus study is actually two sophisticated statistical studies that examine over 2,000 murder cases that occurred in Georgia during the 1970's. The raw numbers collected by Professor Baldus indicate that defendants charged with killing white persons received the death penalty in 11% of the cases, but defendants charged with killing blacks received the death penalty in only 1% of the cases. The raw numbers also indicate a reverse racial disparity according to the race of the defendant: 4% of the black defendants received the death penalty, as opposed to 7% of the white defendants.

Baldus also divided the cases according to the combination of the race of the defendant and the race of the victim. He found that the death penalty was assessed in 22% of the cases involving black defendants and white victims; 8% of the cases involving white defendants and white victims; 1% of the cases involving black defendants and black victims; and 3% of the cases involving white defendants and black victims. Similarly, Baldus found that prosecutors sought the death penalty in 70% of the cases involving black defendants and white victims; 32% of the cases involving white defendants and white victims; 15% of the cases involving black defendants and black victims; and 19% of the cases involving white defendants and black victims.

Baldus subjected his data to an extensive analysis, taking account of 230 variables that could have explained the disparities on nonracial grounds. One of his models concludes that, even after taking account of 39 nonracial variables, defendants charged with killing white victims were 4.3 times as likely to receive a death sentence as defendants charged with killing blacks. According to this model, black defendants were 1.1 times as likely to receive a death sentence as other defendants. Thus, the Baldus study indicates that black defendants, such as McCleskey, who kill white victims have the greatest likelihood of receiving the death penalty.

The District Court * * * denied the petition * * *. The Court of Appeals for the Eleventh Circuit, sitting en banc, * * * affirmed the denial by the District Court of McCleskey's petition for a writ of habeas corpus * * *. We granted certiorari and now affirm.

McCleskey's first claim is that the Georgia capital punishment statute violates the Equal Protection Clause of the Fourteenth Amendment.[7] He argues that race has infected the administration of Georgia's statute in two ways: persons who murder whites are more likely to be sentenced to death than persons who murder blacks, and black murderers are more likely to be sentenced to death than white murderers. As a black defendant who killed a white victim, McCleskey claims that the Baldus study demonstrates that he was discriminated against because of his race and because of the race of his victim. * * * We agree with the Court of Appeals, and every other court that has considered such a challenge, that this claim must fail.

Our analysis begins with the basic principle that a defendant who alleges an equal protection violation has the burden of proving "the existence of purposeful discrimination." A corollary to this principle is that a criminal defendant must prove that the purposeful discrimination "had a discriminatory effect" on him. Thus, to prevail under the Equal Protection Clause, McCleskey must prove that the decisionmakers in *his* case acted

---

[7]    * * * As did the Court of Appeals, we assume the study is valid statistically without reviewing the factual findings of the District Court. Our assumption that the Baldus study is statistically valid does not include the assumption that the study shows that racial considerations actually enter into any sentencing decisions in Georgia. Even a sophisticated multiple-regression analysis such as the Baldus study can only demonstrate a *risk* that the factor of race entered into some capital sentencing decisions and a necessarily lesser risk that race entered into any particular sentencing decision.

with discriminatory purpose. He offers no evidence specific to his own case that would support an inference that racial considerations played a part in his sentence. Instead, he relies solely on the Baldus study. McCleskey argues that the Baldus study compels an inference that his sentence rests on purposeful discrimination. McCleskey's claim that these statistics are sufficient proof of discrimination, without regard to the facts of a particular case, would extend to all capital cases in Georgia, at least where the victim was white and the defendant is black.

The Court has accepted statistics as proof of intent to discriminate in certain limited contexts. First, this Court has accepted statistical disparities as proof of an equal protection violation in the selection of the jury venire in a particular district. Although statistical proof normally must present a "stark" pattern to be accepted as the sole proof of discriminatory intent under the Constitution, "because of the nature of the jury-selection task, ... we have permitted a finding of constitutional violation even when the statistical pattern does not approach [such] extremes." Second, this Court has accepted statistics in the form of multiple-regression analysis to prove statutory violations under Title VII of the Civil Rights Act of 1964.

But the nature of the capital sentencing decision, and the relationship of the statistics to that decision, are fundamentally different from the corresponding elements in the venire-selection or Title VII cases. Most importantly, each particular decision to impose the death penalty is made by a petit jury selected from a properly constituted venire. Each jury is unique in its composition, and the Constitution requires that its decision rest on consideration of innumerable factors that vary according to the characteristics of the individual defendant and the facts of the particular capital offense. Thus, the application of an inference drawn from the general statistics to a specific decision in a trial and sentencing simply is not comparable to the application of an inference drawn from general statistics to a specific venire-selection or Title VII case. In those cases, the statistics relate to fewer entities, and fewer variables are relevant to the challenged decisions.

* * * McCleskey's statistical proffer must be viewed in the context of his challenge. McCleskey challenges decisions at the heart of the State's criminal justice system. "One of society's most basic tasks is that of protecting the lives of its citizens and one of the most basic ways in which it achieves the task is through criminal laws against murder." Implementation of these laws necessarily requires discretionary judgments. Because discretion is essential to the criminal justice process, we would demand exceptionally clear proof before we would infer that the discretion has been abused. The unique nature of the decisions at issue in this case also counsels against adopting such an inference from the disparities indicated by the Baldus study. Accordingly, we hold that the

Baldus study is clearly insufficient to support an inference that any of the decisionmakers in McCleskey's case acted with discriminatory purpose.

McCleskey also suggests that the Baldus study proves that the State as a whole has acted with a discriminatory purpose. He appears to argue that the State has violated the Equal Protection Clause by adopting the capital punishment statute and allowing it to remain in force despite its allegedly discriminatory application. But "discriminatory purpose . . . implies more than intent as volition or intent as awareness of consequences. It implies that the decisionmaker, in this case a state legislature, selected or reaffirmed a particular course of action at least in part because of, not merely in spite of, its adverse effects upon an identifiable group." For this claim to prevail, McCleskey would have to prove that the Georgia Legislature enacted or maintained the death penalty statute *because of* an anticipated racially discriminatory effect. * * * There [is] no evidence * * * that the Georgia Legislature enacted the capital punishment statute to further a racially discriminatory purpose.

Nor has McCleskey demonstrated that the legislature maintains the capital punishment statute because of the racially disproportionate impact suggested by the Baldus study. * * * Accordingly, we reject McCleskey's equal protection claims.

McCleskey also argues that the Baldus study demonstrates that the Georgia capital sentencing system violates the Eighth Amendment. * * * [McCleskey] contends that the Georgia capital punishment system is arbitrary and capricious in *application*, and therefore his sentence is excessive, because racial considerations may influence capital sentencing decisions in Georgia. * * *

To evaluate McCleskey's challenge, we must examine exactly what the Baldus study may show. Even Professor Baldus does not contend that his statistics *prove* that race enters into any capital sentencing decisions or that race was a factor in McCleskey's particular case. Statistics at most may show only a likelihood that a particular factor entered into some decisions. There is, of course, some risk of racial prejudice influencing a jury's decision in a criminal case. There are similar risks that other kinds of prejudice will influence other criminal trials. The question "is at what point that risk becomes constitutionally unacceptable." McCleskey asks us to accept the likelihood allegedly shown by the Baldus study as the constitutional measure of an unacceptable risk of racial prejudice influencing capital sentencing decisions. This we decline to do. * * *

McCleskey's argument that the Constitution condemns the discretion allowed decisionmakers in the Georgia capital sentencing system is antithetical to the fundamental role of discretion in our criminal justice system. Discretion in the criminal justice system offers substantial benefits to the criminal defendant. Not only can a jury decline to impose the death sentence, it can decline to convict or choose to convict of a lesser offense. * * * Similarly, the capacity of prosecutorial discretion to provide individualized justice is "firmly entrenched in American law." * * * Of course, "the power to be lenient [also] is the power to discriminate," but a capital punishment system that did not allow for discretionary acts of leniency "would be totally alien to our notions of criminal justice."

At most, the Baldus study indicates a discrepancy that appears to correlate with race. Apparent disparities in sentencing are an inevitable part of our criminal justice system. * * * In light of the safeguards designed to minimize racial bias in the process, the fundamental value of jury trial in our criminal justice system, and the benefits that discretion provides to criminal defendants, we hold that the Baldus study does not demonstrate a constitutionally significant risk of racial bias affecting the Georgia capital sentencing process.

Two additional concerns inform our decision in this case. First, McCleskey's claim, taken to its logical conclusion, throws into serious question the principles that underlie our entire criminal justice system. The Eighth Amendment is not limited in application to capital punishment, but applies to all penalties. Thus, if we accepted McCleskey's claim that racial bias has impermissibly tainted the capital sentencing decision, we could soon be faced with similar claims as to other types of penalty. Moreover, the claim that his sentence rests on the irrelevant factor of race easily could be extended to apply to claims based on unexplained discrepancies that correlate to membership in other minority groups, and even to gender. * * * Also, there is no logical reason that such a claim need be limited to racial or sexual bias. If arbitrary and capricious punishment is the touchstone under the Eighth Amendment, such a claim could—at least in theory—be based upon any arbitrary variable, such as the defendant's facial characteristics, or the physical attractiveness of the defendant or the victim, that some statistical study indicates may be influential in jury decisionmaking. As these examples illustrate, there is no limiting principle to the type of challenge brought by McCleskey. * * *

Second, McCleskey's arguments are best presented to the legislative bodies. It is not the responsibility—or indeed even the right—of this Court to determine the appropriate punishment for particular crimes. It is the legislatures, the elected representatives of the people, that are "constituted to respond to the will and consequently the moral values of the people." * * * Despite McCleskey's wide-ranging arguments that basically challenge the validity of capital punishment in our multiracial society, the only question before us is whether in his case the law of Georgia was properly applied. We agree with the District Court and the Court of Appeals for the Eleventh Circuit that this was carefully and correctly done in this case.

Accordingly, we affirm the judgment of the Court of Appeals for the Eleventh Circuit.

*It is so ordered.*

JUSTICE BRENNAN, with whom JUSTICE MARSHALL joins, and with whom JUSTICE BLACKMUN and JUSTICE STEVENS join * * *, dissenting.

* * * Since *Furman v. Georgia*, the Court has been concerned with the *risk* of the imposition of an arbitrary sentence, rather than the proven fact of one. * * * Defendants challenging their death sentences thus never have had to prove that impermissible considerations have actually infected sentencing decisions. We have required instead that they establish that the system under which they were sentenced posed a significant risk of such an occurrence. McCleskey's claim does differ, however, in one respect from these earlier cases: it is the first to base a challenge not on speculation about how a system *might* operate, but on empirical documentation of how it *does* operate.

The Court assumes the statistical validity of the Baldus study, and acknowledges that McCleskey has demonstrated a risk that racial prejudice plays a role in capital sentencing in Georgia. Nonetheless, it finds the probability of prejudice insufficient to create constitutional concern. Close analysis of the Baldus study, however, in light of both statistical principles and human experience, reveals that the risk that race influenced McCleskey's sentence is intolerable by any imaginable standard.

The Baldus study indicates that, after taking into account some 230 nonracial factors that might legitimately influence a sentencer, the jury *more likely than not* would have spared McCleskey's life had his victim been black. * * * [In cases] in which the jury has considerable discretion in choosing a sentence * * * death is imposed in 34% of white-victim crimes and 14% of black-victim crimes, a difference of 139% in the rate of imposition of the death penalty. In other words, just under 59%—almost 6 in 10—defendants comparable to McCleskey would not have received the death penalty if their victims had been black.

Furthermore, even examination of the sentencing system as a whole, factoring in those cases in which the jury exercises little discretion, indicates the influence of race on capital sentencing. For the Georgia system as a whole, race accounts for a six percentage point difference in the rate at which capital punishment is imposed. Since death is imposed in 11% of all white-victim cases, the rate in comparably aggravated black-victim cases is 5%. The rate of capital sentencing in a white-victim case is thus 120% greater than the rate in a black-victim case. Put another way, over half—55%—of defendants in white-victim crimes in Georgia would not have been sentenced to die if their victims had been black. * * *

These adjusted figures are only the most conservative indication of the risk that race will influence the death sentences of defendants in Georgia. Data unadjusted for the mitigating or aggravating effect of other factors show an even more pronounced disparity by race. The capital sentencing rate for all white-victim cases was almost *11 times* greater than the rate for black-victim cases. Furthermore, blacks who kill whites are sentenced to death at nearly *22 times* the rate of blacks who kill blacks, and more than *7 times* the rate of whites who kill blacks. In addition, prosecutors seek the death penalty for 70% of black defendants with white victims, but for only 15% of black defendants with black victims, and only 19% of white defendants with black victims. Since our decision upholding the Georgia capital sentencing system in *Gregg*, the State has executed seven persons. All of the seven were convicted of killing whites, and six of the seven executed were black. Such execution figures are especially striking in light of the fact that, during the period encompassed by the Baldus study, only 9.2% of Georgia homicides involved black defendants and white victims, while 60.7% involved black victims. * * *

The statistical evidence in this case thus relentlessly documents the risk that McCleskey's sentence was influenced by racial considerations. This evidence shows that there is a better than even chance in Georgia that race will influence the decision to impose the death penalty: a majority of defendants in white-victim crimes would not have been sentenced to die if their victims had been black. In determining whether this risk is acceptable, our judgment must be shaped by the awareness that "the risk of racial prejudice infecting a capital sentencing proceeding is especially serious in light of the complete finality of the death sentence," and that "it is of vital importance to the defendant and to the community that any decision to impose the death sentence be, and appear to be, based on reason rather than caprice or emotion." In determining the guilt of a defendant, a State must prove its case beyond a reasonable doubt. That is, we refuse to convict if the chance of error is simply less likely than not. Surely, we should not be willing to take a person's life if the chance that his death sentence was irrationally imposed is *more* likely than not. In light of the gravity of the interest at stake, petitioner's statistics on their face are a powerful demonstration of the type of risk that our Eighth Amendment jurisprudence has consistently condemned.

Evaluation of McCleskey's evidence cannot rest solely on the numbers themselves. We must also ask whether the conclusion suggested by those numbers is consonant with our understanding of history and human experience. Georgia's legacy of a race-conscious criminal justice system, as well as this Court's own recognition of the persistent danger that racial attitudes may affect criminal proceedings, indicates that McCleskey's claim is not a fanciful product of mere statistical artifice.

For many years, Georgia operated openly and formally precisely the type of dual system the evidence shows is still effectively in place. The criminal law expressly differentiated between crimes committed by and against blacks and whites, distinctions whose lineage traced back to the time of slavery. During the colonial period, black slaves who killed whites in Georgia, regardless of whether in self-defense or in defense of another, were automatically executed.

By the time of the Civil War, a dual system of crime and punishment was well established in Georgia. The state criminal code contained separate sections for "Slaves and Free Persons of Color" and for all other persons. The code provided, for instance, for an automatic death sentence for murder committed by blacks, but declared that anyone else convicted of murder might receive life imprisonment if the conviction were founded solely on circumstantial testimony *or* simply if the jury so recommended. The code established that the rape of a free white female by a black "shall be" punishable by death. However, rape by anyone else of a free white female was punishable by a prison term not less than 2 nor more than 20 years. The rape of *blacks* was punishable "by fine and imprisonment, at the discretion of the court." A black convicted of assaulting a free white person with intent to murder could be put to death at the discretion of the court, but the same offense committed against a black, slave or free, was classified as a "minor" offense whose punishment lay in the discretion of the court, as long as such punishment did not "extend to life, limb, or health." Assault with intent to murder by a white person was punishable by a prison term of from 2 to 10 years. * * *

The ongoing influence of history is acknowledged, as the majority observes, by our " 'unceasing efforts' to eradicate racial prejudice from our criminal justice system." These efforts, however, signify not the elimination of the problem but its persistence. Our cases reflect a realization of the myriad of opportunities for racial considerations to influence criminal proceedings * * *.

The discretion afforded prosecutors and jurors in the Georgia capital sentencing system creates such opportunities. No guidelines govern prosecutorial decisions to seek the death penalty, and Georgia provides juries with no list of aggravating and mitigating factors, nor any standard for balancing them against one another. * * * The Georgia sentencing system therefore provides considerable opportunity for racial considerations, however subtle and unconscious, to influence charging and sentencing decisions.

History and its continuing legacy thus buttress the probative force of McCleskey's statistics. Formal dual criminal laws may no longer be in effect, and intentional discrimination may no longer be prominent. Nonetheless * * * "subtle, less consciously held racial attitudes" continue to be of concern and the Georgia system gives such attitudes considerable room to operate.

* * * Enhanced willingness to impose the death sentence on black defendants, or diminished willingness to render such a sentence when blacks are victims, reflects a devaluation of the lives of black persons. When confronted with evidence that race more likely than not plays such a role in a capital sentencing system, it is plainly insufficient to say that the importance of discretion demands that the risk be higher before we will act—for in such a case the very end that discretion is designed to serve is being undermined. * * *

The Court next states that its unwillingness to regard petitioner's evidence as sufficient is based in part on the fear that recognition of McCleskey's claim would open the door to widespread challenges to all aspects of criminal sentencing. Taken on its face, such a statement seems to suggest a fear of too much justice. Yet surely the majority would acknowledge that if striking evidence indicated that other minority groups, or women, or even persons with blond hair, were disproportionately sentenced to death, such a state of affairs would be repugnant to deeply rooted conceptions of fairness. The prospect that there may be more widespread abuse than McCleskey documents may be dismaying, but it does not justify complete abdication of our judicial role. The Constitution was framed fundamentally as a bulwark against governmental power, and preventing the arbitrary administration of punishment is a basic ideal of any society that purports to be governed by the rule of law. * * *

The Court also maintains that accepting McCleskey's claim would pose a threat to all sentencing because of the prospect that a correlation might be demonstrated between sentencing outcomes and other personal characteristics. Again, such a view is indifferent to the considerations that enter into a determination whether punishment is "cruel and unusual." Race is a consideration whose influence is expressly constitutionally proscribed. We have expressed a moral commitment, as embodied in our fundamental law, that this specific characteristic should not be the basis for allotting burdens and benefits. * * * That a decision to impose the death penalty could be influenced by *race* is thus a particularly repugnant prospect, and evidence that race may play even a modest role in levying a death sentence should be enough to characterize that sentence as "cruel and unusual." * * *

Finally, the Court justifies its rejection of McCleskey's claim by cautioning against usurpation of the legislatures' role in devising and monitoring criminal punishment. The Court is, of course, correct to emphasize the gravity of constitutional intervention and the importance that it be sparingly employed. * * * [However t]he judiciary's role in this society counts for little if the use of governmental power to extinguish life does not elicit close scrutiny.

* * * "[T]he methods we employ in the enforcement of our criminal law have aptly been called the measures by which the quality of our civilization may be judged." Those whom we would banish from society or from the human community itself often speak in too faint a voice to be heard above society's demand for punishment. It is the particular role of courts to hear these voices, for the Constitution declares that the majoritarian chorus may not alone dictate the conditions of social life. The Court thus fulfills, rather than disrupts, the scheme of separation of powers by closely scrutinizing the imposition of the death penalty, for no decision of a society is more deserving of "sober second thought."

It is tempting to pretend that minorities on death row share a fate in no way connected to our own, that our treatment of them sounds no echoes beyond the chambers in which they die. Such an illusion is ultimately corrosive, for the reverberations of injustice are not so easily confined. "The destinies of the two races in this country are indissolubly linked together," and the way in which we choose those who will die reveals the depth of moral commitment among the living. * * *

[JUSTICE BLACKMUN's dissenting opinion has been omitted.]

# APPENDIX

■ ■ ■

## I.   THE CONSTITUTION OF THE UNITED STATES OF AMERICA
### (selected Amendments)
### Amendment IV

The right of the people to be secure in their persons, houses, papers, and effects, against unreasonable searches and seizures, shall not be violated, and no Warrants shall issue, but upon probable cause, supported by Oath or affirmation, and particularly describing the place to be searched, and the persons or things to be seized.

### Amendment V

No person shall be held to answer for a capital, or otherwise infamous crime, unless on a presentment or indictment of a Grand Jury, except in cases arising in the land or naval forces, or in the Militia, when in actual service in time of War or public danger; nor shall any person be subject for the same offense to be twice put in jeopardy of life or limb; nor shall be compelled in any criminal case to be a witness against himself, nor be deprived of life, liberty, or property, without due process of law; nor shall private property be taken for public use, without just compensation.

### Amendment VI

In all criminal prosecutions, the accused shall enjoy the right to a speedy and public trial, by an impartial jury of the State and district wherein the crime shall have been committed, which district shall have been previously ascertained by law, and to be informed of the nature and cause of the accusation; to be confronted with the witnesses against him; to have compulsory process for obtaining witnesses in his favor, and to have the Assistance of Counsel for his defense.

### Amendment VIII

Excessive bail shall not be required, nor excessive fines imposed, nor cruel and unusual punishments inflicted.

### Amendment XIV
### Section 1

All persons born or naturalized in the United States, and subject to the jurisdiction thereof, are citizens of the United States and of the State wherein they reside. No State shall make or enforce any law which shall abridge the privileges or immunities of citizens of the United States; nor shall any State deprive any person of life, liberty, or property, without due process of law; nor deny to any person within its jurisdiction the equal protection of the laws. * * *

## II. FEDERAL RULES OF CRIMINAL PROCEDURE

### RULE 6: THE GRAND JURY

Federal Rules of Criminal Procedure
U.S. Gov't Printing Office, 2014

**(a) Summoning a Grand Jury.**

**(1) In General.** When the public interest so requires, the court must order that one or more grand juries be summoned. A grand jury must have 16 to 23 members, and the court must order that enough legally qualified persons be summoned to meet this requirement.

**(2) Alternate Jurors.** When a grand jury is selected, the court may also select alternate jurors. Alternate jurors must have the same qualifications and be selected in the same manner as any other juror. Alternate jurors replace jurors in the same sequence in which the alternates were selected. An alternate juror who replaces a juror is subject to the same challenges, takes the same oath, and has the same authority as the other jurors.

**(b) Objection to the Grand Jury or to a Grand Juror.**

**(1) Challenges.** Either the government or a defendant may challenge the grand jury on the ground that it was not lawfully drawn, summoned, or selected, and may challenge an individual juror on the ground that the juror is not legally qualified.

**(2) Motion to Dismiss an Indictment.** A party may move to dismiss the indictment based on an objection to the grand jury or on an individual juror's lack of legal qualification, unless the court has previously ruled on the same objection under Rule 6(b)(1). The motion to dismiss is governed by 28 U.S.C. § 1867(e). The court must not dismiss the indictment on the ground that a grand juror was not legally qualified if the record shows that at least 12 qualified jurors concurred in the indictment.

**(c) Foreperson and Deputy Foreperson.** The court will appoint one juror as the foreperson and another as the deputy foreperson. In the foreperson's absence, the deputy foreperson will act as the foreperson. The foreperson may administer oaths and affirmations and will sign all indictments. The foreperson—or another juror designated by the foreperson—will record the number of jurors concurring in every indictment and will file the record with the clerk, but the record may not be made public unless the court so orders.

**(d) Who May Be Present.**

**(1) While the Grand Jury Is in Session.** The following persons may be present while the grand jury is in session: attorneys for the government, the witness being questioned, interpreters when needed, and a court reporter or an operator of a recording device.

**(2) During Deliberations and Voting.** No person other than the jurors, and any interpreter needed to assist a hearing-impaired or speech-impaired juror, may be present while the grand jury is deliberating or voting.

**(e) Recording and Disclosing the Proceedings.**

**(1) Recording the Proceedings.** Except while the grand jury is deliberating or voting, all proceedings must be recorded by a court reporter or by a suitable recording device. But the validity of a prosecution is not affected by the unintentional failure to make a recording. Unless the court orders otherwise, an attorney for the government will retain control of the recording, the reporter's notes, and any transcript prepared from those notes.

**(2) Secrecy.**

**(A)** No obligation of secrecy may be imposed on any person except in accordance with Rule 6(e)(2)(B).

**(B)** Unless these rules provide otherwise, the following persons must not disclose a matter occurring before the grand jury:

   **(i)** a grand juror;

   **(ii)** an interpreter;

   **(iii)** a court reporter;

   **(iv)** an operator of a recording device;

   **(v)** a person who transcribes recorded testimony;

   **(vi)** an attorney for the government; or

   **(vii)** a person to whom disclosure is made under Rule 6(e)(3)(A)(ii) or (iii).

**(3) Exceptions.**

**(A)** Disclosure of a grand-jury matter—other than the grand jury's deliberations or any grand juror's vote—may be made to:

**(i)** an attorney for the government for use in performing that attorney's duty;

**(ii)** any government personnel—including those of a state, state subdivision, Indian tribe, or foreign government—that an attorney for the government considers necessary to assist in performing that attorney's duty to enforce federal criminal law; or

**(iii)** a person authorized by 18 U.S.C. § 3322.

**(B)** A person to whom information is disclosed under Rule 6(e)(3)(A)(ii) may use that information only to assist an attorney for the government in performing that attorney's duty to enforce federal criminal law. An attorney for the government must promptly provide the court that impaneled the grand jury with the names of all persons to whom a disclosure has been made, and must certify that the attorney has advised those persons of their obligation of secrecy under this rule.

**(C)** An attorney for the government may disclose any grand-jury matter to another federal grand jury.

**(D)** An attorney for the government may disclose any grand-jury matter involving foreign intelligence, counterintelligence (as defined in 50 U.S.C. § 3003), or foreign intelligence information (as defined in Rule 6(e)(3)(D)(iii)) to any federal law enforcement, intelligence, protective, immigration, national defense, or national security official to assist the official receiving the information in the performance of that official's duties. An attorney for the government may also disclose any grand-jury matter involving, within the United States or elsewhere, a threat of attack or other grave hostile acts of a foreign power or its agent, a threat of domestic or international sabotage or terrorism, or clandestine intelligence gathering activities by an intelligence service or network of a foreign power or by its agent, to any appropriate federal, state, state subdivision, Indian tribal, or foreign government official, for the purpose of preventing or responding to such threat or activities.

**(i)** Any official who receives information under Rule 6(e)(3)(D) may use the information only as necessary in the conduct of that person's official duties subject to any limitations on the unauthorized disclosure of such information. Any state, state subdivision, Indian tribal, or foreign government official who receives information under Rule 6(e)(3)(D) may use the information only in a manner consistent with any guidelines issued by the Attorney General and the Director of National Intelligence.

**(ii)** Within a reasonable time after disclosure is made under Rule 6(e)(3)(D), an attorney for the government must file, under seal, a notice with the court in the district where the grand jury convened stating that such information was disclosed and the departments, agencies, or entities to which the disclosure was made.

**(iii)** As used in Rule 6(e)(3)(D), the term "foreign intelligence information" means:

> **(a)** information, whether or not it concerns a United States person, that relates to the ability of the United States to protect against—
>
> - actual or potential attack or other grave hostile acts of a foreign power or its agent;
> - sabotage or international terrorism by a foreign power or its agent; or
> - clandestine intelligence activities by an intelligence service or network of a foreign power or by its agent; or
>
> **(b)** information, whether or not it concerns a United States person, with respect to a foreign power or foreign territory that relates to—
>
> - the national defense or the security of the United States; or
> - the conduct of the foreign affairs of the United States.

**(E)** The court may authorize disclosure—at a time, in a manner, and subject to any other conditions that it directs—of a grand-jury matter:

> **(i)** preliminarily to or in connection with a judicial proceeding;
>
> **(ii)** at the request of a defendant who shows that a ground may exist to dismiss the indictment because of a matter that occurred before the grand jury;
>
> **(iii)** at the request of the government, when sought by a foreign court or prosecutor for use in an official criminal investigation;

**(iv)** at the request of the government if it shows that the matter may disclose a violation of State, Indian tribal, or foreign criminal law, as long as the disclosure is to an appropriate state, state-subdivision, Indian tribal, or foreign government official for the purpose of enforcing that law; or

**(v)** at the request of the government if it shows that the matter may disclose a violation of military criminal law under the Uniform Code of Military Justice, as long as the disclosure is to an appropriate military official for the purpose of enforcing that law.

**(F)** A petition to disclose a grand-jury matter under Rule 6(e)(3)(E)(i) must be filed in the district where the grand jury convened. Unless the hearing is ex parte—as it may be when the government is the petitioner—the petitioner must serve the petition on, and the court must afford a reasonable opportunity to appear and be heard to:

**(i)** an attorney for the government;

**(ii)** the parties to the judicial proceeding; and

**(iii)** any other person whom the court may designate.

**(G)** If the petition to disclose arises out of a judicial proceeding in another district, the petitioned court must transfer the petition to the other court unless the petitioned court can reasonably determine whether disclosure is proper. If the petitioned court decides to transfer, it must send to the transferee court the material sought to be disclosed, if feasible, and a written evaluation of the need for continued grand-jury secrecy. The transferee court must afford those persons identified in Rule 6(e)(3)(F) a reasonable opportunity to appear and be heard.

**(4) Sealed Indictment.** The magistrate judge to whom an indictment is returned may direct that the indictment be kept secret until the defendant is in custody or has been released pending trial. The clerk must then seal the indictment, and no person may disclose the indictment's existence except as necessary to issue or execute a warrant or summons.

**(5) Closed Hearing.** Subject to any right to an open hearing in a contempt proceeding, the court must close any hearing to the extent necessary to prevent disclosure of a matter occurring before a grand jury.

**(6) Sealed Records.** Records, orders, and subpoenas relating to grand-jury proceedings must be kept under seal to the extent and as long as necessary to prevent the unauthorized disclosure of a matter occurring before a grand jury.

**(7) Contempt.** A knowing violation of Rule 6, or of any guidelines jointly issued by the Attorney General and the Director of National Intelligence under Rule 6, may be punished as a contempt of court.

**(f) Indictment and Return.** A grand jury may indict only if at least 12 jurors concur. The grand jury—or its foreperson or deputy foreperson—must return the indictment to a magistrate judge in open court. To avoid unnecessary cost or delay, the magistrate judge may take the return by video teleconference from the court where the grand jury sits. If a complaint or information is pending against the defendant and 12 jurors do not concur in the indictment, the foreperson must promptly and in writing report the lack of concurrence to the magistrate judge.

**(g) Discharging the Grand Jury.** A grand jury must serve until the court discharges it, but it may serve more than 18 months only if the court, having determined that an extension is in the public interest, extends the grand jury's service. An extension may be granted for no more than 6 months, except as otherwise provided by statute.

**(h) Excusing a Juror.** At any time, for good cause, the court may excuse a juror either temporarily or permanently, and if permanently, the court may impanel an alternate juror in place of the excused juror.

**(i) "Indian Tribe" Defined.** "Indian tribe" means an Indian tribe recognized by the Secretary of the Interior on a list published in the Federal Register under 25 U.S.C. § 479a–1.

## RULE 7: THE INDICTMENT AND THE INFORMATION
Federal Rules of Criminal Procedure
U.S. Gov't Printing Office, 2014

**(a) When Used.**

**(1) Felony.** An offense (other than criminal contempt) must be prosecuted by an indictment if it is punishable:

    **(A)** by death; or

    **(B)** by imprisonment for more than one year.

**(2) Misdemeanor.** An offense punishable by imprisonment for one year or less may be prosecuted in accordance with Rule 58(b)(1).

**(b) Waiving Indictment.** An offense punishable by imprisonment for more than one year may be prosecuted by information if the defendant—in open court and after being advised of the nature of the charge and of the defendant's rights—waives prosecution by indictment.

**(c) Nature and Contents.**

**(1) In General.** The indictment or information must be a plain, concise, and definite written statement of the essential facts constituting the offense charged and must be signed by an attorney for the government. It need not contain a formal introduction or conclusion. A count may incorporate by reference an allegation made in another count. A count may allege that the means by which the defendant committed the offense are unknown or that the defendant committed it by one or more specified means. For each count, the indictment or information must give the official or customary citation of the statute, rule, regulation, or other provision of law that the defendant is alleged to have violated. For purposes of an indictment referred to in section 3282 of title 18, United States Code, for which the identity of the defendant is unknown, it shall be sufficient for the indictment to describe the defendant as an individual whose name is unknown, but who has a particular DNA profile, as that term is defined in that section 3282.

**(2) Citation Error.** Unless the defendant was misled and thereby prejudiced, neither an error in a citation nor a citation's omission is a ground to dismiss the indictment or information or to reverse a conviction.

**(d) Surplusage.** Upon the defendant's motion, the court may strike surplusage from the indictment or information.

**(e) Amending an Information.** Unless an additional or different offense is charged or a substantial right of the defendant is prejudiced, the court may permit an information to be amended at any time before the verdict or finding.

**(f) Bill of Particulars.** The court may direct the government to file a bill of particulars. The defendant may move for a bill of particulars before or within 14 days after arraignment or at a later time if the court permits. The government may amend a bill of particulars subject to such conditions as justice requires.

## RULE 11: PLEAS

Federal Rules of Criminal Procedure
U.S. Gov't Printing Office, 2014

**(a) Entering a Plea.**

**(1) In General.** A defendant may plead not guilty, guilty, or (with the court's consent) nolo contendere.

**(2) Conditional Plea.** With the consent of the court and the government, a defendant may enter a conditional plea of guilty or nolo contendere, reserving in writing the right to have an appellate court review an adverse determination of a specified pretrial motion. A defendant who prevails on appeal may then withdraw the plea.

**(3) Nolo Contendere Plea.** Before accepting a plea of nolo contendere, the court must consider the parties' views and the public interest in the effective administration of justice.

**(4) Failure to Enter a Plea.** If a defendant refuses to enter a plea or if a defendant organization fails to appear, the court must enter a plea of not guilty.

**(b) Considering and Accepting a Guilty or Nolo Contendere Plea.**

**(1) Advising and Questioning the Defendant.** Before the court accepts a plea of guilty or nolo contendere, the defendant may be placed under oath, and the court must address the defendant personally in open court. During this address, the court must inform the defendant of, and determine that the defendant understands, the following:

**(A)** the government's right, in a prosecution for perjury or false statement, to use against the defendant any statement that the defendant gives under oath;

**(B)** the right to plead not guilty, or having already so pleaded, to persist in that plea;

**(C)** the right to a jury trial;

**(D)** the right to be represented by counsel—and if necessary have the court appoint counsel—at trial and at every other stage of the proceeding;

**(E)** the right at trial to confront and cross-examine adverse witnesses, to be protected from compelled self-incrimination, to testify and present evidence, and to compel the attendance of witnesses;

**(F)** the defendant's waiver of these trial rights if the court accepts a plea of guilty or nolo contendere;

**(G)** the nature of each charge to which the defendant is pleading

**(H)** any maximum possible penalty, including imprisonment, fine, and term of supervised release;

**(I)** any mandatory minimum penalty;

**(J)** any applicable forfeiture;

**(K)** the court's authority to order restitution;

**(L)** the court's obligation to impose a special assessment;

**(M)** in determining a sentence, the court's obligation to calculate the applicable sentencing-guideline range and to consider that range, possible departures under the Sentencing Guidelines, and other sentencing factors under 18 U.S.C. § 3553(a);

**(N)** the terms of any plea-agreement provision waiving the right to appeal or to collaterally attack the sentence; and

**(O)** that, if convicted, a defendant who is not a United States citizen may be removed from the United States, denied citizenship, and denied admission to the United States in the future.

**(2) Ensuring That a Plea Is Voluntary.** Before accepting a plea of guilty or nolo contendere, the court must address the defendant personally in open court and determine that the plea is voluntary and did not result from force, threats, or promises (other than promises in a plea agreement).

**(3) Determining the Factual Basis for a Plea.** Before entering judgment on a guilty plea, the court must determine that there is a factual basis for the plea.

**(c) Plea Agreement Procedure**

**(1) In General.** An attorney for the government and the defendant's attorney, or the defendant when proceeding pro se, may discuss and reach a plea agreement. The court must not participate in these discussions. If the defendant pleads guilty or nolo contendere to either a charged offense or a lesser or related offense, the plea agreement may specify that an attorney for the government will:

**(A)** not bring, or will move to dismiss, other charges;

**(B)** recommend, or agree not to oppose the defendant's request, that a particular sentence or sentencing range is appropriate or that a particular provision of the Sentencing

Guidelines, or policy statement, or sentencing factor does or does not apply (such a recommendation or request does not bind the court); or

**(C)** agree that a specific sentence or sentencing range is the appropriate disposition of the case, or that a particular provision of the Sentencing Guidelines, or policy statement, or sentencing factor does or does not apply (such a recommendation or request binds the court once the court accepts the plea agreement).

**(2) Disclosing a Plea Agreement.** The parties must disclose the plea agreement in open court when the plea is offered, unless the court for good cause allows the parties to disclose the plea agreement in camera.

**(3) Judicial Consideration of a Plea Agreement.**

**(A)** To the extent the plea agreement is of the type specified in Rule 11(c)(1)(A) or (C), the court may accept the agreement, reject it, or defer a decision until the court has reviewed the presentence report.

**(B)** To the extent the plea agreement is of the type specified in Rule 11(c)(1)(B), the court must advise the defendant that the defendant has no right to withdraw the plea if the court does not follow the recommendation or request.

**(4) Accepting a Plea Agreement.** If the court accepts the plea agreement, it must inform the defendant that to the extent the plea agreement is of the type specified in Rule 11(c)(1)(A) or (C), the agreed disposition will be included in the judgment.

**(5) Rejecting a Plea Agreement.** If the court rejects a plea agreement containing provisions of the type specified in Rule 11(c)(1)(A) or (C), the court must do the following on the record and in open court (or, for good cause, in camera):

**(A)** inform the parties that the court rejects the plea agreement;

**(B)** advise the defendant personally that the court is not required to follow the plea agreement and give the defendant an opportunity to withdraw the plea; and

**(C)** advise the defendant personally that if the plea is not withdrawn, the court may dispose of the case less favorably toward the defendant than the plea agreement contemplated.

**(d) Withdrawing a Guilty or Nolo Contendere Plea.** A defendant may withdraw a plea of guilty or nolo contendere:

**(1)** before the court accepts the plea, for any reason or no reason; or

**(2)** after the court accepts the plea, but before it imposes sentence if:

**(A)** the court rejects a plea agreement under Rule 11(c)(5); or

**(B)** the defendant can show a fair and just reason for requesting the withdrawal.

**(e) Finality of a Guilty or Nolo Contendere Plea.** After the court imposes sentence, the defendant may not withdraw a plea of guilty or nolo contendere, and the plea may be set aside only on direct appeal or collateral attack.

**(f) Admissibility or Inadmissibility of a Plea, Plea Discussions, and Related Statements. The admissibility or inadmissibility of a plea, a plea discussion, and any related statement is governed by Federal Rule of Evidence 410.**

**(g) Recording the Proceedings.** The proceedings during which the defendant enters a plea must be recorded by a court reporter or by a suitable recording device. If there is a guilty plea or a nolo contendere plea, the record must include the inquiries and advice to the defendant required under Rule 11(b) and (c).

**(h) Harmless Error.** A variance from the requirements of this rule is harmless error if it does not affect substantial rights.

## RULE 12.1: NOTICE OF AN ALIBI DEFENSE

Federal Rules of Criminal Procedure
U.S. Gov't Printing Office, 2014

**(a) Government's Request for Notice and Defendant's Response.**

**(1) Government's Request.** An attorney for the government may request in writing that the defendant notify an attorney for the government of any intended alibi defense. The request must state the time, date, and place of the alleged offense.

**(2) Defendant's Response.** Within 14 days after the request, or at some other time the court sets, the defendant must serve written notice on an attorney for the government of any intended alibi defense. The defendant's notice must state:

**(A)** each specific place where the defendant claims to have been at the time of the alleged offense; and

**(B)** the name, address, and telephone number of each alibi witness on whom the defendant intends to rely.

**(b) Disclosing Government Witnesses.**

**(1) Disclosure.**

**(A) In General.** If the defendant serves a Rule 12.1(a)(2) notice, an attorney for the government must disclose in writing to the defendant or the defendant's attorney:

**(i)** the name of each witness—and the address and telephone number of each witness other than a victim—that the government intends to rely on to establish that the defendant was present at the scene of the alleged offense; and

**(ii)** each government rebuttal witness to the defendant's alibi defense.

**(B) Victim's Address and Telephone Number.** If the government intends to rely on a victim's testimony to establish that the defendant was present at the scene of the alleged offense and the defendant establishes a need for the victim's address and telephone number, the court may:

**(i)** order the government to provide the information in writing to the defendant or the defendant's attorney; or

**(ii)** fashion a reasonable procedure that allows preparation of the defense and also protects the victim's interests.

**(2) Time to Disclose.** Unless the court directs otherwise, an attorney for the government must give its Rule 12.1(b)(1) disclosure within 14 days after the defendant serves notice of an intended alibi defense under Rule 12.1(a)(2), but no later than 14 days before trial.

**(c) Continuing Duty to Disclose.**

**(1) In General.** Both an attorney for the government and the defendant must promptly disclose in writing to the other party the name of each additional witness—and the address and telephone number of each additional witness other than a victim—if:

**(A)** the disclosing party learns of the witness before or during trial; and

**(B)** the witness should have been disclosed under Rule 12.1(a) or (b) if the disclosing party had known of the witness earlier.

**(2) Address and Telephone Number of an Additional Victim Witness.** The address and telephone number of an additional victim witness must not be disclosed except as provided in Rule 12.1(b)(1)(B).

**(d) Exceptions.** For good cause, the court may grant an exception to any requirement of Rule 12.1(a)–(c).

**(e) Failure to Comply. If a party fails to comply with this rule, the court may exclude the testimony of any undisclosed witness regarding the defendant's alibi. This rule does not limit the defendant's right to testify.**

**(f) Inadmissibility of Withdrawn Intention.** Evidence of an intention to rely on an alibi defense, later withdrawn, or of a statement made in connection with that intention, is not, in any civil or criminal proceeding, admissible against the person who gave notice of the intention.

## RULE 16: DISCOVERY AND INSPECTION
Federal Rules of Criminal Procedure
U.S. Gov't Printing Office, 2014

**(a) Government's Disclosure.**

**(1) Information Subject to Disclosure.**

**(A) Defendant's Oral Statement.** Upon a defendant's request, the government must disclose to the defendant the substance of any relevant oral statement made by the defendant, before or after arrest, in response to interrogation by a person the defendant knew was a government agent if the government intends to use the statement at trial.

**(B) Defendant's Written or Recorded Statement.** Upon a defendant's request, the government must disclose to the defendant, and make available for inspection, copying, or photographing, all of the following:

**(i)** any relevant written or recorded statement by the defendant if:

- the statement is within the government's possession, custody, or control; and

- the attorney for the government knows—or through due diligence could know—that the statement exists;

**(ii)** the portion of any written record containing the substance of any relevant oral statement made before or after arrest if the defendant made the statement in response to interrogation by a person the defendant knew was a government agent; and

**(iii)** the defendant's recorded testimony before a grand jury relating to the charged offense.

**(C) Organizational Defendant.** Upon a defendant's request, if the defendant is an organization, the government must disclose to the defendant any statement described in Rule 16(a)(1)(A) and (B) if the government contends that the person making the statement:

**(i)** was legally able to bind the defendant regarding the subject of the statement because of that person's position as the defendant's director, officer, employee, or agent; or

**(ii)** was personally involved in the alleged conduct constituting the offense and was legally able to bind the defendant regarding that conduct because of that person's position as the defendant's director, officer, employee, or agent.

**(D) Defendant's Prior Record.** Upon a defendant's request, the government must furnish the defendant with a copy of the defendant's prior criminal record that is within the government's possession, custody, or control if the attorney for the government knows—or through due diligence could know—that the record exists.

**(E) Documents and Objects.** Upon a defendant's request, the government must permit the defendant to inspect and to copy or photograph books, papers, documents, data, photographs, tangible objects, buildings or places, or copies or portions of any of these items, if the item is within the government's possession, custody, or control and:

**(i)** the item is material to preparing the defense;

**(ii)** the government intends to use the item in its case-in-chief at trial; or

**(iii)** the item was obtained from or belongs to the defendant.

**(F) Reports of Examinations and Tests.** Upon a defendant's request, the government must permit a defendant to inspect and to copy or photograph the results or reports of any physical or mental examination and of any scientific test or experiment if:

**(i)** the item is within the government's possession, custody, or control;

**(ii)** the attorney for the government knows—or through due diligence could know—that the item exists; and

**(iii)** the item is material to preparing the defense or the government intends to use the item in its case-in-chief at trial.

**(G) Expert witnesses.**—At the defendant's request, the government must give to the defendant a written summary of any testimony that the government intends to use under Rules 702, 703, or 705 of the Federal Rules of Evidence during its case-in-chief at trial. If the government requests discovery under subdivision (b)(1)(C)(ii) and the defendant complies, the government must, at the defendant's request, give to the defendant a written summary of testimony that the government intends to use under Rules 702, 703, or 705 of the Federal Rules of Evidence as evidence at trial on the issue of the defendant's mental condition. The summary provided under this subparagraph must describe the witness's opinions, the bases and reasons for those opinions, and the witness's qualifications.

**(2) Information Not Subject to Disclosure.** Except as permitted by Rule 16(a)(1)(A)–(D), (F), and (G), this rule does not authorize the discovery or inspection of reports, memoranda, or other internal government documents made by an attorney for the government or other government agent in connection with investigating or prosecuting the case. Nor does this rule authorize the discovery or inspection of statements made by prospective government witnesses except as provided in 18 U.S.C. § 3500.

**(3) Grand Jury Transcripts.** This rule does not apply to the discovery or inspection of a grand jury's recorded proceedings, except as provided in Rules 6, 12(h), 16(a)(1), and 26.2.

**(b) Defendant's Disclosure.**

**(1) Information Subject to Disclosure.**

**(A) Documents and Objects.** If a defendant requests disclosure under Rule 16(a)(1)(E) and the government complies, then the defendant must permit the government, upon request, to inspect and to copy or photograph books, papers, documents, data, photographs, tangible objects, buildings or places, or copies or portions of any of these items if:

**(i)** the item is within the defendant's possession, custody, or control; and

**(ii)** the defendant intends to use the item in the defendant's case-in-chief at trial.

**(B) Reports of Examinations and Tests.** If a defendant requests disclosure under Rule 16(a)(1)(F) and the government complies, the defendant must permit the government, upon request, to inspect and to copy or photograph the results or reports of any physical or mental examination and of any scientific test or experiment if:

> **(i)** the item is within the defendant's possession, custody, or control; and

> **(ii)** the defendant intends to use the item in the defendant's case-in-chief at trial, or intends to call the witness who prepared the report and the report relates to the witness's testimony.

**(C) Expert witnesses.**—The defendant must, at the government's request, give to the government a written summary of any testimony that the defendant intends to use under Rules 702, 703, or 705 of the Federal Rules of Evidence as evidence at trial, if—

> **(i)** the defendant requests disclosure under subdivision (a)(1)(G) and the government complies; or

> **(ii)** the defendant has given notice under Rule 12.2(b) of an intent to present expert testimony on the defendant's mental condition.

This summary must describe the witness's opinions, the bases and reasons for those opinions, and the witness's qualifications.

**(2) Information Not Subject to Disclosure.** Except for scientific or medical reports, Rule 16(b)(1) does not authorize discovery or inspection of:

> **(A)** reports, memoranda, or other documents made by the defendant, or the defendant's attorney or agent, during the case's investigation or defense; or

> **(B)** a statement made to the defendant, or the defendant's attorney or agent, by:

> > **(i)** the defendant;

> > **(ii)** a government or defense witness; or

> > **(iii)** a prospective government or defense witness.

**(c) Continuing Duty to Disclose.** A party who discovers additional evidence or material before or during trial must promptly disclose its existence to the other party or the court if:

**(1)** the evidence or material is subject to discovery or inspection under this rule; and

**(2)** the other party previously requested, or the court ordered, its production.

**(d) Regulating Discovery.**

**(1) Protective and Modifying Orders.** At any time the court may, for good cause, deny, restrict, or defer discovery or inspection, or grant other appropriate relief. The court may permit a party to show good cause by a written statement that the court will inspect ex parte. If relief is granted, the court must preserve the entire text of the party's statement under seal.

**(2) Failure to Comply.** If a party fails to comply with this rule, the court may:

**(A)** order that party to permit the discovery or inspection; specify its time, place, and manner; and prescribe other just terms and conditions;

**(B)** grant a continuance;

**(C)** prohibit that party from introducing the undisclosed evidence; or

**(D)** enter any other order that is just under the circumstances.

## RULE 26.2: PRODUCING A WITNESS'S STATEMENT

Federal Rules of Criminal Procedure
U.S. Gov't Printing Office, 2014

**(a) Motion to Produce.** After a witness other than the defendant has testified on direct examination, the court, on motion of a party who did not call the witness, must order an attorney for the government or the defendant and the defendant's attorney to produce, for the examination and use of the moving party, any statement of the witness that is in their possession and that relates to the subject matter of the witness's testimony.

**(b) Producing the Entire Statement.** If the entire statement relates to the subject matter of the witness's testimony, the court must order that the statement be delivered to the moving party.

**(c) Producing a Redacted Statement.** If the party who called the witness claims that the statement contains information that is privileged or does not relate to the subject matter of the witness's testimony, the court must inspect the statement in camera. After excising any privileged or unrelated portions, the court must order delivery of the redacted statement to the moving party. If the defendant objects to an excision, the court must preserve the entire statement with the excised portion indicated, under seal, as part of the record.

**(d) Recess to Examine a Statement.** The court may recess the proceedings to allow time for a party to examine the statement and prepare for its use.

**(e) Sanction for Failure to Produce or Deliver a Statement.** If the party who called the witness disobeys an order to produce or deliver a statement, the court must strike the witness's testimony from the record. If an attorney for the government disobeys the order, the court must declare a mistrial if justice so requires.

**(f) "Statement" Defined.** As used in this rule, a witness's "statement" means:

**(1)** a written statement that the witness makes and signs, or otherwise adopts or approves;

**(2)** a substantially verbatim, contemporaneously recorded recital of the witness's oral statement that is contained in any recording or any transcription of a recording; or

**(3)** the witness's statement to a grand jury, however taken or recorded, or a transcription of such a statement.

**(g) Scope.** This rule applies at trial, at a suppression hearing under Rule 12, and to the extent specified in the following rules:

**(1)** Rule 5.1(h) (preliminary hearing);

**(2)** Rule 32(i)(2) (sentencing);

**(3)** Rule 32.1(e) (hearing to revoke or modify probation or supervised release);

**(4)** Rule 46(j) (detention hearing); and

**(5)** Rule 8 of the Rules Governing Proceedings under 28 U.S.C. § 2255.

## RULE 29: MOTION FOR A JUDGMENT OF ACQUITTAL
Federal Rules of Criminal Procedure
U.S. Gov't Printing Office, 2014

**(a) Before Submission to the Jury.** After the government closes its evidence or after the close of all the evidence, the court on the defendant's motion must enter a judgment of acquittal of any offense for which the evidence is insufficient to sustain a conviction. The court may on its own consider whether the evidence is insufficient to sustain a conviction. If the court denies a motion for a judgment of acquittal at the close of the government's evidence, the defendant may offer evidence without having reserved the right to do so.

**(b) Reserving Decision.** The court may reserve decision on the motion, proceed with the trial (where the motion is made before the close of all the evidence), submit the case to the jury, and decide the motion either before the jury returns a verdict or after it returns a verdict of guilty or is discharged without having returned a verdict. If the court reserves decision, it must decide the motion on the basis of the evidence at the time the ruling was reserved.

**(c) After Jury Verdict or Discharge.**

**(1) Time for a Motion.** A defendant may move for a judgment of acquittal, or renew such a motion, within 14 days after a guilty verdict or after the court discharges the jury, whichever is later.

**(2) Ruling on the Motion.** If the jury has returned a guilty verdict, the court may set aside the verdict and enter an acquittal. If the jury has failed to return a verdict, the court may enter a judgment of acquittal.

**(3) No Prior Motion Required.** A defendant is not required to move for a judgment of acquittal before the court submits the case to the jury as a prerequisite for making such a motion after jury discharge.

**(d) Conditional Ruling on a Motion for a New Trial.**

**(1) Motion for a New Trial.** If the court enters a judgment of acquittal after a guilty verdict, the court must also conditionally determine whether any motion for a new trial should be granted if the judgment of acquittal is later vacated or reversed. The court must specify the reasons for that determination.

**(2) Finality.** The court's order conditionally granting a motion for a new trial does not affect the finality of the judgment of acquittal.

**(3) Appeal.**

**(A) Grant of a Motion for a New Trial.** If the court conditionally grants a motion for a new trial and an appellate court later reverses the judgment of acquittal, the trial court must proceed with the new trial unless the appellate court orders otherwise.

**(B) Denial of a Motion for a New Trial.** If the court conditionally denies a motion for a new trial, an appellee may assert that the denial was erroneous. If the appellate court later reverses the judgment of acquittal, the trial court must proceed as the appellate court directs.

## III. FEDERAL STATUTES

### FEDERAL BAIL REFORM ACT OF 1984

18 U.S.C.A. §§ 3141, 1342
West 2015

### 18 U.S.C.A. § 3141—Release and Detention Authority Generally

**(a) Pending trial.**—A judicial officer authorized to order the arrest of a person under section 3041 of this title before whom an arrested person is brought shall order that such person be released or detained, pending judicial proceedings, under this chapter.

**(b) Pending sentence or appeal.**—A judicial officer of a court of original jurisdiction over an offense, or a judicial officer of a Federal appellate court, shall order that, pending imposition or execution of sentence, or pending appeal of conviction or sentence, a person be released or detained under this chapter.

### 18 U.S.C.A. § 3142—Release or Detention of a Defendant Pending Trial

**(a) In general.**—Upon the appearance before a judicial officer of a person charged with an offense, the judicial officer shall issue an order that, pending trial, the person be—

**(1)** released on personal recognizance or upon execution of an unsecured appearance bond, under subsection (b) of this section;

**(2)** released on a condition or combination of conditions under subsection (c) of this section;

**(3)** temporarily detained to permit revocation of conditional release, deportation, or exclusion under subsection (d) of this section; or

**(4)** detained under subsection (e) of this section.

**(b) Release on personal recognizance or unsecured appearance bond.**—The judicial officer shall order the pretrial release of the person on personal recognizance, or upon execution of an unsecured appearance bond in an amount specified by the court, subject to the condition that the person not commit a Federal, State, or local crime during the period of release and subject to the condition that the person cooperate in the collection of a DNA sample from the person if the collection of such a sample is authorized pursuant to section 3 of the DNA Analysis Backlog Elimination Act of 2000 (42 U.S.C. 14135a), unless the judicial officer determines that such release will not reasonably assure the appearance of the person as required or will endanger the safety of any other person or the community.

**(c) Release on conditions.—**

**(1)** If the judicial officer determines that the release described in subsection (b) of this section will not reasonably assure the appearance of the person as required or will endanger the safety of any other person or the community, such judicial officer shall order the pretrial release of the person—

**(A)** subject to the condition that the person not commit a Federal, State, or local crime during the period of release and subject to the condition that the person cooperate in the collection of a DNA sample from the person if the collection of such a sample is authorized pursuant to section 3 of the DNA Analysis Backlog Elimination Act of 2000 (42 U.S.C. 14135a); and

**(B)** subject to the least restrictive further condition, or combination of conditions, that such judicial officer determines will reasonably assure the appearance of the person as required and the safety of any other person and the community, which may include the condition that the person—

**(i)** remain in the custody of a designated person, who agrees to assume supervision and to report any violation of a release condition to the court, if the designated person is able reasonably to assure the judicial officer that the person will appear as required and will not pose a danger to the safety of any other person or the community;

**(ii)** maintain employment, or, if unemployed, actively seek employment;

**(iii)** maintain or commence an educational program;

**(iv)** abide by specified restrictions on personal associations, place of abode, or travel;

**(v)** avoid all contact with an alleged victim of the crime and with a potential witness who may testify concerning the offense;

**(vi)** report on a regular basis to a designated law enforcement agency, pretrial services agency, or other agency;

**(vii)** comply with a specified curfew;

**(viii)** refrain from possessing a firearm, destructive device, or other dangerous weapon;

**(ix)** refrain from excessive use of alcohol, or any use of a narcotic drug or other controlled substance, as defined in section 102 of the Controlled Substances Act (21 U.S.C. 802), without a prescription by a licensed medical practitioner;

**(x)** undergo available medical, psychological, or psychiatric treatment, including treatment for drug or alcohol dependency, and remain in a specified institution if required for that purpose;

**(xi)** execute an agreement to forfeit upon failing to appear as required, property of a sufficient unencumbered value, including money, as is reasonably necessary to assure the appearance of the person as required, and shall provide the court with proof of ownership and the value of the property along with information regarding existing encumbrances as the judicial office may require;

**(xii)** execute a bail bond with solvent sureties; who will execute an agreement to forfeit in such amount as is reasonably necessary to assure appearance of the person as required and shall provide the court with information regarding the value of the assets and liabilities of the surety if other than an approved surety and the nature and extent of encumbrances against the surety's property; such surety shall have a net worth which shall have sufficient unencumbered value to pay the amount of the bail bond;

**(xiii)** return to custody for specified hours following release for employment, schooling, or other limited purposes; and

**(xiv)** satisfy any other condition that is reasonably necessary to assure the appearance of the person as required and to assure the safety of any other person and the community.

In any case that involves a minor victim under section 1201, 1591, 2241, 2242, 2244(a)(1), 2245, 2251, 2251A, 2252(a)(1), 2252(a)(2), 2252(a)(3), 2252A(a)(1), 2252A(a)(2), 2252A(a)(3), 2252A(a)(4), 2260, 2421, 2422, 2423, or 2425 of this title, or a failure to register offense under section 2250 of this title, any release order shall contain, at a minimum, a condition of electronic monitoring and each of the conditions specified at subparagraphs (iv), (v), (vi), (vii), and (viii).[a]

**(2)** The judicial officer may not impose a financial condition that results in the pretrial detention of the person.

**(3)** The judicial officer may at any time amend the order to impose additional or different conditions of release. * * *

**(e)** Detention.

**(1)** If, after a hearing pursuant to the provisions of subsection (f) of this section, the judicial officer finds that no condition or combination of conditions will reasonably assure the appearance of the person as required and the safety of any other person and the community, such judicial officer shall order the detention of the person before trial.

**(2)** In a case described in subsection (f)(1) of this section, a rebuttable presumption arises that no condition or combination of conditions will reasonably assure the safety of any other person and the community if such judicial officer finds that—

**(A)** the person has been convicted of a Federal offense that is described in subsection (f)(1) of this section, or of a State or local offense that would have been an offense described in

---

[a] In 2006, Congress enacted the Adam Walsh Act, which, among other things, mandates specific conditions for the pretrial release of persons charged with certain offenses, including child pornography, sexual exploitation, offenses involving a minor victim, and the offense of failing to register as a sex offender. In these cases, a release order "shall contain, at a minimum, a condition of electronic monitoring" even if the Magistrate Judge does not make a specific finding that electronic monitoring is necessary to assure the defendant's appearance or the safety of the community. Several U.S. district courts have struck down the electronic monitoring provision of the Adam Walsh Act as violating the Due Process Clause of the Fifth Amendment and/or the Eighth Amendment's prohibition against excessive bail. *See, e.g.* United States v. Polouizzi, 697 F. Supp. 2d 381, 394 (E.D.N.Y. 2010) (finding that the Adam Walsh Act's mandatory pretrial release condition of electronic monitoring for all defendants charged with possession or receipt of child pornography violated defendant's procedural due process rights and the Eighth Amendment's prohibition against excessive bail); United States v. Arzberger, 592 F. Supp. 2d 590, 601 (S.D.N.Y. 2008) (finding that imposition of electronic monitoring on certain defendants without providing the defendant with any opportunity to contest whether such monitoring is necessary to ensure his return to court or the safety of the community violates the Due Process Clause of the Fifth Amendment); United States v. Karper, 847 F. Supp. 2d 350, 360 (N.D.N.Y. 2011) (finding that the provision of the Adam Walsh Act that mandates conditions, such as electronic monitoring, on certain pretrial detainees without affording them an opportunity to contest the restriction on their freedom of movement violates procedural due process); United States v. Torres, 566 F. Supp. 2d 591 (W.D. Tex. 2008) (finding that the provision of the Adam Walsh Amendments to the Federal Bail Reform Act, mandating electronic monitoring, as set forth in 3142(c)(1)(B), violates the Due Process Clause of the Fifth Amendment and the Eighth Amendment's prohibition against excessive punishment); United States v. Smedley, 611 F. Supp. 2d 971 (E.D. Mo. 2009) (finding that provision of Adam Walsh Act imposing home detention with electronic monitoring as a condition of pretrial release violates due process); United States v. Merritt, 612 F. Supp. 2d 1074 (D. Neb. 2009) (finding that the Adam Walsh Amendments violate the Due Process Clause because they mandate certain release conditions in child pornography cases, such as electronic monitoring and a curfew, without a judicial determination of whether such restrictions are necessary to ensure the defendant's appearance at trial or to protect the public).

subsection (f)(1) of this section if a circumstance giving rise to Federal jurisdiction had existed;

**(B)** the offense described in subparagraph (A) was committed while the person was on release pending trial for a Federal, State, or local offense; and

**(C)** a period of not more than five years has elapsed since the date of conviction, or the release of the person from imprisonment, for the offense described in subparagraph (A), whichever is later.

**(3)** Subject to rebuttal by the person, it shall be presumed that no condition or combination of conditions will reasonably assure the appearance of the person as required and the safety of the community if the judicial officer finds that there is probable cause to believe that the person committed—

**(A)** an offense for which a maximum term of imprisonment of ten years or more is prescribed in the Controlled Substances Act (21 U.S.C. 801 et seq.), the Controlled Substances Import and Export Act (21 U.S.C. 951 et seq.), or chapter 705 of title 46 [46 USCS § 70501 et seq.];

**(B)** an offense under section 924(c), 956(a), or 2332b of this title [18 USCS § 924(c), 956(a), or 2332b];

**(C)** an offense listed in section 2332b(g)(5)(B) of title 18, United States Code [18 USCS § 2332b(g)(5)(B)], for which a maximum term of imprisonment of 10 years or more is prescribed;

**(D)** an offense under chapter 77 of this title [18 USCS §§ 1581 et seq.] for which a maximum term of imprisonment of 20 years or more is prescribed; or

**(E)** an offense involving a minor victim under section 1201, 1591, 2241, 2242, 2244(a)(1), 2245, 2251, 2251A, 2252(a)(1), 2252(a)(2), 2252(a)(3), 2252A(a)(1), 2252A(a)(2), 2252A(a)(3), 2252A(a)(4), 2260, 2421, 2422, 2423, or 2425 of this title [18 USCS § 1201, 1591, 2241, 2242, 2244, (a)(1), 2245, 2251, 2251A, 2252(a)(1), 2252(a)(2), 2252(a)(3), 2252A(a)(1), 2252A(a)(2), 2252A(a)(3), 2252A(a)(4), 2260, 2421, 2422, 2423, or 2425].

**(f)** **Detention hearing.**—The judicial officer shall hold a hearing to determine whether any condition or combination of conditions set forth in subsection (c) of this section will reasonably assure the appearance of such person as required and the safety of any other person and the community—

**(1)** upon motion of the attorney for the Government, in a case that involves—

**(A)** a crime of violence;

**(B)** an offense for which the maximum sentence is life imprisonment or death;

**(C)** an offense for which a maximum term of imprisonment of ten years or more is prescribed in the Controlled Substances Act (21 U.S.C. 801 et seq.), the Controlled Substances Import and Export Act (21 U.S.C. 951 et seq.), or the Maritime Drug Law Enforcement Act (46 U.S.C. App. 1901 et seq.); or

**(D)** any felony if such person has been convicted of two or more offenses described in subparagraphs (A) through (C) of this paragraph, or two or more State or local offenses that would have been offenses described in subparagraphs (A) through (C) of this paragraph if a circumstance giving rise to Federal jurisdiction had existed, or a combination of such offenses; or

**(2)** upon motion of the attorney for the Government or upon the judicial officer's own motion, in a case that involves—

**(A)** a serious risk that such person will flee; or

**(B)** a serious risk that such person will obstruct or attempt to obstruct justice, or threaten, injure, or intimidate, or attempt to threaten, injure, or intimidate, a prospective witness or juror.

The hearing shall be held immediately upon the person's first appearance before the judicial officer unless that person, or the attorney for the Government, seeks a continuance. Except for good cause, a continuance on motion of such person may not exceed five days (not including any intermediate Saturday, Sunday, or legal holiday), and a continuance on motion of the attorney for the Government may not exceed three days (not including any intermediate Saturday, Sunday, or legal holiday). During a continuance, such person shall be detained, and the judicial officer, on motion of the attorney for the Government or sua sponte, may order that, while in custody, a person who appears to be a narcotics addict receive a medical examination to determine whether such person is an addict. At the hearing, such person has the right to be represented by counsel, and, if financially unable to obtain adequate representation, to have counsel appointed. The person shall be afforded an opportunity to testify, to present witnesses, to cross-examine witnesses who appear at the hearing, and to present information by proffer or otherwise. The rules concerning admissibility of evidence in criminal trials do not apply to the presentation and consideration of information at the hearing. The facts the judicial officer uses to support a finding pursuant to subsection (e) that no condition or combination of conditions will reasonably assure the safety of any other person and the community shall be supported by clear and convincing evidence. The person may be detained pending completion of the hearing. The hearing may be reopened, before or after a determination by the judicial officer, at any time before trial if the judicial officer finds that information exists that was not known to the movant at the time of the hearing and that has a material bearing on the issue whether there are conditions of release that will reasonably assure the appearance of such person as required and the safety of any other person and the community.

**(g) Factors to be considered.**—The judicial officer shall, in determining whether there are conditions of release that will reasonably assure the appearance of the person as required and the safety of any other person and the community, take into account the available information concerning—

**(1)** the nature and circumstances of the offense charged, including whether the offense is a crime of violence, a violation of section 1591, a Federal crime of terrorism, or involves a minor victim or a controlled substance, firearm, explosive, or destructive device;

**(2)** the weight of the evidence against the person;

**(3)** the history and characteristics of the person, including—

**(A)** the person's character, physical and mental condition, family ties, employment, financial resources, length of residence in the community, community ties, past conduct, history relating to drug or alcohol abuse, criminal history, and record concerning appearance at court proceedings; and

**(B)** whether, at the time of the current offense or arrest, the person was on probation, on parole, or on other release pending trial, sentencing, appeal, or completion of sentence for an offense under Federal, State, or local law; and

**(4)** the nature and seriousness of the danger to any person or the community that would be posed by the person's release. In considering the conditions of release described in subsection (c)(1)(B)(xi) or (c)(1)(B)(xii) of this section, the judicial officer may upon his own motion, or shall upon the motion of the Government, conduct an inquiry into the source of the property to be designated for potential forfeiture or offered as collateral to secure a bond, and shall decline to accept the designation, or the use as collateral, of property that, because of its source, will not reasonably assure the appearance of the person as required.

**(h) Contents of release order.**—In a release order issued under subsection (b) or (c) of this section, the judicial officer shall—

**(1)** include a written statement that sets forth all the conditions to which the release is subject, in a manner sufficiently clear and specific to serve as a guide for the person's conduct; and

**(2)** advise the person of—

**(A)** the penalties for violating a condition of release, including the penalties for committing an offense while on pretrial release;

**(B)** the consequences of violating a condition of release, including the immediate issuance of a warrant for the person's arrest; and

**(C)** sections 1503 of this title (relating to intimidation of witnesses, jurors, and officers of the court), 1510 (relating to obstruction of criminal investigations), 1512 (tampering with a witness, victim, or an informant), and 1513 (retaliating against a witness, victim, or an informant).

**(i) Contents of detention order.**—In a detention order issued under subsection (e) of this section, the judicial officer shall—

**(1)** include written findings of fact and a written statement of the reasons for the detention;

**(2)** direct that the person be committed to the custody of the Attorney General for confinement in a corrections facility separate, to the extent practicable, from persons awaiting or serving sentences or being held in custody pending appeal;

**(3)** direct that the person be afforded reasonable opportunity for private consultation with counsel; and

**(4)** direct that, on order of a court of the United States or on request of an attorney for the Government, the person in charge of the corrections facility in which the person is confined deliver the person to a United States marshal for the purpose of an appearance in connection with a court proceeding.

The judicial officer may, by subsequent order, permit the temporary release of the person, in the custody of a United States marshal or another appropriate person, to the extent that the judicial officer determines such release to be necessary for preparation of the person's defense or for another compelling reason.

**(j) Presumption of innocence.**—Nothing in this section shall be construed as modifying or limiting the presumption of innocence.

## THE JENCKS ACT: DEMANDS FOR PRODUCTION OF STATEMENTS AND REPORTS OF WITNESSES
18 U.S.C.A. § 3500
West 2015

**(a)** In any criminal prosecution brought by the United States, no statement or report in the possession of the United States which was made by a Government witness or prospective Government witness (other than the defendant) shall be the subject of subpoena, discovery, or inspection until said witness has testified on direct examination in the trial of the case.

**(b)** After a witness called by the United States has testified on direct examination, the court shall, on motion of the defendant, order the United States to produce any statement (as hereinafter defined) of the witness in the possession of the United States which relates to the subject matter as to which the witness has testified. If the entire contents of any such statement relate to the subject matter of the testimony of the witness, the court shall order it to be delivered directly to the defendant for his examination and use.

**(c)** If the United States claims that any statement ordered to be produced under this section contains matter which does not relate to the subject matter of the testimony of the witness, the court shall order the United States to deliver such statement for the inspection of the court in camera. Upon such delivery the court shall excise the portions of such statement which do not relate to the subject matter of the testimony of the witness. With such material excised, the court shall then direct delivery of such statement to the defendant for his use. If, pursuant to such procedure, any portion of such statement is withheld from the defendant and the defendant objects to such withholding, and the trial is continued to an adjudication of the guilt of the defendant, the entire text of such statement shall be preserved by the United States and, in the event the defendant appeals, shall be made available to the appellate court for the purpose of determining the correctness of the ruling of the trial judge. Whenever any statement is delivered to a defendant pursuant to this section, the court in its discretion, upon application of said defendant, may recess proceedings in the trial for such time as it may determine to be reasonably required for the examination of such statement by said defendant and his preparation for its use in the trial.

**(d)** If the United States elects not to comply with an order of the court under subsection (b) or (c) hereof to deliver to the defendant any such statement, or such portion thereof as the court may direct, the court shall strike from the record the testimony of the witness, and the trial shall proceed unless the court in its discretion shall determine that the interests of justice require that a mistrial be declared.

**(e)** The term "statement", as used in subsections (b), (c), and (d) of this section in relation to any witness called by the United States, means—

> **(1)** a written statement made by said witness and signed or otherwise adopted or approved by him
>
> **(2)** a stenographic, mechanical, electrical, or other recording, or a transcription thereof, which is a substantially verbatim recital of an oral statement made by said witness and recorded contemporaneously with the making of such oral statement; or
>
> **(3)** a statement, however taken or recorded, or a transcription thereof, if any, made by said witness to a grand jury.

## IV. AMERICAN BAR ASSOCIATION STANDARDS

### PROSECUTION FUNCTION
CRIMINAL JUSTICE STANDARDS FOR THE PROSECUTION FUNCTION
AM. BAR ASS'N, 4th ed. 2015

### Standard 3–1.2: Functions and Duties of the Prosecutor

**(a)** The prosecutor is an administrator of justice, a zealous advocate, and an officer of the court. The prosecutor's office should exercise sound discretion and independent judgment in the performance of the prosecution function.

**(b)** The primary duty of the prosecutor is to seek justice within the bounds of the law, not merely to convict. The prosecutor serves the public interest and should act with integrity and balanced judgment to increase public safety both by pursuing appropriate criminal charges of appropriate severity, and by exercising discretion to not pursue criminal charges in appropriate circumstances. The prosecutor should seek to protect the innocent and convict the guilty, consider the interests of victims and witnesses, and respect the constitutional and legal rights of all persons, including suspects and defendants.

**(c)** The prosecutor should know and abide by the standards of professional conduct as expressed in applicable law and ethical codes and opinions in the applicable jurisdiction. The prosecutor should avoid an appearance of impropriety in performing the prosecution function. A prosecutor should seek out, and the prosecutor's office should provide, supervisory advice and ethical guidance when the proper course of prosecutorial conduct seems unclear. A prosecutor who disagrees with a governing ethical rule should seek its change if appropriate, and directly challenge it if necessary, but should comply with it unless relieved by court order.

**(d)** The prosecutor should make use of ethical guidance offered by existing organizations, and should seek to establish and make use of an ethics advisory group akin to that described in Defense Function Standard 4–1.11.

**(e)** The prosecutor should be knowledgeable about, consider, and where appropriate develop or assist in developing alternatives to prosecution or conviction that may be applicable in individual cases or classes of cases. The prosecutor's office should be available to assist community efforts addressing problems that lead to, or result from, criminal activity or perceived flaws in the criminal justice system.

**(f)** The prosecutor is not merely a case-processor but also a problem-solver responsible for considering broad goals of the criminal justice system. The prosecutor should seek to reform and improve the administration of criminal justice, and when inadequacies or injustices in the substantive or procedural law come to the prosecutor's attention, the prosecutor should stimulate and support efforts for remedial action. The prosecutor should provide service to the community, including involvement in public service and Bar activities, public education, community service activities, and Bar leadership positions. A prosecutorial office should support such activities, and the office's budget should include funding and paid release time for such activities.

### Standard 3–1.6: Improper Bias Prohibited

**(a)** The prosecutor should not manifest or exercise, by words or conduct, bias or prejudice based upon race, sex, religion, national origin, disability, age, sexual orientation, gender identity, or socioeconomic status. A prosecutor should not use other improper considerations, such as partisan or political or personal considerations, in exercising prosecutorial discretion. A prosecutor should strive to eliminate implicit biases, and act to mitigate any improper bias or prejudice when credibly informed that it exists within the scope of the prosecutor's authority.

**(b)** A prosecutor's office should be proactive in efforts to detect, investigate, and eliminate improper biases, with particular attention to historically persistent biases like race, in all of its work. A prosecutor's office should regularly assess the potential for biased or unfairly disparate impacts of its policies on communities within the prosecutor's jurisdiction, and eliminate those impacts that cannot be properly justified.

## Standard 3–1.12: Duty to Report and Respond to Prosecutorial Misconduct

**(a)** The prosecutor's office should adopt policies to address allegations of professional misconduct, including violations of law, by prosecutors. At a minimum such policies should require internal reporting of reasonably suspected misconduct to supervisory staff within the office, and authorize supervisory staff to quickly address the allegations. Investigations of allegations of professional misconduct within the prosecutor's office should be handled in an independent and conflict-free manner.

**(b)** When a prosecutor reasonably believes that another person associated with the prosecutor's office intends or is about to engage in misconduct, the prosecutor should attempt to dissuade the person. If such attempt fails or is not possible, and the prosecutor reasonably believes that misconduct is ongoing, will occur, or has occurred, the prosecutor should promptly refer the matter to higher authority in the prosecutor's office including, if warranted by the seriousness of the matter, to the chief prosecutor.

**(c)** If, despite the prosecutor's efforts in accordance with sections (a) and (b) above, the chief prosecutor permits, fails to address, or insists upon an action or omission that is clearly a violation of law, the prosecutor should take further remedial action, including revealing information necessary to address, remedy, or prevent the violation to appropriate judicial, regulatory, or other government officials not in the prosecutor's office.

## Standard 3–4.2: Decisions to Charge are the Prosecutor's

**(a)** While the decision to arrest is often the responsibility of law enforcement personnel, the decision to institute formal criminal proceedings is the responsibility of the prosecutor. Where the law permits a law enforcement officer or other person to initiate proceedings by complaining directly to a judicial officer or the grand jury, the complainant should be required to present the complaint for prior review by the prosecutor, and the prosecutor's recommendation regarding the complaint should be communicated to the judicial officer or grand jury.

**(b)** The prosecutor's office should establish standards and procedures for evaluating complaints to determine whether formal criminal proceedings should be instituted.

**(c)** In determining whether formal criminal charges should be filed, prosecutors should consider whether further investigation should be undertaken. After charges are filed the prosecutor should oversee law enforcement investigative activity related to the case.

**(d)** If the defendant is not in custody when charged, the prosecutor should consider whether a voluntary appearance rather than a custodial arrest would suffice to protect the public and ensure the defendant's presence at court proceedings.

## Standard 3–4.3: Minimum Requirements for Filing and Maintaining Criminal Charges

**(a)** A prosecutor should seek or file criminal charges only if the prosecutor reasonably believes that the charges are supported by probable cause, that admissible evidence will be sufficient to support conviction beyond a reasonable doubt, and that the decision to charge is in the interests of justice.

**(b)** After criminal charges are filed, a prosecutor should maintain them only if the prosecutor continues to reasonably believe that probable cause exists and that admissible evidence will be sufficient to support conviction beyond a reasonable doubt.

**(c)** If a prosecutor has significant doubt about the guilt of the accused or the quality, truthfulness, or sufficiency of the evidence in any criminal case assigned to the prosecutor, the prosecutor should disclose those doubts to supervisory staff. The prosecutor's office should then determine whether it is appropriate to proceed with the case.

**(d)** A prosecutor's office should not file or maintain charges if it believes the defendant is innocent, no matter what the state of the evidence.

## Standard 3–4.4: Discretion in Filing, Declining, Maintaining, and Dismissing Criminal Charges

**(a)** In order to fully implement the prosecutor's functions and duties, including the obligation to enforce the law while exercising sound discretion, the prosecutor is not obliged to file or maintain all criminal charges which the evidence might support. Among the factors which the prosecutor may properly consider in exercising discretion to initiate, decline, or dismiss a criminal charge, even though it meets the requirements of Standard 3–4.3, are:

    **(i)** the strength of the case;

    **(ii)** the prosecutor's doubt that the accused is in fact guilty;

    **(iii)** the extent or absence of harm caused by the offense;

    **(iv)** the impact of prosecution or non-prosecution on the public welfare;

    **(v)** the background and characteristics of the offender, including any voluntary restitution or efforts at rehabilitation;

    **(vi)** whether the authorized or likely punishment or collateral consequences are disproportionate in relation to the particular offense or the offender;

    **(vii)** the views and motives of the victim or complainant;

    **(viii)** any improper conduct by law enforcement;

**(ix)** unwarranted disparate treatment of similarly situated persons;

**(x)** potential collateral impact on third parties, including witnesses or victims;

**(xi)** cooperation of the offender in the apprehension or conviction of others;

**(xii)** the possible influence of any cultural, ethnic, socioeconomic or other improper biases;

**(xiii)** changes in law or policy;

**(xiv)** the fair and efficient distribution of limited prosecutorial resources;

**(xv)** the likelihood of prosecution by another jurisdiction; and

**(xvi)** whether the public's interests in the matter might be appropriately vindicated by available civil, regulatory, administrative, or private remedies.

**(b)** In exercising discretion to file and maintain charges, the prosecutor should not consider:

**(i)** partisan or other improper political or personal considerations;

**(ii)** hostility or personal animus towards a potential subject, or any other improper motive of the prosecutor; or

**(iii)** the impermissible criteria described in Standard 1.6 above.
\* \* \*

**(d)** The prosecutor should not file or maintain charges greater in number or degree than can reasonably be supported with evidence at trial and are necessary to fairly reflect the gravity of the offense or deter similar conduct.
\* \* \*

**(f)** The prosecutor should consider the possibility of a noncriminal disposition, formal or informal, or a deferred prosecution or other diversionary disposition, when deciding whether to initiate or prosecute criminal charges. The prosecutor should be familiar with the services and resources of other agencies, public or private, that might assist in the evaluation of cases for diversion or deferral from the criminal process.

### Standard 3–4.5: Relationship with a Grand Jury

**(a)** In presenting a matter to a criminal grand jury, and in light of its *ex parte* character, the prosecutor should respect the independence of the grand jury and should not preempt a function of the grand jury, mislead the grand jury, or abuse the processes of the grand jury.

**(b)** Where the prosecutor is authorized to act as a legal advisor to the grand jury, the prosecutor should appropriately explain the law and may, if permitted by law, express an opinion on the legal significance of the evidence, but should give due deference to the grand jury as an independent legal body.

**(c)** The prosecutor should not make statements or arguments to a grand jury in an effort to influence grand jury action in a manner that would be impermissible in a trial.

**(d)** The entirety of the proceedings occurring before a grand jury, including the prosecutor's communications with and presentations and instructions to the grand jury, should be recorded in some manner, and that record should be preserved. The prosecutor should avoid off-the-record communications with the grand jury and with individual grand jurors.

### Standard 3–4.6: Quality and Scope of Evidence Before a Grand Jury

**(a)** A prosecutor should not seek an indictment unless the prosecutor reasonably believes the charges are supported by probable cause and that there will be admissible evidence sufficient to support the charges beyond reasonable doubt at trial. A prosecutor should advise a grand jury of the prosecutor's opinion that it should not indict if the prosecutor believes the evidence presented does not warrant an indictment.

**(b)** In addition to determining what criminal charges to file, a grand jury may properly be used to investigate potential criminal conduct, and also to determine the sense of the community regarding potential charges.

**(c)** A prosecutor should present to a grand jury only evidence which the prosecutor believes is appropriate and authorized by law for presentation to a grand jury. The prosecutor should be familiar with the law of the jurisdiction regarding grand juries, and may present witnesses to summarize relevant evidence to the extent the law permits.

**(d)** When a new grand jury is empaneled, a prosecutor should ensure that the grand jurors are appropriately instructed, consistent with the law of the jurisdiction, on the grand jury's right and ability to seek evidence, ask questions, and hear directly from any available witnesses, including eyewitnesses.

**(e)** A prosecutor with personal knowledge of evidence that directly negates the guilt of a subject of the investigation should present or otherwise disclose that evidence to the grand jury. The prosecutor should relay to the grand jury any request by the subject or target of an investigation to testify before the grand jury, or present other non-frivolous evidence claimed to be exculpatory.

**(f)** If the prosecutor concludes that a witness is a target of a criminal investigation, the prosecutor should not seek to compel the witness's testimony before the grand jury absent immunity. The prosecutor should honor, however, a reasonable request from a target or subject who wishes to testify before the grand jury.

**(g)** Unless there is a reasonable possibility that it will facilitate flight of the target, endanger other persons, interfere with an ongoing investigation, or obstruct justice, the prosecutor should give notice to a target of a grand jury investigation, and offer the target an opportunity to testify before the grand jury. Prior to taking a target's testimony, the prosecutor should advise the target of the privilege against self-incrimination and obtain a voluntary waiver of that right.

**(h)** The prosecutor should not seek to compel the appearance of a witness whose activities are the subject of the grand jury's inquiry, if the witness states in advance that if called the witness will claim the constitutional privilege not to testify, and provides a reasonable basis for such claim. If warranted, the prosecutor may judicially challenge such a claim of privilege or seek a grant of immunity according to the law.

**(i)** The prosecutor should not issue a grand jury subpoena to a criminal defense attorney or defense team member, or other witness whose testimony reasonably might be protected by a recognized privilege, without considering the applicable law and rules of professional responsibility in the jurisdiction.

**(j)** Except where permitted by law, a prosecutor should not use the grand jury in order to obtain evidence to assist the prosecution's preparation for trial of a defendant who has already been charged. A prosecutor may, however, use the grand jury to investigate additional or new charges against a defendant who has already been charged.

**(k)** Except where permitted by law, a prosecutor should not use a criminal grand jury solely or primarily for the purpose of aiding or assisting in an administrative or civil inquiry.

### Standard 3–5.4: Identification and Disclosure of Information and Evidence

**(a)** After charges are filed if not before, the prosecutor should diligently seek to identify all information in the possession of the prosecution or its agents that tends to negate the guilt of the accused, mitigate the offense charged, impeach the government's witnesses or evidence, or reduce the likely punishment of the accused if convicted.

**(b)** The prosecutor should diligently advise other governmental agencies involved in the case of their continuing duty to identify, preserve, and disclose to the prosecutor information described in (a) above.

**(c)** Before trial of a criminal case, a prosecutor should make timely disclosure to the defense of information described in (a) above that is known to the prosecutor, regardless of whether the prosecutor believes it is likely to change the result of the proceeding, unless relieved of this responsibility by a court's protective order. (Regarding discovery prior to a guilty plea, see Standard 3–5.6(f) below.) A prosecutor should not intentionally attempt to obscure information disclosed pursuant to this standard by including it without identification within a larger volume of materials.

**(d)** The obligations to identify and disclose such information continue throughout the prosecution of a criminal case.

**(e)** A prosecutor should timely respond to legally proper discovery requests, and make a diligent effort to comply with legally proper disclosure obligations, unless otherwise authorized by a court. When the defense makes requests for specific information, the prosecutor should provide specific responses rather than merely a general acknowledgement of discovery obligations. Requests and responses should be tailored to the case and "boilerplate" requests and responses should be disfavored.

**(f)** The prosecutor should make prompt efforts to identify and disclose to the defense any physical evidence that has been gathered in the investigation, and provide the defense a reasonable opportunity to examine it.

**(g)** A prosecutor should not avoid pursuit of information or evidence because the prosecutor believes it will damage the prosecution's case or aid the accused.

**(h)** A prosecutor should determine whether additional statutes, rules or caselaw may govern or restrict the disclosure of information, and comply with these authorities absent court order.

### Standard 3–5.5: Preservation of Information and Evidence

**(a)** The prosecutor should make reasonable efforts to preserve, and direct the prosecutor's agents to preserve, relevant materials during and after a criminal case, including

    **(i)** evidence relevant to investigations as well as prosecutions, whether or not admitted at trial;

    **(ii)** information identified pursuant to Standard 3–5.4(a); and

    **(iii)** other materials necessary to support significant decisions made and conclusions reached by the prosecution in the course of an investigation and prosecution.

**(b)** The prosecutor's office should develop policies regarding the method and duration of preservation of such materials. Such policies should be consistent with applicable rules and laws (such as public records laws) in the jurisdiction. These policies, and individual preservation decisions, should consider the character and seriousness of each case, the character of the particular evidence or information, the likelihood of further challenges to judgments following conviction, and the resources available for preservation. Physical evidence should be preserved so as to reasonably preserve its forensic characteristics and utility.

**(c)** Materials should be preserved at least until a criminal case is finally resolved or is final on appeal and the time for further appeal has expired. In felony cases, materials should be preserved until post-conviction litigation is concluded or time-limits have expired. In death penalty cases, information should be preserved until the penalty is carried out or is precluded.

**(d)** The prosecutor should comply with additional statutes, rules or caselaw that may govern the preservation of evidence.

### Standard 3–6.3: Selection of Jurors

**(a)** The prosecutor's office should be aware of legal standards that govern the selection of jurors, and train prosecutors to comply. The prosecutor should prepare to effectively discharge the prosecution function in the selection of the jury, including exercising challenges for cause and peremptory challenges. The prosecutor's office should also be aware of the process used to select and summon the jury pool and bring legal deficiencies to the attention of the court.

**(b)** The prosecutor should not strike jurors based on any criteria rendered impermissible by the constitution, statutes, applicable rules of the jurisdiction, or these standards, including race, sex, religion, national origin, disability, sexual orientation or gender identity. The prosecutor should consider contesting a defense counsel's peremptory challenges that appear to be based upon such criteria.

**(c)** In cases in which the prosecutor conducts a pretrial investigation of the background of potential jurors, the investigative methods used should not harass, intimidate, or unduly embarrass or invade the privacy of potential jurors. Absent special circumstances, such investigation should be restricted to review of records and sources of information already in existence and to which access is lawfully allowed. If the prosecutor uses record searches that are unavailable to the defense, such as criminal record databases, the prosecutor should share the results with defense counsel or seek a judicial protective order.

**(d)** The opportunity to question jurors personally should be used solely to obtain information relevant to the well-informed exercise of challenges. The prosecutor should not seek to commit jurors on factual issues likely to arise in the case, and should not intentionally present arguments, facts or evidence which the prosecutor reasonably should know will not be admissible at trial. Voir dire should not be used to argue the prosecutor's case to the jury, or to unduly ingratiate counsel with the jurors.

**(e)** During voir dire, the prosecutor should seek to minimize any undue embarrassment or invasion of privacy of potential jurors, for example by seeking to inquire into sensitive matters outside the presence of other potential jurors, while still enabling fair and efficient juror selection.

**(f)** If the court does not permit voir dire by counsel, the prosecutor should provide the court with suggested questions in advance, and request specific follow-up questions during the selection process when necessary to ensure fair juror selection.

**(g)** If the prosecutor has reliable information that conflicts with a potential juror's responses, or that reasonably would support a "for cause" challenge by any party, the prosecutor should inform the court and, unless the court orders otherwise, defense counsel.

### Standard 3–7.2: Sentencing

**(a)** The severity of sentences imposed should not be used as a measure of a prosecutor's effectiveness.

**(b)** The prosecutor should be familiar with relevant sentencing laws, rules, consequences and options, including alternative non-imprisonment sentences. Before or soon after charges are filed, and throughout the pendency of the case, the prosecutor should evaluate potential consequences of the prosecution and available sentencing options, such as forfeiture, restitution, and immigration effects, and be prepared to actively advise the court in sentencing.

**(c)** The prosecutor should seek to assure that a fair and informed sentencing judgment is made, and to avoid unfair sentences and disparities.

**(d)** In the interests of uniformity, the prosecutor's office should develop consistent policies for evaluating and making sentencing recommendations, and not leave complete discretion for sentencing policy to individual prosecutors.

**(e)** The prosecutor should know the relevant laws and rules regarding victims' rights, and facilitate victim participation in the sentencing process as the law requires or permits.

## DEFENSE FUNCTION
CRIMINAL JUSTICE STANDARDS FOR THE DEFENSE FUNCTION
AM. BAR ASS'N, 4th ed. 2015

### Standard 4–1.1: The Scope and Function of These Standards

**(a)** As used in these Standards, "defense counsel" means any attorney—including privately retained, assigned by the court, acting pro bono or serving indigent defendants in a legal aid or public defender's office—who acts as an attorney on behalf of a client being investigated or prosecuted for alleged criminal conduct, or a client seeking legal advice regarding a potential, ongoing or past criminal matter or subpoena, including as a witness. These Standards are intended to apply in any context in which a lawyer would reasonably understand that a criminal prosecution could result. The Standards are intended to serve the best interests of clients, and should not be relied upon to justify any decision that is counter to the client's best interests. The burden to justify any exception should rest with the lawyer seeking it.

**(b)** These Standards are intended to provide guidance for the professional conduct and performance of defense counsel. They are not intended to modify a defense attorney's obligations under applicable rules, statutes or the constitution. They are aspirational or describe "best practices," and are not intended to serve as the basis for the imposition of professional discipline, to create substantive or procedural rights for clients, or to create a standard of care for civil liability. They may be relevant in judicial evaluation of constitutional claims regarding the right to counsel. For purposes of consistency, these Standards sometimes include language taken from the Model Rules of Professional Conduct; but the Standards often address conduct or provide details beyond that governed by the Model Rules of Professional Conduct. No inconsistency is ever intended; and in any case a lawyer should always read and comply with the rules of professional conduct and other authorities that are binding in the specific jurisdiction or matter, including choice of law principles that may regulate the lawyer's ethical conduct.

**(c)** Because the Standards for Criminal Justice are aspirational, the words "should" or "should not" are used in these Standards, rather than mandatory phrases such as "shall" or "shall not," to describe the conduct of lawyers that is expected or recommended under these Standards. The Standards are not intended to suggest any lesser standard of conduct than may be required by applicable mandatory rules, statutes, or other binding authorities.

**(d)** These Standards are intended to address the performance of criminal defense counsel in all stages of their professional work. Other ABA Criminal Justice Standards should also be consulted for more detailed consideration of the performance of criminal defense counsel in specific areas.

### Standard 4–1.2: Functions and Duties of Defense Counsel

**(a)** Defense counsel is essential to the administration of criminal justice. A court properly constituted to hear a criminal case should be viewed as an entity consisting of the court (including judge, jury, and other court personnel), counsel for the prosecution, and counsel for the defense.

**(b)** Defense counsel have the difficult task of serving both as officers of the court and as loyal and zealous advocates for their clients. The primary duties that defense counsel owe to their clients, to the administration of justice, and as officers of the court, are to serve as their clients' counselor and advocate with courage and devotion; to ensure that constitutional and other legal rights of their clients are protected; and to render effective, high-quality legal representation with integrity.

**(c)** Defense counsel should know and abide by the standards of professional conduct as expressed in applicable law and ethical codes and opinions in the applicable jurisdiction. Defense counsel should seek out supervisory advice when available, and defense counsel organizations as well as others should provide ethical guidance when the proper course of conduct seems unclear. Defense counsel who disagrees with a governing ethical rule should seek its change if appropriate, and directly challenge it if necessary, but should comply with it unless relieved by court order.

**(d)** Defense counsel is the client's professional representative, not the client's alter-ego. Defense counsel should act zealously within the bounds of the law and standards on behalf of their clients, but have no duty to, and may not, execute any directive of the client which violates the law or such standards. In representing a client, defense counsel may engage in a good faith challenge to the validity of such laws or standards if done openly.

**(e)** Defense counsel should seek to reform and improve the administration of criminal justice. When inadequacies or injustices in the substantive or procedural law come to defense counsel's attention, counsel should stimulate and support efforts for remedial action. Defense counsel should provide services to the community, including involvement in public service and Bar activities, public education, community service activities, and Bar leadership positions. A public defense organization should support such activities, and the office's budget should include funding and paid release time for such activities.

**(f)** Defense counsel should be knowledgeable about, and consider, alternatives to prosecution or conviction that may be applicable in individual cases, and communicate them to the client. Defense counsel should be available to assist other groups in the community in addressing problems that lead to, or result from, criminal activity or perceived flaws in the criminal justice system.

**(g)** Because the death penalty differs from other criminal penalties, defense counsel in a capital case should make extraordinary efforts on behalf of the accused and, more specifically, review and comply with the ABA Guidelines for the Appointment and Performance of Defense Counsel in Death Penalty Cases.

### Standard 4–1.3: Continuing Duties of Defense Counsel

Some duties of defense counsel run throughout the period of representation, and even beyond. Defense counsel should consider the impact of these duties at all stages of a criminal representation and on all decisions and actions that arise in the course of performing the defense function. These duties include:

**(a)** a duty of confidentiality regarding information relevant to the client's representation which duty continues after the representation ends;

**(b)** a duty of loyalty toward the client;

**(c)** a duty of candor toward the court and others, tempered by the duties of confidentiality and loyalty;

**(d)** a duty to communicate and keep the client informed and advised of significant developments and potential options and outcomes;

**(e)** a duty to be well-informed regarding the legal options and developments that can affect a client's interests during a criminal representation;

**(f)** a duty to continually evaluate the impact that each decision or action may have at later stages, including trial, sentencing, and post-conviction review;

**(g)** a duty to be open to possible negotiated dispositions of the matter, including the possible benefits and disadvantages of cooperating with the prosecution;

**(h)** a duty to consider the collateral consequences of decisions and actions, including but not limited to the collateral consequences of conviction.

### Standard 4–1.6: Improper Bias Prohibited

**(a)** Defense counsel should not manifest or exercise, by words or conduct, bias or prejudice based upon race, sex, religion, national origin, disability, age, sexual orientation, gender identity, or socioeconomic status. Defense counsel should strive to eliminate implicit biases, and act to mitigate any improper bias or prejudice when credibly informed that it exists within the scope of defense counsel's authority.

**(b)** Defense counsel should be proactive in efforts to detect, investigate, and eliminate improper biases, with particular attention to historically persistent biases like race, in all of counsel's work. A public defense office should regularly assess the potential for biased or unfairly disparate impacts of its policies on communities within the defense office's jurisdiction, and eliminate those impacts that cannot be properly justified.

### Standard 4–4.1: Duty to Investigate and Engage Investigators

**(a)** Defense counsel has a duty to investigate in all cases, and to determine whether there is a sufficient factual basis for criminal charges.

**(b)** The duty to investigate is not terminated by factors such as the apparent force of the prosecution's evidence, a client's alleged admissions to others of facts suggesting guilt, a client's expressed desire to plead guilty or that there should be no investigation, or statements to defense counsel supporting guilt.

**(c)** Defense counsel's investigative efforts should commence promptly and should explore appropriate avenues that reasonably might lead to information relevant to the merits of the matter, consequences of the criminal proceedings, and potential dispositions and penalties. Although investigation will vary depending on the circumstances, it should always be shaped by what is in the client's best interests, after consultation with the client. Defense counsel's investigation of the merits of the criminal charges should include efforts to secure relevant information in the possession of the prosecution, law enforcement authorities, and others, as well as independent investigation. Counsel's investigation should also include evaluation of the prosecution's evidence (including possible re-testing or re-evaluation of physical, forensic, and expert evidence) and consideration of inconsistencies, potential avenues of impeachment of prosecution witnesses, and other possible suspects and alternative theories that the evidence may raise.

**(d)** Defense counsel should determine whether the client's interests would be served by engaging fact investigators, forensic, accounting or other experts, or other professional witnesses such as sentencing specialists or social workers, and if so, consider, in consultation with the client, whether to engage them. Counsel should regularly re-evaluate the need for such services throughout the representation.

**(e)** If the client lacks sufficient resources to pay for necessary investigation, counsel should seek resources from the court, the government, or donors. Application to the court should be made *ex parte* if appropriate to protect the client's confidentiality. Publicly funded defense offices should advocate for resources sufficient to fund such investigative expert services on a regular basis. If adequate investigative funding is not provided, counsel may advise the court that the lack of resources for investigation may render legal representation ineffective.

## Standard 4–5.2: Control and Direction of the Case

**(a)** Certain decisions relating to the conduct of the case are for the accused; others are for defense counsel. Determining whether a decision is ultimately to be made by the client or by counsel is highly contextual, and counsel should give great weight to strongly held views of a competent client regarding decisions of all kinds.

**(b)** The decisions ultimately to be made by a competent client, after full consultation with defense counsel, include:

**(i)** whether to proceed without counsel;

**(ii)** what pleas to enter;

**(iii)** whether to accept a plea offer;

**(iv)** whether to cooperate with or provide substantial assistance to the government;

**(v)** whether to waive jury trial;

**(vi)** whether to testify in his or her own behalf;

**(vii)** whether to speak at sentencing;

**(viii)** whether to appeal; and

**(ix)** any other decision that has been determined in the jurisdiction to belong to the client.

**(c)** If defense counsel has a good faith doubt regarding the client's competence to make important decisions, counsel should consider seeking an expert evaluation from a mental health professional, within the protection of confidentiality and privilege rules if applicable.

**(d)** Strategic and tactical decisions should be made by defense counsel, after consultation with the client where feasible and appropriate. Such decisions include how to pursue plea negotiations, how to craft and respond to motions and, at hearing or trial, what witnesses to call, whether and how to conduct cross-examination, what jurors to accept or strike, what motions and objections should be made, what stipulations if any to agree to, and what and how evidence should be introduced.

**(e)** If a disagreement on a significant matter arises between defense counsel and the client, and counsel resolves it differently than the client prefers, defense counsel should consider memorializing the disagreement and its resolution, showing that record to the client, and preserving it in the file.

## Standard 4–5.4: Consideration of Collateral Consequences

**(a)** Defense counsel should identify, and advise the client of, collateral consequences that may arise from charge, plea or conviction. Counsel should investigate consequences under applicable federal, state, and local laws, and seek assistance from others with greater knowledge in specialized areas in order to be adequately informed as to the existence and details of relevant collateral consequences. Such advice should be provided sufficiently in advance that it may be fairly considered in a decision to pursue trial, plea, or other dispositions.

**(b)** When defense counsel knows that a consequence is particularly important to the client, counsel should advise the client as to whether there are procedures for avoiding, mitigating or later removing the consequence, and if so, how to best pursue or prepare for them.

**(c)** Defense counsel should include consideration of potential collateral consequences in negotiations with the prosecutor regarding possible dispositions, and in communications with the judge or court personnel regarding the appropriate sentence or conditions, if any, to be imposed.

### Standard 4–5.5: Special Attention to Immigration Status and Consequences

**(a)** Defense counsel should determine a client's citizenship and immigration status, assuring the client that such information is important for effective legal representation and that it should be protected by the attorney-client privilege. Counsel should avoid any actions that might alert the government to information that could adversely affect the client.

**(b)** If defense counsel determines that a client may not be a United States citizen, counsel should investigate and identify particular immigration consequences that might follow possible criminal dispositions. Consultation or association with an immigration law expert or knowledgeable advocate is advisable in these circumstances. Public and appointed defenders should develop, or seek funding for, such immigration expertise within their offices.

**(c)** After determining the client's immigration status and potential adverse consequences from the criminal proceedings, including removal, exclusion, bars to relief from removal, immigration detention, denial of citizenship, and adverse consequences to the client's immediate family, counsel should advise the client of all such potential consequences and determine with the client the best course of action for the client's interests and how to pursue it.

**(d)** If a client is convicted of a removable offense, defense counsel should advise the client of the serious consequences if the client illegally returns to the United States.

### Standard 4–8.3: Sentencing

**(a)** Early in the representation, and throughout the pendency of the case, defense counsel should consider potential issues that might affect sentencing. Defense counsel should become familiar with the client's background, applicable sentencing laws and rules, and what options might be available as well as what consequences might arise if the client is convicted. Defense counsel should be fully informed regarding available sentencing alternatives and with community and other resources which may be of assistance in formulating a plan for meeting the client's needs. Defense counsel should also consider whether consultation with an expert specializing in sentencing options or other sentencing issues is appropriate.

**(b)** Defense counsel's preparation before sentencing should include learning the court's practices in exercising sentencing discretion; the collateral consequences of different sentences; and the normal pattern of sentences for the offense involved, including any guidelines applicable for either sentencing and, where applicable, parole. The consequences (including reasonably foreseeable collateral consequences) of potential dispositions should be explained fully by defense counsel to the client.

**(c)** Defense counsel should present all arguments or evidence which will assist the court or its agents in reaching a sentencing disposition favorable to the accused. Defense counsel should ensure that the accused understands the nature of the presentence investigation process, and in particular the significance of statements made by the accused to probation officers and related personnel. Defense counsel should cooperate with court presentence officers unless, after consideration and consultation, it appears not to be in the best interests of the client. Unless prohibited, defense counsel should attend the probation officer's presentence interview with the accused and meet in person with the probation officer to discuss the case.

**(d)** Defense counsel should gather and submit to the presentence officers, prosecution, and court as much mitigating information relevant to sentencing as reasonably possible; and in an appropriate case, with the consent of the accused, counsel should suggest alternative programs of service or rehabilitation or other non-imprisonment options, based on defense counsel's exploration of employment, educational, and other opportunities made available by community services.

**(e)** If a presentence report is made available to defense counsel, counsel should seek to verify the information contained in it, and should supplement or challenge it if necessary. Defense counsel should either provide the client with a copy or (if copying is not allowed) discuss counsel's knowledge of its contents with the client. In many cases, defense counsel should independently investigate the facts relevant to sentencing, rather than relying on the court's presentence report, and should seek discovery or relevant information from governmental agencies or other third-parties if necessary.

**(f)** Defense counsel should alert the accused to the right of allocution. Counsel should consider with the client the potential benefits of the judge hearing a personal statement from the defendants as contrasted with the possible dangers of making a statement that could adversely impact the sentencing judge's decision or the merits of an appeal.

**(g)** If a sentence of imprisonment is imposed, defense counsel should seek the court's assistance, including an on-the-record statement by the court if possible, recommending the appropriate place of confinement and types of treatment, programming and counseling that should be provided for the defendant in confinement.

**(h)** Once the sentence has been announced, defense counsel should make any objections necessary for the record, seek clarification of any unclear terms, and advise the client of the meaning and effects of the judgment, including any known collateral consequences. Counsel should also note on the record the intention to appeal, if that decision has already been made with the client.

**(i)** If the client has received an imprisonment sentence and an appeal will be taken, defense counsel should determine whether bail pending appeal is appropriate and, if so, request it.

### Standard 4–9.6: Challenges to the Effectiveness of Counsel

**(a)** If appellate or post-appellate counsel is satisfied after appropriate investigation and legal research that another defense counsel who served in an earlier phase of the case did not provide effective assistance, new counsel should not hesitate to seek relief for the client.

**(b)** If defense counsel concludes that he or she did not provide effective assistance in an earlier phase of the case, counsel should explain this conclusion to the client. Unless the client clearly wants counsel to continue, counsel in this situation should seek to withdraw from further representation of the client with an explanation to the court of the reason, consistent with the duty of confidentiality to the client. Counsel should recommend that the client consult with independent counsel if the client desires counsel to continue with the representation. Counsel should continue with the representation only if the client so desires after informed consent and such further representation is consistent with applicable conflict of interest rules.

**(c)** Defense counsel whose conduct in a criminal case is drawn into question is permitted to testify concerning the matters at issue, and is not precluded from disclosing the truth concerning the matters raised by his former client, even though this involves revealing matters which were given in confidence. Former counsel must act consistently with applicable confidentiality rules, and ordinarily may not reveal confidences unless necessary for the purposes of the proceeding and under judicial supervision.

**(d)** In a proceeding challenging counsel's performance, counsel should not rely on the prosecutor to act as counsel's lawyer in the proceeding, and should continue to consider the former client's best interests.

# INDEX

References are to Pages. For any index entries referring to pages 9–618, please refer to *Lee, Richardson, and Lawson's Criminal Procedure, Cases and Materials, 2nd Edition* (ISBN 978-1-64020-204-7)